The EBONY Cookbook
A Date with a Dish

The EBONY Cookbook
A DATE WITH A DISH

by

FREDA DE KNIGHT

with a foreword by

GERTRUDE BLAIR

and drawings by

HERBERT TEMPLE

Revised edition
JOHNSON PUBLISHING COMPANY, INC.
Chicago, 1973

We gratefully acknowledge the use of
color photograpy from

INSTITUTIONS MAGAZINE

LIBRARY OF CONGRESS CATALOGING IN

PUBLICATION DATA

De Knight, Freda, 1910-1963

The Ebony cookbook. First published in
1948 under title: A date with a dish

1. Cookery, American. 2. Cookery, Negro.
I. Ebony. II. Title. III. Title: A date with a dish.
TX715.D326   1973   641.5   72-13963
ISBN 0-87485-003-7

First printing, 1962; Second printing, 1969;
Third printing, 1970 Revised edition, 1973
            Fifth printing, 1978
Sixth printing, 1980, Seventh printing, 1982
            Eighth Printing, 1984

MANUFACTURED IN THE UNITED STATES OF AMERICA

To my mother

ELEANOR LEE ALEXANDER

and to

JOHN H. JOHNSON

who has given my

Date with a Dish

international exposure

Preface

THERE HAS LONG BEEN A NEED for a non-regional cookbook that would contain recipes, menus and cooking hints from Negroes all over America. I have attempted to present in these pages, with my own contributions, as complete a collection as can be found anywhere in the land. New recipes . . . old recipes brought back to life that are original, traditional and exciting.

It is a fallacy, long disproved, that Negro cooks, chefs, caterers and homemakers can adapt themselves only to the standard Southern dishes, such as fried chicken, greens, corn pone and hot breads. Like other Americans living in various sections of the country they have naturally shown a desire to become versatile in the preparation of any dish, whether it is Spanish, Italian, French, Balinese or East Indian in origin.

Years ago some of our greatest culinary artists were unable to read or write but their ingenuity, mother wit and good common sense made them masters in their profession without the aid of measuring equipment or science. Needless to say, the old methods they used were tried and true, and no matter how advanced the art of cooking is today, therein lies the basic success of the "old school" cookery.

There are no set rules for dishes created by most Negroes. They just seem to have a "way" of taking a plain everyday dish and improvising a gourmet's delight. Whether acquired or inherent, this love for food has given them the desire to make their dishes different, well-seasoned and eye-appealing.

The recipes in this book have been tested for the average cook to master, the culinary artist to elaborate upon, the homemaker to experiment with, the gourmet and the family to enjoy.

"A Date With A Dish" has been written to help you! So make the most of it and plan your menus so that they will be worthy of praise and give your efforts the professional touch. Then you will enjoy to the fullest the meaning of "Culinary Art."

FREDA DE KNIGHT

THIS 1973 EDITION OF THE EBONY COOKBOOK has been corrected and revised, and we are grateful to readers who have pointed out omissions and suggested additions. In the original edition cooking times and oven temperatures were occasionally left to the imagination; in this revision we have tried to be more specific. In all other respects, this "Date with a Dish" is as the late Freda DeKnight left it, and we hope it will continue to make new friends among those who love to cook and to eat good food.

There's Magic in a Cookbook

CONFIRMED COLLECTORS OF RECIPES are eternally on the prowl for new treasures to add to their cooking lore. Ten minutes or ten thousand miles from home, there's no telling when or where a prize may be found. And of this choice company is Freda De Knight. She boasts, with not the slightest humility, of having assiduously collected over a thousand wonderful recipes from Negro sources, during the last twenty years.

At seven, she started her schooling in Salem, South Dakota, but she spent her summers cutting out recipes and playing cook instead of cutting out paper dolls and playing house. I feel a great kinship with those youthful culinary pursuits of Freda De Knight's. When I was eight years old, it was my special privilege to prepare the mid-day lunch during the summer holidays. I remembered that I loved gravy. So there was gravy every day, often strange of hue and texture; mostly so thick it could be cut like a pudding! I doted on tomatoes. Day after day we had them fried and baked and stewed and sliced and es-calloped. I wonder now how the family survived.

But young Freda was different—by the time she was five, she was able to bake her first loaf of bread, garnish plates, make biscuits and generally make herself useful. Even at the tender age of five, Freda's efforts smacked of artistry. You can know by this that Freda must surely have begun to gather her wonderful collection of special recipes at quite an early age. Today's version of that energetic little girl is a slender, bright-eyed and charming woman with a fine zest for living and with quite an independent turn of mind as well.

Freda De Knight is a cultivated Negro woman, writing the first book of its kind, a cookbook of American Negro cooking. I purposely mention this fact far from the beginning of my introduction to her work. *It is important that here is an authentic collection of very fine Negro recipes.* It is equally important that the book can stand on its own merit in competition with any other cookbook. It can be appreciated for its practical handling of directions for cooking and table service, equally valuable in homes of very limited means and those of greater comfort.

All in all, need I say that this cookbook puts magic into cooking. I can urgently recommend it for every household where cooking sometimes seems to sink into the doldrums. There are many Negro chefs' recipes given here that have some special little twist that makes them lively and different. Such is the Damson Pie that comes from the famous caterers George and Daisy Harris of Richmond. Possibly you have served a Tomato Cream Soup made by a recipe that includes salt pork. I had not, but I followed Freda De Knight's directions and from this time forth, Freda's Tomato Cream Soup will have first place in my recipe file.

Freda De Knight is a brave woman, too; she plays no favorites. A delectable Filet Mignon—expensive as expensive!—prepared with chicken liver paste, fresh mushrooms and garlic, takes its place in her book to serve your more expensive moments. An Apricot Bread is to be found on another page. It is not exactly Plain Jane, but inexpensive to prepare. A Buttermilk Pie should tempt the gourmet. Smiling peanut cookies fill the cooky jar for all the children.

THERE'S MAGIC IN A COOKBOOK

There is the savor of good living in every page of this book, stamped unmistakably with the personality of its author. In your leisure moments you will enjoy reading it.

GERTRUDE BLAIR

Table of Contents

The EBONY Cookbook
A Date with a Dish

1.

A Guide for
the Housewife

HERE IS THE LITTLE BROWN CHEF'S
guide for the housewife. If you read
it thoroughly, you are bound to know
all the answers of how to prepare and cook most any of the
dishes you eat. Do you know your oven? Watch your
baking, broiling and deep-fat temperatures and tests. Know
your measurements and can sizes and how to buy. Attach a
great deal of importance to all these facts for your own
benefit and efficiency. Remember, cooking is not a problem.
It's just knowing *how* and mastering the little tricks of
the profession with "thought."

A GLOSSARY OF COOKING TERMS

Bake—To cook in an oven by dry heat.
Barbecue—To roast meats, fowl or other foods over or before
    an open flame or glowing coals. Often done on a revolving
    spit or frame when meat is in large pieces.
Baste—To moisten roasted, baked or broiled meat or other food
    while in the process of cooking with drippings or additional
    liquids or sauces.
Beat—To mix vigorously with over and over strokes.
Blanch—To plunge into and quickly out of boiling water.
Blend—To mix two or more ingredients until well combined.
Boil—To cook in liquid, usually water, in which bubbles con-
    tinuously rise to the surface and break.

1

A GUIDE FOR THE HOUSEWIFE

Braise—To brown meat in a hot heavy pot or skillet in a small amount of fat. Then simmering slowly in a tightly covered pan to which a small amount of liquid is added.

Broil—To cook food that is exposed directly to the heat.

PAN-BROILING—Cooking food in a heavy, hot pan or griddle with just enough fat to prevent burning. If excess fat accumulates, it should be poured off at once or food will fry.

Brown (or Sauté)—To cook in a small amount of fat under a low fire until brown.

Brush—To spread lightly over food with a pastry brush, soft cloth or even paper.

Chop—To cut into small pieces with a chopper or sharp knife.

Cream—To stir and mix butter or other fat with sugar until it is of a light creamy consistency. Usually applied in cake and dessert-making.

Cut In—To blend together shortening and flour with two knives, knife and fork, or pastry blender until fat and dry ingredients are blended and the fat remains in tiny particles.

Dice—To cut into small cubes.

Dissolve—To change a solid ingredient to a liquid by combining with a liquid.

Dredge—To cover lightly but completely with flour or meal.

Fold In—To mix with as few strokes as possible, using a large fork or spoon.

Fry—To cook in fat.

PAN FRY—To cook in a small amount of fat.

DEEP-FAT FRY—To cook in enough fat to cover food completely.

Garnish—To ornament a completed food dish with some other food which is colorful and bright.

Glacé—To coat with a thin sugar syrup or honey.

Grate—To rub firmly on a grater so that food is reduced to small pieces.

Grind—To reduce food to particles of various sizes by using a food chopper with different sizes of chopping blades.

Knead—To work in with the fingers until smooth and elastic. Usually applied to making of bread and roll dough.

Marinate—To soak food before cooking in wine, vinegar, lemon juice, et cetera.

Mince—To chop very fine.

Mold—To place food in a pan or mold, allowing it to become firm so that food assumes the desired shape.

Parboil—To boil a raw food until just partially cooked.

Pare, Peel—To cut off outside skin or surface. Applied to potatoes, vegetables, fruits, et cetera.

Poach—To cook slowly in enough hot liquid to cover.

Roast—To cook slowly by dry heat, usually in oven.

Sauté—To cook in a small amount of fat over a low fire being careful not to burn, stirring frequently.

Scald Milk—To heat liquid to a temperature just below the boiling point.

Shred—To cut in very thin strips or slices.

Simmer—To cook slowly at a steady temperature without boiling.

Skewer—To pierce or fasten meat or poultry together with metal or wooden skewers.

Steam—To cook with the heat from boiling water, such as cooking in the top of a double-boiler or placing a vessel covered tightly into a large pot of boiling water.

OVEN TEMPERATURES

Very slow oven	250° F. to 300° F.
Slow oven	300° F. to 350° F.
Moderate oven	350° F. to 400° F.
Hot oven	400° F. to 450° F.
Very hot oven	450° F. to 550° F.

DEEP-FAT FRYING TEMPERATURES

Temperature by Thermometer	Bread Test
360° F.	When an inch cube of bread becomes golden brown in 60 seconds.
375° F.	When an inch cube of bread becomes golden brown in 40 seconds.
395° F.	When an inch cube of bread becomes golden brown in 20 to 25 seconds.

3

A GUIDE FOR THE HOUSEWIFE

MEASUREMENTS

A dash or pinch	=	less than ⅛ teaspoon
3 teaspoons	=	1 tablespoon
4 tablespoons	=	¼ cup
5 tablespoons plus 1 teaspoon	=	⅓ cup
8 tablespoons	=	½ cup
16 tablespoons	=	1 cup
2 cups	=	1 pint
4 cups	=	1 quart
4 quarts	=	1 gallon
4 cups flour	=	1 pound
2 cups rice	=	1 pound
1 square chocolate	=	1 ounce
1 package raisins	=	3 cups
1 pound cranberries	=	4 cups
1 envelope unflavored gelatin	=	1 tablespoon
1 ounce granulated sugar	=	2 tablespoons
2 cups granulated sugar	=	1 pound
2¼ cups firmly packed brown sugar	=	1 pound
3⅓ cups sifted confectioners' sugar	=	1 pound

BUYING GUIDE FOR CANNED GOODS

Standard Size Cans	Average Net Weight	Average Cupfuls
8 ounces	8 ounces	1
Picnic (No. 1 Eastern)	11 ounces	1⅓
No. 1 tall	16 ounces	2
No. 2	20 ounces	2½
No. 2½	28 ounces	3½
No. 3	33 ounces	4
No. 10	6 pounds, 10 ounces	13

SPICES AND HERBS

Negroes and Latin races are famous for spicy foods. In certain parts of the country, where many of the herbs are grown in one's own garden or back yard, it is so easy to use them. Don't be afraid to season foods; that's what spices are for. Some Negroes have never had the pleasure of reading spice hints, but they most certainly have the knack of adding the right spice at the right time to the right food.

Plain foods are made tasty by adding seasoning. If you follow the recipes and use the amounts given, you will find that spices play a most important role in completing a successful meal. Keep simple spices on your pantry shelf; they are not expensive, but they are so essential.

Nowadays, there is a spice to pep up every dish you prepare, and convenient little booklets on their usage can be bought for a song.

If your family does not like the aftertaste of garlic, a few dashes of garlic salt may be used as a substitute.

"The flavor is simply wonderful. What, may I ask, have you used for a seasoning?" This is a question so often asked. When I tell them, they know why their dish doesn't taste like mine.

Spices and seasonings and the use of herbs are almost personal issues. Many folk can't differentiate between tastes. But a well-seasoned dish never goes untouched! It has a fascinating flair for inveigling folk to taste it. Sometimes the old method of a bit of this or a pinch of that is best for the individual taste. When in doubt, however, use the amounts given, as they strike a happy medium. You can vary measurements and be safe, and you won't ruin a good dish or a good meal.

Buy a complete set of spices! Keep your shelf well stocked. If you like concocting mysterious and unusual dishes, the use of spices and herbs certainly helps.

BASIC SPICES AND HERBS

Allspice	*Chili Peppers*
Basil	*Chili Powder*
Bay Leaf	*Chives*
Capers	*Chutney*
Caraway	*Cinnamon*
Cayenne Pepper	*Cinnamon Sticks*
Celery Salt	*Cloves*
Celery Seed	*Cumin Seed*

A GUIDE FOR THE HOUSEWIFE

Curry Powder	*Oregano*
Dill	*Paprika*
Garlic	*Pepper (black, white, red)*
Garlic Salt	*Poppy Seed*
Ginger	*Poultry Seasoning*
Hickory Salt	*Rosemary*
Mace	*Sage*
Marjoram	*Salt*
Mint	*Savory*
Mustard (dry, prepared)	*Season-all*
Nutmeg	*Season Salt*
Onion Salt	*Thyme*

GLOSSARY OF SPICES

Allspice—A dried berry of the pimiento tree of the West Indies. Used as a condiment. The name derives from the flavor which resembles a combination of cloves, cinnamon and nutmeg.

Caraway—A biennial herb with an aromatic fruit usually known as caraway seeds. Used in breads, cookies, cakes, candies, salads and cheese. Marketed whole or ground.

Cinnamon—True cinnamon is the inner bark of cinnamon zeylanicum which grows only in Ceylon. It has a very mild flavor. Cassia cinnamon grown also in the Far East is generally used and has a more full-bodied flavor. The dried bark is sold in sticks or ground.

Cloves—The flower buds of a tree which is grown in the Netherlands East Indies, Zanzibar and Madagascar. Sold whole or ground.

Ginger—The root of an herbaceous perennial grown in semitropical countries.

BLACK GINGER—Unscraped rootstock.

WHITE GINGER—Scraped and peeled rootstock. Often candied.

Mace—The network around the nutmeg kernel. It is a vivid red when fresh and dries to a light orange. It is sold whole as blades or ground and is used to flavor sauces, gravies, cakes and pies. The aroma is similar to nutmeg but it has a different flavor.

Mincemeat Spice—A mixture of spices such as cloves, all-spice, cinnamon, etc. Used to flavor mincemeat, cakes, cookies and sauces.

Nutmeg—The kernel of a fruit of the Myristica tree grown in the Netherlands East Indies and British West Indies. The whole fruit resembles an apricot in shape and size. It has four parts: the outer husk, the mace, the inner shell and the seed or nutmeg. Sold whole or ground.

Oregano—Known as a Mexican sage and grown principally in Mexico. Used in making chili powder and for chili con carne and very spicy dishes. Also good for pork and beef dishes as well as egg omelets.

GLOSSARY OF HERBS

Basil—An annual plant cultivated in Western Europe. Leaves are dried, ground and powdered. Used to flavor soups, sauces, sausages and stews. The flavor combines well with tomatoes.

Bay Leaf—The aromatic leaf of the sweet-bay or laurel tree. Dried whole and used to flavor soups, meats and pickles.

Capers—The flower buds of Capparis spinosa grown in Mediterranean countries. Used as a condiment and for pickles.

Celery Salt—Mixture of ground celery seed and fine white salt. Used in meats, salads and many other dishes.

Celery Seed—Seed of a small plant similar in appearance and taste to celery. Used whole or ground to flavor soups, stews, cheese, pickles and some salads. Southern France, India and the United States are producers.

Chili—A hot pepper. Used as a base for chili sauce and other spicy dishes.

Chives—Similar to green onions though smaller and milder.

Cumin Seed—Dried fruit of Cuminum cyminum. Has a slightly bitter flavor. Used for flavoring meats, sausages, pickles and as an ingredient of curry powder.

Curry Powder—A yellow condiment from India containing various spices.

Dill—An annual herb grown for its aromatic seed. Used in pickles and sauces. Grown mostly in India.

7

A GUIDE FOR THE HOUSEWIFE

Garlic—A strongly flavored plant of the lily family, cloves of which are used to flavor meats, salads, etc.

Garlic Salt—Mixture of garlic and fine white salt used in meats, salads, etc.

Marjoram—A fragrant annual of the mint family. Leaves are dried and used whole or powdered to flavor soups, salads, stuffings, meats and sausages. The best grade comes from France, although it is also grown in Northern Africa and Chile.

Mint—A fragrant plant, the leaves of which are used (either fresh or dried) to flavor certain soups, vegetables, fruits and beverages.

Mustard—A plant, the seeds of which are used either whole or ground. Also combined with spices and vinegar to make a moist product known as prepared mustard. Used in pickles, meats, salads, etc.

Paprika—A sweet red pepper which is dried and ground after seeds and stem are removed. Its mild flavor is good with shellfish, fish and salad dressings. The best brands are made of Spanish and Hungarian paprikas.

Rosemary—An evergreen plant, the leaves and flowers of which are used to flavor and garnish fish, stews and sauces.

Sage—A perennial mint, the leaves of which are dried and used in stuffings and meats.

Scallion—Small onion.

Thyme—An herb, the powdered leaves of which are used to season meat, poultry and clams.

EBONY'S CURRY POWDER

No. 1 Curry Powder (medium hot)

1 pound ground turmeric	1½ ounces ground cayenne pepper
¾ pound ground coriander seed	1½ ounce ground cardamon seed
3 ounces ground ginger	2 teaspoons ground cloves
2 ounces ground black pepper	½ ounce ground caraway seed

8

Mix all ingredients thoroughly. Store in a tightly covered glass jar.

No. 2 Curry Powder (hot)

2 pounds ground turmeric
4 pounds ground coriander
  seed
1½ pounds finely ground
  red chilies

1 pound ground caraway
  seed
1 pound ground fenugreek
1 pound ground black pepper

Mix all ingredients thoroughly. Store in a tightly covered glass jar.

LIVEN UP YOUR COOKING WITH SPICES

Can you imagine an apple pie without cinnamon or nutmeg, a baked ham without cloves or a pizza without oregano? Without spices our food would be pretty dull and uninteresting.

Here are some herb and spice additions to show you how spices and herbs are used to add interest and variety to your seasoning shelf and imagination to your cooking.

MEATS

Beef roasts, loaves and patties: Basil, garlic powder or salt, mace, marjoram, nutmeg, parsley, savory, thyme, ginger, dry mustard, celery salt or rosemary.

Beef pot roasts: All the above plus bay leaf, mixed pickling spices and sage.

Beef soups and stews: All the above plus bay leaf, whole black peppers, cinnamon stick, whole cloves, whole mace.

Lamb chops or patties broiled: Cumin, garlic, oregano, garlic salt, onion powder or salt.

Lamb roasts: Marjoram, onion powder or salt, mixed pickling spices, poultry seasoning, rosemary, savory and thyme.

Lamb stews and soups: Whole coriander seed, basil, bay leaf, garlic salt or powder, mixed pickling spices, onion salt or powder, rosemary, savory, curry powder or thyme.

Fresh pork chops or roasts: Cayenne pepper, chili powder, curry powder, garlic powder or salt, marjoram, paprika, onion powder or salt, thyme, caraway seed, rosemary, poultry seasoning, savory or oregano.

Smoked pork roasted: Whole cloves, dry mustard.

Smoked pork boiled: Bay leaf, dill seed, whole cloves, mixed pickling spices and whole mace.

Veal roast and pot roasts: Basil, celery seed, ginger, marjoram, oregano, thyme and garlic powder.

Veal stews: Bay leaf, cayenne pepper, celery seed, chili powder, curry powder, ginger, marjoram, nutmeg, paprika, rosemary and thyme.

POULTRY

Chicken and turkey, broiled or roasted: Cayenne pepper, curry powder, garlic powder or salt, onion powder or salt, paprika, marjoram, saffron, rosemary, thyme and savory.

Duck, roasted: Curry powder or ginger.

Goose, roasted: Caraway seed, juniper berries, marjoram, poultry seasoning or sage.

Pheasant: Same seasonings as chicken.

FISH AND SEAFOODS

Fish, baked or broiled: Basil, celery seed, chives, curry powder, marjoram, dry mustard, onion flakes, rosemary, savory, saffron, tarragon or thyme.

Lobster, boiled: Bay leaf, chili powder, curry powder, garlic powder or salt, onion powder or salt, oregano, thyme or tarragon.

Shrimp, boiled: Same seasonings as for lobster.

EGGS

Omelet, scrambled or shirred: Basil, chives, curry powder, marjoram, thyme, rosemary, savory, paprika, onion salt or dry mustard.

Deviled eggs: Cayenne pepper, celery seed, chives, ground cumin seed, curry powder, dry mustard, paprika or savory.

VEGETABLES

Asparagus: Basil, dry mustard, nutmeg, savory, sesame seed, tarragon or thyme.

Beets: Allspice, basil, caraway seed, celery seed, dill seed, mustard seed, onion powder, nutmeg or thyme.

Broccoli: Basil, caraway seed, curry powder, dill seed or nutmeg.

Brussels Sprouts: Basil, curry powder, dill seed or mustard.

Cabbage: Basil, caraway seed, celery seed, cumin seed, dry mustard or tarragon.

Carrots: Basil, bay leaf, parsley, rosemary, savory, fennel, ginger, mace, marjoram, mint, nutmeg or thyme.

Cauliflower: Rosemary, savory, tarragon, thyme or basil.

Cucumber: Dill seed, basil, tarragon, thyme or chives.

Mushrooms: Rosemary or thyme.

Onions: Caraway seed, dill seed, marjoram, dry mustard, rosemary, sage or thyme.

Green Peas: Basil, chives, ginger, marjoram, dry mustard, nutmeg, rosemary, celery seed or paprika.

Potatoes: Basil, caraway seed, celery seed, chives, curry powder, dill seed, dry mustard, poppy seed or thyme.

Sweet Potatoes: Cinnamon, ginger or nutmeg.

Spinach: Allspice, mace, marjoram, nutmeg, oregano, rosemary or thyme.

Green Beans: Basil, curry powder, dill seed, garlic, dry mustard, nutmeg, oregano, sesame seed.

Squash: Allspice, cinnamon, cloves, curry powder or nutmeg.

Tomatoes: Basil, caraway seed, celery salt, chives, cloves, curry powder, dill seed, garlic powder, oregano, tarragon, thyme or sesame seed.

Turnips: Allspice, basil, celery seed, dill seed, nutmeg, onion or chives.

FRUITS

Apples: Cardamon seed, cinnamon, cloves, coriander seed, mace, nutmeg or allspice.

Apricots: Cinnamon, cloves, allspice or ginger.

Blueberries: Cinnamon, nutmeg, cloves or allspice.

Cherries: Allspice, cinnamon, cloves, ginger or nutmeg.

Cranberries: Allspice, cinnamon, cloves or ginger.

Lemon or Lime: Cloves, nutmeg, mace or ginger.

Peaches: Cinnamon, cloves or ginger.

Pears: Cinnamon, cloves, allspice or ginger.

Pineapple: Ginger, cinnamon, mace or nutmeg.

Plums: Cinnamon and cloves.

Rhubarb: Allspice, cinnamon, cloves, ginger, mace or nutmeg.

BREADS AND CAKES

Breads, coffee, cakes, muffins: caraway seed, cardamon seed, cinnamon, fennel seed, nutmeg, poppy seed, saffron or sesame seed.

Cakes: Anise seed, caraway seed, cinnamon, coriander seed, cloves, ginger, nutmeg, mace, saffron or allspice.

DESSERTS AND PASTRIES

Ice Cream: Cinnamon or nutmeg.

Pies: Caraway seed, coriander seed, nutmeg, cinnamon, cloves or sesame seed.

Custard and Puddings: Cardamon seed, coriander seed, cinnamon, nutmeg or mace.

BEVERAGES

Chocolate: Cinnamon or nutmeg.

Coffee: Cardamon seed, whole cloves or cinnamon.

Tea: Whole cloves or cinnamon sticks.

Milk: Allspice, cinnamon, cloves, mace or nutmeg.

CHEESE

American or Cheddar, cooked: Cayenne pepper, ginger, dry mustard, paprika, chili powder or curry powder.

Cottage Cheese: Caraway seed, chives, dill, garlic powder, paprika, poppy seed or sesame seed.

2.

Appetizers

TAKE THE LITTLE Brown Chef's advice for big cocktail parties, and don't try to prepare too many fancy hot dishes. Don't work yourself to death! Create a picture in your mind, and arrange your spreads and tidbits so that they will look attractive and taste better. For instance:

Place a bowl of any one of the tasty sauces given in the center of a large flat plate. Decorate the plate with parsley. In sections, arrange cooked shrimp, carrot strips, celery strips, and tomato wedges on toothpicks.

Or your plate might contain tiny cheese balls on toothpicks, green pepper strips, tiny hot sausages, olives, tiny tuna fish balls rolled in parsley.

Other good appetizers are tiny strips of salami, potato chips, sautéed mushroom and pickle on a toothpick, strips of Swiss cheese, cream cheese and onion balls on toothpicks. You may serve a plate of tiny hot frankfurters or hot codfish balls with the sauce in the center of a plate of all raw vegetables such as carrots, cucumber strips, string beans, celery, cauliflower.

Then make a bowl of your best spreads such as The Brown Chef suggests. Place bowl in center of plate or tray. Decorate, surround with potato chips, rye bread strips, assorted crackers, melba toast or white bread squares. Be sure there are plenty of spreads on your table so each person can help himself, and you will be saved many headaches.

Don't overlook the easy varieties of meat rolls that take only a little time, such as: On thin slices of salami, spread a mixture of horseradish and cream cheese, roll, cut in half if too large. Place on toothpicks. Chill.

ANCHOVY AND ONION BALLS

1 flat tin anchovy fillet	*1 teaspoon paprika*
1 teaspoon dry mustard	*24 small pickled onions*

Drain oil from anchovy fillets. Roll 1 anchovy around an onion. Mix mustard and paprika. Roll anchovy and onion ball in mustard mixture. Place on a toothpick.

AVOCADO BALLS

2 ripe avocados	*2 tablespoons minced or*
1 tablespoon lemon juice	*grated onion*
1 teaspoon salt	*3 or 4 grated carrots*
1 teaspoon paprika	*¼ cup chopped parsley*

Peel and mash avocado. Add lemon juice and salt with chopped parsley. Form into small balls and roll in grated carrots. Serve on toothpick.

AVOCADO EMERALD

2 medium avocados	*1 lemon*
1 teaspoon salt	*1 teaspoon paprika*
1 cup crab meat or tuna	*½ cup minced celery*
½ cup cream cheese	*2 tablespoons grated onion*
1 teaspoon Season-all	*1 head lettuce*
½ teaspoon Tabasco sauce	

Peel avocado. Cut carefully in ¼-inch rings around seed until it can be removed without breaking. Cut lemon in half. Squeeze juice of half lemon over avocado rings. Sprinkle with salt and chill. Cut remaining lemon in 6 thin slices and twist each slice. Mix crab or tuna with celery, cheese and onion. Season with season salt and Tabasco sauce. Form into balls. Roll in paprika.

Shred lettuce. Place a slice of avocado on each plate, a ball of fish mixture in the center and the lemon twist on the side. Serves 6 to 8.

BASIC SPREADS FOR HORS D'OEUVRES

Increase the amount of basic butter spread for hors d'oeuvres by adding any of the following ingredients to ½ cup butter:

¼cup prepared mustard	¼ cup horseradish
¼ cup tomato catsup	2 tablespoons grated onion

Salad dressing may be substituted for butter. It adds zest and is economical.

BITE SIZE HAMBURGERS

1 pound chuck beef, ground twice	½ teaspoon red pepper
	½ teaspoon garlic salt
2 tablespoons grated onion	1 teaspoon salt
1 teaspoon prepared mustard	1 tablespoon Worcestershire sauce
1 egg	½ cup flour

Combine all ingredients except flour until they are very well mixed. Form into tiny balls about ½ inch in diameter. Flatten slightly to resemble hamburgers. Roll lightly in flour. Fry in hot fat, turning as required. Place in hot chafing dish. Serve with spicy cocktail sauce or barbecue sauce. Serve with crackers or on toothpicks.

CHEDDAR CHEESE AND RUM

3 cups grated sharp American cheddar cheese	1 cup grated minced onion
	1 cup dark rum

Mix together thoroughly. Store in tightly covered glass jars in refrigerator. Use as spread on crackers.

CHEESE, HAM AND PICKLE PATTIES

1 package cream cheese, at room temperature	dash of hot sauce or ⅛ teaspoon pepper
1 cup grated American cheese	1 teaspoon celery salt
1 cup ground ham	½ cup parsley, finely chopped
¼ cup red pickle relish, strained	1 teaspoon paprika

Cream softened cheese, grated cheese and ham with pickle relish, hot sauce or pepper and celery salt. Make ham and cheese mixture into rolls approximately 2 inches long and ¼ inch in diameter. Put chopped parsley on waxed paper and sprinkle with paprika. Roll sandwich in parsley and paprika. Chill.

CHICKEN LIVER FILLING

½ cup chopped cooked chicken livers
¼ teaspoon savory salt

½ tablespoon cream
2 hard-cooked eggs
1 teaspoon grated onion

Combine ingredients, add just enough cream to moisten. Spread on toast, crackers or potato chips. Good for stuffing tomatoes or served on pieces of pepper or celery or even tomato slices.

CLAM SPREAD

1 can minced clams, well drained
3 4-ounce packages cream cheese
1 teaspoon onion juice or

¼ cup chopped green onion
1 tablespoon salad dressing
1 teaspoon paprika
1 tablespoon Tabasco sauce

Combine all ingredients thoroughly until well blended. Cover; chill. Serve in bowl with crackers or potato chips. Garnish with parsley.

COCKTAIL OYSTERS

4 to 5 dozen oysters
½ cup white wine
½ cup chopped parsley and chives
1 tablespoon lemon juice
1 tablespoon butter

1 can mushrooms
½ cup heavy cream
1 small onion
salt and pepper to taste
2 egg yolks

Drain and finely chop oysters. Sauté mushrooms, onion, parsley and oysters in butter. Add seasonings. Simmer 20 minutes. Beat egg yolks and cream until very light. Add to oysters. Simmer over low fire 2 to 3 minutes. Remove from fire. Add lemon juice. Place in chafing dish or casserole to keep hot. Serve as hors d'oeuvre.

COTTAGE CHEESE SPREAD

1 pint cottage cheese
2 carrots, grated
1 teaspoon paprika
2 tablespoons salad dressing
2 small onions, grated

1 tablespoon prepared
    mustard
1 bunch green onions and
    tops
1 teaspoon tomato catsup

Mix all ingredients well. Chill. Serve with crackers.

CHEESE AND OLIVE BISCUITS

To your favorite biscuit dough recipe add:

1 cup coarse cheese, grated
1 cup stuffed olives, chopped

1 tablespoon catsup
dash paprika

Mix cheese, olives and catsup. Roll dough ½ inch thick. Cut in small rounds. Place ½ teaspoon of mixture on each biscuit, then place another plain biscuit on top. Press together, sprinkle with paprika and bake 15 minutes in a moderate oven, 350° F. Yield: approximately 24 biscuits.

CRAB MEAT AND CHEESE PUFFS

1 can crab meat, drained
    and flaked
¼ cup grated onion
¼ cup grated green pepper
1 tablespoon prepared
    horseradish
1 teaspoon celery salt
1 teaspoon prepared mustard
2 tablespoons salad dressing

24 bread rounds (1 inch
    in diameter)
3 tablespoons soft butter
1 egg yolk
¼ teaspoon salt
1 cup grated American
    cheese
paprika

Combine crab meat, onion, green pepper, horseradish, celery salt, mustard and salad dressing. Add egg yolk and mix thoroughly. Cut bread rounds and butter lightly. Place about 1 tablespoon of crab mixture on each round of bread. Beat egg white and salt until stiff; fold in grated cheese. Top each round with egg white mixture; add a dash of paprika. Place rounds under broiler for 8 to 10 minutes until cheese is melted and they are puffed. Serve hot.

APPETIZERS

EBONY'S OYSTERS

1 pint fresh oysters
1 cup chili sauce
1 teaspoon basil
1 teaspoon garlic salt
1 teaspoon oregano

¼ cup finely chopped
  parsley
2 tablespoons smoked
  hickory salt
2 tablespoons soft butter

Drain juices from oysters. Combine chili sauce, basil, garlic salt, oregano, parsley, hickory salt and butter in a chafing dish. Add oysters, cover and steam for 10 minutes. Serve hot on crackers or with toothpicks.

FRIED MEAT BALLS AND CRAB MEAT

1½ pounds finely ground
  lean pork
¼ pound cooked crab meat
  or
1 can crab meat, drained
  and flaked
½ cup chopped mushrooms
½ cup chopped canned
  water chestnuts

2 teaspoons salt
½ teaspoon pepper
1 teaspoon sugar
1 cup cornstarch
2 eggs, beaten
2 tablespoons water
fat for frying

Combine finely chopped pork, crab meat, mushrooms and water chestnuts with salt, pepper and sugar in bowl. Shape in 1-inch balls. Roll balls in cornstarch; set aside. Combine beaten eggs and water. Dip each ball in egg mixture and fry in 350° F. fat for 8 to 10 minutes. Serve with sliced cucumbers.

Balls are excellent as hors d'oeuvre; spear each one on a toothpick with a thin slice of cucumber and tomato.

GRAPEFRUIT AND MINT

1 bunch fresh mint
½ cup crème de menthe
½ cup confectioners' sugar

1 can grapefruit sections,
  chilled
1 bottle green maraschino
  cherries

Wash and remove mint leaves from stems. Place leaves in a bowl. Add crème de menthe and confectioners' sugar and crush with mint leaves. Drain juice from grapefruit sections.

18

Add sections to sugar and mint mixture; coat sections carefully. Cover and chill until ready to serve. Place in cocktail glasses or a low bowl. Garnish with cherries and serve.

HAM AND EGG CARROTS

1 package cream cheese
1 cup finely ground cooked
  ham
¼ cup minced celery
¼ cup minced green pepper
1 finely chopped hard-cooked
  egg
¼ cup salad dressing
1 bunch finely chopped
  green onions

1 tablespoon prepared
  mustard
1 teaspoon salt
1 teaspoon paprika
3 raw grated carrots
1 tablespoon meat sauce
celery leaves
minced parsley

Cream cheese until smooth. Add ham, celery, green pepper, egg, salad dressing, onions, mustard, salt and paprika. Mix ingredients well. Shape into 12 small carrots. Roll in grated carrots. Garnish top with celery leaves and minced parsley. Chill in refrigerator before serving.

HAM ROLLS

8 to 10 slices boiled ham
¼ cup grated celery
½ cup chopped cooked
  string beans
¼ cup salad dressing
4 medium white potatoes

¼ cup chopped parsley
1 tablespoon prepared
  mustard
dash onion salt
salt and pepper to taste

Boil potatoes, cool and dice very small. Add other ingredients, mix well, mashing with a fork. Place mixture on ham slices and roll. Hold roll together with toothpicks. Set in refrigerator to chill. Remove picks. Serve with cocktails or, if used for picnic lunches, wrap individually in waxed paper.

Any one of your favorite cold sliced meats may be substituted in this recipe.

HOT DUNK FOR SEA FOOD

3 tablespoons butter
3 tablespoons flour

1 teaspoon onion salt
1 teaspoon celery salt

19

1 teaspoon garlic salt	½ cup A-1 sauce
1 cup milk	¼ cup Worcestershire sauce
½ cup mayonnaise	½ cup prepared mustard
½ cup catsup	½ teaspoon pepper

Melt butter in heavy saucepan. Stir in flour, pepper and the three salts until quite smooth. Add milk all at once. Stir constantly over medium heat until mixture boils, then reduce heat and continue to stir until thick and smooth. Remove from heat. Stir in all remaining ingredients. Bring to boil, and cook until thick, stirring constantly. Serve hot as dunk for cocktail, franks or sausages, shrimps or miniature meat balls.

LIVERWURST BALLS

1 pound liverwurst	1 teaspoon pepper sauce
1 tablespoon grated onion	1 cup chopped parsley

Mash liverwurst with pepper sauce and onion. Blend well. If necessary, add a bit of salad dressing to mix. Form into balls. Roll in parsley and serve.

Tiny pickled onions may be placed in the center of each ball if desired. Serves 12.

LIVER SAUSAGE COCKTAIL BITS

½ pound liver sausage	2 tablespoons finely diced
2 tablespoons grated onion	green peppers
1 teaspoon curry powder	1 tablespoon prepared
¼ cup finely ground bread	mustard
crumbs	1 egg, beaten
	fine bread crumbs for coating

Combine liver sausage, onion, curry powder, ¼ cup bread crumbs, green pepper and mustard. Mix thoroughly. Shape into ½-inch or 1-inch balls. Dip balls in beaten egg; roll in bread crumbs. Fry in deep fat heated to 350° F. for 1 to 2 minutes or until crisp and golden brown all over. Turn once. Drain on absorbent paper.

OYSTER APPETIZER

12 small oysters	12 strips bacon
12 stuffed olives	Tabasco sauce
bread crumbs	

Drain oysters well. Roll in crumbs. Wrap each in a strip of bacon with an olive in center of each oyster. Bacon should go around oyster and olive in ball form. Hold together with toothpick. Place under broiler 10 minutes. Shake pan or use large fork to turn. Dot with Tabasco sauce. Serve hot.

OYSTER TURNOVER

Canapés and hors d'oeuvres need not always be elaborate productions. There are many simple, easy canapés that are tasty and give little or no trouble to the amateur chef. For instance, here is what can be done with rich biscuit dough and several combinations for piping hot "taste teasers."

To your favorite biscuit dough recipe add:

2 dozen small oysters　　　*1 cup cracker crumbs*
1 tablespoon garlic salt　　*1 teaspoon paprika*
¼ cup melted butter　　　　*1 teaspoon celery salt*

Roll dough thin and cut in 2-inch squares. Sprinkle with celery salt. Drain oysters well. Roll in crumbs to which garlic salt has been added. Place an oyster in each biscuit dough square. Press into dough. Fold ends over tightly to meet. Ends may be held together with toothpick. Brush with melted butter. Sprinkle with paprika. Bake in hot oven 15 minutes. Serve hot. Yield: 24 biscuits.

RAW VEGETABLE APPETIZER

½ cup finely chopped　　　*1 bunch finely chopped*
　string beans　　　　　　　*onions*
1 bunch finely chopped　　　*2 finely chopped red peppers*
　water cress　　　　　　　　*½ cup prepared mustard*
2 finely chopped green　　　*1 quart cottage cheese*
　peppers　　　　　　　　　*1 teaspoon paprika*
6 small finely chopped　　　*2 tablespoons horseradish*
　carrots　　　　　　　　　*1 teaspoon garlic salt*
　　　　　　　　　　　　　　juice of 1 lemon

Blend ingredients. Chill and serve with crackers, potato chips or tiny squares of bread.

ROQUEFORT CHEESE AND BRANDY

1 pound Roquefort cheese   *1 teaspoon paprika*
½ cup brandy

Mash cheese, add brandy and paprika; mix thoroughly. Pack in tightly covered glass jar. Store in refrigerator. Use as spread for crackers.

ROLLED DRIED BEEF RINGS

6 to 8 large slices of dried   *red pepper*
   beef   *2 tablespoons salad dressing*
1 package pimiento or
   cream cheese

Mix salad dressing and cheese. Sprinkle with red pepper. Spread thinly on slices of beef and roll as jelly roll. Chill. Slice in ¼ inch wedges and serve.

SALAMI ROLLS

¼ pound Salami (Italian)   *½ teaspoon paprika*
   sliced paper thin   *½ teaspoon hot sauce*
1 package cream cheese   *2 pimientos*

Blend chopped pimientos, cheese and hot sauce into a paste. Spread on slice of Salami sparingly. Roll as jelly roll. Place in refrigerator to set. Place on toothpick.

Tiny sweet pickles may be placed in center if desired.

SALMON MIX

2 cans red salmon   *1 cup finely chopped*
1 cup grated onion   *pickle (drained)*
2 tablespoons lemon juice   *¼ cup mustard*
1 cup salad dressing   *1 cup cream cheese*
1 tablespoon paprika   *1 cup finely chopped celery*

Drain salmon, remove bones. Mix all ingredients and season. Blend in cheese. Place in a large bowl surrounded with potato chips, crackers or toast. Serves 10 to 15.

SARDINE SPECIAL

2 medium cans sardines   *2 packages cream cheese*
2 tablespoons lemon juice   *2 tablespoons salad dressing*

1 teaspoon paprika
1 cup finely chopped green
    peppers
2 tablespoons prepared
    mustard

6 sweet pickles, diced or
    ½ cup drained relish
1 tablespoon Tabasco sauce
salt and pepper to taste

Drain oil from sardines. Mash with fork. Add seasonings and blend in cheese mixture so that paste will be thin enough to spread without running. More cream cheese may be added if necessary. Serve in a bowl. Surround with melba toast strips.

STUFFED EGGS AND CRAB MEAT

6 hard-cooked eggs
2 tablespoons mustard
2 tablespoons lemon juice
¼ cup grated onion
2 tablespoons finely
    chopped green peppers

paprika to taste
1 teaspoon salt
¾ cup mayonnaise
1 cup crab meat
½ cup finely chopped celery
dash Tabasco sauce

Cut eggs in half, crosswise. Remove yolks. Mash and combine with other ingredients. Fill whites and sprinkle with paprika. Yield: 12 halves.

STUFFED EGGS WITH SARDINES

12 hard-cooked eggs
2 tablespoons lemon juice
1 finely chopped pimiento
1 tablespoon prepared
    mustard
½ cup finely chopped
    parsley

1 can sardines
1 small grated onion
1 teaspoon salt
⅓ cup salad dressing
paprika to taste
celery salt to taste
1 tablespoon Tabasco sauce

Cut eggs in half and remove yolks. Sprinkle whites with salt and celery salt. Mash yolks to a powder, or run through a sieve. Blend onion, mashed sardines, pimiento, lemon juice, mustard, Tabasco sauce and salad dressing. Season to taste. Fill egg whites. Garnish or roll in chopped parsley. Yield: 24 halves.

Serve as hors d'oeuvre or on a bed of lettuce as a salad. For variety in stuffed eggs, place a rolled anchovy in each half (omit sardines) and fill with yolk mixture. Instead of sardines use ½ cup anchovy paste, or add 1 cup grated carrot and ¼ cup chopped green onions.

APPETIZERS

TINY WIENER APPETIZERS

To your favorite biscuit dough recipe add:

3 dozen tiny frankfurters   *2 tablespoons prepared*
1 cup sauerkraut, chopped   *mustard*

Roll dough thin. Cut in circles about 3 inches in diameter. Spread each circle sparingly with mustard. Place 1 tablespoon sauerkraut and one frankfurter in center. Roll tightly, place on a greased baking sheet and bake in a hot oven for 20 minutes. Serve hot. Yield: approximately 36 biscuits.

TUNA FISH SURPRISE

To your favorite biscuit recipe dough add:

1 cup tuna fish   *2 tablespoons grated onion*
1 chopped dill pickle   *1 tablespoon butter*
1 teaspoon prepared mustard   *¼ cup chopped parsley*

Roll biscuit dough ½-inch thick. Cut in very small rounds. Blend tuna, onion and pickle together. With teaspoon, make opening in center of biscuit. Fill with mixture and press top together. Brush with butter and mustard which have been previously mixed. Bake in hot oven 15 minutes. Makes 24 to 30 small biscuits.

COCKTAIL SAUCES

⅓ cup tomato catsup   *(1)*
2 tablespoons horseradish   *4 tablespoons lemon juice*
dash Tabasco sauce   *celery salt to taste*

½ cup chili sauce   *(2)*
2 tablespoons   *¼ cup salad dressing*
    Worcestershire sauce   *2 tablespoons mustard*

⅓ cup mustard   *(3)*
⅓ cup mayonnaise   *2 tablespoons lemon juice*
1 teaspoon Tabasco sauce   *1 teaspoon garlic salt*

The above variations may be used for fish, vegetable, cheese cocktails, and hors d'oeuvres, as well as vegetable, meat and cheese platters.

3.

Cheese

THE LITTLE BROWN CHEF SAYS: "In dating good dishes, we all know the benefits of cheese; how much nutritional value it contains, how it can take the place of meat. So let's go ahead and use it. Try new combinations and new dishes. Be a cheese explorer! There are so many varieties to explore and experiment with." Here's a list that's bound to help with your shopping and cooking:

AMERICAN CHEESE

Brick—Rennet cheese, with strong sweetish flavor, an elastic texture and many small round eyes or holes.

Cheddar—Similar to English made Cheddar.

Cottage—Soft curds. Made commercially from pasteurized sour milk with or without rennet. Also known as smierkase.

Cream—A soft rich cheese with mild flavor. Genuine cream cheese is made from pasteurized rich cream thickened by souring or from sweet cream thickened with rennet. It is also made from thin cream thickened with rennet and from whole milk.

Hand—Soft; sharp pungent taste and odor. Made from sour milk and shaped by hand. Caraway seeds are sometimes added.

Herkimer—Aged Cheddar.

CHEESE

Liederkranz—Semi-soft, resembles Limburger in flavor. Ripened by a red-slime growth on surface.

Process Cheese—Cheese blended with an emulsifying agent and pasteurized.

Swiss—Similar to Swiss-made Emmenthaler.

ENGLISH CHEESES

Cheddar—Hard, sharp; white or yellow color. Made from sweet milk and sold as "full cream" (when whole milk is used), "part skim" or "skim," depending on the type of milk used.

Cheshire—Hard rennet cheese somewhat like Cheddar.

Stilton—Hard rennet cheese with green or blue mold and wrinkled or ridged skin or rind.

FRENCH CHEESES

Brie—Soft, rennet cheese; definite odor, sharp flavor with a red color on the surface. Made from whole or partly skimmed milk.

Camembert—Soft, rennet cheese covered with a firm rind of molds and dried cheese.

Gruyere—Hard, blended rennet cheese of the Swiss type produced in France. Nutlike flavor.

GERMAN CHEESES

Limburger—Soft rennet cheese with strong, characteristic odor.

Münster—Semi-hard rennet cheese, caraway seeds or aniseed added. Made of whole milk.

HOLLAND CHEESES

Edam—Hard rennet cheese, round with a red rind.

Gouda—Hard rennet cheese, slightly round and flat.

ITALIAN CHEESES

Gorgonzola—Semi-hard rennet cheese with streaks of mold.

Parmesan—Hard, rennet cheese made from partly skimmed milk. Green or black rind.

Provole or Provolona—Hard, round and held by a net.

CHEESE HINTS

Melted cheese makes a delicious topping for vegetables, as well as cheese sauces of all varieties.

Remember, to make cheese sauces—simply add ½ to 1 whole cup of grated cheese to your white sauce. A tablespoon prepared mustard may be added too!

CHEDDAR CHEESE AND RUM

Three cups Cheddar cheese blended with one cup dark rum. Place in jars and set aside to ripen.

AMERICAN CHEESE AND SHERRY

1 cup American cheese (soft type)	½ cup sherry wine 1 tablespoon cream

Blend together. Place in jar to ripen.

Remember when blending cheese for spreads, cheese should be room temperature so that it will blend easily.

Just before serving, a bit of chopped chives may be blended into spreads.

CHEESE AND PIMIENTO TIDBITS

To your favorite biscuit dough add:

2 cups grated sharp cheese (coarse)	1 teaspoon catsup 1 cup chopped pimiento

Divide in 3 parts. Roll each part into a thin rectangle. Mix cheese, pimiento and catsup. Spread ⅓ of mixture on dough. Roll as jelly roll. Cut in thin slices (repeat with rest of dough). Place on greased sheet and bake 10 minutes in hot oven, 400° F. Dough is divided so the slices will be tiny rounds, or about bite size. Yield: 48 small pieces.

CHEESE AND OLIVE APPETIZERS

1 jar smoky cheese	12 small stuffed olives
1 cup chopped parsley	1 teaspoon celery salt
12 1-inch squares of toast (optional)	

Place 1 teaspoon cheese in center of hand. Mold around olive. Roll in parsley. Chill. Serve plain or place on toast squares and set in oven for 10 minutes. Serve hot.

CHEESE

WELSH RAREBIT

4 tablespoons butter
2 cups American or store
    cheese, grated
1 tablespoon
    Worcestershire sauce

½ cup milk
1 teaspoon dry mustard
2 eggs

Melt butter in top of double boiler over hot water. Add cheese, stirring constantly until cheese is melted. Add mustard, salt and Worcestershire sauce. Add milk gradually. Continue to stir. Add slightly beaten egg and cook until thick. Serve at once on thin crisp toast. Sprinkle with paprika and garnish with parsley. Serves 4.

The old folk say "Rarebit ain't rarebit without beer." So, if you wish, you can substitute beer for milk.

RAREBIT WITH ZIP

2 cups hot milk
2 tablespoons flour
1 small green pepper,
    chopped
1 medium onion, chopped

4 tablespoons butter
1 tablespoon chopped
    parsley
3 tablespoons flour
pinch garlic salt
1 teaspoon Tabasco sauce

Sauté onions and pepper in butter. Add flour and milk. Place in double boiler. Cook until thick. Add cheese and spices. Heat thoroughly and serve over toasted bread squares.

CHEESE SOUP

3 cups milk
1 tablespoon chopped
    onion
½ teaspoon salt
1 tablespoon chopped
    celery
½ cup grated aged or
    snappy cheese

1 cup grated sharp,
    American, or Cheddar
    cheese
1 teaspoon paprika
½ teaspoon curry powder
1 tablespoon butter

Sauté vegetables in butter. Add flour, seasoning and milk which has been scalded. Cook until it becomes thick, stirring constantly. Just before serving add cheese and Tabasco sauce. Serve at once with crackers or toast.

COTTAGE CHEESE PATTIES

2 cups cottage cheese
2 tablespoons grated onion
2 tablespoons chopped
    parsley
½ teaspoon paprika
1 egg

2 cups bread crumbs
1 small green pepper, grated
1 teaspoon pepper
1 cup milk
½ cup grated carrots

Combine cheese, vegetables, bread crumbs, seasonings and milk. Form into patties. Dip in a mixture of 1 egg beaten with 2 tablespoons milk or water. Then roll in bread or cracker crumbs. Fry in deep hot fat until brown on all sides.

BAKED CHEESE AND OLIVE CASSEROLE
(With Vegetables)

1 cup cooked peas
1 cup corn
1 cup boiled celery
1 cup cooked lima beans
½ cup chopped parsley
1 cup milk
1 cup cooked string beans
2 tablespoons butter
1 cup cooked green pepper

1 cup chopped olives
    (stuffed)
2 cups grated cheese
1 cup bread crumbs
1 cup chopped boiled onion
1 cup tomato sauce
1 teaspoon garlic salt
salt, pepper, paprika to taste

Mix cheese and tomato sauce in double boiler until well blended. Add milk. Mix all vegetables together. Add salt, pepper, paprika. Sauté bread crumbs in butter. Place a layer of vegetables in greased casserole. Add layer of bread crumbs, then vegetables, and alternate until full.

Pour the cheese and tomato sauce over top of casserole and bake in moderate oven 35 to 40 minutes. Serve with a salad for a complete meal.

4.

Soups

SOME PEOPLE THINK of soup as anything from an extra added attraction to a full meal in itself. And indeed it might be either. Soups, like vegetables, lend themselves to versatility.

When country folk make a pot of soup on a cold wintry day, it is really a production. When you travel along the Eastern Shore, there is nothing better than fish chowders. The justly famous gumbos and bisques of New Orleans are definitely all-in-one meals.

Then there is the tiny cup that teases your appetite and the cold jellied consommés for hot days. Creamed soup, plain soup, thick soup, thin soup, fancy soup, too. Versatile soups are in abundance.

Soups and stews are one of the oldest forms of cookery. We must value them because their age-old charm has been cultivated to modern taste, and we have discovered many vitamins and minerals in soups that are indispensable health-givers. Soup has become a *must* on American menus.

I've seen soup made from costly delicacies, and it was "scrumptious." I've tasted soup made from leftovers by the poor, and it was breath-takingly good. Whether it's served in a palace or a shack, it's good for us. So let's try it!

GARNISHES FOR SOUPS

Bacon and onions: Add chopped crisp bacon and onions sautéed in bacon fat to tomato, celery or bean soup.

Cheese: Sprinkle grated cheese over chowders.

Croutons: Sprinkle over any kind of soup.

Parsley: Sprinkle over any kind of soup.

Macaroni rings: Cut cooked macaroni into thin slices, making tiny rings and sprinkle over soup or chowder.

Olive rings: Slice stuffed olives very thin and serve as a garnish for jellied consommé.

Whipped cream: Serve slightly salted whipped cream in cream soups and sprinkle with paprika, or top with a tiny sprig of parsley or a bit of pimiento cut in an attractive shape.

BLACK BEAN SOUP

2 cups black beans	dash mace, red pepper, salt,
10 cups water	black pepper
¼ pound salt pork or bacon	2 hard-cooked eggs, sliced
ends	1 small garlic clove
½ cup sherry	6 slices lemon
3 whole cloves	3 minced onions

Wash and soak beans overnight. Drain water. Add water and meat which has been finely chopped, onions, garlic and seasonings. Cover and cook slowly 3 hours until beans are very soft. Run through a sieve. Place in a saucepan. Heat. Add sherry. Serve in a tureen or soup plate with a slice of egg and a slice of lemon. A sprig of parsley may be added if desired. Serves 8.

LOUISIANA BEAN SOUP

½ pound navy beans	1 finely chopped onion
2 cups milk	½ cup finely chopped celery
1 garlic clove	several sprigs chopped
2 teaspoons salt	parsley
2 cups tomatoes	1 sprig leaf thyme
½ cup finely chopped green	¼ pound chopped bacon
peppers	

Soak beans overnight. Drain. Cook with onion, bacon and garlic in salted water until very soft. Press through sieve when

31

done. Sauté in butter, celery, pepper and parsley in large pan. Add flour and mix well. Add milk and spices. Heat tomatoes and bean purée. Add to milk mixture. Heat thoroughly. Do not boil. Serves 6.

CRAB AND TOMATO BISQUE

1 cup flaked crab meat	3 tablespoons butter
2 tablespoons flour	2 cups milk
½ teaspoon salt	½ teaspoon Season-all
1 cup tomato juice	pinch sugar
½ cup finely chopped chives	dash garlic salt
dash red pepper	

Melt butter. Add flour and blend. Add milk gradually. Cook until thick. Add seasonings and crab meat. Heat tomato juice and sugar. Add gradually into crab mixture.

Sprinkle chives on top of each serving. Serves 6.

Lobster may be used instead of crab meat.

GREEN PEA SOUP

2 cups stock	½ teaspoon marjoram
1 quart water	1 tablespoon flour
3 cups green peas	2 tablespoons butter
¼ cup diced celery	1 teaspoon salt
1 onion or 4 green onions	¼ teaspoon pepper
and tops	½ teaspoon paprika
1 teaspoon sugar	

Combine brown stock, water, 2½ cups peas, celery, onion and marjoram. Cook until vegetables are tender. Rub through a sieve. Thin with stock or water, if necessary. Blend flour and butter and season with salt, pepper and sugar. Add to puréed vegetables gradually. Heat to boiling point. Stir constantly. Add remaining whole peas, cook until tender and serve. Serves 6.

If green onions are used, chop tops fine and add to soup with whole peas before serving.

MOCK BISQUE SOUP

1 pint tomatoes	1 quart milk
1 small onion	5 tablespoons butter

4 tablespoons flour   white pepper to taste
1 teaspoon salt   1 teaspoon sugar

Stew tomatoes and onion until soft enough to strain easily. Melt the butter in a saucepan, add the flour and stand aside to cool. Then stir in cold milk and cook for 5 minutes. Add salt, pepper, sugar and strained tomatoes.

If tomatoes are very acid, ½ teaspoon baking soda may be added before straining. Do not allow the soup to boil. Serve immediately. Serves 6.

CREAM OF ASPARAGUS SOUP

1 pound asparagus   4 cups scalded milk
2 tablespoons butter   2 tablespoons flour
1 teaspoon salt   ¼ teaspoon pepper
½ teaspoon celery salt   ½ teaspoon onion salt

Wash asparagus, cut off tips 1½ inches from top, cover with boiling water and cook uncovered until tender. Remove and set aside. Add remainder of asparagus and cook until tender. Drain, rub through a sieve and add to milk. Melt butter, blend in flour, salt, and pepper. Add asparagus mixture gradually and heat, stirring constantly. Cook 3 minutes. Add asparagus tips and serve hot with toasted crackers. Serves 6.

2 cups chicken stock and 2 cups milk may be used in place of 4 cups milk.

CORN-TOMATO CHOWDER

¼ pound salt pork or bacon   1 small onion, sliced
2½ cups (1 No. 2 can corn)   2 cups diced potatoes
1½ cups tomatoes   1 teaspoon salt
1 tablespoon sugar   ½ teaspoon celery salt
½ teaspoon paprika   dash pepper
1 quart boiling water   1 cup evaporated milk

Cut pork into small pieces and fry slowly to a golden brown in a large saucepan. Add onion and cook slowly without browning for 5 minutes. Add corn, potatoes and tomatoes. Sprinkle with salt, sugar and pepper. Add water and cook slowly until potatoes are tender. Remove from stove and stir milk in slowly. Serves 6 to 8.

SOUPS

OLD-FASHIONED SPLIT PEA SOUP

2 to 3 *pounds ham ends or*
   salt pork
1 *onion*
3 *quarts boiling water*
2 *tablespoons catsup*
2 *carrots, chopped*
2 *potatoes*
1 *cup split peas*
1 *bay leaf*

Place ham ends or salt pork, carrots, onion, whole potatoes and boiling water in a kettle. Boil 1 hour. Remove ham. Strain vegetables. Skin ham and return to the stock with strained vegetables. Add split peas and boil for 1 hour. Add bay leaf, salt and pepper. Add catsup. Remove ham and serve as the meat course. Milk may be added if desired. Serves 6.

Thin soup with boiling water if too thick.

BOUILLON

2 *pounds beef and soup bone*
4 *peppercorns*
2 *cloves*
1 *blade mace*
1 *carrot, diced*
1 *stalk celery, diced*
1 *teaspoon salt*
2 *quarts cold water*
1 *bay leaf*
1 *teaspoon sweet basil*
1 *small onion, diced*
2 *thin turnips, diced*
1 *sprig parsley*

Cut meat into small pieces. Combine with other ingredients in a kettle. Heat to boiling point slowly and simmer 3 to 4 hours. Strain stock through a fine strainer or several thicknesses of cheesecloth, and cool. When cool, remove fat from top. Reheat and serve hot. Yields 1 quart stock.

If a darker colored stock is desired, brown meat in 2 tablespoons shortening before adding water and other ingredients.

For vegetable soup, add 1 cup diced vegetables, uncooked or cooked, to bouillon. If uncooked vegetables are used, simmer in bouillon until tender. It may be necessary to add more salt.

CONSOMMÉ

1 *pound beef*
1 *bone, split*
1½ *quarts cold water, or 1*
   pint cold water and 1 pint
   chicken stock
2 *peppercorns*
1 *sprig parsley*
1 *clove*
½ *teaspoon sweet herbs*
2 *stalks diced celery*

2 diced carrots   1 teaspoon salt
1 diced onion

Cut meat into small pieces. Combine all ingredients in a kettle, heat slowly to boiling and simmer 3 to 4 hours. Strain consommé through several thicknesses of cheesecloth and cool. When cold, remove fat from top. Reheat and serve hot. Yields 1 quart consommé.

GARDEN LETTUCE AND CORN SOUP

2 cups finely chopped lettuce   1 small onion, or 6 green
3 tablespoons flour   onions and tops
1 teaspoon celery salt   1 quart milk
1 8-ounce can golden cream   1 teaspoon Season-all
    style corn   ⅓ cup butter
½ teaspoon salt   dash nutmeg
dash pepper   ½ teaspoon paprika

Sauté lettuce and onion in butter about 5 minutes. Add flour and mix well. Place in a large pot. Add milk and seasonings. Stir until thick. Press corn through a sieve or, if desired, add as is. Add to soup. Reheat. Add a dash of nutmeg and serve. Serves 6.

CREAM OF TOMATO SOUP

2 cups cooked tomatoes   2 tablespoons flour
1 small minced onion   1 quart scalded milk
¼ teaspoon pepper   2 teaspoons sugar
dash cayenne   dash garlic salt
2 tablespoons butter or   1 teaspoon salt
    substitute

Cook tomatoes, onion, salt, pepper, cayenne and sugar together for 15 minutes. Strain. Melt butter, blend in flour, add milk gradually, stirring constantly. Add tomato mixture gradually to milk mixture, stirring constantly. Serve immediately with water cress, parsley, or whipped cream. Serves 6.

Tomato-Cheese Soup

Add 1 cup grated strong American cheese just before serving.

Tomato-Oyster Soup

Heat 1 pint oysters in 1 tablespoon fat until edges curl. Add to milk.

CLAM CHOWDER

2 dozen fresh clams	salt and pepper to taste
6 strips diced bacon	2 tablespoons flour
1 stalk diced celery	2 medium diced onions
2 large diced white	1 diced green pepper
potatoes	2 carrots (optional)
3 sprigs parsley	1 tablespoon paprika
1 tablespoon thyme	1 can tomato soup or purée

Steam clams in enough water to cover for 15 minutes. Drain broth and set aside. Chop clams fine and sprinkle with flour. Add diced bacon, onions, celery, pepper, potatoes, carrots and parsley to clam broth. Simmer 15 minutes. Add paprika, salt, pepper and thyme. Add clams, tomato soup or purée. Cook an additional 10 minutes and serve. Serves 8.

CHICKEN AND OYSTER GUMBO

3 to 4 pound stewing	1 cup diced celery
chicken	2 dozen oysters
1 pound fat beef, cubed	3 or 4 tomatoes
½ pound diced okra	1 garlic clove
2 teaspoons salt	2 small onions, chopped
2 quarts water	1 bay leaf
1 teaspoon paprika	1 sprig leaf thyme

Cut up chicken and beef. Cover with water. Add bay leaf and thyme. Boil 1 hour or until chicken is tender. Cool. Remove from bone and return to stock. Add vegetables. Cook 30 minutes. When vegetables are tender add oysters and juice. Steam about 12 minutes. Serve with rice. Filé powder (see p. 352) may be added if desired. Serves 8 to 10.

GARDEN VEGETABLE SOUP

1 soup bone	1 teaspoon salt
1 pound soup meat	1 cup fresh peas
6 carrots	½ teaspoon pepper
3 or 4 stalks celery	2 or 3 white turnips, diced
1 can tomatoes	1 bay leaf

½ pound okra

½ pound string beans

1 bunch green onions and
   tops

1 garlic clove

several sprigs parsley

½ teaspoon celery salt

3 or 4 white potatoes

½ teaspoon sugar

2 large onions

1 green pepper

2 parsnips

Have soup bone split. Place in a large pot. Cut meat in cubes and place in pot with bone. Cover with water. Add spices and simmer 2 hours. Add tomatoes and all vegetables which have been peeled and diced. Add rest of seasonings. Cook until vegetables are tender. Add more salt if necessary. Remove bone before serving. Serve with crackers.

OXTAIL SOUP

1 oxtail

1 tablespoon fat

1 large finely chopped onion

3 pints stock

1 stalk diced celery

1 diced carrot

1 bay leaf

1 sprig thyme

1 cup Dubonnet wine

2 sprigs parsley

1 tablespoon Worcestershire
   sauce

½ cup chopped tomatoes

salt to taste

6 peppercorns

Wash oxtail well and split in small joints. Melt fat, add pieces of meat, and when it starts to brown, add chopped onion. Sauté until onion is a deep gold, then add stock, carrot, celery, thyme, parsley and bay leaf (tied securely together in a cheesecloth bag), tomatoes and wine. Season with Worcestershire sauce, crushed peppercorns and salt and boil. Place over a low heat and simmer until meat is tender, about 3 hours. Remove herbs. Remove meat from bones, reheat and serve a little in each plate of soup. Serves 6.

FRENCH ONION SOUP

4 medium onions

2 tablespoons butter

1 quart water

1 teaspoon Worcestershire
   sauce

4 rounds of toast

salt and pepper to taste

grated Parmesan cheese

Slice onions thin and brown in butter. Add water, Worcestershire sauce, salt and pepper and simmer until onions are tender. Pour soup into an earthen jar or casserole. Arrange toast on top of soup, sprinkle with grated cheese and place under broiler until cheese melts and browns. Serves 4.

Rub casserole or toast with cut clove of garlic.

FISH CHOWDER

2 large onions diced
1 green pepper, diced
1 small stalk celery
several sprigs parsley
1 teaspoon garlic salt
salt, pepper and paprika to
   taste

2 bay leaves
1 pound fillet of sole
½ pound shrimp, cleaned
   and cut
2 cups milk
several strips of bacon, diced
2 tablespoons flour

Clean and prepare shrimp and cut raw fish in small pieces. Sprinkle with seasonings and flour. Set aside. Sauté bacon—do not brown. Put diced vegetables and bacon in pot with 2 cups water. Add bay leaves and boil for ½ hour. Add fish and milk which has been *heated.* Simmer 15 to 20 minutes and serve *hot!* Serves 8.

BROWN STOCK

5-pound beef soup bone
3 quarts cold water
8 peppercorns
3 sprigs thyme
1 stalk celery
½ cup diced turnips

5 cloves
1 bay leaf
2 sprigs parsley
1 tablespoon salt
½ cup diced carrots
2 large onions, sliced

Cut lean meat from the bones and brown ⅓ of it in the marrow taken from the bones. Put the rest of the meat and bones in a large kettle, cover with water and let stand 1 hour. Add browned meat and seasonings and bring to a boil. Reduce heat and simmer for 5 hours. Add the vegetables and cook 1½ hours longer. Strain through a cheesecloth and cool. When cold remove layer of fat which forms on top. Serves 10.

ANGAROLA ONION SOUP

2 large onions, thinly sliced
¼ cup parsley, chopped

2 tablespoons celery leaves,
   chopped

1 clove garlic, juiced or 1
   tablespoon garlic juice
½ cup butter
salt and pepper
4 cups beef broth

1 teaspoon paprika
pinch thyme
grated Swiss cheese
toast

Melt butter in large, heavy cooking pot. Add onions, parsley, celery leaves and garlic juice and cook gently until onion and celery are soft but not colored. Add beef broth, salt, pepper, paprika and thyme. Bring to boil; simmer for 5 minutes. Place a thin slice of toast in bottom of individual baking casserole. Place 2 tablespoons grated cheese on top of toast and fill casserole with soup.

J. P. C. BEAN SOUP

1 cup dried navy beans
1 ham hock, smoked bacon
   or salt pork
3 branches of celery with
   green leaves

1 medium onion
1 garlic clove
1 bay leaf
1 teaspoon paprika
salt and pepper

Wash beans well, cover with cold water and soak 2 hours. Place ham in pot and cover with water. Bring to a boil. Add celery, onion, garlic spices and navy beans; cover and cook slowly until beans are tender, about 2 hours. Strain broth from beans, remove meat, press beans through sieve, add to broth. If necessary, add more water, or a can of beef broth to make 6 cups of liquid. Heat. Serve with chopped parsley or chives.

VARIATIONS:

It is not necessary to strain soup. Beans may be left whole if desired. Before serving sieved bean soup, add ½ cup of sherry wine or 1 teaspoon of curry powder to make soup a gourmet treat. Grated fresh carrots added to hot soup gives added color. Add ⅓ cup of tomatoes or a can of tomato sauce to meat.

CHICKEN AND TOASTED ALMOND SOUP

4 cups chicken broth or
   stock (with 1 cup
   chopped chicken)
1 small onion, grated

several stalks celery,
   chopped
1 cup toasted almonds,
   chopped

1 teaspoon paprika
several drops of almond
  seasoning
4 tablespoons butter
4 tablespoons flour

2 cups of milk
1 cup cream
2 tablespoons parsley,
  chopped
1 teaspoon dry ginger

Sauté onion, celery and almonds in butter for 5 minutes. Add flour and spices. Add chicken broth and simmer slowly for 15 minutes. Add milk, cream, parsley, salt and pepper to taste, and serve.

CREAM OF TOMATO SOUP

1 quart ripe tomatoes
1 pint chicken stock
1 pint warm cream
sprig thyme
¼ pound salt pork, diced
small bay leaf

1 tablespoon sugar
½ teaspoon soda
2 tablespoons flour
1 teaspoon paprika
2 tablespoons butter
salt and pepper to taste

Cook tomatoes, chicken stock and salt pork for 40 minutes or until salt pork is tender. Strain and add sugar and soda. Blend butter and flour in large pot. Add cream and stir well. Add tomato mixture gradually with thyme and bay leaf. Simmer 20 minutes. Add ½ teaspoon white pepper and salt to taste. Serve with crackers or croutons. Serves 8.

CHICKEN OKRA SOUP

Remove the breast from a raw fowl, and with the remaining chicken make a chicken broth. Dice breast in small pieces. Put in a vessel with a chopped onion and a chopped green pepper and a small amount of butter. Simmer until the onion is soft, then add the chicken broth, 2 peeled tomatoes, diced small, or some canned tomatoes, salt and pepper to taste. Boil slowly for ½ hour then add 1 pound of okra cut in pieces ¾ of an inch in length, and cook until the okra is soft. Add 1 teaspoon of Worcestershire sauce and a cup of boiled rice and serve with chopped parsley. If desired, a slice of ham may be cut in small squares and added at the same time as the chicken breast.

NEW ENGLAND OYSTER STEW

1 quart oysters	1 tablespoon butter
2 cups scalded milk	½ teaspoon salt
2 cups evaporated milk, or cream	⅛ teaspoon pepper

Remove oysters carefully from shells. Add ¾ cup water and cook until oysters are plump and edges curl. Remove oysters and add to milk. Add salt and pepper, then strained oyster juice. Add butter, heat and serve. Serves 6.

PEANUT SOUP

1 quart milk	2 tablespoons butter
2 tablespoons flour	1 cup peanuts

Cook peanuts until soft. Remove skins, mash or grind until very fine. Boil milk and add the peanuts. Cook 20 minutes. Mix flour into a smooth paste with milk. Add butter to the peanuts and milk. Stir in the flour. Season with salt and pepper to taste. Serve hot. Serves 6.

MULLIGATAWNY SOUP

3-pound fat stewing chicken	salt and pepper to taste
2 whole mace	1 bay leaf
4 whole allspice, or 1 teaspoon ground allspice	1 small garlic clove
1 tablespoon curry	¼ cup rice, uncooked
¼ cup ground coconut	1 quart hot water
	1 pint milk

Clean and cut chicken. Put several small pieces of chicken fat in stew pan. Sauté enough so that chicken does not stick to pan. Add chicken, mace, allspice, bay leaf, curry and coconut. Brown slowly, turning chicken on all sides. Add water, garlic, rice and milk. Cook slowly until chicken is tender. Remove chicken from soup. Cut meat from bones and chop. Return chopped chicken to soup. Add salt and pepper to taste. Serves 8.

5.

Relishes

RELISHES ADD A VERY SPECIAL something to foods. Although crisp celery, radishes and carrot sticks are definitely an asset, there is nothing quite like a spicy relish or fruit for that extra tang. Stuffed pears, peaches, or apples served with roasts and fowl contribute atmosphere as well as flavor, and you should try them often. It takes a little more time, but it is well worth the effort.

There are many simple, easy-to-prepare relishes you can make in addition to those you can buy ready-prepared, so, why not take the advice of the Little Brown Chef and try these simple relish recipes.

BRANDIED PEACHES

1 stick cinnamon	6 to 8 peaches
2 cloves	½ cup vinegar
½ cup brandy	salt to taste
2 tablespoons brown sugar	1 cup water

Wash and peel peaches. Cut in halves and remove stones if desired. Place vinegar, cinnamon, cloves and brown sugar in a sauce pan. Bring to a boil. Add peaches and continue boiling 10 to 12 minutes. Add brandy and set aside for 2 to 3 hours. Serve with meats, roasts or fowls. Serves 12 to 16.

GRATED CARROTS AND ONION RELISH

An unusual relish, good for fish and meats. To be used at once.

1 bunch large carrots, grated medium	3 medium onions
1 cup grated celery	1 teaspoon celery seeds
1 tablespoon salt	8 to 10 cloves
1 bay leaf	2 tablespoons sugar
1 cup vinegar	1 teaspoon lemon juice

Boil cloves, bay leaf and celery seeds in vinegar for 10 minutes. Strain. Add sugar and salt. Heat to boiling point and add vegetables which have been grated. Serve when cool. Yield: 1 pint.

CARROT RELISH

1 cup grated carrot	½ cup chopped onion
2 sweet pickles, chopped	½ cup salad dressing
1 teaspoon lemon juice	1 teaspoon Tabasco sauce
½ teaspoon Savory salt	

Blend ingredients with salt and pepper to taste. Yield: approximately 2½ cups.

SPECIAL CAULIFLOWER "FLOWERS"

1 whole head cauliflower	1 teaspoon lemon juice
½ cup vinegar	1 tablespoon sugar
1 onion, diced	1 tablespoon pickle spices
1 teaspoon celery seed	2 red pepper pods
salt and pepper to taste	

Separate cauliflower into flowers, being careful not to cut off too much of the stem. Parboil in salted boiling water 10 minutes. Drain. Boil spices, sugar, onion, vinegar and lemon juice for 20 minutes. Add red pepper. Strain over cauliflower buds and boil an additional 10 minutes or until tender. Cool. Serve with salads, as hors d'oeuvres, as a vegetable, or as a relish.

May be tinted with vegetable coloring if desired.

RAW CRANBERRY RELISH

4 cups fresh cranberries	1 lemon
2 raw apples	1 orange
1 cup sugar	½ teaspoon salt

Wash and pick berries. Put through the food chopper. Wash orange, lemon and apples. Cut into pieces. Remove seeds and put through food chopper. Add sugar. Place in refrigerator several hours before serving. Yield: approximately 1 quart.

PINEAPPLE RELISH

½ cup crushed pineapple
1 tablespoon lemon juice
2 teaspoons prepared
* horseradish*
1 teaspoon grated lemon rind
½ teaspoon salt
2 tablespoons salad dressing
½ teaspoon paprika

Drain juice from pineapple. Add horseradish. Place in a sauce pan and heat 5 minutes. Do not boil! Add lemon juice, rind, salt, paprika and salad dressing. Cool. Serve with lamb chops or lamb roast. Yield: 1 cup.

HOT SPICED PEAS

2 pounds frozen peas, cooked
* and drained*
1 head green lettuce,
* chopped fine*
1 teaspoon paprika
white pepper
1 cup chopped mushrooms,
* cooked*
1 teaspoon garlic salt
1 cup French dressing,
* heated*

Mix peas, lettuce, paprika and mushrooms. Add garlic salt and French dressing. Sprinkle with white pepper. Serve with turkey salad.

GINGER PEARS

1 pound sugar
2 cups water
3 to 4 pounds pears
2 lemons, grated
1 stick ginger
1 teaspoon salt

Boil sugar and water. Add lemon. While boiling, add ginger root cut in very thin slices or broken fine. Peel, core and soak pears in salt water 15 to 20 minutes. Pour off water and drop in boiling syrup. Cook ½ hour. Pears may be chopped or sliced. Place in clean sterile glasses or jars and cover with paraffin. Serve with meats.

RED CHERRY RELISH

1 can pitted, tart red cherries
¾ cup brown sugar
1 stick cinnamon
1 tablespoon lemon juice

2 whole cloves	1/4 cup nut meats
1/2 teaspoon nutmeg	1/2 teaspoon salt

Place cherries and syrup from can, brown sugar, spices and lemon juice in sauce pan. Simmer 20 minutes. Remove spices and drain juice. Chop cherries fine. Cook syrup until about 1/2 cup is left. Add nut meats and cherries. Cook another 5 minutes and chill. Serve with meats or fish. Yield: 1 pint.

PICKLED CHERRIES

2 pounds cherries with stems	1 cup vinegar
1 teaspoon salt	1 cup water
6 to 8 cloves	1/4 cup sugar

Select large fresh cherries. Wash well, without removing stems. Pack in sterilized jars. Place vinegar, sugar, salt and water in sauce pan. Place spices in a tiny white cloth bag. Bring to a boil. Remove spice bag and cool. Pour liquid over cherries. Seal and set to ripen. Yield: approximately 2 pint jars.

Serve with meats, salads, or as hors d'oeuvres.

PEPPER RELISH

6 red peppers	2 teaspoons salt
6 green peppers	1 teaspoon celery seed
4 medium onions	3/4 cup sugar or white syrup
1 cup vinegar	hot water

Grind peppers and onions medium fine. Place in sauce pan with hot water to cover. Simmer 15 minutes. Drain. Add vinegar and sugar with salt and celery seed. Cook 15 minutes over slow fire. Cool and serve. Yield: 1 pint.

SPICED APPLES

1/2 cup sugar	1/2 teaspoon whole cloves
1/2 cup dark brown sugar	8 medium apples
2 cups boiling water	1/2 cup wine
1 4-inch stick cinnamon	

Combine sugar, syrup, water, cinnamon and half of the cloves. Bring to boil. Meanwhile, pare, halve and remove cores from 4 of the apples. Cook covered in syrup, keeping temperature just

45

below boiling point for 30 minutes or until apples are tender. Remove from syrup.

Halve and remove cores from remaining 4 apples. Add remaining cloves to syrup. Cook unpeeled apples in this syrup, following procedure used above. Remove apples and divide syrup in two equal parts.

SPICED APPLE HALVES: Cover unpeeled halves with part of the syrup. Chill and serve with baked ham.

SPICED PEACHES

2 tablespoons pickle spices	1 cup vinegar
1 stick cinnamon	1 teaspoon salt
1 cup brown sugar	rind of 1 lemon
½ cup water	5 pounds peaches

Place spices in a cheesecloth bag or thin white cloth. Mix vinegar, sugar and water. Bring to a boil. Add lemon rind and spices. Boil 15 minutes. Remove rind and spice bag. Wash and peel peaches, leave whole or cut in half, and remove stones. Drop fruit in hot syrup. Cook 10 minutes. Seal in jars which have been sterilized. Be sure the syrup fills jars to top.

SPICED CRABAPPLES

1 cup brown sugar (light)	1 teaspoon salt
1½ cups vinegar (white)	2 tablespoons corn syrup, or
1 teaspoon celery seed	white sugar
1 tablespoon whole cloves	5 pounds apples with stems
1 stick cinnamon	

Select small, firm apples. Leave stems on and wash well. Soak for 2 to 3 hours in ¼ teaspoon alum, 1 teaspoon salt and enough water to cover. Make a syrup of brown sugar, water and vinegar. Boil for 10 minutes. Drop cinnamon stick in boiling mixture. Add cloves and celery seed. Boil 10 minutes longer. Drain apples. Drop in hot syrup. Cook 15 minutes. Place apples carefully in sterile jars so as not to break stems. Pour syrup over fruit and seal jars. Syrup may be strained before pouring over apples if desired. Delicious for roasts or as hors d'oeuvres.

PEPPER HASH

1 dozen red peppers
½ cup brown sugar
pepper to taste
hot water

15 medium onions (red skin)
3 tablespoons salt
vinegar

Grind onions and peppers. Cover with hot water and let stand overnight. Add brown sugar, salt and pepper. Cover with vinegar and heat thoroughly. Do *not* boil! Store in sterile jars for future use.

A tasty relish for all meats and fowl.

GREEN TOMATO PICKLES

1 peck green tomatoes
12 hot peppers

salt to taste

Wash tomatoes and slice about ¼ inch thick. Place a layer of green tomatoes in a heavy crock or glass with wide top. Sprinkle generously with salt and add a few peppers. Continue layers until jar is full. Weight with iron or a rock and let stand 5 days.

Economical and tasty. Delicious with meats, sandwiches or beans.

CRANBERRY CHUTNEY

1½ pounds (1½ cans)
    whole cranberry
½ cup finely cut blanched
    almonds
1½ cups white vinegar

2 cups firmly packed brown
    sugar
1 cup seedless raisins
1 teaspoon garlic salt
1 teaspoon ground ginger
½ teaspoon red pepper

Blend all ingredients into heavy saucepan. Cook over low heat, stirring constantly, until chutney is fairly thick. Pour into hot sterile jars and seal immediately.

6.

Sauces for meats, fish and vegetables

A SAUCE CAN MAKE any dull dish perk up and take on a "new" look.

There are all kinds and colors of sauces, sweet, tart, sour and zesty. Your main job, of course, is finding the right sauce for the right dish. And the ingredients make the *right* sauce.

Follow recipes carefully, using fresh spices and ingredients. Above all, use your imagination. Don't serve thin sauces on plates containing several vegetables. Use side dishes or paper cups. Keep your dishes neat and appetizing.

WHITE SAUCE No. 1

White sauce is used as a basic sauce for meats, fish, vegetables and soups and can be changed by many little tricks. For instance, paprika adds that rosy glow, chopped pimientos, a real festive look. Parsley, green olives, green onion tops and celery can also be effectively used. An egg yolk will lend a rich golden hue for special occasions. You can change your white sauce for each menu as you would your hat to match each outfit!

3 tablespoons butter
1½ cups milk
½ teaspoon garlic salt
(optional)

2 tablespoons flour
½ teaspoon salt
dash white pepper

Melt butter without browning. Add flour and blend well. Add milk slowly, stirring constantly to keep from sticking. When mixture begins to reach the boiling point and thicken, remove from stove and beat well. Season and serve. Yield: 1⅓ cups.

If a brown sauce is desired, brown the butter slightly and add 2 tablespoons Worcestershire sauce.

WHITE SAUCE No. 2

2 tablespoons butter	*2 tablespoons flour*
1 cup milk	*dash paprika*
salt and pepper to taste	

Melt butter. Add flour. Stir until well blended. Add milk gradually. Cook until thick, stirring constantly. Season and serve. Yield: approximately 1 cup.

For variations, add to white sauce:

(1) 1 hard-cooked egg finely chopped.

(2) ½ cup grated cheese.

(3) ½ cup finely chopped olives.

(4) ½ cup finely chopped pimientos.

(5) 3 tablespoons capers.

(6) Chopped clams, shrimp or lobster may be added with 2 tablespoons Worcestershire sauce.

(7) If egg sauce is desired, add 1 slightly beaten egg to sauce just before removing from fire to serve.

(8) If a very rich sauce is desired, use cream instead of milk as well as egg.

(9) Chopped salted nuts or parsley may be added for the special touch.

TARTAR SAUCE FOR FISH

1 tablespoon minced onion	*2 tablespoons chopped sweet*
1 teaspoon minced capers	*pickle*
(optional)	*1 tablespoon minced parsley*
¾ cup salad dressing	*1 tablespoon wine or tarragon*
1 teaspoon paprika	*vinegar*

Add pickle (well drained), onion, capers and parsley to salad dressing, then vinegar. Blend well. Serve in tiny paper cups or on individual lettuce leaves.

SAUCES FOR MEATS, FISH AND VEGETABLES

DRAWN BUTTER

(Use approximately 2 teaspoons of butter for each serving of drawn butter to be made).

(1) Melt butter, allow salt to settle. Pour over fish or serve in small cups.

(2) Melt butter, add 1 teaspoon Worcestershire sauce with 1 teaspoon lemon juice.

(3) Add to melted butter, 1 tablespoon chopped parsley, 1 teaspoon salt and 2 tablespoons lemon juice.

(4) Sauté in butter 1 grated onion, ½ cup celery leaves chopped fine, and a dash of Tabasco sauce. Add 2 tablespoons lemon juice.

(5) Sauté in butter the tops from a bunch of green onions. Add 1 tablespoon vinegar, a dash of paprika and red pepper.

TOMATO SAUCE

2 tablespoons fat
1 small finely chopped
   onion
1 bay leaf

salt and pepper to taste
1 cup tomato sauce or purée
dash mace
3 cloves

Sauté onion in fat. Combine and add other ingredients. Simmer 20 minutes. Strain. Add salt and pepper to taste. Yield: 1 cup.

MUSTARD SAUCE FOR HAM

2 tablespoons dry mustard
1 tablespoon flour
¼ cup brown sugar, or
   syrup
1 teaspoon salt

¼ teaspoon celery seed
dash clove (optional)
2 tablespoons vinegar
1 teaspoon paprika
1 cup water

Mix mustard, flour, brown sugar, vinegar, salt, paprika and celery seed. Add water. Mix well. Pour into sauce pan. Cook 15 minutes. Serve on ham, *hot!*

HORSERADISH SAUCE

¼ cup prepared
   horseradish, drained
1 tablespoon vinegar
dash pepper

1 teaspoon salt
½ cup mayonnaise, salad
   dressing, or whipped
   cream

SAUCES FOR MEATS, FISH AND VEGETABLES

Mix ingredients thoroughly. Fold in mayonnaise, salad dressing or whipped cream. Serve. Yield: 1 cup.

NEWBURG SAUCE

2 tablespoons butter
salt and pepper
1 egg yolk, beaten

1 teaspoon flour
¼ cup evaporated milk
2 tablespoons sherry

Melt butter. Add flour, pepper and milk. Cook until thick, stirring constantly. When ready to use, add egg yolk and sherry. Blend. Yield: approximately ⅓ cup.

MUSTARD SAUCE

2 tablespoons butter
dash pepper
1½ cups milk
1 teaspoon salt

2 tablespoons flour
2 teaspoons dry mustard
1 tablespoon lemon juice,
    or white vinegar

Melt butter. Add flour, salt and pepper. Mix well. Add mustard. Blend in milk gradually and cook until thick, stirring constantly. Cool. Add lemon juice and reheat when ready to serve. Yield: 1½ cupfuls.

CREOLE SAUCE

1 small finely chopped onion
1 finely chopped garlic clove
½ teaspoon red pepper
salt and pepper to taste

1 finely chopped green
    pepper
¼ cup butter or bacon fat
2 cups cooked tomatoes, or
    sauce

Sauté vegetables in fat. Add tomatoes and seasonings. Serve on broiled or baked fish. One-half cup mushrooms or chopped olives may be added if desired. Yield: approximately 3 cups.

LEMON BUTTER FOR FISH

½ cup butter
3 tablespoons lemon juice

1 teaspoon paprika

Cream butter, add lemon juice and paprika gradually. Spread on hot fish. Yield: ½ cup.

SPANISH SAUCE

1 can tomato paste

1 finely chopped green
    pepper

1 finely chopped onion
1 garlic clove
3 or 4 slices bacon
1 bay leaf
pinch thyme

2 red pepper pods
1 cup water
1/4 teaspoon oregano
1/2 cup finely chopped parsley

Sauté chopped bacon, onion, pepper and celery. Add spices, brown. Add tomato paste and water. Cook 15 minutes. Just before serving, add parsley. Yield: 3 cups.

RAISIN SAUCE FOR HAM

1 cup raisins
2 cloves
1 tablespoon cornstarch,
    or 2 tablespoons flour
1 tablespoon butter
1/4 teaspoon Worcestershire
    sauce

1 cup water
1/2 cup brown sugar
1/2 teaspoon salt
1/4 teaspoon pepper
2 tablespoons vinegar
1 teaspoon lemon juice

Cover raisins with water. Add cloves and vinegar. Simmer 15 minutes. Add sugar blended with flour, salt and pepper. Stir over low flame until thick. Add lemon juice and serve warm over ham. Yield: 2 cups.

CURRY SAUCE

1 tablespoon butter
1 onion, grated
1 tablespoon curry powder

2 tablespoons chutney
1 cup beef or chicken stock

Brown butter. Add onion and chutney. Cook thoroughly before adding stock and curry. Cook again about 20 minutes. Either meat or hard-cooked eggs can be added to curry sauce. Yield: 1 cup.

EASY HOLLANDAISE SAUCE

2 tablespoons butter
2 tablespoons flour
1 teaspoon salt
2 tablespoons lemon juice

1/4 teaspoon cayenne
3/4 cup milk
2 egg yolks

Melt butter, remove from heat; add flour and seasoning. Mix well. Add milk and cook slowly until thickened, stirring constantly. Remove from heat. Pour mixture over slightly beaten egg yolks. Place in double boiler and cook like custard for 5 to 8 minutes. Add 2 tablespoons lemon juice. Yield: approximately 1⅓ cups.

MOCK HOLLANDAISE SAUCE

2 tablespoons butter
1 teaspoon flour
1 cup warm milk

salt and pepper to taste
4 egg yolks
juice of 1 lemon

Melt butter in top of double boiler. Work in flour and seasonings. Blend in warm milk. Simmer 15 minutes. Blend in egg yolks slowly. Simmer another 10 minutes over hot water. Just before ready to serve, add lemon juice. Serves 6 to 8.

Good with broccoli, beans, fish and cauliflower.

CURRY SAUCE

½ cup butter or margarine
¼ cup finely chopped onion
⅓ cup finely diced raw carrot
2 cups meat stock or canned consommé

1 teaspoon curry powder
1 tablespoon flour
1 cup tomato sauce
3 slices apple

Melt butter or margarine in heavy saucepan. Add onions and carrots; cook over medium heat until vegetables are tender; onions a very light golden color but not brown. Stir in curry powder and flour until smooth. Add meat stock all at once. Stirring continually, bring mixture to boil. Stir over medium heat until quite smooth. Add ½ cup tomato sauce and sliced apples. Cover and cook over very low heat for about 30 minutes. Skim off excess butter; blend well. Serve hot over hard-cooked eggs, or baked or pan fried fish fillets with fluffy rice.

SHRIMP SAUCE

½ cup cooked shrimp
juice of 1 lemon
½ teaspoon hot sauce
2 cups white sauce

1 hard-cooked egg, diced
1 teaspoon paprika
chopped parsley

Cut shrimp in half, soak ½ hour in lemon and hot sauce. Add to white sauce with finely chopped egg and parsley. Add paprika and serve over hot baked or broiled fish.

53

7.

Beverages

TEA, COFFEE, FRUIT JUICES, such as lemon, orange or grape, may be frozen in cubes for your drinks. A red or green cherry, as well as mint leaves and pineapple may be added to each cube before freezing.

CAFÉ AU LAIT, COLD

3 cups strong coffee
3 cups milk

½ jigger brandy or sherry
(sugar if desired)

Combine coffee and milk in heavy saucepan. Heat to under boil. Cool, add brandy or sherry. Pour over cracked ice. Serve with sugar on the side for those who wish to sweeten it. Yield: 6 servings.

JETER'S HOT POT

1 dozen eggs
2½ cups sugar
2 quarts milk
2 quarts cream
1 pint bourbon whisky
1 pint rum

2 teaspoons ginger
2 teaspoons cinnamon
2 teaspoons allspice
2 teaspoons nutmeg
½ teaspoon salt
1 cup brandy

Beat yolks until light. Add sugar and continue beating until fluffy. Add milk, cream, ginger, cinnamon, allspice, nutmeg and salt. Stir well while adding. Pour whisky, rum and brandy into mixture in a large roomy pot and mix constantly. Place on stove with low flame, stirring constantly until mixture thickens. Never bring to boiling point. Makes total of 6 quarts.

GINGER ALE AND CREAM SODA FLOATS

Fill tall glasses ⅔ full of beverage. Add a scoop of pineapple or orange sherbert. Garnish with mint. Serve with straws.

MINT COCOA OR HOT CHOCOLATE

Boil several fresh sprigs of mint in 1 cup of water. Blend together 2 squares chocolate, ½ cup sugar, a dash of salt, and the mint water over hot water. Stir until well blended. Add 3 cups of milk and ½ cup cream. Beat with rotary egg beater until well blended.

A dash of whipped cream and a fresh mint leaf may be added to each cup. Serves 6. A most unusual party or tea drink.

MINT TEA

2 cups sugar	*¾ cup water*
4 oranges	*1 lemon*
2 quarts strong tea	*several sprigs mint*

Squeeze juice of oranges and lemon, cut rind in small pieces. Add water and several sprigs of mint. Boil 10 minutes. Strain, add sugar. Stir until melted. Cool. Mix tea and juices. Rub edge of glasses with mint leaves. Put crushed ice in glasses and pour tea mixture over ice. To garnish add a mint leaf and slice of lemon or orange. More sugar may be added if necessary.

ICED GINGER TEA

Boil several pieces of ginger root in 2 cups of water, 3 to 5 minutes. Add juice of ½ lemon. Strain, sweeten and pour over ice cubes or cracked ice, as desired.

COFFEE NOG

1 cup strong coffee (warm)	*dash salt*
2 cups cream	*1 teaspoon vanilla*
2 eggs	*½ cup sugar*

Blend coffee, sugar, and salt into beaten egg yolks. Cook over hot water until thick. Remove from fire and cool. Add flavoring. Whip egg whites and cream until thick but not stiff. Fold into coffee mixture.

BEVERAGES

GRAPE JUICE PUNCH

(Pineapple with Mint)

2 cups pineapple juice
2 cups grape juice
mint
½ cup sugar
juice of 1 lemon
½ cup pineapple, crushed
or pieces

Crush mint. Mix lemon juice and sugar. Add to mint. Mix well. Add pineapple, grape and lemon juices. Cool. Serve over ice with a green minted cherry to decorate.

FROSTED APRICOT DRINK

1 cup cooked apricots and
juice
½ pint vanilla ice cream
3 cups milk

Press apricots through a sieve. Mix apricot pulp and milk. Put ice cream in a pitcher. Pour milk mixture over ice cream. Stir until slightly mixed. Serves 4 to 6.

PINEAPPLE MINT PUNCH

3 cups cold milk
¾ cup cream
1½ teaspoons lemon juice
12 mint leaves
2 cups cold pineapple juice
¼ cup sugar
dash salt

Crush mint leaves in a bowl before mixing. Remove leaves. Combine all ingredients and beat until foamy. Pour into tall glasses, garnish with sprigs of mint and serve immediately. Serves 6.

TEA PUNCH

2 cups orange juice
1 cup lemon juice
1 cup crushed pineapple
few sprigs mint
1 cup raspberry syrup
1¼ cups sugar melted in 1
cup hot water
1½ cups strong tea
1 quart carbonated water

Blend sugar and hot water. Add tea and juices. Mix well. Add pineapple and raspberry syrup. Cool. Pour into punch bowl over ice. Add carbonated water and mint leaves. Yield: 6 quarts.

56

GINGER PUNCH

½ pound Canton ginger, chopped
1 cup sugar
1 cup water

1 quart carbonated water
½ cup orange juice
½ cup lemon juice

Chop ginger, add sugar and water. Boil 15 minutes. Add fruit juices and strain. Pour over large piece of ice. Add carbonated water. Yield: 2 quarts.

HOT POT

12 egg yolks
2½ cups sugar
2 quarts milk
2 quarts cream
2 teaspoons ginger
2 teaspoons cinnamon

2 teaspoons allspice
2 teaspoons nutmeg
½ teaspoon salt
1 pint bourbon whisky
1 pint rum
1 cup brandy

Beat egg yolks until light. Add sugar gradually and continue beating until thick and fluffy. Add milk, cream, ginger, cinnamon, allspice, nutmeg and salt; blend well. Add whisky, rum and brandy. Pour into a large, heavy pot, stirring constantly. Place on stove over low flame. Stir until mixture thickens. *Do not bring to a boil!*

PARTY ICE CUBES

½ cup lemon juice
⅓ cup maraschino cherry liquid
1 cup sugar

3 cups cold water
mint leaves
maraschino cherries

Mix together lemon juice, cherry liquid, sugar and cold water, stirring until sugar is completely dissolved. Place ice dividers in 2 ice cube trays. Place 1 maraschino cherry and 1 mint leaf in each ice cube section. Pour lemon mixture on top carefully. Freeze. Use ice cubes in iced tea, lemonade or fruit punch.

COOKING WITH WINES

If you wish to be formal, consult a wine chart for the right wine at the right time with the right food.

Use sherry and Madeira in soups; dry white wine with fish;

dry red wine in meats; port, sweet sherry or sweet Madeira, liquers, brandy, rum in desserts. Follow the above suggestions until you become familiar with the flavor-effect of wines and spirits. Then your own food sense will tell you which wine you are likely to enjoy most in any given dish.

SOUP—Almost any soup, hot, jellied, or canned is better with a tablespoon or two of dry sherry or dry Madeira, or a small amount of Dubonnet.

OYSTER STEW—Add a little sherry just before serving.

FISH—Pour some white wine into the water in which you boil shrimp or any fish.

BEEF—Soak pot roast in red wine overnight. Then cook as usual, using the wine as liquid.

GRAVY—For roast beef or pot roast, add a tablespoon of rum to the fat; thicken and season as usual. Add a dash of sherry to chicken gravy.

HAMBURGER PATTIES—Pour a little dry red wine over the patties while cooking.

FRUIT OR MELON CUP—Cover with sauterne, sherry, port, blackberry or apricot brandy. Chill.

CREAM PIES—Add one tablespoon of rum to the cooked mixture after it is removed from the heat.

CUSTARDS—Wine changes a simple pudding to a sophisticated dessert. Pour Bavet brandy or Crème de Cacao over it as a sauce.

SOFT-BOILED CUSTARD—Light rum or brandy poured over sliced fruit is delicious. Chill before serving.

HOT TEA—Pep up with a dash of rum or brandy.

SPONGE CAKE OR POUND CAKE—Moisten a slice of cake with apricot or any fruit liqueur. Top with whipped cream. Also try hot buttered rum.

WHIPPED CREAM—may be flavored with chartreuse, brandy, or cordials.

8.

Meats

ALL MEATS no matter how inexpensive the cut, contain iron, protein, minerals, and vitamins.

The best way to confront meat with confidence is with a sound knowledge of the various cuts and methods of preparation. Experiment with unfamiliar cuts, new recipes, and gloat over the results. Try fresh combinations and concentrates seasonings for extra taste thrills.

Above all, remember not to overcook! Pour half a cup of vinegar or lemon juice over lamb, pork, or veal before roasting; you will be delighted with the results. Do not rush roasts or you will ruin their tenderness and flavor. Use rolled corn or bran flakes for extra crispness in breading croquettes, patties, or chops.

Plan your dinner menus two or three days in advance so that you can use leftover meats in successive menus. You will save time and money. Build your menus around meats. They are the foundation of a well-balanced meal.

TIME-TABLE FOR COOKING MEAT
Broiling or Panbroiling

Steak

1 inch thick, medium rare	8 to 10 minutes
1½ to 2 inches thick, medium rare	20 to 25 minutes

MEATS

Lamb Chops

Loin, single, ¾ to 1 inch thick	10 to 15 minutes
double, 1½ to 2 inches thick	25 to 30 minutes
Rib, single	10 to 15 minutes
double	30 to 35 minutes
Shoulder	10 to 15 minutes

Ham

¼ inch thick	10 minutes
½ to ¾ inch thick	20 minutes
1 inch thick	30 minutes

Roasting

Beef Ribs

Sear   20 to 30 minutes at 500° F.; finish roasting at 300° F.
Allow 16 minutes per pound for rare roast
Allow 22 minutes per pound for medium roast
Allow 30 minutes per pound for well-done roast

Pork

Sear   15 minutes at 500° F.; finish roasting at 300° F.
Allow 30 minutes per pound plus searing for 4 to 5 pound
loin
Allow 25 to 30 minutes per pound plus searing for fresh
shoulder
Allow 25 to 30 minutes per pound plus searing for fresh
ham
Allow 45 to 50 minutes per pound plus searing
for fresh butt

Ham

Allow 25 minutes per pound for 10 to 12 pound ham
Allow 20 minutes per pound for larger hams
Allow 30 minutes per pound for half hams

Lamb

Sear   30 minutes at 500° F.; finish roasting at 300° F.
Allow 35 minutes per pound

Veal

Sear   25 minutes at 500° F.
Allow 23 minutes per pound at 260° F.

Braising

Pot-Roast

4 to 6 pounds	3 to 3½ hours
Swiss Steak	1¼ to 1¾ hours
Veal Cutlets	45 minutes to 1 hour

Pork Chops

(depending on thickness)	30 to 45 minutes

Simmering

Beef

4 to 5 pounds	3 hours
Ham	25 minutes per pound

EBONY'S BARBECUED SPARERIBS

6 pounds spareribs	*several bay leaves*
paprika to taste	*salt and pepper to taste*
3 finely chopped garlic cloves	*hickory salt to taste*
juice of 1 lemon	

Sauce

3 medium finely chopped	*1 can tomato paste*
onions	*½ cup finely chopped celery*
bacon fat	*½ cup chili sauce*
1 tablespoon dry mustard	*2 tablespoons Worcestershire*
2 tablespoons cumin seed	*sauce*
1 tablespoon thyme or sage	*several red pepper pods*
2 tablespoons sugar	*2 tablespoons chili powder*
(optional)	*1 cup vinegar*

Cut ribs into small pieces and place in a flat glass or enamel vessel. Sprinkle with salt, pepper, paprika and hickory salt. Add chopped garlic, bay leaves, lemon juice. Let stand several hours, or overnight if desired.

Prepare sauce as follows. Sauté onions and celery in bacon fat. When well done but not brown, add chili sauce, mustard, Worcestershire sauce, thyme or sage, chili powder, cumin seed, red pepper, tomato sauce, vinegar and sugar.

Marinate ribs in sauce on both sides. Cook under broiler, turning and basting every 15 minutes until well done and very brown. Oven temperature, 300° F. Approximate cooking time for 6 pounds of ribs is 2 hours. Keep ribs warm in oven until ready to serve. Serves 6 to 8.

BARBECUED RIBS

5 pounds fresh spareribs
salt, pepper and paprika to
    taste
2 onions, quartered
5 garlic cloves, crushed
juice of 1 lemon and grated
    rind
2 tablespoons brown sugar
2 tablespoons
    Worcestershire sauce
1 cup tomato catsup
2 tablespoons pepper sauce

2 tablespoons chili powder
1 cup water
1/4 cup prepared mustard
2 tablespoons butter or
    bacon fat
1 can tomato sauce
1 teaspoon sweet basil
1 teaspoon celery seed
1 teaspoon leaf thyme
1 teaspoon cumin seed
1 teaspoon paprika
2 tablespoons hickory salt

Wipe ribs with clean damp cloth and cut into pieces for individual servings. Sprinkle with salt, pepper and paprika. Set aside. Place all ingredients except ribs in large heavy frying pan. Simmer 20 to 30 minutes. Cool. Place ribs in large shallow flat dish and marinate well with sauce on both sides. Cover and store in refrigerator for several hours. If ribs are barbecued on a pit, leave them in a slab form. If cooked in oven, they can be cut into smaller serving pieces.

BARBECUE SAUCE No. 1

1 grated onion
1 cup tomato catsup
1 teaspoon celery salt
1 teaspoon dry mustard
2 tablespoons brown sugar

juice of 1 lemon
salt, red and black pepper
    to taste
2 teaspoons hickory salt

Mix ingredients which will yield 1½ cups of sauce. Marinate ribs or meat. Barbecue. Turn and baste ribs or meat often with a spoon or brush.

BARBECUE SAUCE No. 2

2 teaspoons savory salt
½ cup brown sugar
2 bay leaves

2 tablespoons
    Worcestershire sauce
1 teaspoon salt

¼ cup prepared mustard
2 garlic cloves
½ cup vinegar

2 tablespoons red pepper
sauce

Boil ingredients. Marinate meat and barbecue as directed in first recipe. May be barbecued in an open pit or oven. Yield: 1 cup sauce. Makes sauce for 4 pounds of ribs.

BARBECUE SAUCE No. 3

½ cup finely chopped celery
bacon fat
½ cup tomato catsup or chili
sauce
2 tablespoons prepared
mustard
1 can tomato sauce
1 cup vinegar
1 tablespoon chili powder
salt to taste

3 medium finely chopped
onions
2 garlic cloves
2 tablespoons Worcestershire
sauce
1 can tomato paste
2 bay leaves
1 tablespoon sweet basil
several red pepper pods

Sauté onions, celery and garlic in bacon fat. Add remaining ingredients. Yield: 1 quart sauce; enough for 10 to 12 pounds of ribs.

BARBECUE SAUCE No. 4

1 grated onion
2 tablespoons butter
2 tablespoons vinegar
2 tablespoons brown sugar
2 cloves
1 teaspoon chili powder
1 tablespoon flour
2 cups water

⅓ cup lemon juice
1 tablespoon paprika
1 cup chopped parsley
3 tablespoons Worcestershire
sauce
1 teaspoon oregano
2 teaspoons hickory salt
1 teaspoon garlic salt

Sprinkle 5 pounds ribs with garlic salt, hickory salt, and flour. Mix rest of ingredients. Boil 20 minutes and marinate ribs. Barbecue. Yield: 3 cups.

SWEET AND SOUR SPARERIBS

3 pounds lean spareribs
2 cups cooking sherry wine
1 teaspoon salt

¼ teaspoon pepper
¼ teaspoon paprika
5 tablespoons brown sugar

2 tablespoons Chinese soya
    sauce
1 tablespoon vinegar

1 tablespoon lemon juice
2 ounces candied ginger or
    ginger root

Trim excess fat from ribs and wipe ribs with a clean, damp cloth. Cut ribs into small pieces. Place sherry in a heavy saucepan and add salt, pepper and paprika and stir until blended. Add spareribs to the wine mixture, making sure that each piece is covered. Cover and bring mixture to boil, stirring frequently. Reduce heat to the simmering stage. Cook very slowly until ribs are tender when tested with a fork. Place brown sugar in a heavy skillet and add remaining wine mixture from the cooked ribs. Add soya sauce, vinegar and lemon juice. Cut candied ginger into small pieces or use fresh ginger root and add to mixture. Stir until ingredients are well blended. Place cooked, drained ribs in skillet and marinate with the ginger and brown sugar sauce until well coated. Cover and simmer ribs over low heat until brown sauce is absorbed. Serve remaining sauce over ribs.

SPARERIBS WITH A FUTURE

4 pounds spareribs, cut in
    small pieces
2 small onions
1 bay leaf
1 garlic clove
1 cup chopped parsley
1 cup chopped celery
2 tablespoons flour

1 teaspoon salt
½ teaspoon pepper
1 teaspoon paprika
1 teaspoon rosemary
2 cups boiling water
½ teaspoon ginger
3 tablespoons fat

Dredge ribs in flour and seasonings. Sauté ribs in fat until brown in a heavy iron skillet or Dutch oven. Add hot water, onions, celery, garlic and spices. Cover and simmer until tender. Add chopped parsley and serve with rice, mashed potatoes or noodles and buttered lima beans and pimiento. Serves 4 to 6.

RIBS IN TOMATO SAUCE

4 to 6 pounds ribs, cut in very
    small pieces
1 tablespoon salt

2 small onions
1 can tomato sauce or paste
2 tablespoons flour

2 tablespoons bacon fat
1 teaspoon paprika
1 tablespoon chili powder

1 garlic clove
1 can mushrooms and juice
1 teaspoon celery salt

Sprinkle ribs with salt, pepper, and flour. Sauté in fat. Place onion and spices over ribs. Add tomato sauce, mushrooms, and juice. Cover and simmer about 2 hours until tender. Serve with rice. Serves 6.

HINTS ON COOKING HAM

Try using sherry or port wines on ham instead of fruit juices, and if you like a zesty, pungent taste, place tiny pieces of garlic through the fat! It's different!

An extra one half cup of cream added just before removing from oven will make a ham gravy.

If the day is too hot and lighting the oven is out of the question, try preparing any of the following recipes in a deep, heavy skillet. Cover for the first half hour of cooking! Keep heat *very low!*

You can add cooked sweet potatoes during the last half hour of cooking.

Baked whole apples with ham are time-savers, too. Simply core apples, fill with sugar and spice, and bake in the same pan with the ham.

An unpeeled whole pear baked with stem and covered with whole cloves add a festive touch that is really "sumpthin."

BAKED HAM SLICES IN CREAM

1 2-inch slice tender ham
2 tablespoons prepared
  mustard
½ cup maple syrup
½ cup fruit juice (pineapple,

orange, or grapefruit)
½ teaspoon allspice
½ teaspoon paprika
¼ teaspoon mace
1 cup cream

Cover ham with mustard and place in baking pan. Pour syrup and juice over it. Sprinkle with paprika, mace and allspice. Bake ½ hour at 350° F. Remove from oven. Add cream and replace in oven for ½ hour.

Serve with escalloped potatoes or yams, a green vegetable, and an escarole salad. Serves 4 to 6.

MEATS

BAKED HAM-FRUIT SLICES

2 slices tender ham, 1½ to 2
  inches thick
½ cup brown sugar
1 cup fruit juice
½ teaspoon cinnamon
¼ cup pickle juice, or 1

tablespoon lemon juice
½ teaspoon mace
6 to 8 slices fruit, or 1 cup
  crushed pineapple,
  apricot, or apple
½ cup honey

Place 1 slice of ham on baking dish. Cover with cinnamon, mace, lemon juice, and brown sugar. Add second slice and cover in same manner. Pour fruit juice over ham and bake 30 to 45 minutes at 350° F. Remove ham from oven. Arrange fruit artistically on top and cover with honey. Bake ½ hour longer; cut in wedges like pie and serve. Serves 6 to 8.

Cooked crushed cranberries may be used to add a festive and tasty effect. Crushed fruit may be placed between slices with mustard and brown sugar. Add second slice and bake as directed.

BAKED HAM SLICES WITH BROWN GRAVY

1 large tenderized ham
2 tablespoons peanut butter
1 cup ginger ale
1 cup pineapple juice

2 tablespoons prepared
  mustard
¼ cup brown or white sugar
½ pint thin cream

Blend mustard, peanut butter, and sugar. Spread on ham, covering well. Pour ginger ale and pineapple juice over ham. Place in a moderate oven (350° F.) and bake for 45 minutes. Remove and pour cream over ham. Bake 30 minutes longer. Cut in slices and serve. Serves 6.

Try the same delicious recipe with apricots, peaches, pineapple or crushed cranberries placed on top of ham after the mustard mixture has been added. Serve with baked macaroni, spinach and tomatoes. Lemon chiffon pie for dessert.

ROAST FRESH HAM

1 fresh ham, 5 to 7 pounds
salt and pepper to taste
2 garlic cloves
2 small finely chopped
  onions

1 tablespoon
  Worcestershire sauce
1 tablespoon sugar
1 teaspoon paprika

½ cup vinegar

¼ cup tomato catsup purée

⅓ cup lemon juice and water

or chili sauce

Combine chopped onions, sugar, paprika, vinegar, lemon juice, water, Worcestershire sauce and catsup. Set aside. Remove excess fat and skin from ham. Peel and cut slices of garlic thin. Make small inserts with a sharp knife in meat and insert garlic. Sprinkle well with salt and pepper. Place fat side down in an open roasting pan. Cook in moderate oven 1 hour. Remove from oven, drain off fat. Cover ham with onion and vinegar mixture. Return to oven. Baste with drippings every 20 minutes until done. Allow 40 minutes to each pound. Serve with sweet potato puff, corn and bean succotash and hot corn sticks.

BAKED HAM SLICES WITH PEANUT BUTTER

1 2-inch slice ham

½ teaspoon cloves

1 tablespoon horseradish

2 tablespoons syrup or sugar

2 tablespoons milk

1 tablespoon pickle relish

½ cup peanut butter

dash paprika

Mix all ingredients in a bowl to form a paste. Spread over top and sides of ham. Place in a baking dish with a small amount of water or milk. Bake slowly 1 hour. A few ground salted peanuts and parsley may be sprinkled on top. If gravy is desired, add 1 cup fruit juice or milk the last 15 minutes of baking.

Serve with squash, baked pineapple slices, or buttered cauliflower. Serves 6.

BAKED HAM SLICES WITH APRICOTS

2 large ham slices, 1-inch thick

1 cup sherry wine

1 can apricot halves

¼ cup prepared mustard

12 maraschino cherries

¼ cup peanut butter

½ cup honey

2 cups fruit juice, orange, pineapple or apricot

Mix peanut butter and mustard together. Spread a layer on each ham slice placing one slice on top of the other. Place in large shallow baking pan; pour fruit juice over ham and bake in 350° F. oven for ½ hour. Remove from oven and pour sherry wine over ham. Bake 1 hour. Remove from oven and place apricot halves and cherries on top of ham.

PEPPY BAKED HAM

1 tenderized ham (about 12 pounds)
1 pint ginger ale
1 pint pineapple juice

½ cup brown sugar
1 tablespoon ground cloves
1 tablespoon dry ginger
1 tablespoon horseradish

Ham should be at room temperature. Remove outside wrapper, and wipe with damp cloth. Mix ginger, horseradish and cloves; rub over ham and place fat side down in roaster. Do not cover. Bake in a slow oven, 325°F. Pour ginger ale over ham and continue to bake, turning at least 3 times. During last ½ hour of baking, remove from oven. Make a series of cuts across fat in squares or diamonds. Pour pineapple and brown sugar over ham. Return to oven and bake until done, basting occasionally. Serve with candied yams and apple slices, broccoli, steamed prune pudding for dessert. Serves 15 to 20.

Allow ham to bake approximately 18 to 20 minutes per pound.

HAM WITH WINE

1 ham, 10 to 12 pounds (tenderized)
2 small garlic cloves
1 teaspoon cloves, ground

¼ cup prepared mustard
2 tablespoons brown sugar
1 cup fruit juice
2 cups wine, sherry or port

Blend cloves, mustard and sugar into a paste. Place ham in a baking dish. Remove excess fat. Cut garlic in small pieces and stick through fat of ham. Cover entire ham with mustard mixture. Pour fruit juice and wine over ham. Cover and bake in moderate oven, 400° F., 1½ hours. Turn at least 3 times. Remove ham from oven. Make a series of cuts across fat in squares and sprinkle with brown sugar or honey. Garnish with cloves and pineapple if desired. (Pineapple may be held in place with toothpicks.) Return to oven uncovered and cook 45 minutes longer.

Serve with sweet potatoes, spinach and spiced fruits. Serves 10 to 12.

HAM PATTIES

If your leftover boiled or baked ham is 1 cup . . . or 4 cups, judge your ingredients accordingly. Make a large amount to fit your family needs by adding leftover potatoes or vegetables. Make into patties, and fry in deep fat or bake.

1 cup chopped ham	1 teaspoon paprika
1 small onion, grated	½ teaspoon pepper
½ cup chopped celery	½ cup green pepper
2 cups leftover cooked vege-	1 egg
tables, mashed or fried	1 cup bread crumbs or
potatoes	cornflakes

Grind ham, onion and celery. Mix mashed potatoes and cooked vegetables. Add seasoning and egg. Add ham mixture. Shape into patties and roll in cornflakes or bread crumbs. Fry in deep fat.

JENNY JETER'S HAM LOAF

1 pound lean pork, ground	2 cups soft bread crumbs
1 pound smoked ham, ground	¼ teaspoon pepper
1 egg, unbeaten	1 teaspoon salt
1 cup milk	

Put ground meat in mixing dish. Add unbeaten egg, milk, bread crumbs and seasonings. Mix and form into loaf. Put in pan. Bake in oven at 375° F. for 1 hour. Serves 6 to 8.

LUCILLE'S BAKED HAM

1 10- to 12-pound ham	1 cup brown sugar
water to cover	½ cup corn meal
1 pint pineapple juice	whole cloves

Cut hock from ham. Put ham into a large pot and cover with cold water. Let water come slowly to a boil and boil 2 hours. Tie a bag of cloves (1 tablespoon) and drop into pot to boil with ham. When ham is tender, remove from water. Cool and skin. Cross-cut the fat side of ham. Place on baking pan and stud with cloves. Mix corn meal and brown sugar. Rub evenly over ham. Baste with pineapple juice. Bake about 1 hour at 300° F., basting 3 times with remainder of juice. Cool and slice. Serves 20.

SMITHFIELD HAM WITH CLOVES

Soak a 10- to 12-pound ham in water for 12 to 14 hours. Drain water. Cover again and cook slowly for approximately 5 hours or until tender. Cool in stock. When cool, remove the skin. (Trim extra fat if desired.) Make a series of cuts across fat in squares. Sprinkle top of ham with about ½ cup brown sugar, 1 teaspoon black pepper. Stud ham with cloves. Pour 1 cup of sherry over ham if desired or ¼ cup vinegar and ¼ cup water. Bake in hot oven 25 to 30 minutes. Garnish with spiced apples and water cress.

HAM BANANA ROLL
(Mrs. F. Alexander)

6 slices boiled ham	1 teaspoon butter
3 bananas	1 tablespoon flour
1 tablespoon mustard	¼ cup milk
½ cup grated cheese	

Melt butter. Add flour. Blend in milk and cheese. Cook until thick. Spread each slice of ham with mustard. Peel and cut bananas in half. Wrap a slice of ham around each banana. Hold together with a toothpick. Pour cheese sauce over banana and ham. Bake in a moderate oven 30 minutes until bananas are tender. Remove from oven. Place on hot platter, pour sauce over roll and serve. Serves 6.

HAM HOCKS

Don't shun ham hocks as poor folks' food . . . "cause they ain't!" However they can do a terrific job in budget slashing. They can be used in a variety of ways; boiled and seasoned, or, after boiling, the meat can be cut from the bone, ground, and made into croquettes or hash, or cut up for creamed ham or ham salad.

The stock from boiled ham hocks is good for soups and gravies too. Don't throw out the juice! Store it in the refrigerator for later use.

PORK

In a quaint little cabin in Tennessee where old post cards and Christmas cards are used as wallpaper and decoration I met a dear old lady, aged 70, known to her friends as "Ma Liz," the best pork-cooker in the territory. She said she "mothered" pork from the time the pig was a little suckling until it was ready to be slaughtered. All her folk had been pork cooks back to slavery days. To her, pork cooked just right is what pheasant is to the gourmet. She said, "You don't overcook, you jest cook it right."

Pork is not too hard to digest. But when half cooked and rushed, it is certainly *not* good for pork—or for you! It is true that pork can taste like chicken when carefully prepared.

STUFFED PORK CHOPS

6 double pork chops	1 tablespoon parsley
1 teaspoon salt	1½ cups bread crumbs
½ teaspoon pepper	1 teaspoon sage
3 tablespoons bacon fat	½ teaspoon leaf thyme
1 tablespoon grated onion	1 teaspoon paprika
¼ cup chopped celery leaves	3 tablespoons water

Cut pocket in the bone side of each chop. Sprinkle with salt and pepper inside and out. Sauté onions, celery, and parsley in bacon fat. Add bread crumbs and seasonings. Stuff chops with dressing and brown on both sides in skillet in a little fat. Add water and bake in a slow oven about 50 minutes or until tender.

STUFFED PORK CHOPS WITH VEGETABLES

6 chops, ¾ inch or more thick	½ cup chopped green pepper
salt and pepper to taste	¼ teaspoon pepper
1 tablespoon prepared mustard	1 tablespoon poultry seasoning
½ cup chopped green onion tops	1 cup bread or cracker crumbs
½ cup finely chopped celery	¼ teaspoon butter
½ cup whole kernel corn	½ cup flour
	¼ teaspoon paprika

Make a large gash or pocket into the side of each chop. Sprinkle with salt and pepper. Rub mustard on outside. Mix onion, celery, corn, pepper, seasoning and bread crumbs. Fill each pocket with dressing and sew open sides. Rub chop with butter and sprinkle with flour and paprika. Place in an open baking pan, add a bit of water and cook slowly for 1½ hours. Brown under broiler before serving. Serves 6.

Serve with baked potatoes, buttered summer squash or peas.

PORK CHOPS AND CREAM GRAVY

4 large, thick pork chops
1 cup milk or light cream
salt and pepper to taste
⅓ cup flour
1 teaspoon paprika
2 tablespoons bacon fat

½ teaspoon celery salt
½ teaspoon Season-all
½ teaspoon garlic salt
1 garlic clove, chopped
½ cup water

Mix flour and seasonings together. Dredge chops in flour. Save remaining flour. Sauté chops in fat on both sides until brown; cover and steam thoroughly for about 30 minutes. Remove cover, add balance of flour and brown. Mix with fat. Pour milk or cream over chops. Add water. Simmer another 15 minutes until gravy is thick. Serves 4.

Serve with fluffy mashed potatoes.

BAKED SWEET AND SOUR CHOPS

6 pork chops
1 teaspoon ginger
1 cup pineapple juice
1 teaspoon salt
½ teaspoon pepper
1 tablespoon butter

1 teaspoon paprika
¼ cup flour
3 tablespoons brown sugar
2 tablespoons white vinegar
2 fresh tomatoes, sliced

Mix flour, ginger, salt and pepper and paprika. Set aside in a flat bowl. Place pork chops in a pan. Dot each chop with butter. Place under broiler and brown on both sides and remove from oven. Dredge each chop in flour mixture, covering both sides well. Return to pan. Mix sugar, vinegar, pineapple juice and pour over chops. Cook slowly in oven 1 hour. Add tomato slices. Just before serving, place under broiler to brown. Serves 6.

Serve with broiled pineapple slices, parsley, rice, peas and mushrooms, water cress and cottage cheese salad.

PORK CHOPS A LA GABBY

4 to 6 lean pork chops
salt and pepper to taste
2 tablespoons Worcestershire
  sauce

1 teaspoon paprika
1 green pepper
¼ cup flour
garlic, onion, or celery salt

2 tablespoons fat
3 medium apples

1 tablespoon brown sugar
½ cup hot water

Mix salt, pepper and paprika in flour. Dredge chops on both sides with seasoned flour. Place in a heavy skillet which has been preheated with fat. Brown chops slowly, turning often. Slice green pepper in rings and lay on top of chops. Cut apples in half, remove core, place on top of pepper rings. Mix water, Worcestershire sauce and sugar. Pour over apples. Simmer 40 minutes.

Serve with mashed potatoes, broccoli, hearts of lettuce with cheese sauce and blueberry dumplings.

PORK BALLS

1½ pounds pork, ground
3 tablespoons raw rice
⅓ cup milk
1 small onion, chopped
1 teaspoon salt

¼ teaspoon pepper
½ green pepper, chopped
1 tablespoon pimiento
1 can condensed tomato soup
1 cup water

Mix all ingredients except soup and water. Form into balls. Place in casserole. Mix soup with water and pour over meat balls. Bake in moderate oven, 350° F., 1 hour. Serves 6 to 8.

BAKED PORK CHOPS

6 to 8 pork chops
1 tablespoon prepared
    mustard
salt, pepper, paprika, celery
    and garlic salts to taste

¼ cup flour
2 large onions
1 green pepper
2 teaspoons grated lemon
    rind

Cover chops with mustard. Sprinkle with pepper, seasoned salts, paprika and flour. Brown in a heavy skillet in a small amount of fat. Place in flat baking dish. Cover with onion and green pepper rings, water, and lemon rind. Bake in a slow oven (325° F.) approximately 45 minutes. Bake potatoes at the same time.

BAKED PORK CHOPS WITH RICE

6 pork chops, 1 inch thick
flour
salt and pepper to taste
fat

6 large slices of onion
1 green pepper
6 tablespoons uncooked rice
6 tomatoes

MEATS

Sprinkle chops with salt, pepper, and flour. Brown on both sides in a little fat and place in a baking dish. Put a slice of onion on each chop, then a ring cut from the green pepper. Put 1 tablespoon of rice in center of pepper. Cook for 1 hour in a slow oven. When nearly done, put tomatoes on top of rice and cook until done. Make about 1 quart of rich gravy and pour over chops. Bake 10 to 15 minutes more. Serves 6.

ROAST LOIN OF PORK

1 loin of pork
juice of 1 lemon
salt and pepper to taste

Season-all to taste
1 teaspoon ginger
2 teaspoons prepared
mustard

Have butcher trim and prepare meat. Cover roast with lemon on all sides. Sprinkle with salt, pepper, Season-all and ginger. Hickory salt may be used if desired. Place in roasting pan. Bake in uncovered roaster in moderate oven at 350° F. Allow 30 minutes per pound. Baste with lemon juice or vinegar and mustard. Cook slowly until well done and brown.

Serve with browned potatoes, apple sauce and string beans.

PORK TENDERLOIN

2 pounds smoked pork
tenderloin
3 or 4 whole cloves
2 tablespoons prepared
mustard

¼ cup brown sugar
½ cup water
½ cup orange juice

Simmer tenderloin and cloves in enough water to cover for 45 minutes. Drain. Mix sugar and mustard. Place tenderloin in baking pan and spread with mustard mixture. Pour orange juice and water into pan. Bake in a hot oven 30 minutes. Baste with orange juice. Serve sliced, hot or cold. Serves 4 to 6.

Serve with creamed potatoes, spinach, cranberry sauce.

PICKLED PORK

1 meaty shoulder or leg of
pork
8 peppercorns

1 teaspoon celery seed
2 small red peppers
3 to 4 cups white vinegar

2 bay leaves | 1 whole onion, sliced
1 garlic clove | 1 teaspoon mustard seed

Place shoulder or leg of pork in a deep crock or pottery dish. Marinate with vinegar and remaining ingredients. Set in a cool place for 2 to 3 days. Remove from marinade and roast in moderate oven, 35 minutes for each pound of meat. Baste with vinegar mixture. Serves 6 to 8.

SPICED PIGS' FEET

6 pigs' feet | salt and pepper to taste
1 teaspoon cloves | 2 bay leaves
1 red pepper pod | 1 teaspoon dry mustard
1 tablespoon paprika | 1 teaspoon celery seed
2 cups wine or tarragon | 2 onions
   vinegar | pinch marjoram

Select young, tender pigs' feet. Have them split. Wash well, cover with cold salted water, and soak. Drain. Place in a stew pot. Cover with cold water and cook about 1 hour. Add spices, vinegar, and onions. Simmer slowly until tender. Serves 6 to 8.
Serve with a tasty red and green cabbage slaw.

PIGS' FEET IN TOMATO SAUCE

6 medium pigs' feet | 2 red pepper pods
3 large chopped onions | 3 stalks chopped celery and
1 garlic clove | tops
1 chopped green pepper | salt, pepper and paprika to
several bay leaves | taste
½ cup vinegar | 1 can tomato purée

Split pigs' feet in half, wash, rub with lemon juice, place in water to cover. Cook ½ hour. Add pepper, onions, garlic, celery and tops, vinegar and seasonings. When the water boils add tomato purée. Cook slowly until well done. Serve with hot potato salad. Serves 6 to 8.

BAKED PIGS' FEET A LA BYNUM

6 medium pigs' feet | 1 tablespoon salt
2 bay leaves | 2 red pepper pods
⅓ cup vinegar | several garlic cloves

salt and pepper to taste
2 tablespoons
    Worcestershire sauce
2 finely chopped onions
1 green pepper

1 large can tomato purée
1 teaspoon celery seed
several finely chopped
    celery stalks

Have feet split. Wash well, cover with water. Add vinegar, salt, bay leaves, celery seed, and peppers. Boil until tender, but not too done. Drain water, place feet in a baking pan. Sauté onion, garlic, pepper and celery in bacon fat or butter. Add purée, Worcestershire sauce, salt, and pepper. Simmer 15 minutes. Pour over pigs' feet and cover. Cook in moderate oven for 40 minutes. Place on a platter and sprinkle with paprika and chopped parsley. Serve with cole slaw or potato salad, rye bread, and beer if desired. Serves 8.

ROAST SUCKLING PIG

1 very young, tender pig
    (not over 6 weeks old)
1 teaspoon pepper
1 tablespoon lemon juice

1 tablespoon dry mustard
2 teaspoons salt
1 teaspoon paprika
1 tablespoon vinegar

Clean and scald pig well. Salt and pepper inside and out as you would fowl. Fill with your favorite dressing and sew.

Rub outside of pig with a paste made from salt, pepper, paprika, lemon juice, vinegar, and mustard.

Place pig in roasting pan and bake 3½ to 4 hours, basting from time to time. When ready to serve, remove from oven and place a red apple in pig's mouth. Garnish with water cress or parsley. Serves 10 to 12.

Serve with candied sweet potatoes and a spicy apple sauce.

CHITTERLINGS No. 1

5 pounds chitterlings
2 garlic cloves
1 lemon, cut in quarters
1 teaspoon pepper
1 teaspoon clove
1 tablespoon thyme
several sprigs parsley

2 bay leaves
2 medium onions
1 teaspoon salt
1 teaspoon mace
1 teaspoon allspice
1 tablespoon marjoram
¼ cup vinegar

Soak chitterlings overnight. Wash through 4 or 5 waters. Turn inside out, remove excess fat but leave a small amount for seasoning. Add all spices and cover with water. Boil over low heat for 6 hours until tender. Cut in small pieces. During the last 30 minutes of cooking, add ½ cup tomato catsup or 1 cup tomato sauce and hot pepper to taste. Serve with a tasty cole slaw.

FRIED CHITTERLINGS

Prepare chitterlings and boil as in above recipe. Omit tomato sauce or catsup and vinegar. When tender, drain. Cut in 2-inch squares. Dip in a good fritter batter and fry in deep fat. Drain.

Serve hot with assorted salad plate and pickles.

CHITTERLINGS No. 2

10 pounds chitterlings	*4 garlic cloves*
2 large onions	*5 to 8 red pepper pods*
¼ cup vinegar	*2 celery stalks with tops*
2 bay leaves	*2 teaspoons salt*
2 teaspoons black pepper	

Thaw and wash chitterlings. Remove excess fat. Add spices and cover with water. Boil over low heat for 6 hours or until tender. Serve with spaghetti, cole slaw and corn bread.

SCRAPPLE

3 to 4 pounds pork with bone	*2 finely chopped onions*
3 quarts water	*1 tablespoon salt*

Boil pork until tender and save liquids. Remove meat from bones. Add 2 cups corn meal to the liquid and cook until mixture becomes a thick mush. Stir constantly. Chop pork and add to mush with juice of one onion. Add salt and pepper to taste. Pour into a greased loaf pan to cool and set. Slice and fry in hot skillet for breakfast. Makes 2 pounds scrapple.

Neck bones may be used in making scrapple if desired.

ROAST BEEF

1 5-pound beef roast	*1 teaspoon salt*
¼ cup flour	*½ teaspoon pepper*

Wipe meat with a damp cloth. Rub with salt and sprinkle with flour. Place on rack in a well-floured roasting pan, skin-side down. Place in hot oven, 475° F., until the surface is well seared. When flour in pan browns, reduce the heat. Baste roast every 15 minutes with fat and drippings. If flour begins to burn in pan, add a small amount of water. The water, however, is unnecessary if the pan is of sufficient size and the temperature is correct.

When your roast is half done, turn, taking care to avoid piercing roast with fork which would allow juices to escape. Sprinkle lightly with flour and cook according to time chart for roast beef. Serve with browned potatoes, Yorkshire pudding and fresh string beans, lettuce and tomato salad.

Roast beef may be served with or without gravy. If gravy is desired, try the following recipe.

ROAST BEEF GRAVY

Remove some of the fat from pan, leaving about 3 tablespoons. Add 3 tablespoons flour and stir until brown. When the flour is brown, it should give additional color to the gravy. Add 1½ cups boiling water gradually and cook 5 minutes. Season with salt and pepper and strain.

GOULASH

1 pound lean beef	1 cup strained tomatoes
1 pound lean veal	1 teaspoon salt
1 large diced onion	½ teaspoon pepper
3 tablespoons drippings	8 small white potatoes
	1 large diced carrot

Cut meat into fairly large pieces and brown with onion in the drippings. When meat is brown, add tomatoes, salt and pepper; and cook slowly one hour, keeping pan covered. After cooking ½ hour, add potatoes and carrots. If gravy has cooked down, add tomato juice to cover potatoes. Serves 4.

BEEF GOULASH

3 pounds brisket of beef cut up	2 medium onions, sliced
salt, pepper, and paprika to taste	¼ cup coarsely chopped celery
1 tablespoon garlic salt	1 clove
½ cup flour	1 bay leaf
fat	2 to 3 cups boiling water

Sprinkle salt, pepper, garlic salt, paprika and flour over meat. Brown in a small amount of fat. Add onion, celery, clove and bay leaf, then boiling water. Steam 1½ to 2 hours. Add tomato sauce. Simmer 30 minutes longer or until meat is tender. Add diced potatoes and carrots if desired. Serves 6 to 8.

Dumplings add an extra special touch. If potatoes are omitted, serve with rice or noodles, a green salad and a tasty dessert.

YORKSHIRE PUDDING

1 cup milk	*2 eggs*
1 cup flour	*¼ tablespoons salt*

Mix salt and flour and add milk gradually to form a smooth paste. Add eggs which have been lightly beaten. Cover bottom of hot pan with some of the beef fat from roast and pour mixture in pan ½ inch deep. Bake 20 minutes in hot oven and baste with fat after pudding has risen.

Roast beef is not quite complete without Yorkshire Pudding.

ANDY'S YORKSHIRE PUDDING

1 quart milk	*4½ cups sifted flour*
8 eggs	*1 teaspoon salt*
¼ pound beef suet	

Beat eggs until light. Add milk, flour and salt. Add ground suet and beat until smooth. Place in a well greased hot roasting pan. Bake for 1 hour, the first ½ hour at 375° F., then reduce to 325°F. for the second ½ hour.

STEAK FOR YOUR MEMOIRS

6 filets, or 2 small T-bone steaks, or 1 large sirloin steak	*salt and pepper to taste*
	1 teaspoon paprika
	1 tablespoon lemon juice
1 garlic clove, crushed	*1 tablespoon Tabasco sauce*
½ cup olive oil	

Crush garlic, add paprika, lemon juice and Tabasco sauce. Marinate steak in mixture. Place under broiler and broil. Sprinkle freely with salt and paprika before serving. Sauté 1 pound of mushrooms in ¼ cup butter. Add ½ cup cream, 1 teaspoon steak sauce and pour over steak.

Filet mignon is really a treat roasted in a whole piece and sliced.

If you want that extra touch of flavor, use Worcestershire steak sauce.

FILET MIGNON WITH CHICKEN LIVER PASTE

4 tenderloin steaks
2 cans chicken liver paste
4 tablespoons fat
5 tablespoons flour
2 cups brown stock
1 clove garlic

salt, pepper and paprika to
taste
1 small onion
1 cup fresh mushrooms,
sliced

Rub steaks with garlic. Make a pocket in each and stuff with chicken liver paste. Broil to your taste, medium, rare, or well done. Cover with mushroom sauce made by sautéing onion in fat with mushrooms. Add flour and brown. Add stock or water. Simmer and add seasonings. Place the steak and sauce on a very hot plank, trim with mashed potatoes (run through a pastry tube). Arrange tiny carrots, peas and a few cauliflower buds around potatoes. Garnish with parsley and celery. Serves 4.

GOLDEN BROWN STEW

2 pounds chuck or brisket
   beef
½ teaspoon garlic salt
1 teaspoon salt
4 cups boiling water
1 medium onion, chopped
1 teaspoon lemon juice
6 carrots
½ teaspoon curry powder
¼ cup flour

1 teaspoon Worcestershire
   sauce
several whole cloves
2 bay leaves
dash nutmeg
8 to 10 small onions
6 to 8 small potatoes
½ teaspoon pepper
1 teaspoon sugar

Sprinkle meat with flour and seasonings. Brown on all sides in a small amount of fat. Add boiling water, lemon juice, curry powder, Worcestershire sauce, chopped onion, cloves, and other spices and simmer 2 hours. Add whole onions, carrots and potatoes. Cook 20 minutes longer. Serve piping hot. Lamb or veal may be used also in this tasty stew. Serves 5.

ROLLED ROUND STEAK

2 pounds round steak
2 medium onions finely
    chopped
1 green pepper, finely
    chopped
1 teaspoon salt
¼ teaspoon paprika
1 teaspoon poultry seasonings
2 cups bread crumbs

4 tablespoons bacon fat
4 stalks celery, finely
    chopped
1 garlic clove, finely chopped
1 teaspoon thyme
1 teaspoon pepper
¼ cup water or tomato sauce
2 tablespoons flour

Sauté onions, celery, green pepper and garlic in bacon fat. Add salt, pepper, paprika, thyme, poultry seasoning, water or tomato sauce and simmer 10 minutes. Add bread crumbs. Sprinkle round steak with seasoning and salt. Cut steak ½ inch thick. Cover with dressing. Roll as a jelly roll and tie with clean white string. Grease well on all sides with bacon fat and sprinkle lightly with flour. Place in a roasting pan with small amount of water. Bake 2½ hours, or until tender. Serves 4 to 6.

Make a rich brown gravy and serve with browned potatoes and apple sauce. You will be surprised to find that round steak prepared in this manner tastes something like turkey.

Baked or braised breast of lamb or short ribs may be prepared in the same method. A barbecue sauce may be used for braising lamb for variety.

MARINATED STEAKS

6 garlic cloves
1 cup salt
juice from 1 lemon
2 tablespoons paprika
¼ cup olive oil

pinch thyme
pinch basil
2 tablespoons celery salt
¾ cup red wine
tender beef steaks

Place garlic in a small wooden bowl and crush to a pulp. Remove the skins. Add salt, pouring into bowl gradually and mixing until garlic and salt are completely blended. Add juice of 1 lemon and blend with salt and garlic mixture. Add paprika, thyme, basil, celery salt and blend well. Rub seasoning on both sides of steak with fingers. Place steaks in flat dish.

Combine wine and olive oil and pour over seasoned steaks. Cover. Let steaks marinate in liquid for 2 to 3 hours in refrigerator. This will allow seasoning to penetrate throughout meat. Remove steaks from dish and place on broiler pan. Place under broiler at 450° F. for 10 minutes. Baste in wine sauce and turn. Broil another 10 minutes and baste. Increase heat to 500° F. and baste until brown.

When steaks are done to desired taste remove from oven.

STEAK SAUCE

remainder of wine	*oil*
2 tablespoons Worcestershire sauce	*mushrooms*

Brown mushrooms in oil, add remainder of wine and Worcestershire sauce. Serve over steaks.

POT ROAST

3 to 4 pounds chuck or rump	*2 tablespoons flour*
1 onion	*2 cloves*
2 red peppers	*2 cups boiling water*
1 bay leaf	*2 tablespoons fat*
2 teaspoons salt	*1 teaspoon paprika*
pinch thyme	

Mix flour, salt, and paprika. Dredge meat well in mixture. Brown meat slowly on both sides in heavy Dutch oven or pan. Add water, cloves, bay leaf and thyme. Cover and simmer 3 hours or until meat is tender. During the last half hour of cooking, add the remaining flour, potatoes, and whole onion. Serves 4 to 6.

A cup of tomatoes or a cup of chopped parsley will change the entire picture or try whole tomatoes for a colorful treat.

A cup of sour cream added just before serving is really "something." Carrots, peas and turnips also help to give variety.

Tomato sauce should be omitted when cream is used.

BRAISED BEEF

3 pounds beef, from lower part of round or face of rump	*2 thin slices salt pork*
	6 peppercorns
	3 cloves

¼ cup flour
1 small bunch diced carrots
2 small diced turnips
2 small diced onions

¼ cup diced celery
salt and pepper
1 bay leaf
¼ teaspoon ginger

Sauté salt pork until brown and remove from drippings. Wipe meat, sprinkle with salt, ginger and pepper. Dredge with flour and brown entire surface in pork fat. Place in deep baking dish and surround with vegetables, peppercorns and 3 cups boiling water. Cover and bake 4 hours in very slow oven, basting every ½ hour and turning after second hour. The liquid should be kept below the boiling point while cooking. Serve with horseradish sauce or with brown sauce made from liquid in pan. Serves 4.

SHORT RIBS OF BEEF

4 to 5 pounds lean short ribs
several bay leaves
1 garlic clove, chopped
1 teaspoon salt
1 cup tomato purée or sauce
    (sour cream, if preferred)

1 cup water
½ cup flour
½ teaspoon pepper
1 teaspoon paprika

Cut meat so that there will be a bone in each piece. Roll meat in flour to which salt, pepper and paprika have been added. Place in a heavy skillet and brown on all sides. Add bay leaves, garlic, water, tomato purée or sour cream. Cover tightly and simmer until tender. Onions and vegetables may be added if desired. Serves 6.

Oxtail or breast of lamb may be prepared with this same recipe, or use barbecue sauce for braising lamb.

PLAIN STEW

2 pounds breast of veal
    (meat and bone)
2 teaspoons salt
2 whole cloves
½ teaspoon pepper
1 quart water or stock

3 potatoes
1 tablespoon butter
3 small onions
3 carrots
3 turnips

MEATS

Cut meat in small pieces. Place in sauce pan. Add salt, pepper, cloves, and cold water or stock. Simmer 2 or 3 hours until tender. Cut vegetables into small pieces, brown them in butter and add to the stew. Allow at least ½ hour for vegetables to cook. When vegetables are done, thicken gravy with 2 tablespoons flour and 2 tablespoons water, mixed into a thin paste. Cook 5 minutes longer, and serve. Serves 4.

Lamb can be substituted for veal in this recipe.

OXTAILS

2 oxtails, cut in pieces
½ cup diced carrots
½ cup diced onions
2 whole allspice or cloves
salt, pepper, and paprika
    to taste

1 quart hot water
½ cup celery, chopped
⅓ cup flour
1 can tomatoes
1 bay leaf
¼ cup fat

Sprinkle oxtails with salt and pepper and dredge in flour. Sauté in a heavy pot with fat. Brown well on all sides and add 1 quart of hot water or vegetable water. Add spices and cook slowly about 1 hour. Add remaining vegetables. Continue to cook until tender. Serve with mashed potatoes or rice. If desired, potatoes may be added to oxtails a half hour before serving. Serves 6.

MEAT LOAF

2 pounds ground beef
1 egg
1 small minced onion
2 teaspoons salt
½ teaspoon pepper

1 cup bread crumbs
1 cup tomato soup or sauce
1 teaspoon allspice
1 teaspoon prepared mustard

Mix meat and onion in a large bowl. Add bread crumbs, egg and seasonings. Blend well. Add ½ cup tomato soup to meat mixture and shape into a loaf. Place in a greased baking dish. Pour rest of tomato soup over meat and bake in a moderate oven 1½ hours or until done.

Mix ½ cup tomato catsup, ⅓ cup water and 2 tablespoons bacon fat and baste roast every 15 minutes until done to keep moist and form its own gravy. Serves 6.

Serve with mashed potatoes, French string beans and a tasty salad.

GROUND ROUND TURNOVER

¼ cup finely chopped onions
1 teaspoon celery salt
1 crushed garlic clove
1 teaspoon salt
⅛ teaspoon pepper
1 teaspoon paprika
1 teaspoon sage
2 pounds ground beef
⅓ cup flour

1 onion, sliced in rings
2 green peppers, sliced in rings
1 cup hot water
1 tablespoon Worcestershire sauce
1 tablespoon prepared mustard

Add onions, seasonings to ground beef. Mix thoroughly. Shape into one large flat cake about 2 inches thick. Sprinkle with flour on both sides. Place in large, hot, greased heavy frying pan. Brown meat on both sides, turning carefully. Place onion and green pepper rings on top. Cover tightly. Turn heat low and simmer for about 40 minutes. Place on large hot platter. Garnish with parsley.

UNIQUE HAMBURGERS

3 to 4 slices old bread
1 cup evaporated milk
5 pounds ground round steak
2 medium-sized onions, grated
½ cup prepared mustard

½ cup oil
1 tablespoon garlic salt
1 tablespoon paprika
2 tablespoons salt
1 tablespoon black pepper
dill pickle slices

Soak bread in milk. Add ground steak and mix thoroughly. Add remaining ingredients except pickle slices and oil and mix thoroughly. Shape into medium-sized balls. Press a dill pickle slice in center of each. Flatten out into pattie and sprinkle both sides lightly with flour. Fry quickly on both sides in hot fat, then place in a shallow baking pan in 325° F. oven to finish cooking and keep hot.

COMPANY MEAT LOAF

1 pound ground veal
1 pound ground beef

½ cup chopped green pepper

1 medium onion, chopped
2 cups bread crumbs or
    mashed potatoes
1 can mushroom slices and
    juice
½ cup chopped celery

2 eggs
2 tablespoons horseradish
½ cup tomato catsup
½ cup milk
1 teaspoon garlic and
    celery salt

Add vegetables and bread crumbs to meat. Blend in eggs and milk with seasonings. Shape into loaf. Sprinkle with salt, pepper and flour. Bake 45 minutes in a medium oven. Pour mushrooms mixed with horseradish and catsup over meat. Continue to cook another ½ hour. Sprinkle with parsley and serve. Make gravy if desired. Serves 6.

Mushroom soup may be used in place of sliced or whole mushrooms.

BREAKFAST HASH

4 medium white potatoes
1 small onion
3 tablespoons bacon fat or
    butter
2 tablespoons flour
2 cups cooked meat

1 teaspoon salt
½ teaspoon pepper
½ teaspoon paprika
1 teaspoon Worcestershire
    sauce
2 to 3 cups hot water

Peel and dice potatoes and onion. Sauté in fat. Add flour and brown lightly. Add meat, seasonings and water. Simmer 20 minutes. Sprinkle with chopped parsley. Serve.

CORNED BEEF HASH CUPS

2 small onions
2 small green peppers
2 tablespoons fat
2 cans corned beef hash
8 eggs

salt and pepper to taste
2 tablespoons chopped
    parsley
dash paprika

Sauté onions and peppers in fat. Add hash and set aside to cool. Shape into cups, molding with hands. Be sure the bottom of patty is about ½ inch thick. Place on a buttered baking dish. Fill each cup with a small egg. Sprinkle with salt, paprika, pepper and parsley. Bake in a slow oven until eggs are firm. Serve on a bed of parsley. Serves 8.

VEAL LOAF

1 full cup bread crumbs
¼ cup milk
1 egg
1 teaspoon poultry
   seasoning or sage
1 teaspoon salt, pepper,
   garlic salt, paprika

1 rib of celery, chopped
2 tablespoons grated green
   pepper
1 grated onion
2 pounds ground veal
2 tablespoons bacon fat or
   butter

Soak bread crumbs in milk. Add egg and seasonings. Blend celery, grated pepper and onion into veal. Add egg mixture. Form into a loaf and place in a greased loaf pan. Bake in a moderate oven, 350° F., 1½ to 2 hours. Baste roast with melted shortening in hot water or 1 tablespoon catsup or Worcestershire sauce. Serve hot with tomato sauce or brown gravy.

Veal loaf is delicious served cold for summer salads and cold cut platters.

Leftover mashed potatoes may be used instead of bread crumbs. Chopped pimientos or olives added to veal loaf lend a distinguished touch.

For a very fancy and special dish, add 1 cup chopped pistachio nuts to loaf!

VEAL AND PEPPERS No. 1

2 pounds veal steak
6 green peppers, cut in long
   strips
2 tablespoons soya sauce
1 teaspoon paprika
1½ cups warm water

3 large onions
1 garlic clove
¼ cup flour
2 tablespoons bacon fat
1 teaspoon salt

Cut veal in 2- or 3-inch strips. Sprinkle with flour, sauté in fat until brown. Add peppers, celery, onions and garlic. Cover and simmer on low flame about 25 minutes. Add remaining flour, soya sauce, paprika, salt and pepper. Add 1½ cups warm water, and continue to cook 15 to 20 minutes longer. Serve with rice. Serves 6.

MEATS

VEAL AND PEPPERS No. 2

2 pounds veal steak
2 medium onions, sliced
3 green peppers, cut in strips
several stalks celery, in small
    strips
1 can tomato sauce
3 tablespoons flour
1 cup hot water

1 tablespoon Worcestershire
    sauce
1 teaspoon paprika
1 teaspoon garlic salt
salt and pepper to taste
2 tablespoons fat
1 bay leaf

Cut veal in 1¼- to 1½-inch strips. Sprinkle with salt, pepper and flour. Place in heavy hot skillet with fat and sauté until brown on all sides. Add pepper, celery, and onion and sauté slowly. Add remaining flour, hot water, tomato sauce, and seasoning. Simmer for 45 minutes. Serve hot with rice and green peas.

TO BOIL TRIPE

Wash tripe carefully in several waters before boiling. Place in a kettle of cold water. Add 1 tablespoon salt and 2 tablespoons vinegar and boil at least 4 hours until tender. Drain well. It is best to prepare tripe the day before use, then you need not be rushed.

Tripe may be fried after boiling. Drain, cut in strips. Dip in beaten egg and roll in bread crumbs. Drop in very hot fat and fry to a crisp golden brown. Serve with a snappy sauce if desired.

SPICED TRIPE EDYTHE

2 pounds cut boiled tripe
4 small onions
2 small green peppers
6 cloves
6 allspice
3 bay leaves
1 teaspoon thyme
¼ cup white vinegar
6 firm tomatoes

6 carrots
2 garlic cloves
3 tablespoons bacon fat
2 tablespoons Worcestershire
    sauce
½ cup chopped parsley
½ teaspoon red pepper
salt and pepper to taste

Lay tripe in large pan. Slice onion, pepper and carrots in rings. Add bacon fat, spices and garlic and cover with tomato slices.

Cook until vegetables are tender. Add salt, pepper and vinegar. Do not stir. Steam 20 minutes longer. Just before serving, add Worcestershire sauce. Serves 4 to 6.

TRIPE A LA CREOLE

2 pounds tripe
2 tablespoons butter
2 medium onions, chopped
1 small green pepper,
    chopped
2 garlic cloves, crushed
½ teaspoon oregano
2 sprigs parsley

2 sprigs Spanish thyme
2 bay leaves
½ teaspoon paprika
½ teaspoon each, red and
    black pepper
¼ cup diced ham or bacon
1 No. 2 can tomatoes
salt to taste

Clean tripe well. Boil until tender. Cut in slices about 2 inches long and ½ inch wide. Melt butter in pan. Add chopped onions, pepper and garlic. Add all spices and simmer until brown. Add diced ham or bacon and tomatoes. Cook 15 minutes. Add salt and pepper. Add tripe. Cover and cook additional 30 minutes or until tender and well seasoned. Tomato purée may be used instead of canned tomatoes. Serves 4 to 6.

ROAST LEG OF LAMB IN WINE

1 leg of lamb, 6 to 8 pounds
salt and pepper to taste
1 teaspoon paprika

½ teaspoon dry mustard
2 tablespoons bacon fat
2 cups madeira or sherry wine

Rub leg of lamb with mixture of salt, pepper, paprika, mustard and fat. Place in baking dish and roast in a slow oven, allowing 20 minutes per pound. After first 40 minutes of roasting, baste with wine until done (about 2 hours). If lamb browns too fast, cover with damp heavy brown paper. Serves 8. Serve with green peas or asparagus, potatoes, mint sauce and chopped green water cress salad.

LAMB CHOPS AND FRESH PINEAPPLE SLICES

6 rib lamb chops
1 tablespoon flour
1 teaspoon garlic salt

1 teaspoon paprika
½ lemon
1 tablespoon butter

½ teaspoon nutmeg
salt and pepper to taste

6 slices fresh pineapple
water cress

Sprinkle chops on both sides with salt, pepper, paprika and garlic salt. Heat heavy skillet and brown chops. When brown on both sides, remove from pan. Peel and slice pineapple. Place slices which have been well drained in pan with butter. Brown, sprinkle with nutmeg. Place chops on top of each slice of fruit. Cover and simmer 20 minutes. Serve on a bed of water cress. Squeeze lemon juice over water cress. Serve with asparagus and potato balls.

LAMB PATTIES

1½ pounds ground lamb
    shank or shoulder
1 teaspoon garlic salt
6 slices bacon

salt and pepper to taste
2 tablespoons grated onion
1 teaspoon paprika
bacon fat or butter

Mix seasoning with ground lamb. Shape into patties about 2 inches thick. Wrap with slices of bacon. Sprinkle with salt and pepper and rub with fat and place under broiler for 15 to 20 minutes, turning at least twice. Serve hot on heated plates. May be panbroiled or baked. Serves 6.

Delicious with minted pineapple slices or sprinkled with mushrooms and parsley.

Minted Pineapple Slices:
  6 pineapple slices   *1 jar mint jelly*

Melt jelly. Drain pineapple and lay in melted jelly. Simmer a few minutes on each side. A few sprigs of chopped fresh mint may be added.

SMOTHERED BREAST OF LAMB

breast or shoulder of lamb
    (about 5 lbs.)
2 carrots, diced
1 cup fresh peas
sprig thyme
1 cup bread crumbs
2 tablespoons butter

1 teaspoon saffron
2 sprigs parsley
2 onions
½ can tomatoes
1 bay leaf
pinch sage
1 garlic clove

Have butcher remove all bones. Wipe meat with clean damp cloth. Sauté onion, garlic and parsley in fat. Add bread crumbs which have been dampened and tomatoes. Sauté 5 minutes. Add all spices and place dressing in open side of meat. Roll and tie with string. Place in heavy iron pot. Sauté meat and brown all sides. Simmer about 1 hour until tender. Add diced carrots, 1 cup hot water and peas during last 20 minutes of cooking.

BAKED BREAST OF LAMB WITH VEGETABLES

3 to 4 pounds breast of lamb
(one large breast)
1 teaspoon salt
1 teaspoon sugar

6 small carrots
1 garlic clove
¼ cup vinegar
6 medium potatoes

Rub breast of lamb with garlic. Sprinkle with salt. Place in baking pan. Pour vinegar to which sugar has been added, over lamb. Place in hot oven, 400° F., for 15 to 20 minutes, basting and turning. Reduce heat to 350° F. Cook 1½ hours, or until tender, crisp and brown, basting occasionally. During last half hour of cooking, add raw potatoes from which the centers have been cut out. Insert a small carrot through each potato and bake for 30 minutes. Serves 4 to 6.

ROAST LEG OF LAMB WITH BROWN GRAVY

1 leg of lamb (about
6 pounds)
2 garlic cloves
juice of 1 lemon, or
½ cup white vinegar

1 teaspoon ginger
salt, pepper and paprika
to taste

Wipe meat with clean, damp cloth. Remove excess fat and outside skin. Make several cuts in meat. Place slices of garlic through meat. Cover lamb with ginger, salt, pepper and paprika. Pour lemon juice or vinegar over lamb. Place in roaster fat side up. Roast uncovered in a slow oven until tender. Allow 30 to 35 minutes per pound. Remove roast from pan.

For gravy, add 3 tablespoons flour to drippings in roaster and brown. Add 1 tablespoon Worcestershire sauce, 1 teaspoon paprika and 2 to 3 cups water.

During the last half hour of baking, add tiny new potatoes

and carrots. Sprinkle with salt and finish baking. Garnish and serve. Serves 8.

BRAISED LAMB SHANKS

4 lamb shanks	¼ teaspoon marjoram
2 tablespoons drippings	½ teaspoon salt
1 sliced onion	⅛ teaspoon black pepper
1 bay leaf	1 cup hot tomato juice

Heat drippings in small heavy roaster and brown shanks over high heat. Add onion, bay leaf, marjoram, salt, and pepper to hot tomato juice. Pour over browned shanks. Cover tightly. Braise or bake slowly in moderate oven, 350° F., 2½ hours or until tender. Serve on bed of fluffy rice. Serves 4.

LAMB PATTIES ON PINEAPPLE

3 pounds lamb, chopped or ground	1 teaspoon garlic salt
	8 pineapple rings
1 bunch green onions, chopped	8 green pepper rings
	½ cup mint jelly
1 tablespoon prepared mustard	melted butter

Mix lamb with green onions, mustard and garlic salt. Mold into 8 slices about ½ inch thick. Place patties on pineapple rings, top with green pepper rings and mint jelly and place on wire rack in shallow baking pan. Bake in a 350° F. oven for 15 minutes. Brush with butter and place under broiler for 15 minutes.

LAMB KIDNEYS

6 to 8 strips cooked bacon	1 cup water
6 to 8 lamb kidneys	1 cup celery
½ cup red wine	1 cup green pepper
½ cup mushrooms	1 cup onions
½ teaspoon garlic salt	2 tablespoons flour

Wash and peel thin skin from kidney. Soak 2 hours. Drain, dry, dip in flour and garlic salt. Sauté in hot fat until brown. Remove from pan. Add chopped onion, pepper, and celery. Brown. Add flour, mushrooms and 1 cup water and wine. Return kidneys to pan and simmer covered 15 minutes. Serve on platter. Surround with toast triangles and bacon. Serves 4.

CURRY OF LAMB

1½ pounds lean lamb, cut in 1-inch pieces
2 tablespoons shortening
½ cup finely chopped onion
1 garlic clove, crushed
1 apple, pared, cored and cubed

3 tomatoes peeled and cut in pieces
2 cups water or meat stock
1 teaspoon salt
⅛ teaspoon pepper
3 tablespoons flour
1 tablespoon curry powder

Melt shortening in deep, heavy cooking pot. Add lamb and onions. Cook over medium heat until meat is browned. Add all ingredients except flour. Cover pot and bring to a boil. Use low heat and simmer until tender, about 1½ hours. Remove lamb and set aside. Strain sauce and mix flour to a smooth paste. Simmer until thick and smooth. Place meat in sauce and heat. Serve with hot cooked rice. Yield: 4.

OPOSSUM AND SWEET POTATOES

1 opossum
1 teaspoon pepper
1 teaspoon leaf sage
4 or 5 slices bacon
2 teaspoons salt

1 teaspoon paprika
2 garlic cloves
6 to 8 medium sweet potatoes

Clean, dress, and wash opossum well. Place overnight in freezing compartment of refrigerator or on ice. Drain and wipe dry. Rub well with a mixture of spices. Lay in a baking pan. Cover with thin slices of bacon and set in a slow oven about 300° F. Bake and baste for 1 to 1½ hours. During the last half of baking, arrange sweet potatoes that have been parboiled around meat. Bake until brown, basting with drippings.

Here is an adventure in good eating. Serve with a country salad, corn bread and buttermilk.

STEWED TURTLE

2 pounds turtle meat
1½ lemons
5 bay leaves

2 finely chopped onions
2 finely chopped peppers
6 garlic cloves

MEATS

5 sprigs fresh thyme
½ bunch green onions
1 can tomato paste
1 can tomatoes
6 tablespoons parsley
½ cup fat

4 tablespoons flour
6 red pepper pods
salt, pepper, cayenne to
   taste
2 pints water

Steam turtle meat. Drain and fry turtle meat in fat for 15 minutes. Add onions, peppers, garlic, green onions, parsley and fry 2 minutes. Add flour and fry until brown. Add tomatoes, tomato paste, water, lemon, salt, pepper, bay leaves, thyme. Cook with cover for 45 minutes or until tender.

NECKBONES
(Mrs. C. Tinkchell)

4 pounds neckbones
1 tablespoon salt
1 teaspoon black pepper

¼ teaspoon sage (optional)
3 tablespoons bacon fat
1 medium onion, sliced

Wash meat in lukewarm water. Drain well or damp dry. Combine salt, pepper, and sage and use to season neckbones well. Heat bacon fat and brown on all sides. Place in pot of lukewarm water to cover. Add leftover seasonings, cover, and simmer gently for 1 hour or until meat begins to become tender. Add onion and continue to simmer for 20 to 30 minutes or until meat comes away from bone with a fork. Add a little flour to liquid if gravy is desired. Serves 4 to 6.

9.

Fowl

TIME-TABLE FOR ROASTING POULTRY

Fowl	Oven Temp.	Time per pound
Capon	325° F.	22 to 30 minutes
Chicken, roasting	300° F.	30 to 45 minutes
Duck	325° F.	20 to 30 minutes
Turkey		
8- to 10-pound	300° F.	20 to 25 minutes
10- to 16-pound	300° F.	18 to 20 minutes
18- to 25-pound	300° F.	15 to 18 minutes
Wild Duck or Goose		
(rare)	325° F.	10 to 12 minutes
(well done)	325° F.	15 to 20 minutes

TURKEY

Why not try roasting your turkey in a Spanish sauce; if not for Thanksgiving, perhaps as a September or October dish? It is a treat cut in quarters and roasted without dressing.

Use a very small turkey, cut in quarters. Baste with milk or cream, salt, pepper, paprika, grated onions, and mushrooms. Bake slowly, letting turkey form its own gravy, until very tender. This is a dish that is rich and different!

Or you might try baked or roasted turkey legs. Many markets feature turkey and chicken parts. It is different to serve only these choice parts, and we all like to be different at times, to test our ingenuity and creative powers to please our family and thrill our guests.

OLD-FASHIONED ROAST TURKEY

12- to 15-pound turkey
1 tablespoon salt
1 tablespoon paprika

2 tablespoons bacon fat
1 teaspoon garlic salt
½ teaspoon pepper

Rinse turkey with cold water, and pat dry. Rub inside and out with salt and pepper. Fill with your favorite dressing. Sew or close with skewers; neck cavity may be filled with stuffing, if desired. Fold wing tips under back. (Never stuff turkey tightly —allow for expansion.)

Rub turkey well with bacon fat, salt, pepper, paprika, and garlic salt. Cover with a clean white cloth which has been dipped in melted fat or milk. Cover well. Roast slowly uncovered, making sure cloth stays damp at oven temperature, 300° F. Allow 20 minutes per pound. Baste from time to time with drippings, turning turkey completely to brown on all sides. Cloth may be removed during the last half hour, so the turkey skin will be brown and crisp.

Boil giblets and neck with celery tops, onions and seasonings to make gravy. Allow ½ to ¾ pound per person.

ROAST TURKEY IN PORT WINE

12- to 15-pound turkey
1 bottle Port wine
salt, pepper, paprika, garlic
    salt to taste

3 tablespoons bacon fat
1 clean heavy brown
    paper bag

Rinse turkey inside and out. Rub with salt, pepper, and garlic salt. Fill with your favorite dressing. Rub turkey with bacon fat, place in oven. Pour 2 cups of wine over the turkey. Start in hot oven. Cook 2 hours, basting with wine and turning every half hour. Reduce heat. Dip paper bag in warm water and squeeze out lightly. Place over turkey. Cook until done, basting in wine and turning from time to time. Gravy may be made the usual way by browning flour and adding stock. Allow ¾ pound to each person.

There is no set rule about a cover for roasting turkey. I've tasted some grand turkeys, juicy brown and crisp, roasted with and without a cover. Just don't rush your turkey! Consult a time-table, and take your time.

ROAST TURKEY IN PEANUT BUTTER

10- to 12-pound turkey
1 tablespoon flour
½ cup peanut butter
1 tablespoon salt
1 teaspoon pepper
1 tablespoon paprika
1 teaspoon celery salt
⅓ cup milk or cream (enough to make a medium paste)

Mix flour, salt, pepper, paprika, celery salt and peanut butter into a paste. Blend with cream or milk.

Wash, clean and stuff bird. Place in roasting pan. Spread paste over entire bird, covering well. Add 1 cup water in pan. Place in moderate oven, 400° F., for 3 hours, basting every 30 minutes and turning at least twice to brown on all sides. One cup stock can be substituted for 1 cup of water. Allow ¾ pound per person.

TURKEY PIE

3 or 4 cups leftover turkey
1 medium onion
2 whole cloves
4 carrots
½ cup flour
½ teaspoon nutmeg
2 cups vegetable stock; meat, turkey or chicken broth (canned broth may be used)
1 teaspoon salt
½ teaspoon pepper
1 teaspoon lemon juice
¼ cup butter
½ cup celery, chopped
2 cups evaporated milk

Parboil carrots, onion, cloves, celery, and garlic in soup or stock. Blend flour and butter. Add vegetables and stock, cook until thick. Add milk, diced turkey and lemon juice. Season to taste. Place in deep pie pan or casserole. Place rich pastry on top. (Made from your favorite rich pastry recipe.) Brush with milk. Bake in a hot oven, 400° F., for 15 minutes. Reduce heat, continue to bake 10 minutes longer until brown. Serves 8.

Serve with a green salad bowl and pumpkin chiffon pie, coffee.

Turkey pies may be baked individually in small casseroles. A rich biscuit dough may be used for the crust if desired.

CREAMED TURKEY WITH PISTACHIO NUTS

Do you want a color scheme for your Holiday bridge? Try this recipe for red and green.

6 cups cold turkey	1 tablespoon paprika
1 cup celery	pinch mace
1 cup parsley	½ cup diced pimiento
½ cup flour	½ cup pistachio nuts,
2 cups cream or evaporated	chopped
milk	salt to taste
2 cups milk	¼ cup butter

Chop and boil celery in milk. Add cream, and heat. Blend flour and butter. Add milk and celery mixture. Cook until thick. Add turkey, pimiento, parsley, nuts and seasoning. Simmer until well heated. Serve on toast, in patty shells, or with tiny hot biscuits. Serves 12.

A spiced red pear salad filled with cottage cheese and chives on crisp endive with French dressing makes a very festive plate.

CHICKEN

Gravy is a matter of choice with chicken. In making gravy, either brown or cream, drain off excess grease; brown flour well; add seasoning, water or milk.

Mushrooms, onions, parsley, and peppers can be added effectively to chicken gravy.

To roast chicken, follow same simple method as for turkey. Baste often and watch your cooking time. Use your favorite dressing. Small chickens may be split in halves and roasted without dressing.

Fresh killed chickens have a tendency to be a little stringy, especially if cooked immediately after killing and cleaning. It is best to let chickens cool in the refrigerator for several hours before cooking.

When you put flour and seasonings in a paper bag to flour your frying chicken, use a dash of nutmeg and paprika or garlic salt for a new taste thrill.

Many people feel that fried chicken belongs to the South, but I have encountered just as many who have never been below the Mason-Dixon line who are definitely fried chicken experts. It is a matter of taste. So, for your varied tastes, here are recipes from Negro cooks in the South, North, East, and even West. They are all good!

FRIED CHICKEN IN BATTER

1 young fryer (about
   3 pounds)
1½ cups flour
1 egg, beaten
1 teaspoon salt

½ teaspoon pepper
½ cup milk
1 teaspoon baking powder
½ teaspoon paprika

Cut chicken in small pieces. Wash and dry. Sprinkle with salt and pepper. Mix flour, baking powder and salt. Add egg and milk. Let stand ½ hour. Dip chicken in batter. Be sure it is well coated. Fry in deep hot fat, turning to brown on all sides. Be sure chicken is well done—as batter prevents chicken from cooking thoroughly. Serves 4.

Raw chicken may be steamed in a small amount of water, dried and cooled, dipped in same batter to fry.

FRIED CHICKEN IN CREAM

3-pound fryer (cut up)
½ cup butter or shortening
2 tablespoons chopped
   parsley
salt and pepper to taste

1 cup cream
¼ cup flour
1 teaspoon paprika
dash nutmeg

Put flour, salt, pepper, paprika, and nutmeg in a paper bag. Shake well. Cut chicken in small pieces. Wash and dry. Sprinkle with garlic salt and place in paper bag with other seasonings. Marinate well with flour and seasoning mixture. Place in hot skillet with fat. Brown on all sides. Cover and simmer ½ hour. Remove cover. Add cream and parsley and cook an additional 20 minutes. Serve hot with mashed potatoes. Serves 4.

FRIED CHICKEN No. 1

1 2- to 3-pound chicken, cut, washed and well dried	salt, pepper, paprika to taste
1 teaspoon garlic salt	½ cup flour
	1 cup fat

Place salt, pepper, paprika, and flour in a paper bag. Shake well. Sprinkle cut chicken with garlic salt and nutmeg. Place 2 or 3 pieces of chicken in bag at one time and shake so that each piece will be well coated. Drop into hot fat and cook 15 to 20 minutes on each side. Avoid sticking fork into meat of chicken because juices will escape and pop in hot fat! When brown and crisp on both sides, remove from pan, drain on paper and serve. Serves 4.

If gravy is desired, drain all fat except about 2 tablespoons, add 2 tablespoons of remaining flour. Brown and add 2 cups hot water, salt and pepper. Simmer. Chicken may be added to gravy if desired.

FRIED CHICKEN No. 2

1 3- to 4-pound chicken	½ teaspoon pepper
1 lemon	1 grated onion
1 teaspoon paprika	½ teaspoon garlic salt
1 teaspoon salt	1 cup flour

Clean, wash and cut chicken. Dry well. Marinate with juice from lemon. Sprinkle with garlic salt. Let stand overnight or for several hours in refrigerator. Add seasonings to flour in paper bag or bowl. Flour chicken well. Fry in medium deep fat for about 45 minutes, turning to brown on all sides.

Top may be placed on pan after chicken is brown. Keep your flame moderate! Serves 6.

MARYLAND FRIED CHICKEN

1 young fryer (3 to 3½ pounds)	1 cup water
	½ cup flour
1 teaspoon salt	½ teaspoon pepper
½ teaspoon paprika	⅔ cup fat

Quarter chicken, wash and singe. Dry well. Dip in mixture of flour, salt, pepper, and paprika. Place in hot fat in a heavy skillet. Brown on all sides. Allow about 15 minutes each side. Reduce heat. Cover and simmer 15 to 20 minutes. Remove from pan. Add 2 to 3 tablespoons flour and brown. Add 1 cup water. Mix well. Place chicken in gravy. Simmer another additional 15 minutes. Serve with rice or potatoes, hot biscuits and honey. Serves 6.

ROAST CAPON

6- to 7-pound capon	1 teaspoon paprika
1 teaspoon salt	1 cup heavy cream
2 cups celery and leaves	1 teaspoon season salt
1 small onion, minced	2 tablespoons fat or butter
½ teaspoon poultry seasoning	

Clean and dress capon. Sprinkle inside with salt. Stuff with your favorite dressing. Sew up or tie opening. Sauté in fat, onion, and celery. Cool and add cream. Sprinkle with seasonings. Place in baking pan. Cover capon with cream and onion mixture. Place some of the mixture in bottom of pan. Place capon with breast up and bake in slow oven, 325° F., 25 to 30 minutes per pound. Baste frequently with cream. When capon begins to brown, cover with a cloth dipped in milk and wrung out (brown paper may be used as well). Continue cooking until done. Use drippings for gravy. Serves 8.

BROILED CHICKEN

4 small broilers	¼ cup Sherry wine
juice 1 lemon	4 small onions
1 teaspoon ginger	½ cup evaporated milk, or cream
salt, pepper, paprika to taste	

Split chickens in half. Rub with onions, sprinkle with salt, pepper and paprika. Pour juice of lemon over them and set in refrigerator for several hours.

Mix wine and ginger. Place chicken in flat pan. Marinate with wine. Bake under broiler (very low) for 30 minutes, turning every 15 minutes. When brown, place in oven for another 30 minutes and pour cream over chicken. Serves 8.

SAUCE FOR CHICKEN

3 tablespoons fat
2 medium onions
½ cup chili sauce
2 tablespoons Worcestershire
    sauce
1 teaspoon thyme
1 bay leaf

2 garlic cloves
½ cup grated celery
2 tablespoons prepared
    mustard
2 tablespoons hickory salt
1 cup tomato sauce
several pods red pepper

Sauté onions, garlic, and celery in fat. Add remaining ingredients and simmer 30 minutes.

When ready to cook, remove chicken from refrigerator and dip in sauce. Place chicken on broiler pan and cook slowly under broiler, turning every 15 minutes with fork until done. Temperature should remain about 325° F. Baste chicken with sauce at regular intervals to keep from drying. Chicken should be a deep brown on all sides. Approximate time is from 1½ to 2 hours. Place in a warm oven until ready to serve. Serve barbecue hot or cold, with or without sauce. Trimmings should include a delicious shell macaroni salad garnished with romaine lettuce, endive, green onions, and celery.

CHICKEN GIBLET STEW

You've heard the old stories about the Sunday when the preacher came to dinner and the kids got only the neck, wings, and back of the chicken.

But in these days, when you can buy any part and as much of the chicken as you want, the stories are not especially pertinent.

I, for one, have always loved the giblets, wings, and necks best in stew. So, the preacher can have what he thinks is the best and I'll take the rest.

Chicken giblets, wings, and
    necks
2 onions
2 celery stalks, diced
2 green peppers
2 tablespoons butter
salt and pepper to taste

1 bay leaf
1 can tomatoes or sauce
2 tablespoons flour
1 garlic clove
2 tablespoons chopped
    parsley

Boil giblets, wings, and backs (optional) with salt, pepper, bay leaf, and garlic in enough water to cover. Sauté onions, celery, and peppers in fat. Add flour and tomatoes. When giblets are tender, add onion and tomato sauce. Simmer 15 to 20 minutes. Add chopped parsley and serve with rice, green peas and salad. Serves 4.

CHICKEN PIE

1 large fowl	*water*
1 onion	*sprig parsley*
1 clove (whole)	*1 bay leaf*
1½ teaspoons salt	*1 teaspoon celery salt*
6 to 8 cooked carrots, diced	*pepper and paprika to taste*
or quartered	*6 to 8 small onions, cooked*
1 cup cooked celery	*1 cup cream or milk*
⅓ cup chopped parsley	*⅓ cup flour*

Cut chicken in pieces. Place in stewing pan with onion and spices. Cover with boiling water. Cook slowly until tender. Remove chicken from pot. Cool, cut meat from bones in large pieces. To remaining chicken stock, which should be about 2½ cups, add milk. Sprinkle flour over vegetables and add to chicken stock. Simmer until thickened, stirring carefully so that vegetables will not break. Remove from fire and pour over chicken in baking dish. Cover with pastry and bake until crust is done, 15 to 20 minutes. Serves 6.

Green peas and potatoes may be added if desired. Serve chicken pie with tasty pineapple salad or mixed garden salad. It's a meal in itself.

EBONY'S BARBECUED CHICKEN

Step 1 (chicken)

Select small fryer-broilers. Clean and split chickens in half lengthwise. Sprinkle lightly with garlic salt, paprika and hickory salt. Cover; let stand in refrigerator several hours or overnight.

Step 2 (sauce)	*½ cup finely chopped*
2 tablespoons chicken fat or	*celery*
butter	*2 garlic cloves, crushed*
⅔ cup finely chopped onion	*½ cup chili sauce*

1 bay leaf	2 tablespoons hickory salt
2 tablespoons Worcestershire sauce	2 tablespoons prepared mustard
1 teaspoon thyme	6 to 8 dry red pepper pods
1 cup tomato sauce	

Melt fat in 1½ quart heavy saucepan; add onions, celery and garlic; cook over low heat stirring constantly, until celery is just tender. Add all remaining ingredients; simmer gently for 20 to 30 minutes.

Step 3 (oven barbecue)
Dip or brush chicken with sauce and place on broiler pan. Cook slowly under broiler, turning every 15 minutes with fork until tender (about 1½ to 2 hours). Temperature should be about 325° F. Baste chicken with sauce at regular intervals to keep from drying. When done, chicken should be a deep brown on all sides. Keep in warm oven until ready to serve.

EBONY'S STEWED CHICKEN AND DUMPLINGS
Step 1

1 4½- to 5-pound stewing hen	1½ teaspoons salt
2 cups cold water	½ teaspoon Accent
½ cup chopped onion	¼ teaspoon garlic salt
½ cup chopped celery with tops	¼ teaspoon paprika

Cut chicken in pieces and place in large, heavy cooking pot with water, and seasonings. Cover. Bring to boil, turn heat low and simmer gently until chicken is almost completely tender, (2 to 3½ hours, depending on the age and quality of bird.) Add dumplings and cook as directed.

Step 2 (dumplings)

1 cup flour	½ teaspoon sugar
2 teaspoons baking powder	2 tablespoons finely chopped parsley
½ cup milk	
½ teaspoon salt	

Sift together all dry ingredients. Add milk and beat to a thick smooth batter. Drop by teaspoon on top of chicken pieces.

Sprinkle with parsley. Cover tightly. Cook 20 minutes without raising the top. Serve chicken on hot platter, with dumplings. Yield: 5 servings.

CHICKEN IN WINE
Step 1

1 3-pound frying chicken
salt and pepper
1 tablespoon paprika
1 medium sized onion, sliced
1 minced garlic clove

½ teaspoon garlic salt
2 cups sweet white wine
½ cup olive oil (or)
½ cup melted butter

Cut chicken in quarters, sprinkle with salt, pepper and paprika. Place in a flat dish. Place onions and garlic or garlic salt over chicken. Cover with wine and oil or melted butter. Cover dish with foil, place in refrigerator over night. Turn at least once so chicken parts are completely marinated. Remove chicken from refrigerator, drain and place in a flat baking dish. Bake in a 350° F. (moderate) oven until brown (about 45 minutes.) Baste with wine and oil mixture frequently.

Step 2

1 can mushrooms
1 bunch green onions, chopped
1 green pepper, chopped
1 bunch celery, chopped

salt and pepper
¼ cup butter
¼ cup sweet white wine
1 tablespoon Worcestershire sauce

Sauté vegetables lightly in butter, about 5 minutes. Add wine and Worcestershire sauce; simmer gently 20 minutes. Pour over chicken just before removing from the oven. Serve with wild rice.

EBONY'S EAST INDIAN CHICKEN
Step 1

4- to 5-pound stewing hen
1 quart cold water
2 cloves
1 cup chopped celery

½ cup butter
1 tablespoon curry powder
1 small onion, diced
2 bay leaves

Cut chicken in pieces; place in large heavy cooking pot with remaining ingredients. Cover; bring to boil; turn heat to low and simmer gently until chicken is tender, about 2½ to 3½ hours. Strain stock and cool. Cut chicken from bones in large pieces; keep cool until ready to use.

Step 2

½ cup butter
1 bunch green onions, chopped
2 cups chopped celery
½ cup cut parsley
2 green peppers, cleaned and chopped
2 tablespoons paprika
2 tablespoons curry powder
½ cup diced pimiento
½ cup coarsely chopped salted almonds
½ cup flour
1 teaspoon Season-all
1 pint milk
1 cup light cream
chicken stock
½ cup chopped chutney
¼ cup chopped ripe olives

Melt butter in heavy cooking pot. Add onions, celery, parsley and green pepper and cook over medium heat until just tender. Stir in seasonings and flour until smooth. Add milk, cream and chicken stock; blend well. Bring to boil; cook over medium heat, stirring continually until thick and smooth. Add chicken, chutney, pimientos and olives. Simmer gently for 30 minutes, adding almonds last 10 minutes of cooking. Serve with rice.

CHICKEN TAMALE PIE

3½- to 4½-pound stewing hen
2½ cups water
2 teaspoons salt
¼ teaspoon pepper
2 tablespoons bacon fat
1 medium onion, chopped
¼ cup parsley, chopped
1 cup celery, chopped
2 green peppers, chopped
2 garlic cloves
½ teaspoon thyme
2 tablespoons chili powder
1 teaspoon paprika
2 bay leaves
1 can whole kernel corn
1 pint ripe olives
1 can tomato purée
2 cups cornmeal
3 cups water
salt, pepper and paprika
¾ cup Italian cheese, grated

Cut chicken in small pieces and place in wide, heavy cooking pot, salt and pepper; cover tightly; simmer gently 2½ to 3½ hours, until tender. Strain. Remove meat from bones and cut in medium sized pieces; set aside. Melt bacon fat, add onions, parsley, celery, and green pepper; garlic, thyme, chili powder, paprika and bay leaves; sauté gently about 20 minutes. Add corn, olives and tomato purée. Simmer 15 minutes longer. Cook cornmeal in water; add salt, pepper and paprika and cook to a thick mush, stirring constantly. Line baking dish with half of the mixed vegetables and chicken and place in casserole. Spread layer of mush over top. Sprinkle with cheese. Bake in a 350° F. (moderate) oven for 45 minutes.

ARROZ CON POLLO

*1 frying chicken, about
   3½ pounds
½ cup lime juice (about
   3 limes)
salt and pepper
⅔ cup oil
¾ cup rice
½ cup chopped onion
½ teaspoon thyme
½ teaspoon sage
½ cup celery, chopped*

*½ cup green pepper,
   chopped
½ teaspoon rosemary
1 cup tomato sauce or purée
1 garlic clove, minced
2 cups boiling water
1 can peas
1 tablespoon butter
salt and pepper to taste
¼ cup parsley, minced
1 jar stuffed olives*

Cut chicken into small pieces and place in shallow pan. Cover with salt, pepper and lime juice. Place in refrigerator for 2 hours or overnight; cover with aluminum foil. Brown chicken pieces in hot oil and remove from pan. Add rice to oil; stir frequently until lightly browned. Add onion, celery, green pepper, parsley, thyme, sage, rosemary, tomato sauce, garlic and water. Mix thoroughly. Place chicken carefully on top; cover tightly and simmer gently 20 to 30 minutes. Heat peas with butter, salt and pepper and place chicken around platter with rice garnished with peas and stuffed olives in center.

HAMP'S STEWED CHICKEN

*4- to 5-pound stewing
   chicken
2 medium onions
2 stalks celery
1 garlic clove
½ teaspoon paprika*

*hot water
¼ cup flour
½ teaspoon pepper
1 small green pepper
1 bay leaf
1 tablespoon salt*

Wash and cut chicken. Sprinkle with seasonings. Dredge with flour. Melt fat in heavy pan. Brown chicken lightly on all sides. Add onion, celery, bay leaf, garlic, and green pepper. Brown 15 minutes. Add hot water to cover. Cook until chicken is tender. Gravy may be thickened, if desired. Serve with rice. Serves 4.

STEWED CHICKEN WINGS

3 pounds chicken wings	1 teaspoon salt
1 green pepper	1 red pepper pod
1 No. 2 can tomatoes	½ teaspoon celery salt
1 garlic clove	2 or 3 carrots
2 medium onions	2 cups water
1 bay leaf	1 teaspoon chili powder

Wash and singe chicken wings. Cover with tomatoes and water. Boil 15 to 20 minutes. Add chopped vegetables with seasonings. Simmer until tender and liquid is almost absorbed. May be thickened, if desired. Serve with rice and green peas. Serves 4.

BROWNED FRICASSEED CHICKEN AND EGG DUMPLINGS

1 stewing chicken (3½- to 4-pound)	2¼ cups bacon fat or shortening
1 small onion	1 teaspoon salt
⅓ cup flour	3 tablespoons fat
1 teaspoon pepper	1 teaspoon paprika
	several stalks celery

Cut, wash and singe chicken. Sprinkle with salt, pepper, paprika and flour. Heat fat in a heavy pan. Add chicken and brown well on all sides. Add about 1 quart warm water, onion and celery. Cook slowly until tender, approximately 2 to 3 hours, in a tightly covered pot.

Egg Dumplings

Mix 1 cup flour, 1 teaspoon chopped parsley, 2 teaspoons baking powder, ½ teaspoon salt. Add 1 egg slightly beaten, and enough milk to make ½ cup. Add to flour. Mix to a thick batter, drop with spoon in boiling chicken. Cover and cook

20 minutes. Do not remove cover. Place chicken on platter with dumplings. Serves 6.

If you wish vegetables in your chicken, add them during the last 30 minutes of cooking or just before adding dumplings.

Leftover vegetables such as peas, carrots, corn may be added.

CHICKEN LIVER SAUTÉ

1 pound chicken livers
½ teaspoon salt
¼ teaspoon pepper
dash garlic salt

2 tablespoons flour
1 onion, diced
1 tablespoon fat
½ cup water or stock

Cut livers in quarters. Sprinkle with salt, pepper and flour. Sauté onion in fat, add livers and brown. Add stock and simmer 5 minutes. Serves 4. Serve on toast or plain.

STEWED CHICKEN AND DUMPLINGS

1 stewing chicken
  (about 4 pounds)
1 small onion
2 tablespoons parsley,
  chopped

salt, pepper, paprika to taste
½ cup celery and leaves
½ teaspoon garlic salt

Dumplings

1 cup flour
2 teaspoons baking powder

½ cup milk
½ teaspoon salt

Place cut chicken, onion, and celery in a pot. Partly cover with water. Add salt and pepper. Cook until tender. Mix flour, baking powder, and salt. Add milk to make a thick batter. Drop with teaspoon into hot chicken broth. Sprinkle with parsley. Cover tightly and cook 20 minutes without raising the top. Place on platter and serve with dumplings. Serves 6.

ROAST DUCK

5-pound duck
1 garlic clove
½ cup raisins

salt and pepper to taste
4 apples, cut in small pieces
1 cup orange juice

Wash, clean and singe duck. Season; rub with garlic and fill with apples and raisins. Place in a roasting pan and roast uncovered in a slow oven, 325° F. Allow 20 to 30 minutes per pound. Baste every 10 minutes using orange juice. Serve with currant jelly and whole baked apples, if desired. Serves 6.

PINEAPPLE DUCK

3-pound duck (dressed and
  cut in small pieces)
½ cup brown sugar
2 tablespoons soya sauce

2 cups boiling water
salt and pepper to taste
1 No. 2 can pineapple,
  crushed

Cover duck with water and simmer 40 minutes. Drain water. Place duck in a baking dish. Cover both sides with brown sugar. Pour crushed pineapple over duck with salt, pepper, and soya sauce. Bake in oven 30 minutes longer, or until crisp and brown. Serves 4.

CORNISH GAME HENS AND RICE STUFFING

2 garlic cloves
2 tablespoons salt
1 teaspoon paprika
1 teaspoon dry ginger
1 teaspoon oregano
½ teaspoon poultry
  seasoning
¼ cup butter
½ cup finely chopped
  celery with tops

1 green pepper, chopped
  fine
6 slices, cooked pineapple,
  diced
2 apples, peeled and diced
2 cups rice (brown, wild or
  white)
¼ cup cut parsley
½ cup water chestnuts

With a pestle and mortar, crush garlic pods with salt until garlic is absorbed by the salt. Blend in paprika, ginger, oregano and poultry seasoning thoroughly. Sauté celery and leaves, green pepper, pineapple and apples in butter for 15 minutes. Add one half of the spice mixture. Cook rice and set aside. Add parsley and water chestnuts along with rice to the pineapple mixture and cook 5 minutes. Mix with cooked rice remaining half of garlic seasonings, rub inside and outside of cleaned hens. Fill cavity with rice stuffiing and truss for baking. Pre-heat oven to 450° F. Bake 20 minutes, basting frequently, then lower heat to 350° F. and cook until done.

10.
Stuffings

CRANBERRY STUFFING

1 cup fresh cranberries,
  chopped
¼ cup sugar
¼ cup celery, chopped
2 tablespoons parsley,
  chopped

2 apples, chopped
4 tablespoons butter
4 cups stale toasted bread
  crumbs
½ teaspoon sweet marjoram
1 teaspoon salt

Combine cranberries, apples, and sugar. Cook celery and parsley in butter for 5 minutes. Combine with bread crumbs, seasonings, and cranberry mixture. Blend well. Remove from heat. Cool. Stuff turkey.

This is a new and delicious stuffing for turkey and other fowl. Also good for pork.

POTATO STUFFING

6 medium white potatoes
1 loaf day-old bread
2 eggs
1 teaspoon salt
1 teaspoon poultry seasoning

3 small onions, chopped
½ stalk celery, chopped
2 sprigs parsley, chopped
½ cup butttr (¼ pound)

Peel potatoes, boil until tender and mash. Moisten bread with water, then press out as dry as possible. Mix mashed potatoes, bread, eggs, salt, and seasoning. Chop onions, celery, and parsley. Simmer in the butter over low heat until tender. Add this mixture to bread mixture, blending thoroughly. Use as stuffing for chicken, goose or turkey.

APPLE STUFFING

1 small onion, minced
½ cup finely chopped
   celery
⅓ cup butter
1 cup day-old bread
   crumbs
¼ teaspoon nutmeg
dash paprika

1 teaspoon ginger
2 cups chopped apples
2 tablespoons parsley,
   chopped
2 tablespoons seedless
   raisins
½ teaspoon salt
pinch poultry seasoning

Add minced onion and celery to the butter and cook 5 minutes. Add remaining ingredients and mix together with a fork until well mixed. Chopped prunes or apricots may be added if desired. Use with pork or veal.

FESTIVE TURKEY STUFFING

1 medium onion, chopped
1 cup diced celery
1 small green pepper,
   chopped
¼ cup chopped parsley
2 tablespoons bacon fat
½ teaspoon garlic salt

1 teaspoon poultry
   seasoning
¼ teaspoon thyme
½ teaspoon paprika
½ cup tomato sauce
6 cups bread crumbs

Sauté chopped onion, celery, pepper and parsley in fat. Add seasonings and tomato sauce. Cook 15 minutes. Pour over bread crumbs until well blended and soft but not soggy. Stuff turkey or chicken, and bake.

CORN BREAD STUFFING

2 cups corn meal
2 cups sour milk or
   buttermilk
3 tablespoons melted
   shortening
2 teaspoons salt
1 teaspoon paprika

2 teaspoons baking powder
1 teaspoon soda
2 eggs
½ cup chopped celery and
   tops
2 onions
¼ cup parsley

1 teaspoon poultry seasoning salt and pepper to taste
½ teaspoon sage hot water or stock

Sift dry ingredients. Add eggs and sour milk. Mix well, pour in melted shortening and place in a greased baking pan. Bake in a hot oven, 425° F., for 25 minutes.

Allow corn bread to cool, then break into small pieces. Sauté celery and onion in a small amount of fat. Add seasonings and mix with bread. Moisten with stock to desired consistency. Fill turkey or chicken. Bake.

SAUSAGE AND ONION STUFFING

1 large loaf stale bread
1½ cups sausage meat
½ cup onion, minced
¼ cup parsley, minced
½ cup celery, chopped
½ teaspoon salt

¼ teaspoon pepper
½ teaspoon sweet marjoram
½ teaspoon poultry
  seasoning
½ teaspoon celery salt

Break bread into small pieces and toast. Sauté sausage meat, onion, celery for 10 minutes. Add bread with remaining ingredients. Add to sausage mixture. Mix well with a fork. Remove from fire. Cool. Stuff fowl.

OLD-FASHIONED BREAD STUFFING

1 large loaf bread
½ cup onions, chopped
½ teaspoon poultry
  seasoning
1 teaspoon salt
½ teaspoon paprika

½ cup chopped celery
  with tops
3 tablespoons butter or bacon
  fat
¼ teaspoon thyme
½ teaspoon pepper

Sauté onion and celery in bacon fat until tender. Add seasoning and bread, which has been crumbled fine. Add a few drops of water, if necessary, to moisten. Mix with a fork. Cool. Stuff chicken or turkey. An egg may be added, if desired.

OYSTER STUFFING

3 tablespoons shortening
2 tablespoons minced onion

2 tablespoons chopped celery
1 tablespoon chopped green
  pepper

113

STUFFINGS

1 cup bread crumbs or half cracker crumbs and half bread crumbs	¼ teaspoon paprika
	½ teaspoon pepper
	½ pint oysters
1 tablespoon parsley	pinch cayenne
½ teaspoon salt	

Cook onion, celery and green pepper slowly in shortening 5 minutes. Add cut oysters and cook 3 minutes, then add salt, dash of cayenne and paprika with pinch of black pepper. Add bread crumbs softened with milk. Yield: 2 cups, sufficient for one medium-sized fowl.

CHESTNUT AND OYSTER STUFFING

1 cup chestnuts	salt, pepper, paprika to taste
½ cup butter or substitute melted in ¼ cup milk	1 pint oysters
	2 cups toasted bread crumbs
1 tablespoon poultry seasoning	¼ cup chopped celery
1 teaspoon Season-all	

Shell and blanch chestnuts. Cook in boiling water with 1 teaspoon salt until tender. Drain and mash. Add salt, pepper, and seasoning with oysters, celery, and bread crumbs. Add milk and fat to moisten. Stuff turkey or chicken and bake.

CHESTNUT AND OYSTER STUFFING

1 cup chestnuts	salt, pepper, paprika to taste
½ cup butter melted in	1 pint oysters
¼ cup milk	2 cups toasted bread crumbs
1 tablespoon poultry seasoning	¼ cup chopped celery
	1 small grated onion
1 teaspoon Season-all	

Shell and blanch chestnuts. Cook in boiling water with 1 teaspoon salt until tender. Drain and mash. Add salt, pepper and seasoning along with oysters, celery, onion and bread crumbs. If necessary, add milk to moisten. Stuff fowl and bake.

STUFFINGS FOR CORNISH GAME HENS
(Wild Rice Stuffing)

1 cup wild rice	1 teaspoon salt
4 cups water	1 small chopped onion

114

1 small chopped green
  pepper
¼ cup chopped celery
1 tablespoon chopped
  parsley

¼ teaspoon oregano
dash of black pepper
1 teaspoon garlic salt
1 teaspoon paprika
1 teaspoon basil

Place rice in saucepan, add water and salt and boil until rice is tender, about 45 minutes. Drain. Sauté chopped onion, green pepper, celery and parsley in butter. Add spices. Add cooked rice (and cooked or diced giblets, if available) to the onion mixture. Toss together until well mixed. Stuff fowl and bake. 1 cup mushrooms may be added if desired.

11.

Fish

FISH IS OFTEN a stepchild on our menus, but its various uses can trim the household budget to a new low. In addition, it is definitely a health food containing a whole alphabet of vitamins. If your family doesn't like fish, however, think twice before blaming them. The fault may be yours for not trying to create unusual, flavorful ways of preparing it.

I was thrilled at the many new methods of preparing fish I had the good fortune of learning while visiting families and friends who live in and about coastal cities. Many could not afford more than occasional meat dishes, and fish became one of their main standbys. They had a way of marinating fish in citric juices, garlic, herbs, and onions that made fish seem more than fish. Their results with all varieties of fish: fried, baked, barbecued, in soups, bisques, stews, were superb. And here are their recipes for your approval.

COURT BOUILLON

Court bouillon is used for boiling fish, in chowders and soups. It can be used more than once if strained and set in the refrigerator after each use. This mixture adds a special something to ordinary fish.

116

2 quarts water
2 tablespoons salt
½ cup vinegar or lemon
    juice
2 diced carrots
2 diced onions
2 bay leaves

½ teaspoon ginger
1 red pepper pod
several stalks celery, diced
4 cloves
1 garlic clove
2 tablespoons butter
sprig parsley

Sauté chopped vegetables in butter. Place in large pan. Add water and spices. Cook 30 minutes. Strain. Bouillon is then ready for use. Yield: 3 quarts.

FISH NESTS

For your bridge party or club luncheon, line individual casseroles with mashed potatoes. Fill center with creamed fish of your choice or fish in tomato or cream sauce. Sprinkle with buttered bread crumbs and bake in moderate oven until brown. Serve hot. Garnish with parsley. Place on a plate with Moss Green salad, broccoli and peppers and hot corn sticks.

BOILED FISH

2 tablespoons butter
½ cup chopped celery
1 red pepper pod
1 small chopped onion
1 teaspoon salt
1 small garlic clove
½ teaspoon ginger

1 teaspoon paprika
1 bay leaf
juice of 1 lemon, or ½ cup
    vinegar
2 cups water
2 pounds cod fish or fish of
    your choice

Place butter in sauce pan. Sauté vegetables in fat. Do not brown. Add spices and water. Boil 15 minutes. Reduce heat. Place fish in a pyrex plate. Tie entire dish in clean white cheesecloth. Lower into hot bouillon. Simmer 15 to 20 minutes depending on size of fish. Serve with your favorite sauce or plain bouillon. Serves 4.

Tomato paste or sauce may be added if desired. In this case, use 1 cup water and 1 cup tomato sauce.

The following types of fish are excellent for boiling:

| Mullet | Red Snapper | Haddock | Cod |
| Halibut | Weak Fish | Bass | Shad |

117

FISH

Salmon   Trout   Fillets (cut thick)   White Fish

If you want to be sure your steamed fish doesn't fall apart or break, try cooking it in a clean piece of cheesecloth!

BOILED OR STEAMED FISH

*3 to 4 pounds fresh fish in
    slices or whole fish
3 tablespoons butter
1 teaspoon salt
¼ teaspoon paprika
½ cup chopped parsley*

*¼ cup water
1 onion, sliced
¼ teaspoon pepper
½ teaspoon celery salt
fresh tomato slices or tomato
    sauce (optional)*

Select whole fish of the white meaty variety, or thick slices of steak fish. Place butter in pan to melt. Add several slices of onion and fish. Lay rest of onion on top of fish. Sprinkle with salt, pepper, paprika, celery salt. Add water. Cover and steam 15 minutes.

Boil gently. Active boiling destroys the flavor. Fresh tomato slices, or several tablespoons of tomato sauce may be added if desired. Just before serving, lift fish gently from the pan with a pancake turner or large flat ladle. Place on platter. Sprinkle freely with parsley. Add a tiny bit of the juice from the pot, and serve. Serves 6.

May we suggest some tasty green peas, cooked with tiny bits of celery, fluffy mashed potatoes and a crisp green salad.

BARBECUED FISH

*1 whole fish, 3 to 4 pounds
1 cup vinegar
1 garlic clove
1 cup tomato sauce
3 or 4 pepper pods*

*1 teaspoon thyme
1 tablespoon hickory salt
1 grated onion
½ teaspoon salt
½ teaspoon pepper*

Select large meaty fish. Cut in half. Remove head and tail. Soak overnight in vinegar, garlic, tomato sauce, thyme, hickory salt, onion, salt, pepper, and red pepper pods, which have been boiled together and cooled. Place under broiler 12 to 15 minutes, basting constantly or over open flame on wire toaster in barbecue pit. (Remember, fish cooks quickly and will break easily.)

BAKING FISH

The beauty of baked fish lies in serving it whole. In other words, from the baking pan to the serving platter are the crucial moments when fish demands the "special handling label."

I have been taught a fish trick that works wonders with baked whole fish. After greasing your baking dish, place a piece of extra heavy brown paper, cut a little larger than the size of the fish in pan. Oil paper lightly before laying on fish. You will find that the paper helps to keep the fish from breaking.

If you are fortunate enough to have a baking plank, then half of your troubles are over. But either way, baked fish, stuffed or plain, is THE LITTLE BROWN CHEF's "must" on menus.

Here are a few of the best types of fish for baking:

Bass	Perch
Blue Fish	Salmon
Cod	Shad
Haddock	Red Snapper
Halibut	White Fish
Mullet	Pike
Lake Trout	

Fish for baking should weigh at least 3 to 5 pounds, and can be baked with or without the head. Be sure, however, that it is well scaled and clean, and above all, it must be *fresh!*

PLANKED FISH

Select any fish suitable for baking. Fish may be split if desired.

Clean and prepare as for baking.

Oil plank and pre-heat in oven. (Do not use too much oil or it will drip into oven.)

Place fish which has been sprinkled with salt and pepper on plank. Brush inside and out with a mixture of:

2 tablespoons lemon juice   1 teaspoon paprika
¼ cup melted butter or oil   dash Tabasco sauce

Do not pour mixture over fish—use pastry brush or substitute. Baste with same method several times. Place in oven, bake 15 minutes at 450° F. Reduce heat, bake 20 to 30 minutes according to size of fish. Allow about 10 minutes per pound. During the last 15 minutes of baking remove fish from oven.

Garnish plank with mashed potatoes and any other cooked vegetable desired. Sprinkle with parsley; finish cooking. Serve hot. Serves 6.

ROLLED STUFFED FILLETS

6 to 8 slices fillet	1 teaspoon salt
½ teaspoon pepper	2 cups bread dressing

Select medium fillets, as uniform in size as possible. Sprinkle with salt and pepper. Fill with your favorite dressing. Roll and tie with clean white string. Bake in a moderate oven 15 to 20 minutes. Serve plain or with sauce. Serves 6 to 8.

Fillets may be stuffed with ½ cup chopped shrimp, 2 tablespoons parsley, 1 small grated onion, 1 cup bread crumbs and 2 tablespoons tomato sauce.

Try chopped clams, 1 cup with ¼ cup celery instead of shrimp. Omit tomato sauce.

RED SNAPPER
(Creole Baked)

1 red snapper (3 to 4 pounds)	1 garlic clove
1 pound boiled shrimp	1 dozen oysters
1½ cups bread crumbs	several crawfish or
2 large tomatoes, or	½ cup crab meat
1 cup canned tomatoes	4 tablespoons chopped celery
1 can mushrooms	sprig parsley
2 or 3 bay leaves	sprig thyme
½ dozen whole allspice	several cloves
1 teaspoon paprika	salt and pepper to taste
2 cups white wine	

Clean fish and remove head. Make 3 diagonal cuts on the skin of fish. Rub fish inside and out with a paste made of mashed garlic, salt, pepper, paprika and thyme.

Make stuffing as follows: Wet bread crumbs and squeeze out water. Sauté onion and celery in butter. Add 2 tablespoons crumbs with salt and pepper. Add 6 oysters cut in pieces and stuff fish. Sew up well. Grease outside of fish. Just before placing fish in oven, pour wine over it. Bake in moderate oven 30 to 40 minutes.

While fish is baking, prepare sauce as follows: Brown onion, parsley, and bay leaf in remaining fat. Stir constantly. Add tomatoes and rest of herbs and remaining oysters and juice. Simmer. Heat shrimp and mushrooms with ½ cup chopped parsley in a small amount of butter. Do not brown. Remove fish from oven and place on a platter. Arrange shrimp around and on top of fish artistically. Pour sauce over fish and serve garnished with parsley. Serves 6.

Crawfish are colorful and may also be used to garnish dish. Sauce may be poured over crawfish and dish may then be placed into oven just before serving.

BAKED STUFFED FISH

1 medium fish (3 to 4 pounds)	*salt and pepper to taste*
½ teaspoon paprika	*3 slices bacon*
1 cup bread crumbs	*¼ cup melted butter*
½ teaspoon thyme	*1 teaspoon sage*
1 small onion, grated	*¼ cup finely chopped celery*
1 teaspoon garlic salt	*water*

Sauté onion and celery in fat. Add seasonings, bread crumbs, and a few drops of water to moisten. Set aside to cool. Wash and clean fish. Dry. Rub inside and out with salt and pepper. Stuff fish with bread crumb mixture and sew up or hold together with skewers. Lay strips of bacon on fish and sprinkle with paprika. Place on a baking sheet or on a very heavy piece of clean brown or white paper. Bake in a hot oven, 450° F., for 15 minutes. Reduce heat and bake 15 to 20 minutes longer. Baste 2 or 3 times. Lift fish carefully from pan with spatula or pancake turner onto platter. Garnish with parsley or serve with a tasty sauce. Serves 6.

BAKED FISH

1 medium fish (3 to 4 pounds)	*¼ cup butter or salad oil*
1 teaspoon garlic salt	*1 lemon*
2 tablespoons Worcestershire sauce	*1 whole onion, sliced*
½ teaspoon paprika	*1 teaspoon pepper*
	⅓ cup chopped parsley

FISH

Wash fish and remove head if desired. Sprinkle with salt and pepper inside and out. Cut three 2-inch slits across outside skin on both sides. Fill fish with onion slices. Squeeze lemon over fish, then cover with butter or oil. Sprinkle garlic salt and pour Worcestershire sauce into slits. Cover with parsley and place in baking pan. Bake in a hot oven, 400° F., for 40 minutes or until brown. Baste frequently. Serves 6.

FRIED FISH

There are so many ways to prepare fried fish that it would be difficult to select one recipe to please each preference. But here are a few simple rules:

(1) Select *fresh* fish!
(2) Removing heads is a matter of choice, and largely depends upon size of fish.
(3) Cut large fish in slices or fillets.
(4) Rub fish with salt, pepper, garlic salt, lemon or mustard. Place in refrigerator overnight or at least several hours to allow seasoning to penetrate fish.
(5) Dip in corn meal, fish fry, or flour. Be sure fish is well coated.
(6) Be sure fat is *very* hot. For ordinary frying at least ⅛ inch of fat is necessary.
(7) Turn and brown on each side, allowing 8 to 10 minutes a side, depending on thickness of fish.
(8) Drain on brown paper before serving.
(9) For French fried fish, use hot deep fat. Fry fast, 5 to 7 minutes. Small pieces of fish are best.
(10) A good tart or hot sauce is a "must" on crisp fried fish.
(11) Sweet basil or thyme and celery, onion, or hickory salt may be rubbed on fish before frying.

FISH FOR FRYING

Butter Fish
Cat Fish
Croaker
Flounder
Herring
Lake Trout

Perch
Pickerel
Porgies
Sheepshead
Smelts
Sole

Sunfish   Weakfish
Whiting

FRENCH FRIED SMELTS

2 pounds melts	½ cup cracker crumbs
1 teaspoon salt	1 teaspoon Season-all
1 teaspoon paprika	½ cup flour
dash red pepper	

Select uniform smelts. Clean and remove heads. Split down center with scissors. Remove bone. Wash, drain and dry. Dip smelts in seasonings and flour which have been mixed together. Be sure they are well coated. Fry in deep fat 12 to 15 minutes.

If a small amount of fat is used, turn fish after first 5 minutes so that they will brown well on both sides. Serves 6.

Serve hot with tartar sauce, shoestring potatoes, and a green vegetable.

NEW ENGLAND CODFISH BALLS

1 cup flaked codfish	crumbs or flour
1 egg, beaten	1½ cups mashed potatoes
2 teaspoons grated onion, or juice	1 tablespoon butter
	1 teaspoon dry mustard
1 cup cracker or bread	salt and pepper to taste

Mix fish, potatoes and egg well. Add remaining ingredients. Beat for about 5 minutes until light and smooth. Shape into balls. Roll in cracker crumbs. Fry in deep fat (very hot) until brown. Serves 6. Balls the size of walnuts may be made and used for appetizers on toothpicks. Yield: 16 to 20.

Mixture may be formed into patties, fried in a small amount of fat and served with the traditional baked beans and brown bread for breakfast or supper.

Boned and flaked salmon or halibut, any canned or leftover fish, may be subsituted for cod in this recipe.

NEW ENGLAND FRIED CLAMS

2 dozen clams (cleaned, shells removed)	1½ cups bread or cracker crumbs

½ teaspoon paprika	½ teaspoon salt
1 egg	dash red pepper

Combine crumbs, salt, pepper and paprika. Beat egg with 1 tablespoon of water. Dip clam in crumb mixture, then in egg and again in crumbs. Sauté quickly in a small amount of fat, then in deep fat and fry 3 to 5 minutes, browning on all sides. Drain on absorbent paper. Serve plain or with chili sauce. Serves 6.

CLAM FRITTERS

1 cup flour	dash nutmeg
¼ teaspoon pepper	½ teaspoon salt
¼ cup milk	⅓ cup clam juice
1½ dozen raw chopped	2 eggs, beaten
clams, or 1 medium can	2 tablespoons butter
1 tablespoon onion	½ teaspoon garlic salt

Mix flour and spices. Add clam juice and milk, then beaten egg, stirring until well blended. Add clams and onion. Drop with spoon into deep fat and fry 5 to 8 minutes. Drain on absorbent paper. Serves 6.

OVEN FRIED OYSTERS

Roll 1 dozen oysters in flour and salt, dip in beaten egg, and roll in bread crumbs. Sprinkle with oil and bake in a hot oven until brown.

OYSTER LOAF

1 long loaf French bread	1 teaspoon salt
2 dozen oysters	½ teaspoon pepper
½ cup cream	2 tablespoons butter
1 tablespoon chopped celery	1 teaspoon Tabasco sauce
1 tablespoon chopped parsley	

Cut off top of entire loaf of bread. Scoop out inside. Butter scooped out bread and toast in oven. Lightly pan-fry oysters in butter. (May be sprinkled with cracker crumbs before frying.) When slightly brown add cream, celery, parsley, salt, pepper and Tabasco sauce with toasted buttered bread. Fill hollowed loaf with this mixture. Cover with top crust and bake 20 minutes. Baste with juice from oysters at least twice. Slice and serve hot! Serves 6.

FRIED OYSTERS

12 large selected oysters	1 egg, beaten
salt and pepper to taste	1 tablespoon water
½ cup bread or cracker crumbs	parsley

Dry oysters thoroughly. Season with salt and pepper. Dip into bread crumbs, then in egg diluted with a little water (1 tablespoon to each egg) and again into bread crumbs. Fry in deep fat. Drain on brown paper, garnish with parsley, and serve on a folded napkin.

If sauce is desired, serve in individual paper cups. Allow 3 to 4 oysters per serving.

OYSTERS IN BROWN SAUCE

3 tablespoons butter	½ teaspoon salt
1 green pepper, chopped	½ teaspoon celery salt
1 small onion, chopped	1 pint oysters
several sprigs of parsley, chopped	2 cups warm milk
2 tablespoons flour	¼ teaspoon red pepper
½ teaspoon paprika	1 tablespoon Worcestershire sauce

Sauté pepper, onion, parsley in butter. Add flour and brown. Add spices, oysters and warm milk. Continue to cook until thick. Add Worcestershire sauce and red pepper. Serve plain or on toast squares. Serves 4 to 6.

Grated sharp cheese may be sprinkled on top if desired.

MA WILLIAMS CRAB CAKES

1 tablespoon butter	1 egg, slightly beaten
¼ cup finely chopped onion	2 tablespoons mayonnaise
2 tablespoons finely chopped celery	1 pound crab meat
⅓ cup finely chopped green pepper	½ teaspoon salt
1½ cups soft bread crumbs	½ teaspoon thyme
	½ teaspoon ground red pepper

Melt butter in heavy frying pan. Add onion, celery and peppers; stir over low heat until vegetables are tender. Remove from heat. Add bread crumbs and mix well. In large bowl, combine beaten egg and mayonnaise. Add vegetables and bread crumbs, crab meat and seasonings; mix thoroughly. Form into 12 cakes and place on waxed paper. Fry in hot deep fat at 375° F. for 5 to 7 minutes or until a golden brown. Drain on paper toweling. Serve with lemon sauce or tartar sauce. Yield: 6.

CRAB FLAKE CUTLETS

To 1 pound of crab meat, add finely chopped parsley, 1 teaspoon Worcestershire sauce, salt, pepper, paprika, and ½ cup thick white sauce. Mix thoroughly. Shape into cutlets, dip into a milk and egg mixture, roll in fresh bread crumbs and fry in deep fat.

SOFT SHELL CRABS

Soft shell crabs are a mighty delectable dish, and you are bound to enjoy them when fried crisp and brown. There are two good methods to follow before cooking. One, soaking crabs in milk; the other, soaking in a salt solution. Either one is sure to please you.

Your fish market will kill and clean crabs at your request.

8 soft shelled crabs	*½ teaspoon pepper*
2 tablespoons salt	*½ cup corn meal*
1 pint water	*¼ cup flour*
1 teaspoon Season-all	

Wash crabs, remove all excess dirt. Lay crabs in a pan. Mix 1 pint water, 2 tablespoons salt and pour over crabs. Soak for 30 minutes. Remove and drain. Dip in corn meal, flour and seasonings. Fry in deep fat, turning until brown and crisp on both sides.

Allow 2 small crabs or 1 large crab per person. Serve with tartar sauce, French fried potatoes and cole slaw.

DEVILED CRABS No. 1

1 pound canned or fresh	*2 tablespoons butter*
crab meat	*1 teaspoon mustard*

2 tablespoons flour
dash Tabasco sauce
1 cup cream or milk
½ cup bread crumbs

2 tablespoons chopped
  parsley
salt and pepper to taste

Remove all shells from crab meat. Sauté onion and parsley in butter. Blend in mustard and flour. Add cream or milk. Cook over low heat until thick and smooth. Add crab meat. Season with salt and pepper. Fill shells or ramekins. Cover with buttered crumbs. Dot with butter, sprinkle with paprika. Bake in hot oven, 400° F., 15 to 20 minutes. Serves 6.

Serve with tomato and cucumber slices, corn sticks, lima beans, and corn succotash.

DEVILED CRABS No. 2

½ pound cooked crab meat,
  shredded
1 hard-cooked egg
3 strips bacon, diced fine
½ teaspoon black pepper
1 teaspoon salt
1 egg

1 teaspoon butter
¾ cup white sauce
1 tablespoon grated onion
2 cups bread crumbs
6 crab shells (small)
¼ teaspoon red pepper

Sauté chopped bacon. Add onion, crab meat and seasonings. Add bread crumbs and white sauce. Fill crab shells if they are to be baked. Sprinkle with bread crumbs and place in baking dish in a hot oven for 15 minutes.

If they are to be fried in deep fat, roll in remaining ½ cup of crumbs. Dip in beaten egg. Then into crumbs again. Wipe off excess crumbs and fry in hot deep fat in wire basket 10 to 12 minutes. Serves 6.

Serve with red and green cole slaw and French fried potatoes.

For variety, use this recipe for tuna fish, lobster meat or shredded shrimp. Fill crab shells as above and bake.

FRIED SOFT SHELL CRABS

6 to 8 soft shell crabs
1 cup milk
1 egg slightly beaten with

2 tablespoons water
½ cup flour
1 tablespoon paprika

FISH

1 tablespoon lemon juice   dash nutmeg
1 teaspoon garlic salt

Clean crabs. Soak overnight in milk. Drain and dry. Mix flour, salt, paprika and nutmeg. Add lemon juice to egg mixture. Dip crabs in egg, then in flour, and fry in deep fat until brown on both sides. Serves 6 to 8.

Serve with carrot slaw, shoestring potatoes, corn muffins. Lemon pudding for dessert.

CRAB JAMBALAYA

½ dozen crabs
1½ cups rice
2 tablespoons butter
1 teaspoon cloves
thyme to taste
2 teaspoons salt
3 quarts water

3 or 4 fresh tomatoes, or 1
    cup canned tomatoes
3 onions
2 tablespoons flour
2 garlic cloves
1 teaspoon chili powder
red and black pepper to taste

Boil and clean crabs. Cut in pieces. Use same method for preparing as Shrimp Jambalaya (p. 132).

Canned beef broth or chicken stock, or even vegetable water may be used instead of water.

CREOLE SHRIMP No. 1

2 pounds cooked cleaned
    shrimp
2 large onions, sliced
1 green pepper, chopped
1 bay leaf, chopped
2 garlic cloves, chopped
1 cup water
¼ teaspoon thyme
dash sugar
salt, pepper, paprika to
    taste

1 No. 2 can tomato purée,
    or 2 cans sauce
1 small bunch celery,
    chopped
2 teaspoons chili powder
2 tablespoons flour
1 tablespoon lemon juice or
    vinegar
¼ cup bacon fat or butter

Sauté onions, celery, garlic and peppers in fat. Blend in flour and seasonings. Add water and tomato sauce. Simmer slowly 30 minutes. Add cooked shrimp and lemon juice or vinegar. Cook 15 minutes longer until shrimp is thoroughly heated.

Serve with fresh cooked rice and green peas. Serves 6.

For fancy variations, sprinkle chopped parsley, mushrooms and paprika through rice. Canned tomatoes may be substituted for tomato sauce. Canned shrimp may be substituted for fresh shrimp.

CREOLE SHRIMP No. 2

2 pounds uncooked shrimp, shelled and cleaned
3 tablespoons shortening
2 stalks celery, chopped
1 small green pepper
1 small onion
dash cayenne

1 can tomato sauce
salt and pepper to taste
¼ cup water
2 cups cooked rice
4 tablespoons grated cheese
1 small garlic clove
½ teaspoon sweet basil

Sauté shrimp, onion, celery, garlic salt, pepper and cayenne in shortening for 10 minutes. Add tomato sauce and simmer slowly. Add water and spices and cook 5 minutes longer. Pour shrimp and half of the sauce into a dish. Add cooked rice to remaining sauce, mix together while still cooking about 3 more minutes. Serve with remaining tomato sauce and shrimp. Sprinkle with grated cheese. Serves 4.

CHATTER EBON

¼ cup salad oil, or melted butter
2 garlic cloves, crushed
2 pounds raw shrimp (cleaned and cut in half)
1 large onion, sliced thin
1 can button mushrooms
1 teaspoon salt
1 small can water chestnuts, drained and sliced thin

4 cups chicken broth
1 tablespoon Accent
1 pound peas, fresh or frozen
3 tablespoons cornstarch
½ cup mushroom liquid
4 large tomatoes, peeled and sliced in quarters
4 cups hot, cooked rice
1 can bamboo shoots, sliced

Heat fat in large frying pan. Add garlic; cook for 5 minutes. Add shrimp, onion and celery and cook for 10 minutes. Add mushrooms, bamboo shoots, salt, water chestnuts, chicken broth, Accent, paprika and peas. Cover tightly and simmer for 15 minutes. Combine cornstarch and cold water until smooth. Add gradually to hot mixture. Stirring constantly, bring mixture to boil. Cook over medium heat continuing to stir until thick and smooth. Add tomato wedges and almonds. Cover tightly and let stand over low heat about 6 minutes. Serve with hot rice.

SHRIMP AT SEA

2 tablespoons butter
½ cup chopped celery
1 chopped green pepper
2 chopped green onions
1 teaspoon paprika
1 teaspoon curry powder

¼ cup mayonnaise
1 cup cream
1 cup bread crumbs
1 pound fresh peeled,
  deveined shrimp

Melt butter; add chopped vegetables, sesasonings and mayonnaise and cook 10 minutes. Add cream and bread crumbs. Blend together. Remove from heat; split shrimps lengthwise. Grease 4 individual shell casseroles well and place 1 tablespoon bread crumb mixture in bottom of each shell. Lay 3 or 4 shrimp halves in each shell. Top with remaining crumb mixture. Bake in 350° F. oven for 35 minutes.

SHELL SHRIMP

2 pounds shrimp
6 to 8 hot red peppers
1 cup vinegar
1 onion, sliced

6 to 8 whole cloves
2 teaspoons salt
1 cup water
½ teaspoon celery seed

Wash shrimp, place in a pan with spices and vinegar. Steam for 20 minutes. Cool. Serve in shells. Good with pretzels for a beer party.

Shrimp may be removed from shells, cleaned and cooked by the same method as above, if desired.

To clean shrimp, remove shells. Cut along back and remove black vein. Wash well to remove all grit. Shrimp may be cleaned either before cooking or after. Personally, I like to clean them before cooking.

SHRIMP CELESTE

3 cups cooked shrimp
1½ cups sliced mushrooms
1¼ cups milk

½ teaspoon seasoned salt
½ teaspoon salt
¼ cup parsley

4 tablespoons *butter*
1 cup *cream*
4 tablespoons *flour*
½ teaspoon *pepper*

1 cup *sherry wine*
¼ pound *chopped salted almonds*

Sauté mushrooms in butter until brown. Add flour, salt and pepper. Mix well and add milk and cream. Cook, stirring constantly, until thick. Add shrimp and place pan over hot water. Add sherry and serve on pastry rings. Sprinkle with parsley and almonds. Serves 6.

MEXICAN SHRIMP WITH RICE

2 pounds *cooked shrimp*
1 can *tomatoes*
½ cup *celery*
2 tablespoons *chili powder*
½ cup *tomato catsup*

2 tablespoons *butter*
2 medium *olives*
4 whole *cloves*
2 tablespoons *paprika*
salt and pepper *to taste*

Sauté onions and celery in fat. Add tomatoes and cloves. Cook 20 minutes. Add cooked shrimp and remaining ingredients. Simmer 15 minutes. Serve with steamed rice. Serves 4 to 6.

SHRIMP AND CRAB GUMBO

2 pounds *shrimp, cleaned and split*
2 medium *hard-shelled crabs*
1 pound *okra, washed and cut up*
2 medium *onions, chopped*
1 garlic *clove, chopped*
1 bay *leaf*
1 large *can tomatoes, or purée*

pinch *sugar*
1 green *pepper, chopped*
½ cup *celery leaves, chopped*
1 teaspoon *thyme*
¼ pound *bacon ends, or chopped ham*
2 quarts *water*
2 *peppercorns*
1 cup *boiled rice*

Boil bacon or ham in water. Add chopped onions, celery leaves, green pepper, garlic, and tomatoes. Boil half hour, add bay leaf and spices. Simmer for 2 hours. Add shrimp, okra and crabs, which have been cleaned. Boil 15 minutes and serve with rice. Serves 8.

SHRIMP JAMBALAYA

2 pounds shrimp	2 large onions, finely chopped
3 or 4 ripe tomatoes or 2 cups canned tomatoes	1 teaspoon chili powder
	sprig thyme leaf
1½ cups rice	2 garlic cloves
2 tablespoons butter	2 bay leaves
2 tablespoons flour	3 quarts water or stock
¼ cup chopped parsley	salt and pepper to taste

Clean and boil shrimp. Place butter in saucepan and add onions. Brown. Add flour and mix well. Add spices. Cook 10 minutes. Add finely chopped tomatoes. Cook 10 to 15 minutes. Add water or stock. Boil, add shrimp and washed rice. Stir often until rice is cooked. Serve hot.

LOBSTER

Lobsters should always be alive when boiled. Heat a large pot of water, put in a handful of salt and bring to a boil. Grasp each live lobster by the middle of its back and plunge it head first into the boiling water. Cover the pot and boil 20 to 30 minutes depending on lobster's size. Remove lobsters and lay them claws down to drain.

SPECIAL LOBSTER

Mother was a typical Easterner and loved shore dinners. Although she couldn't classify herself as a cook, she loved sea food and lobster was a favorite. She had her own special Boston way of preparing it and it was mighty good, too. This recipe was her "company special."

1 boiled chicken lobster	4 tablespoons butter
¼ cup chopped mushrooms	1 garlic clove, minced
1 teaspoon Worcestershire sauce	½ teaspoon lemon juice
	1 teaspoon salt
1 tablespoon parsley	1 tablespoon vinegar
½ teaspoon paprika	1 tablespoon prepared mustard
3 tablespoons grated cheese	

Remove meat from body and claws and chop in fine pieces. Sauté garlic, mushrooms and parsley in butter. Add mustard, Worcestershire sauce, vinegar and lobster meat. Simmer 10 minutes. Fill the shells with lobster mixture. Sprinkle with lemon juice and cover with grated cheese. Place shells in a pan and bake in oven 20 minutes until brown. Serves 2. Allow ½ small lobster to each person.

Serve on a garnished plate with a tasty slaw, or water cress salad, potato chips and olives.

LOBSTER FOR YOUR BEST BRIDGE

2 cups cooked lobster meat	1 cup bread crumbs
1 medium onion	(optional)
1 small can chopped	½ cup chopped celery
pimientos	2 cups medium white sauce
½ cup chopped pistachio	⅓ cup butter
nuts	1 teaspoon paprika
1 green pepper	2 tablespoons Worcestershire
8 to 10 pitted, ripe olives	sauce
2 tablespoons white wine	salt, pepper to taste
dash red pepper	pinch rosemary

Sauté pepper, celery, onion, parsley in butter. Add pimientos and lobster meat, Worcestershire sauce and seasonings. Add sautéed mixture to white sauce together with nuts and olives which have been cut in circles. Simmer until hot. Serves 6.

Add wine and serve in any of the following ways:

If fresh whole lobster is used, refill shells, cover with bread crumbs and paprika. If toast squares or rounds are used, butter and place in center of plate. Cover with mixture, garnish with lemon and parsley. Surround with buttered peas. If patty shells are used, fill and use same procedure as with toast. Lobster prepared in this manner may be served with biscuit shortcake. For extra flavor, pour some lemon juice mixed with garlic salt over lobster before broiling.

Port or white wine and drawn butter poured over broiled lobster is a special treat.

LOBSTER NEWBURG

2 cups lobster meat	salt, pepper and paprika
4 egg yolks	to taste
2 tablespoons melted butter	2½ cups warm milk
½ cup flour	dash Tabasco sauce
parsley	6 to 8 slices toast

Melt butter in double boiler. Add flour and seasonings. Blend in egg yolks. Add warm milk. Simmer 15 minutes, stirring constantly. Add lobster. Cook additional 15 minutes. Serve in pastry shells or on thin toast. Garnish with parsley. Serves 6 to 8.

Serve for your bridge party or luncheon with a fresh green vegetable. Grated cheese may be sprinkled on top of dish or a small amount of pimiento.

LOBSTER AND SHRIMP NEWBURG

2 cups boiled lobster	dash nutmeg
1 cup boiled shrimp, cut in pieces	¼ cup butter
	1 cup Madeira or sherry wine
1½ cups cream	3 egg yolks
½ teaspoon salt	dash red pepper
dash garlic salt	¼ teaspoon dry mustard

Melt butter in a sauce pan and add the lobster and shrimp. Simmer slowly for 5 minutes. Add wine and cook 5 minutes longer. Add beaten egg yolks to mustard and cream. Pour mixture over fish, and shake pan gently until mixture thickens. Be careful not to stir mixture because lobster will break. Since this dish curdles very easily, serve immediately on toast squares or in patty shells. Serves 4.

This can be made in a chafing dish.

LOBSTER FARCIE

Boil the lobster and after it has cooled cut in half. Remove meat very carefully so that the tail and body shells are intact and also remove meat from claws. Cut meat in small pieces. Add a little dry mustard, paprika, finely chopped parsley, Worcestershire sauce, lemon juice, half cup of imported sherry and half cup of Newburg sauce. Return this mixture into the lobster shells. Cover with buttered crumbs and brown in oven.

STEWED RED SNAPPER

Wash, scald, and skin snapper, then cut meat from the shell. Put in a pot, cover with water, season with salt and pepper, boil until very tender. When done, take it out and cool. Then take meat from the bones.

Sauce for Red Snapper: Mash yolks of 5 hard-cooked eggs,

add 1 pint of cream, gradually strain through a small sieve in a sauce pan. Add salt, pepper, and mace, and cook. Thicken with roux, add ½ pint of sherry wine. Put meat in sauce and serve.

CRAWFISH BISQUE

4 dozen medium crawfish
salt, black pepper, cayenne
*   to taste*
juice of 1 lemon
4 bay leaves
1 tablespoon dried or 6
*   sprigs fresh thyme*
2 stalks and tops of celery,
*   chopped*
5 tablespoons chopped
*   parsley*

6 chopped garlic cloves
2 large onions, chopped
3 pods red peppers, finely
*   chopped*
1 green pepper, finely
*   chopped*
6 slices bread, or ½ cup
*   bread crumbs*
½ cup fat
1½ cups flour
1 can tomato sauce

Place crawfish in boiling water to which salt, black pepper, cayenne, lemon, bay leaves and a little thyme have been added. Boil for 10 minutes. Remove and cool. Shell, wash heads thoroughly, and cut meat in ½-inch pieces. Add celery, parsley, garlic, onions, thyme, red peppers, green peppers, moistened bread crumbs, salt, pepper. Mix well. Fry in fat for 20 minutes or until light brown. Cool. Stuff heads with prepared ingredients and roll in 1 cup flour. Brown ½ cup flour. Add tomato sauce and 1 to 2 pints water. Cook 5 minutes. Then add stuffed heads and cook another 5 to 10 minutes. Serve with rice.

BROILED FISH

1 2-pound fish
½ teaspoon pepper
2 tablespoons olive oil

1 teaspoon salt
½ teaspoon paprika
juice of ½ lemon

Select a lean fish. Clean and remove head. Rub fish with salt and pepper; marinate in lemon juice and olive oil. Let stand overnight in refrigerator. When ready to broil, be sure broiler and broiling rack are *hot!* Broil fast and turn with a pancake turner. Serve *hot* on a hot platter. Fish will not be dry. Serves 2 to 4.

SALMON OR LOBSTER MOUSSE

3-pound salmon or lobster meat	truffles
1 wine glass sherry	pinch red pepper
1 teaspoon salt	2 tablespoons Worcestershire sauce
½ teaspoon pepper	1 pint whipped cream

Grease fish mold with butter and line mold with truffles. Put mold in refrigerator to let the truffles set. Put uncooked salmon or lobster meat through a mousse sieve. Add imported sherry, salt, pepper, red pepper, Worcestershire sauce and whipped cream. When thoroughly blended, place mixture into the fish mold. Place mold in a pan of boiling water on range top for about 1 hour. Remove from water. Place mold in moderate oven for 5 to 10 minutes to dry out (not browned). Turn on a silver platter and serve with oyster or Hollandaise sauce.

FAVORITE FISH CHOWDER

2- to 3-pound haddock	2 strips bacon
2 cups diced potatoes	1 tablespoon salt
1 medium onion	1 teaspoon pepper
1 can evaporated milk	3 tablespoons butter

Place head, tail and backbone of fish in pot. Add 4 cups water and bring to boil slowly. Cook about 15 minutes. Dice bacon and place in frying pan with sliced onion. Sauté until brown, about 5 minutes. Dice parboiled potatoes, add potatoes, onion and bacon to liquid drained from bones, then add fish. Cover and simmer. Add milk, butter, salt and pepper. Serves 6 to 8.

12.

All-in-one Dishes

BRUNSWICK STEW

1 chicken or 2 squirrels
2 teaspoons salt
pepper, to taste
1 teaspoon garlic salt
2 tablespoons bacon fat
3 onions, diced
½ cup sherry wine
2 tablespoons
Worcestershire sauce

1 cup corn (fresh, whole
kernel)
1 pound fresh lima beans
2 cups stewed or fresh
tomatoes
½ cup okra
2 tablespoons butter
½ cup breadcrumbs

Clean chicken (or squirrels), add salt and pepper. Sauté onion in bacon fat and add chicken. Sauté until chicken is brown. Place chicken in Dutch oven or deep pan. Add water to cover, sherry and Worcestershire sauce. Cook slowly over low heat about 30 minutes. Add vegetables and simmer 1 hour. Add butter and bread crumbs. Cook 30 minutes longer. Serves 10.

BRUNSWICK STEW No. 2

1 4-pound chicken
4 tablespoons fat
2 diced onions

5 tomatoes, peeled and
quartered
2 cups water

3 cups corn
¼ teaspoon red pepper
salt, pepper, paprika to
  taste

3 cups fresh lima beans
2 teaspoons Worcestershire
  sauce
6 cloves

Disjoint chicken and sauté slowly in the fat until brown. Remove from pan and brown onions slightly. Place chicken, onions, tomatoes, water, red pepper, salt and pepper in a large stewing pan. Cover and simmer until chicken is very tender. Remove the bones from chicken if desired. Add the remaining ingredients and continue cooking about ½ hour until beans are tender. Serves 8.

KIDNEY STEW

2 pounds kidneys (either
  lamb, beef, veal, or pork)
2 cups chopped onion
1 tablespoon Worcestershire
  sauce
4 cups hot water

pinch thyme
1 garlic clove
1½ teaspoons salt
¼ teaspoon black pepper
3 tablespoons fat
4 tablespoons flour

Cut up kidneys and soak at least 1 hour in salted cold water. Drain; dredge kidneys in flour to which salt and pepper have been added. Sauté onion and garlic in fat, add kidneys, hot water, Worcestershire sauce. Cover and simmer 30 minutes. Pour into a greased casserole. Cover with mashed potatoes if desired. Bake 30 minutes. Whole or diced potatoes may be added. Serves 6.

Kidneys may be placed in a large sauce pan on the top of the stove with vegetables added to suit your taste. Mushrooms and tomato sauce with bay leaf or a small amount of marjoram or rosemary lend a delightfully different flavor.

Lamb kidney sautéed with mushrooms, peppers, onions and port wine for luncheon dishes will certainly please your guests.

EAST INDIAN CHICKEN

Glamorous Lena Horne, with her beautiful, sunny disposition and her charming voice, loves delightful food. She is a fairly good cook although she can't devote much time to it. She likes her dishes to be as interesting as her songs and clothes, and as spicy. I love to date her special dish of East Indian Chicken with Rice.

Step 1

1 4-pound chicken	2 bay leaves
2 cloves	¼ pound butter
1 cup celery leaves	1 small onion
1 tablespoon curry powder	2 quarts water

Place chicken in pot and add above ingredients. Boil until tender. Cool. Strain stock and cut chicken from bone into large pieces.

Step 2

Sauté the following in ½ pound butter in a large pot:

1 bunch green onions, chopped	2 green peppers, chopped
1 bunch celery, chopped	2 tablespoons paprika
½ cup parsley, chopped	2 teaspoons curry powder

Sauté ½ cup flour, 1 teaspoon Season-all until slightly brown. Blend 1 pint milk, ½ pint cream and chicken stock. Cook until thick. Add chicken, ½ cup chopped chutney, 2 pimientos, ½ cup salted almonds, 6 to 8 ripe olives, sliced. Simmer 30 minutes. Salt to taste. Serve with pineapple rice. Serves 8 to 10.

CHICKEN HASH (With Water Chestnuts)

2 bunches chopped green onions	4 cups chopped chicken
	⅓ cup flour
1 large stalk chopped celery	3 tablespoons paprika
2 chopped green peppers	1 teaspoon curry powder
½ pound butter or chicken fat	½ teaspoon sweet basil
	1 large can chicken broth or beef
¼ cup slivered salted almonds	bouillon cubes equal to 4 cups
1 No. 2 can water chestnuts, sliced thin	salt, pepper or seasoned salt to taste

Sauté green onions, celery and green peppers in butter or chicken fat. As vegetables begin to brown, add almonds, chestnuts and chicken. Blend together well. Combine flour, paprika, curry powder and sweet basil. Add chicken broth or bouillon cubes, to chicken and vegetable mixture. Cover and steam. Season with salt, pepper and seasoned salt. If a brown gravy is preferred, beef concentrate may be used to darken the hash. Serve this over rice with crushed pineapple, or with pineapple biscuits. Serves 8.

NEW ENGLAND BOILED DINNER

3 pounds corned beef	1 head green cabbage
8 carrots	8 onions
8 potatoes	8 beets
1 teaspoon celery salt	2 red pepper pods
1 teaspoon salt	1 teaspoon paprika

Cover meat with cold water and simmer about 3 hours. Wash and prepare vegetables. Cut cabbage into 6 or 7 wedges. Cook beets separately. Add vegetables to meat. Cook until tender. Season. Drain water from beets and add a small amount of butter, and salt to season. Place meat on platter and surround with vegetables. Sprinkle with paprika. Serve with corn sticks. Serves 6.

SHEPHERD'S PIE

2 cups leftover meat	2 cups mashed potatoes
several stalks celery	1 small green pepper
4 tablespoons bacon fat or butter	6 cooked carrots, diced
3 tablespoons flour	2 small onions
1 tablespoon Worcestershire sauce	2 cups milk
1 cup whole kernel corn	1 beef bouillon cube (optional)
	¼ teaspoon salt

Sauté onions, pepper and celery. Add flour and stir until brown. Add Worcestershire sauce, beef bouillon cube and milk. Blend in meat and cooked vegetables. Place in casserole and cover with mashed potatoes. Brush with beaten egg yolk or melted butter. Bake in moderate oven 20 minutes. Serves 6.

Leftover gravy may be used. If so, omit flour and milk, and blend in gravy with onions, pepper and celery.

MEAT BALL CASSEROLE

2 pounds chopped beef or
  veal
1 finely chopped green
  pepper
1 teaspoon paprika
2 tablespoons bacon fat
1 garlic clove
6 diced potatoes
½ teaspoon ginger
½ teaspoon pepper

2 grated onions
1 teaspoon thyme
1 teaspoon Season-all
¼ cup flour
1 bunch sliced carrots
1 pound fresh peas
1 teaspoon salt
2 tablespoons steak or
  Worcestershire sauce
4 ripe tomatoes

Add grated onions, pepper and all spices (except ginger) to meat and mix well. Form into small balls and roll into flour. Sauté in fat. When meat is brown, add remainder of flour to fat. Cook carrots, peas, and potatoes 15 minutes with ginger and salt. Pour enough water from vegetables into skillet with flour to make gravy to cover meat and vegetables. Add steak sauce and tomatoes which have been cut in half. Sprinkle with salt and bake in moderate oven 40 minutes. Serves 6.

If desired, boiled egg noodles may be added in casserole instead of potatoes. Lima beans may be used instead of peas; canned tomatoes may be substituted for fresh tomatoes.

EBONY'S ALL-IN-ONE DISH

2 or 3 cups leftover lamb,
  pork, chicken or beef cut
  in cubes
4 to 6 small potatoes, sliced
1 cup celery, chopped
1 cup peas, lima or string
  beans
1 cup whole kernel corn
1 teaspoon Season-all

½ teaspoon paprika
1 bunch carrots, sliced
6 small onions, sliced
4 tomatoes, sliced
½ cup chopped parsley
1 teaspoon salt
2 tablespoons Worcestershire
  sauce

Cook vegetables in salted water until tender. Add diced meat. Place in a baking dish. Add leftover gravy and 1 cup of vegetable water. Cover top with sliced tomatoes, corn and parsley. Sprinkle with Season-all. Bake 40 minutes at 350° F. Serves 8.

141

ALL-IN-ONE DISHES

LAMB CASSEROLE

2 pounds lamb shoulder, cut into pieces	1 cup tomatoes
1 onion, chopped	1 garlic clove, chopped
2 tablespoons bacon fat	1 bay leaf
2 tablespoons flour	1 cup mushrooms and juice
1/3 cup chopped parsley	dash rosemary

Sauté meat and onions in bacon fat. Sprinkle with flour. Place in a heavy baking casserole. Add seasonings, tomatoes and mushrooms. Cover with heavy top. Place in oven and bake 1 hour. Sprinkle with chopped parsley. Serve with rice or potatoes. Serves 4 to 6.

Potatoes may be added during last half hour of baking.

RICE WITH CHICKEN, SPANISH STYLE

1 frying chicken, 3 to 4 pounds	2 cups boiling water
1 lime or lemon	1 teaspoon salt
1 teaspoon pepper	1/3 cup shortening or oil
2 cups long grain rice	2 small finely chopped onions
1 small green pepper	several stalks celery
2 tablespoons chopped parlsey	1/2 teaspoon sage
1 garlic clove	1/2 teaspoon thyme
1/4 teaspoon rosemary	1 cup tomato sauce or purée
	1 small jar stuffed olives

Wash and cut chicken into small pieces. Squeeze lime or lemon juice over chicken. Add salt and pepper. Place in refrigerator overnight, or let stand several hours to marinate. When ready to use, fry in oil without flour until brown—but not done! Remove from pan. Add celery, onion, pepper and garlic to remaining oil. Sauté 10 to 15 minutes. Add uncooked rice and continue to sauté, stirring constantly for 10 minutes until all grains are well coated with fat. Add parsley, spices and tomato sauce. Stir with fork until well mixed and add hot water, olives, juice and chicken. Cover tightly and simmer for 20 to 30 minutes on very low heat. When chicken is tender and rice well done, remove from fire. Place rice in center of platter and arrange chicken around rice. Garnish with green peas which have been pre-heated with butter, salt and pepper.

Be sure to use a heavy Dutch oven type vessel so rice will not burn or cook too fast.

RICE AND FRANKFURTER CASSEROLE

6 to 8 frankfurters	*1 teaspoon salt*
¼ cup onion, chopped	*1 teaspoon paprika*
¼ cup green pepper	*1 teaspoon garlic salt*
1 garlic clove	*1 teaspoon chili powder*
2 cups hot water	*¼ cup chopped olives*
2 cups rice (long grain)	*(stuffed)*
¼ cup bacon fat	*½ teaspoon thyme*
2 cans tomatoes or purée	

Sauté onion, olives and green pepper in fat. Add rice, unwashed, and fry until brown, stirring frequently. Add tomatoes, hot water and spices. Add frankfurters which have been split in half. Cover and simmer 30 minutes. Do not remove cover or stir. Serves 6 to 8.

CHILI CON CARNE No. 1

1½ pounds ground beef	*½ pound bacon or salt pork*
2 green peppers, chopped	*4 tablespoons chili powder*
3 medium onions	*1 teaspoon oregano*
2 garlic cloves	*1 teaspoon paprika*
1 large can tomatoes or	*½ teaspoon red pepper*
purée	*2 teaspoons salt*
2 cups red kidney beans	*2 tablespoons bacon fat*
1 bay leaf	*½ teaspoon thyme*

Wash beans. Let soak 2 or 3 hours. Dice bacon and add to beans, with bay leaf and salt. Cover and boil until beans are tender. Sauté onions, peppers and garlic in fat. Add meat, spices and chili powder. Cook 20 minutes. Season to taste. Serves 6 to 8.

Serve with rice and crackers. A green salad or cole slaw makes the meal complete.

CHILI CON CARNE No. 2

1 pound ground beef	1 can red kidney beans
2 onions, diced	½ teaspoon red pepper
3 tablespoons fat	2 tablespoons chili powder
2 cups tomato purée or sauce	1 teaspoon seasoned salt
1 garlic clove	

Sauté onions and garlic in fat. Add beef and seasonings. Pour into a deep sauce pan with tomato purée and beans. Cook 30 minutes. Serve with rice or spaghetti if desired. Serves 6 to 8.

HERBY'S CHICKEN TAMALE PIE

1 3-pound chicken	½ teaspoon thyme
2 green peppers	2 tablespoons chili powder
2 garlic cloves	1 teaspoon paprika
1 small bunch celery	2 bay leaves
several sprigs parsley	2 cups corn meal (yellow or
1 can whole kernel corn	white)
½ cup Italian cheese	3 cups water
1 pint ripe olives	salt, pepper and paprika to
1 medium size can tomato	taste
purée	2 tablespoons bacon fat

Cut chicken in small pieces. Add enough water to cover. Add salt and pepper. Cook until very tender and broth is almost absorbed. Remove meat from bones and cut in medium pieces. Chop onions, peppers, garlic, celery, parsley and spices and sauté in fat. Cook about 20 minutes. Add corn, olives and tomato purée. Simmer 15 minutes longer. Cook corn meal in water with seasonings to make a thick mush. Line baking dish with mush. Add meat and vegetable mixture. Spread layer of mush over top of casserole. Sprinkle with cheese. Bake in a moderate oven for 45 minutes. Serves 8 to 10.

TAMALE PIE

Tamale pie is so easily prepared ahead of time. Bake just before serving.

(1)

2 pounds ground beef	1 can whole kernel corn
2 large onions	1 No. 2 can tomatoes

1 small can tomato sauce or
   purée
1 can or jar ripe olives
2 cups hot water
2 garlic cloves
2 tablespoons bacon fat

2 tablespoons chili powder
1 green pepper chopped
salt and pepper to taste
dash red pepper
1 teaspoon cumin seed
2 cups corn meal

Sauté onion, garlic and pepper in fat for 20 minutes. Add seasonings and chopped meat. Pour into a large pot, add corn, tomatoes and purée. Pour water over corn meal and add to meat and olives. Stir frequently and cook until thick (about 45 minutes).

Pour into deep pottery baking dish. Sprinkle with grated cheese and bake in hot oven 30 minutes.

With tamale pie serve green salad with avocado and bread sticks.

(2)

2 pounds ground meat
3 onions
2 green peppers
2 garlic cloves
½ tablespoon thyme
2 bay leaves
1 teaspoon paprika
2 tablespoons chili powder
1 teaspoon oregano

1 medium can tomato purée
2 cups corn meal
1 can whole kernel corn
1 small bunch celery
several sprigs parsley
1 pint ripe olives
3 cups water
salt and pepper to taste
½ cup Parmesan cheese

Sauté vegetables in fat. Add ground meat and spices. Cook 20 minutes. Add corn, olives and tomato sauce. Simmer 20 minutes longer. Cook corn meal in water with seasonings to make a thick mush. Line baking dish with mush. Add meat and vegetable mixture. Spread layer of mush over top of casserole. Sprinkle with cheese. Bake in moderate oven 45 minutes. Serves 8 to 10.

Serve this festive South-of-the-Border dish with a green garden salad, French bread with garlic butter, and a light dessert such as fresh fruit cup.

ALL-IN-ONE DISHES

JIMMY DANIELS' KEDGEREE

1 cup cooked rice
1 cup cooked and flaked fish
2 tablespoons melted butter
1 hard-cooked egg
1 tablespoon lemon juice

salt, pepper and paprika to
taste
½ teaspoon curry powder
½ cup chopped parsley

Mix ingredients, pack into a buttered bowl. Surround with hot water and steam until heated through. Unmold. Garnish with parsley and serve. (Kedgeree may also be heated in the oven or a chafing dish.) Serves 4.

OYSTER CASSEROLE

1 pint oysters
2 tablespoons grated onions
2 tablespoons grated celery
salt, pepper, paprika to taste
dash mace or nutmeg
1 teaspoon garlic salt

2 tablespoons chopped
parsley
½ cup oyster juice and cream
1½ cups bread crumbs
⅓ cup melted butter

Sauté butter, onions, parsley and celery. Add bread crumbs and seasonings. Brown on top of stove. Grease round or square casserole. Arrange a layer of oysters and cover with half of mixture. Add another layer of oysters and crumbs. Pour oyster juice and cream over mixture and bake 30 minutes in hot oven. Serves 4.

SALMON OR TUNA TWIRLS

1 large can red or pink
    salmon or tuna fish
1 small onion, minced
½ cup celery
1 teaspoon paprika

dash red pepper
1 small green pepper
¼ cup parsley
1 teaspoon seasoned salt
½ teaspoon garlic salt

Sauté onion, celery, parsley and green pepper. Add salmon from which bones have been removed and strained. Simmer 15 minutes. Add paprika, seasoned salt, red pepper, garlic salt. Set aside to cool while you prepare dough.

Dough

2 cups flour
3 teaspoons baking powder

1 teaspoon salt
¼ teaspoon nutmeg

146

6 to 8 tablespoons shortening   1 egg
½ cup milk

Sift dry ingredients. Cut in fat. Beat egg in milk and add to flour mixture to make a medium soft dough. Place on a floured board and knead lightly. Roll dough to ¼ inch thickness in form of a rectangle, approximately 12″ by 14″. Be sure there is very little juice in the filling. Spread filling over dough. Roll up tightly like a jelly roll. Cut in 1½- to 2-inch slices. Arrange on a greased baking pan ½ inch apart. Bake 25 to 30 minutes in a moderate oven (350°-375° F.). Serves 6.

Serve with a cheese sauce, white sauce, or can of prepared clam chowder.

To complete your menu, serve green peas with celery, hearts of lettuce with French dressing, fresh fruit cup and cookies.

SHRIMP WITH CHEESE AND NOODLES

2 pounds shrimp
½ teaspoon red pepper
1 bunch green onions and tops or 1 medium whole onion
½ cup celery tops or parsley (optional)
1 teaspoon garlic salt
¼ teaspoon pepper
½ teaspoon curry powder

3 cups warm milk
1 teaspoon salt
2 tablespoons butter
1 small can pimiento
4 tablespoons flour
1 pound package noodles
¼ teaspoon paprika
½ teaspoon salt
½ cup coarsely grated American cheese

Shell and clean shrimp and split lengthwise. Boil in salted water with a dash of red pepper. Sauté in butter, onions and tops, pimiento cut fine and celery leaves or parsley. Add flour, seasonings and warm milk. Stir until thick. Add cooked shrimp. Simmer 20 minutes over very low heat. Just before removing from fire, add ½ cup coarsely grated American cheese. Serve with plain medium sized noodles that have been boiled and well seasoned with celery, or onion salt, paprika and butter; or make a noodle ring filled with green peas.

A very special dish for your bridge parties, luncheons or dinner for the family. And what to serve with it? A tasty green salad of water cress, avocado, and grapefruit with French dressing and toasted bread sticks. Have a fluffy baked lemon custard for dessert.

TUNA AND SHELL MACARONI CASSEROLE

1 pound shell macaroni	salt and pepper to taste
1 can tuna fish	1/4 cup chopped celery
1 small onion	3 tablespoons butter
3 tablespoons flour	2 1/2 cups milk
1/4 pound grated American cheese	1/2 cup bread crumbs
1/4 cup chopped parsley	1 egg

Cook macaroni in boiling, salted water. Drain and rinse. Sauté onions, celery and parsley in butter. Make a thin white sauce with butter, flour, milk, and seasonings. Remove from fire. Add slightly beaten egg. Place macaroni and tuna fish in baking dish. Pour white sauce over mixture. Add grated cheese and bread crumbs. Bake in greased baking dish at 350° F. for 40 minutes. Serves 8.

13.

Eggs

THERE'S NOTHING
that can surpass a
dainty, delectable
egg dish for your health benefits as well as your eating
pleasure.

Eggs should be included on your menus. They can be as
plain as you please, or as fancy as an Easter Bonnet.
When it comes to variety and budget trimming, eggs are
excellent meat substitutes. Their protein value is as high
as the costliest and finest cut of meat.

Try a variety of omelets, scrambled egg combinations,
eggs with cheese, soufflés, hard-cooked eggs, pickled eggs.
Be an egg explorer, and do as The Little Brown Chef
does—stick your nose into the Egg Basket.

PLAIN OMELET FOR TWO

3 eggs
3 tablespoons milk
½ teaspoon salt

pinch white pepper
dash paprika
1 tablespoon butter

Beat eggs until very light. Add milk and seasonings. Heat pan.
Melt butter and pour omelet into pan. Shake pan back and
forth until mixture is set. Fold omelet away from you and turn
onto a hot platter. Serve at once.

EGG OMELET WITH VARIATIONS

6 eggs, separated	*6 tablespoons milk*
pinch baking powder	*1 teaspoon salt*
dash pepper	*paprika*

Beat yolks and whites separately. Add milk to yolks. Beat in baking powder and seasonings. Blend whites and yolks. Heat butter, turn eggs into roomy skillet, and as mixture cooks on bottom and sides, stick with fork so the egg on top will penetrate cooked surface while eggs are soft. Fold over, let stand a few minutes, turn onto hot dish. Sprinkle with paprika. Serves 4 to 6.

You may add to your omelet:

(1)

1 cup minced lobster	*salt and pepper to taste*
1 tablespoon minced onion	

(2)

1 cup cooked shrimp	*dash chili sauce*
½ cup chopped parsley	

(3)

1 cup cheese (any kind)	*1 tablespoon mustard*

(4)

1 cup Spanish sauce

(5)

1 cup chopped ham, chicken or beef

(6)

1 cup corn and green pepper sautéed

(7)

½ cup cooked rice	*1 cup mushroom and onion sautéed*

(8)

6 to 8 asparagus tips	*2 chopped pimientos*

(9)

½ cup jelly or jam

(10)

1 cup cooked chicken livers, plain or with onions and mushrooms

DUKE ELLINGTON'S SCRAMBLED EGGS

As soothing and fascinating as his music, one would suspect

the same about his taste for food. But when The Little Brown Chef poked his nose into Duke Ellington's ("His Royal Highness") gastronomical tastes, there was indeed a surprise in store for him.

For, as unique as his melodies, is his way of eating. He eats his dessert *first*, whether it is simple pie à la mode or a fancy French pastry. The Duke follows this with a good steak and celery instead of bread or crepe suzettes and a good old-fashioned country boiled dinner. His tastes do not vary over a large range, but he likes substantial dishes.

"But *precisely*," asks The Little Brown Chef, "what can you cook?" Well, that *did* it!

"Cook! There's not a person I know who doesn't go for *my* scrambled eggs. They are definitely a collector's item." So we offer for your musical appetite:

1 dozen eggs	*½ cup butter*
½ cup cream	*1 teaspoon salt*
½ teaspoon paprika	*pinch celery salt*

Separate eggs. Beat yolks, then whites. Add cream and seasonings to yolks and fold in whites. Melt butter. Add eggs to butter, stirring constantly with a large fork. Mix well. Cook 10 minutes. Turn off heat, but continue to scramble until fluffy and light. Pour onto a hot platter and serve. Serves 6.

SCRAMBLED EGGS SUPREME

6 eggs	*1 teaspoon chives*
½ cup cream	*salt, pepper to taste*
paprika	

Beat eggs and add cream, salt, pepper and chives. Scramble lightly, stirring constantly. Serve on toast or with ham, bacon or sausage. Serves 4.

For variations add:

(1)

1 cup grated cheese

(2)

½ cup chopped olives, chopped ham or bacon

(3)

Sauté in butter 6 chopped green onions and 2 tablespoons pimiento. Add eggs and scramble.

151

(4)

Sauté in butter ½ cup chopped celery, ¼ cup chopped parsley and ¼ cup mushrooms. Add eggs and scramble.

BAKED EGGS ON TOAST

6 pieces buttered thin bread   6 eggs
    (crusts removed)   salt and pepper to taste

Fit bread in muffin tins which have been greased. Break egg, place white in bowl, and yolk on bread in muffin tin. Repeat until all 6 tins are filled. Beat whites until stiff. Sprinkle with salt and pepper. Heap whites around egg yolk on bread. Bake in oven 15 to 20 minutes until firm. Sprinkle with paprika. Remove carefully from muffin cups and serve with ham or bacon on wilted lettuce. Serves 6.

BAKED EGGS

(In Custard Cups)

6 eggs   ½ cup chopped parsley
2 tablespoons butter   salt, pepper, paprika to taste

Grease custard cups. Break an egg into each cup. Dot with butter, sprinkle with salt, pepper, paprika and parsley. Bake 20 minutes. Serve in cups. Serves 6.

PICKLED EGGS

1 dozen hard-cooked eggs   2 tablespoons sugar
1 teaspoon salt   1 teaspoon pickle spice
2 cups vinegar   1 garlic clove
1 cup water   ½ teaspoon celery seed

Shell eggs. Boil spices and vinegar with water 10 minutes. Cool and strain. Add garlic cut in small pieces. Pour vinegar mixture over eggs in quart jars. Seal and let stand 2 to 3 days. Eggs may be placed in a covered bowl and set in refrigerator to ripen.

Juices from sweet pickles and pickled beets may be added together and poured over eggs. Cover and set aside to ripen.

SCRAMBLED OR CASSEROLE EGGS AND CORN

2 tablespoons butter   6 green onion tops, finely
¼ cup finely chopped celery   chopped

⅓ cup finely diced cooked
    ham
1 cup, well-drained whole
    kernel corn

4 eggs
¼ cup milk
¼ teaspoon salt
pepper and paprika to taste

Melt butter in medium size, heavy frying pan. Add celery, onion tops and ham and sauté over low heat for 10 minutes, stirring frequently. Pour into bowl to cool. Combine eggs, milk and seasonings; beat enough to mix well; pour into hot, greased frying pan. (If necessary add 1 teaspoon or more butter to hot pan so it will be lightly greased with butter, both bottom and sides.) Place over low heat. Add corn and ham mixture; stir carefully to distribute ham and vegetables. Cook for 8 to 10 minutes over low heat, stirring frequently.

FILLED FRENCH FRIED EGGS

6 hard-cooked eggs
2 tablespoons salad dressing
½ cup finely chopped cooked
    or canned shrimp
2 tablespoons grated onion
1 teaspoon paprika

1 teaspoon celery seed
salt and pepper to taste
dash garlic salt
1 egg, beaten slightly
1 cup fine, dry bread crumbs

Chill hard-cooked eggs. Remove shells. Cut eggs in half lengthwise. Remove yolks and set whites aside. Mash yolks well and mix thoroughly with salad dressing, shrimp, onion and seasonings; blend well. Fill center of whites with this mixture, then press 2 halves together firmly. Dip "whole" stuffed eggs separately in beaten egg, roll in bread crumbs, then fry in deep fat heated to 375° F. for 3 to 5 minutes or until eggs are a golden brown. Drain on paper towels. Serve hot with curry powder. If desired, tuna, lobster, crab meat, ground ham or salmon may be used in place of the shrimp.

BAKED EGG CASSEROLE SURPRISE

6 slices bacon
6 eggs
salt and paprika
6 slices tomato

6 slices American cheese
2 cups sliced mushrooms
¼ cup finely chopped parsley
toast strips

EGGS

Place bacon across bottom of shallow casserole. Break 1 egg across each slice of bacon; sprinkle eggs with salt and paprika. Place 1 slice tomato on top each egg. Place cheese slices on top of tomato slices. Top with mushrooms and parsley. Place in a 325° F. oven until cheese is melted and eggs are firm. Serve with toast strips.

14.

Vegetables on Parade

I ALWAYS LIKED THE autumn season best during my child-hood on the farm. There was so much activity, harvest time, canning, storing food for the long, cold winters. It was all fun. Then there were the weekly trips to market and the county fair which was held in the well-known South Dakota "Corn Palace." Here each farmer exhibited his prize vegetables and produce. What show of color, visions of vegetable sunsets, brilliant rainbow hues!

The Corn Palace became, in my childhood fantasies, a showplace where I visualized a Broadway production with a cast of vegetables. The opening number was a chorus of stately carrot show girls in their orange and green outfits. Then dainty, green onion soubrettes and the red and green pepper boys doing the gay "Corn Cob Polka." The red and green cabbage corps de ballet with their wide crisp leaves. And the stars of the show were Miss Garden Lettuce, stately Sir Cedric Celery, and the villain with a thousand eyes, Potato Paddy. The vocal chorus, the "Parsley and Radish Singers." A production worthy of four stars in any critic's rating.

VEGETABLE HINTS

Green vegetables are vital to health! Use them plentifully in season when they are cheapest and richest in nutritional value. Select only fresh vegetables, and pay attention to their appearance as you would a dress or hat. Use very little water when cooking. Never overcook. Overcooked vegetables lose much of their food value and flavor.

Baking soda is a vitamin thief—use only when called for in recipe. When cooking vegetables, save all vegetable water for gravies, sauces and soups.

In cooking all vegetables, put them into boiling salted water. Use ½ teaspoon salt for each quart of water; ½ to ¾ teaspoon salt when little or no water is used.

Cook vegetables rapidly and only until tender. Time required depends on freshness.

When cooked, drain, if necessary, and season to taste with butter, salt and pepper.

Cream or white sauces may be tinted to suit your color scheme without resorting to artificial coloring—cheese, egg and curry powder for yellow; beet juice, pimiento and paprika for red or pink; parsley and water cress for green.

Try to keep vegetables uniform. If you are serving French style string beans, accompany them with long, slender vegetables, such as asparagus, carrots or shoestring beets. Also potatoes may be cut in strips and boiled. If your string beans are diced, use diced carrots, beets or potatoes. This need not be overdone, but you will find you can arrange your vegetables more artistically with this method.

COLORFUL PLATE COMBINATIONS

At holiday time it's red and green, of course:

Broiled or baked tomato and parsley.

Beets and string beans.

String beans and pimientos.

Green peas and sweet red peppers.

Beets and asparagus.

Beets and green onion tops.

Brussels sprouts with paprika sauce.

Tomatoes and green beans.

Red and green pepper slices.

Spinach and chopped tomato.
Tomatoes and peppers.

For spring, yellow and green color combinations:
Carrots and parsley or peppers.
Carrots and green onion tops.
Yellow turnips and peas.
Corn and green peppers or onion tops.
Asparagus and egg yolks.
Squash with peas.
Spinach and carrots.
Stuffed peppers and corn.
Wax beans and chopped water cress.
Wax beans and onion tops.
Wax beans on wilted lettuce.
Lima beans and corn.

ENGAGING VEGETABLE COMBINATIONS

Cauliflower with mushroom sauce.
String beans, corn, mushrooms and buttered parsley.
Rice, carrots, string beans, celery.
Creamed onions, asparagus.
Baked squash, cherries.
Cauliflower, pistachio nuts.
Carrots, peas, celery.
Cauliflower with Spanish sauce, buttered peas.
Buttered cabbage, onion tops, pimiento.
Carrot rings, chopped lettuce.
Creamed potatoes, peas, mushrooms.
Peas, pistachio nuts, paprika rice.
Fried tomato slices, broccoli with butter.
Mashed potatoes, pimientos, parsley.
Brussels sprouts, tiny onions.
Lima beans, corn sautéed with mushrooms.
Whole boiled green onions, asparagus, pimiento butter.
Parsnips, parsley.
Stuffed baked tomatoes, peas.

ASPARAGUS

Select solid, firm stalks, making sure ends are not wilted. Cut off ends and wash asparagus carefully. Either lay flat in deep fat pan containing boiling salted water, or tie in bunches with clean string. Cook in an open utensil 10 to 15 minutes. Cover, cook 5 minutes longer. Remove carefully and place on serving dish.

Asparagus may be served with your favorite white sauce, cheese sauce, mock or real Hollandaise sauce, pimiento sauce, lemon butter or plain butter. Asparagus is excellent in salads, plain or fancy, as well as soups.

Always save the ends of asparagus and boil to make stock for your gravies or soups.

SPECIAL BOILED ASPARAGUS

1 bunch fresh asparagus	*½ teaspoon garlic salt*
juice of 1 small onion or	*1 teaspoon salt*
grated onion	*1 teaspoon pepper*
3 tablespoons butter	*1 teaspoon paprika*
3 tablespoons cream	*1 hard-cooked egg*

Wash asparagus well. Cut off tough ends and scrape away white roots and stringy ends. Soak in salted water 30 minutes. Place in a pan of boiling water. Cook 20 minutes. Drain well. Sauté onion in butter. Add seasonings and cream. Chop egg. Add to sautéed sauce and pour over asparagus. Cover and steam 3 to 5 minutes. Serves 4 to 6.

Add lemon juice and parsley to your drawn butter for plain boiled asparagus. One tablespoon mustard, Worcestershire, steak or Tabasco sauce gives a delightfully sharp tang.

ASPARAGUS ON TOAST

1 pound asparagus	*1 cup white sauce*
4 slices toast	*2 tablespoons dry bread*
1 hard-cooked egg	*crumbs*
4 slices bacon	*2 tablespoons grated cheese*
nutmeg	*1 tablespoon parsley*

Cook asparagus as directed, drain and set aside. Fry bacon and set aside. Place asparagus on toast in a baking dish. Add chopped egg to white sauce and pour over asparagus. Sprinkle with nutmeg. Lay a slice of bacon on each portion, sprinkle with mixture of bread crumbs and cheese. Bake in a moderate oven, 350° F., about 10 minutes until crumbs are browned. Serves 4.

DRIED BEANS

"Oh no, Mother. Not just plain old beans." How often have those words rung in your ears? But don't be disheartened. You can glorify beans with a few little cooking tricks that are sure to please the family.

To plain boiled lima, navy, red beans or black-eyed peas, try adding chopped onion, several cloves of garlic, a green pepper, a few sprigs of parsley, a few celery leaves, canned tomato sauce or purée and salt. Chop leftover pieces of ham, salt pork, bacon or bacon ends until very fine and add to beans. Remember, be careful to eliminate as much of the fat as possible. You can spoil a tasty dish of beans with excess fat.

Whenever dried beans are served, don't forget that fresh green salads should be included in your menu. Not only are they nutritious but they pep up the beans themselves.

Never overcook beans. Serve them well done, but firm. Don't just put the pot on the stove and forget them. Beans, like all other foods, have wonderful qualities so give them a break.

BOSTON BAKED BEANS No. 1

1 cup navy beans	1/4 pound salt pork (or fat
1 large onion	from ham or bacon ends)
2 tablespoons sugar	1/2 teaspoon dry mustard
2 cups boiling water	2 tablespoons molasses

Soak beans overnight, well-covered with water. Drain and add fresh water. Boil until tender, but not until skins pop off. Drain and place in an earthen pot. Cut salt pork into small cubes. Brown in skillet. Add sliced onion to fat and brown. Add onions and pork cubes to 2 cups of water. Add sugar, molasses, salt and mustard. Pour over beans, cover. Bake 5 to 6 hours in a very slow oven until tender, thoroughly flavored and dry. If needed, add boiling water during baking. Serves 6.

The measurements of sugar, molasses, onions, dry mustard

are approximate rather than absolute. Flavor beans to suit your individual taste.

BOSTON BAKED BEANS No. 2

1 pound California pea beans	1 medium onion
½ pound salt pork	¼ teaspoon salt
1 tablespoon molasses	¼ teaspoon pepper
¼ cup sugar	½ teaspoon mustard

Boil beans until skins can be easily removed. Place salt pork in bottom of bean pot. Then add beans and other ingredients. Cover tightly and bake in a slow oven for 6 hours. Serves 6.

BOSTON BAKED BEANS No. 3

2 cups pea beans	½ teaspoon pepper
1 bay leaf, crushed	½ pound pork or bacon
1 garlic clove	1 large onion
½ cup tomato catsup or chili sauce	¼ cup brown or white sugar
¼ cup molasses	2 teaspoons salt
½ teaspoon thyme	½ teaspoon paprika

Wash beans and cover with water. Soak overnight. Parboil salt pork or bacon ends. When partially done, add salt, bay leaf and grated garlic (optional) to the beans which have been drained. Cook beans about 45 minutes. Remove from heat. Add brown or white sugar, tomato catsup or chili sauce, mustard, molasses, thyme, salt, pepper and paprika. Place beans in a bean pot or casserole (heavy pottery type is better). Pour half of the liquid over the beans, cover tightly and bake in a slow oven 250° to 300° F., baking 5 to 6 hours.

If you plan to keep them in the oven overnight or all day, the temperature of the oven should be from 200° to 250° F. Use remaining liquid to moisten beans if they dry. Try same recipe with red beans for variety.

BLACK-EYED PEAS

Would you like a treat for New Year's? Then try the recipes given for dried black-eyed peas. If you shun them on the market shelves or have never heard of them before, try cooking them as suggested. They are a real New Year's tradition in the

South. Cooked with a tasty hog's head, pigtails, salt pork, ham or bacon, they make a fine dish; not only on New Year's but any day you desire a hearty and delicious nourishing dish.

In the summer and early fall when fresh black-eyed peas are in season, add them regularly to your vegetable list.

PLAIN BLACK-EYED PEAS

*1½ pounds smoked meat or
    bacon ends
1 pound black-eyed peas
1 bay leaf
several red pepper pods*

*1 garlic clove
1 large onion
½ teaspoon dry mustard
salt and pepper to taste
several sprigs parsley*

Parboil meat 30 minutes. Wash and soak peas. Add with onions, garlic and seasonings to meat. Boil slowly. Add salt and pepper using freely since peas need good seasonings to pep them up. They also absorb a lot of water, so be sure they are kept well-covered.

BLACK-EYED PEAS IN SAUCE

*1 pound black-eyed peas
2 pounds ham hocks
1 bay leaf
½ teaspoon sweet basil
1 garlic clove
several red pepper pods,
    chopped*

*several stalks celery,
    chopped
2 medium onions, chopped
1 small can tomato puree
2 tablespoons catsup or
    chili sauce*

Wash and pick peas carefully. Soak 1 hour. Boil meat 30 minutes in enough water to cover. Add all spices, peas and other vegetables, tomato puree and catsup. Cover and boil slowly, 3 to 4 hours or until done. Serves 6.

Serve with rice and a tasty cole slaw or vegetable salad and corn sticks.

Pig tails, bacon ends, ham bone, or smoked spareribs may be used in place of ham hocks.

RED BEANS

Red beans are classified as one of the most nutritious foods. In New Orleans and the Latin countries, as well as in many sections of the South, they are a standard item on the menu. It is a Creole theory that children should be raised on beans and rice to become strong and sturdy adults.

All over America, I guess, there are folk who have never tried red beans or even heard of them. So, may I suggest, if you are in this category, that you try them. You will be convinced that they are "mighty good" as well as nutritious.

I've been told many times: "You haven't lived until you've eaten red beans and rice." Well, I tried them and another fine dish has been added to my list of edibles, a dish definitely in the delicacy class.

Another highly esteemed legume dish is red beans in wine. You can't go wrong serving them prepared this way at your most important dinner parties.

THE MAN, THE HORN, AND RED BEANS

The modern Gabriel, Louis Armstrong, being from New Orleans, loves spicy foods. He doesn't have to depend upon others to cook for him. He can do it himself!

"You can bet," he says, "my sister can make the best Gumbo Filé in Louisiana and I love it! But my favorite of all dishes (when I'm not on my diet and watching my calories) is just plain ham hocks and red beans. No need to make folk think I like fancy foods like quail on toast, chicken and hot biscuits, or steak smothered in mushrooms. Of course they taste good and I can eat them, but have you ever tried ham hocks and red beans? Old man, season them well! Add the right spices at the right time, and man, you have a 'Date with a Dish' that's just about the greatest."

HAM HOCKS AND RED BEANS

1 pound small ham hocks	*1 pound dried red beans*
1 bay leaf	*1 onion, minced*
1 red pepper pod	*1 garlic clove, minced*
salt and pepper to taste	*2 quarts of cold water*

Wash and soak beans 2 to 3 hours, or overnight if preferred. When ready to cook, drain off water and put beans in large pot with 2 quarts cold water. Let water heat thoroughly, then add ham hocks, herbs, and onion. Cook slowly but steadily at least

2 hours or until tender. When done, place in a dish and lay ham hocks on top.

Serve with rice, green salad and corn bread.

RED BEANS IN WINE

1 quart red beans	salt and pepper to taste
3 cloves	1/3 cup butter
1 cup claret or Burgundy wine	1 onion
	pinch thyme or herb bouquet

Wash and soak beans 3 to 4 hours. Drain. Cover with cold water. Add part of butter, onion and cloves. Boil half hour, add wine, stirring frequently. Cook 45 minutes longer, add bouquet and rest of butter. Salt and pepper to taste. Cook about 30 minutes longer or until beans are done. Serve hot and sprinkle with chopped parsley. Serves 6.

RED BEANS WITH TOMATO SAUCE

1 pound dried red beans	2 quarts water
1 small onion, chopped	1 bay leaf
1 tablespoon salt	several cumin seeds
2 red pepper pods	1 chopped garlic clove
ham ends, skin, bone or bacon	1 can tomato sauce
	salt and pepper to taste

If ham or bacon ends are used, chop fine. Cover and boil 10 minutes, add beans which have soaked 2 to 3 hours. (Be sure beans are well washed and picked over.) Add onion, bay leaf, tomato sauce and garlic and cook slowly, tightly covered, for 3 hours or until done. Stir often. Add more water or tomato sauce, if desired.

Red beans can be boiled and then baked with 1 cup molasses or brown sugar, if desired.

Tomato sauce may be omitted and only plain water used.

RED BEANS AND RICE

1 pound red beans	1 pound ham or salt meat
1 onion	1/2 teaspoon pepper
1 garlic clove	1/4 teaspoon red pepper
1/4 teaspoon thyme	1 teaspoon salt
2 quarts water	2 cups cooked dry rice

Wash beans and soak overnight or from 4 to 5 hours in cold water. Drain water. Place in a pot and cover with cold water. Heat slowly. Add seasonings and meat, onion, chopped garlic. Boil at least 2 hours or until beans are tender. Add rice. Mix well and let steam 10 minutes. Serves 6 to 8.

Rice may be served separately, if desired.

HOPPING JOHN

1 cup dried peas	*1 cup uncooked rice*
1 ham bone	*1 chopped onion*
salt and pepper to taste	*dash red pepper*

Wash peas and soak overnight in water. Cover ham bone with water, add onion and cook 2 hours slowly. Add soaked peas and simmer about 1½ hours longer. When peas are tender and water cooked low, add uncooked rice and seasonings. Cook 20 minutes longer. Liquid should be absorbed and rice and peas dry. Serve with a hot sauce. Serves 4 to 6.

STRING BEANS

Whenever boiling string beans as a main dish, French style, or tidbits for the extra green beans, use a dash of garlic salt and a pinch of savory. It will certainly pep them up!

Rich cream sauces and grated cheese are excellent with green beans.

Beans, green or the wax variety, may be cooked with ham, bacon or any smoked meats.

Well-seasoned green beans boiled in smoked spareribs with potatoes is a "dish to remember."

Boiling beans with smoked meats or corned beef requires more time, so be careful not to overcook in order to retain the vitamins.

STRING BEANS AND CORN SUCCOTASH

¼ pound bacon or salt pork, chopped	*salt and pepper to taste*
	1 can whole kernel corn, or 4 ears fresh corn cut off cob
1½ pounds string beans	
1 teaspoon sugar	*1 pod red pepper*

Boil bacon fat in a small amount of water for 20 minutes. Add chopped onions, red pepper, sugar, salt and pepper. Add string beans which have been cut in small pieces. Add corn, cook 30 minutes longer. Serves 6.

Butter may be substituted for bacon after the beans are water drained.

OLD-FASHIONED COUNTRY BEANS

2 pounds green beans
½ pound bacon ends
1 teaspoon sugar
2 teaspoons salt

2 onions
1 pound new potatoes
¼ teaspoon red pepper

Cut bacon in chunks, cover with water, and boil 20 minutes. Wash and cut green beans in half. Add onions, beans, sugar and seasonings. Boil 15 minutes. Add scraped new potatoes, and boil until potatoes are done. Serve with corn bread and garden country salad. Serves 4.

To your green string beans add fresh cut corn from cob.

STRING BEANS UNIQUE

2 pounds fresh string beans
1 cup diced ham and fat
1 medium onion
1 teaspoon salt
2 hot peppers
1 cup cream

1 garlic clove
½ teaspoon sugar
2 tablespoons bacon fat or
    butter
¼ teaspoon pepper

Place ham and diced onion in pan with just enough water to cover. Add chopped garlic, salt, pepper and string beans which have been strung, washed, and cut in half. Add all seasonings, butter and cream. Cover and steam until tender. Serves 6.

STRING BEANS IN TOMATO SAUCE

2 pounds string beans
2 small onions
¼ cup butter or olive oil
1 garlic clove
1 teaspoon sugar
dash red pepper

1 can tomato sauce
1 bay leaf
1 small green pepper
½ teaspoon leaf thyme
1 teaspoon salt

Wash and cut string beans French style. Boil in salted water and sugar 20 minutes. Sauté in butter or oil, onion, pepper, garlic. Add tomato sauce and spices. Cook 15 minutes. Drain water from beans and pour tomato sauce over beans. Steam 5 minutes. Serve. Serves 4 to 6.

May be sprinkled with grated cheese before serving.

STRING BEANS AND WHOLE KERNEL CORN

1 pound string beans	*1 bunch green onions*
1 can whole kernel corn	*1 teaspoon salt*
½ teaspoon sugar	*½ teaspoon paprika*
½ teaspoon celery salt	*¼ cup butter or bacon fat*

Wash and cut string beans in tiny round pieces (to resemble corn). Boil in salted water for 15 minutes. Sauté in butter, onions and tops. Add corn and seasonings. Cook 15 minutes. Strain water from beans and add corn mixture. Steam 10 minutes to let seasonings penetrate. Serves 4 to 6.

STRING BEANS

(With Olives and Mushrooms)

2 pounds fresh string beans	*½ teaspoon paprika*
½ cup stuffed olives, sliced	*2 tablespoons cream*
1 small can mushroom slices	*1 teaspoon salt*
3 tablespoons butter	*¼ teaspoon garlic salt*
½ teaspoon white pepper	

Wash and cut beans in small pieces. Boil in salted water 20 minutes. Strain. Add butter, sliced olives and mushrooms with spices and cream. Steam 10 minutes. Serve.

STRING BEANS IN CREAM, CELERY AND MUSHROOMS

1 pound fresh cut string beans	*1 teaspoon paprika*
2 cups water	*1 tablespoon flour*
1 teaspoon seasoning salt	*1 cup cream*
½ teaspoon pepper	*1 cup thinly sliced mushrooms*
¼ cup bacon drippings	*¼ cup chopped parsley*

Place green beans, water, salt, pepper, bacon fat and paprika in saucepan. Cover and cook 15 minutes until beans are tender. Combine flour with cream and stir into green beans. Bring to boil; cook over medium heat until thick and smooth, stirring constantly. Add mushrooms and parsley and heat thoroughly.

LIMA BEAN AND CORN SUCCOTASH

2 cups cooked beans, fresh or dried
1 tablespoon sugar
1 teaspoon pepper
3 tablespoons butter
3 cups uncooked corn
1 teaspoon salt
1/4 cup milk or cream
1 teaspoon grated onion or juice

Combine ingredients in a saucepan. Simmer slowly 20 minutes and serve. Serves 6.

PHARR'S LIMA BEANS WITH PIGTAILS

1 pound dried lima beans
1 1/2 pounds pigtails
1 small green pepper
1/2 cup chopped parsley
2 teaspoons salt
3 dry chili peppers
1 small onion
1 garlic clove
1/2 teaspoon dry mustard
1 teaspoon chili powder

Wash and pick beans. Soak 2 to 3 hours. Cut pigtails in small pieces. Cover in water and boil 30 minutes. Then add onion, garlic, sliced green pepper, and seasonings to meat. Cook until tender. Add parsley and serve.

BOILED LIMAS IN TOMATO SAUCE

1/4 pound salt pork or bacon ends
2 cups dried lima beans
6 cups water
2 medium onions, chopped
1 garlic clove
1 small green pepper, chopped
1/2 cup celery tops, chopped
1 can tomato sauce or puree
1 bay leaf
salt, pepper, and paprika to taste

Boil salt pork or bacon ends, chopped fine, about 30 minutes. Add lima beans which have been carefully picked and washed. Add onions, pepper, garlic and celery tops. Boil 30 minutes longer. Add tomato sauce, bay leaf, salt and pepper. Simmer until beans are well done. Serves 6.

Serve with sliced ham or pork chops, and a green salad.

Fresh or frozen lima beans may be cooked the same way, using 3 cups of water to approximately a pound of beans.

BEETS

Select small young beets for boiling. Wash, but do not cut.

Cook whole in boiling water until tender. Beets take time! Do not pierce with a fork until after beets have cooked 1 hour or more. When beets are tender, drain and blanch with cold water so that they will peel easily. Serve warm with melted butter, salt and pepper.

SAUTÉED BEETS

4 or 5 large boiled beets
3 strips bacon
2 tablespoons vinegar
1 small chopped onion

1 teaspoon salt
pepper
2 tablespoons sugar

Chop bacon and sauté in skillet. Add chopped onion. Simmer 10 minutes. Chop beets fine. Add to bacon. Add vinegar, salt and sugar together. Pour over beets and serve warm. Serves 6.

SWEET AND SOUR BEETS

6 to 8 medium boiled beets
3 tablespoons butter
2 tablespoons flour
salt and pepper to taste

3 tablespoons sugar
¼ cup lemon juice or vinegar
½ cup water

Slice beets, set aside. Mix flour, sugar, salt and pepper in a pan. Stir lemon juice and water into flour. Bring to a slow boil. Add butter and beets. Heat for 10 minutes. Serve hot. Serves 6.

BEET TOPS

Young tender beet tops are as nutritive as any green vegetable available and may be cooked in the same manner as turnip greens or mixed in your pot of greens!

DANDELION GREENS

3 or 4 bunches of dandelion
    greens
1 pound bacon or salt pork
1 onion
½ teaspoon paprika

½ teaspoon salt
dash red pepper
1 teaspoon sugar
2 cups water

Cut bacon or salt pork in small pieces. Sauté in pot. Add onion and water. Simmer 15 minutes.

Discard greens with buds or blossoms as they will be bitter.

Cut off roots, clean and wash thoroughly. Cut in small pieces. Add greens to bacon and cook for 30 minutes.

BROCCOLI

1 bunch broccoli	dash white pepper
2 tablespoons butter	1 teaspoon lemon rind
6 to 8 chopped green	3 tablespoons lemon juice
onions and tops	½ teaspoon salt

Place broccoli in large pan of salted water. Wash thoroughly and let stand several hours in cold water. Trim edges of stems. Place in boiling salted water. Boil 15 to 20 minutes, then drain. Sauté onion tops in butter. Add seasonings and lemon juice with rind. Pour over broccoli. Steam 5 minutes. Serves 4.

Chopped pimientos may be added to butter if desired. Plain butter may be used as well. White sauce, Hollandaise sauce or rich cheese sauce do a special job on broccoli.

BROCCOLI WITH TOMATOES AND PEPPERS

1 bunch broccoli	2 green peppers, cut in rings
3 or 4 strips bacon	1 teaspoon Tabasco sauce
1 teaspoon butter	½ teaspoon garlic salt
1 large onion, cut in rings	salt and pepper to taste
1 cup chopped celery	3 fresh tomatoes, sliced

Prepare broccoli as directed, only cut in small pieces. Cook the stems first about 10 minutes, then add the tops. Drain. Fry bacon crisp. Remove from pan. Add butter to bacon fat, then sauté onion, celery and green pepper. Add all seasonings, sauté 10 to 15 minutes longer. Add sliced tomatoes. Simmer 15 minutes. Pour over broccoli. Serves 5.

Don't overcook the broccoli—be sure it is firm.

HONEY GLAZED CARROTS

6 to 8 carrots	1 tablespoon parsley
2 tablespoons honey	2 tablespoons orange juice
1 tablespoon butter	salt to taste

Scrape or peel carrots. Cook in a small amount of water until tender—but not soft—about 15 minutes. Remove from water. Place in a greased baking pan. Mix honey and orange juice, pour over carrots. Bake 15 minutes in moderate oven, 350° F. Sprinkle with parsley. Serves 6.

Carrots may be rolled in honey mixture, then bread crumbs and baked.

CARROTS 'N' ONIONS

1 bunch carrots	¼ cup cream
1 bunch green onions	1 teaspoon grated lemon rind
1 teaspoon salt	2 tablespoons parsley
¼ teaspoon sugar	pinch dry mustard
2 tablespoons butter	

Wash and peel carrots and onions. Do not cut away tops of onions. Cut carrots and onions in rings. Cover with cold water, add salt, sugar, mustard. Boil until tender, about 15 minutes. Drain. Add butter and cream. Steam 5 minutes. Just before serving, sprinkle with parsley and grated lemon rind. Serves 6.

BOILED CARROTS, SWEET AND SOUR

8 carrots	½ cup water
3 tablespoons lemon juice	¼ cup chopped parsley
3 tablespoons butter	2 tablespoons sugar
salt, pepper and paprika to taste	several whole cloves

Wash and peel carrots. Cut in half or leave whole. Mix lemon juice, butter, sugar, cloves and water in pan. Boil 10 minutes. Sprinkle carrots with salt and pepper. Pour liquid over them. Cover and steam 25 to 30 minutes. Just before serving, sprinkle chopped parsley and paprika over carrots. Serves 6.

CARROTS 'N' CHEESE

1 bunch carrots	1 tablespoon Worcestershire sauce
2 tablespoons flour	¼ teaspoon paprika
2 tablespoons butter	½ teaspoon Season-all
1 cup milk	½ teaspoon salt
1 green pepper	
½ cup cheese	

Peel and cut carrots in thin, long slices; then French style, making strips approximately 2 inches long. Cover with water and boil until tender. Drain. Sprinkle with Season-all. Melt butter. Add green pepper. Sauté 10 minutes. Blend in flour, salt, paprika and Worcestershire sauce with milk. Stir in cheese. Cook 5 minutes. Place carrots in dish and pour sauce over them and serve. Serves 6.

CABBAGE

Try cabbage in your old-fashioned boiled dinner pot. Do not overcook or have too much fat in it—it's not necessary, and it's not good for you. So don't abuse the cabbage, and it won't abuse you.

OLD-FASHIONED CABBAGE DINNER

1 medium head green cabbage, 3 or 4 pounds	¼ teaspoon celery seed
	¼ teaspoon pepper
1 bunch carrots	8 small onions
6 to 8 new potatoes	2 green peppers
2 pounds corned beef or smoked ham hocks	1 teaspoon salt
	½ teaspoon paprika

Wash and cut cabbage in 6 to 8 sections. Scrape carrots and potatoes. Cut peppers in quarters. Let vegetables stand in cold water. Boil corned beef or ham hocks until well done. Be sure there is not over 2 cups of water left in the pot with the meat. Add vegetables to meat. Sprinkle onions and all vegetables with salt, pepper, paprika, and celery seed. Boil no longer than ½ hour. When potatoes and carrots are done, your cabbage will be ready to eat. Place vegetables and meat attractively on a large platter. Sprinkle with fresh chopped parlsey, and serve with tasty, crunchy corn sticks. Serves 6.

Slices of whole fresh tomatoes may be added in the last 10 minutes of cooking for a colorful touch.

For variety you can supplement cabbage with string beans.

CABBAGE 'N' BUTTER

1 medium head green cabbage	dash pepper
	½ teaspoon paprika
1 teaspoon salt	pinch sugar
⅓ cup butter	1 small onion

Wash and shred cabbage and onion. Cover with water. Simmer 10 to 15 minutes. Drain off most of water. Add salt, pepper, sugar and butter. Steam 15 minutes longer. Remove from heat. Chop very fine and garnish with parsley and paprika. Serves 4 to 6.

SWEET AND SOUR RED CABBAGE

2 pounds red cabbage (shredded)	1 small onion
	2 tablespoons bacon fat
1 cup water	1 teaspoon lemon juice or
1 tablespoon sugar	vinegar
1/8 teaspoon salt	1/2 teaspoon pepper

Brown 1 onion, chopped, in bacon fat or butter. Add red cabbage, water, sugar, salt and pepper. Cook 15 minutes with cover. Uncover; add 1 tablespoon lemon juice or vinegar. Cook 5 minutes longer. Serves 4 to 6.

SPECIAL BOILED CAULIFLOWER

1 head cauliflower	2 cups milk
1 teaspoon salt	water

Trim green leaves and stems and all dark spots from cauliflower, being careful not to cut apart. Place in a pan of salted water. Soak 30 minutes. Drain. Place in a pan with milk and salted water to cover. Boil 20 to 25 minutes until tender. Serve with drawn butter sauce.

For variety, try a medium white sauce over cauliflower. Arrange whole almonds into head artistically, or chop medium fine and sprinkle over vegetable. Serves 4 to 6.

CAULIFLOWER À LA HOLLANDAISE

Remove leaves, cut off stalk, and soak 30 minutes (head down) in cold water to cover. Cook (head up) 20 minutes or until soft, in boiling salted water. Drain and serve with Hollandaise sauce.

PLAIN BOILED CAULIFLOWER

Trim cauliflower. Wash well and drain. Cook head down in boiling water for about 20 minutes. Be careful not to overcook. Add salt.

CELERY

Little celery triplets ... the hearts that win your favor ...
crisp, fresh and sweet ... the lovely soft, green leaves ...
blended into yellow, then white. The use of celery is not limited to salads and appetizers. Although it gives every menu
that extra touch and brightens up the table, you must not overlook the fact it is a wonderful vegetable with vitamin qualities.

I overlooked it, too, until I met a mother who spends her
days creating inexpensive dishes that will please her large
family. When she finishes her job as a cook and has left over
celery leaves and stalks, she invents things to do with them.
Here they are—good, edible and unusual.

BOILED CELERY AND ONIONS

3 cups chopped celery and   *1 teaspoon salt*
*   leaves*   *½ teaspoon celery salt*
1 cup chopped onions (if   *½ teaspoon pepper*
*   green onions are used,*   *1 cup water*
*   add tops)*   *2 tablespoons butter*
1 teaspoon sugar

Place celery, onions and water in a pan. Steam 15 minutes.
Add seasonings and butter. Steam 5 minutes more. Serves 4
to 6.

Omit onions for plain boiled celery and increase celery to
4 cups.

CREAMED CELERY AND CORN

4 large, firm green peppers   *1 cup whole kernel corn*
2 stalks green celery, diced   *1 onion, diced*
1 cup thick white sauce   *½ cup buttered bread*
paprika to taste   *   crumbs*

Wash peppers, cut off tops, and remove seeds. Soak in salted
water 15 minutes. Cut celery in small pieces and add onion.
Boil 15 minutes in salted water. Drain well. Add corn and thick
white sauce. Fill peppers which have been drained and salted
inside. Top with buttered bread crumbs. Place in a greased
baking dish and bake in moderate oven 25 minutes. Serves 4.

Save celery water for soups or gravies.

CREAMED CELERY

3 cups celery cut in medium pieces	salt, pepper and paprika to taste
2 tablespoons grated onion	½ teaspoon salt
2 tablespoons chopped green peppers	⅓ cup butter
2 cups milk	4 tablespoons flour
1 cup water	1 tablespoon grated cheese

Simmer celery, green pepper and onion in water about 15 minutes. Add salt, pepper and paprika. Melt butter in pan. Add flour. Blend well. Add cheese, then milk. Cook slowly until medium thick. Add celery and bring to a slow boil. Pour into a dish to serve. Sprinkle with paprika. Serves 4 to 6.

Try cooking celery with your string beans or green peas. Don't overlook its importance in soups, stews, goulash and gumbo!

CORN

Combine green or red sweet peppers, onions and tops, celery and mushrooms with corn.

Combine creamed corn with lima beans, whole kernel corn, string beans, tomatoes, or peas for variations.

When fresh corn is in season, *use it;* the flavor is definitely different!

The recipes are given for fresh corn since they are from country homes where corn is grown and utilized to save pennies. Canned whole kernel, creamed or frozen corn may be used just as well.

Try corn on the cob, buttered and rolled in grated cheese— or parsley, paprika or lemon butter.

FRIED CORN

1 dozen ears fresh corn or 1 can whole kernel corn	dash paprika
	1 minced onion
¼ cup bacon fat or butter	2 tablespoons milk
¼ cup minced parsley	1 teaspoon sugar

Cut corn from cob. Mix all ingredients in a bowl and season. Add onion to fat and sauté in frying pan. Add corn and cook about 20 minutes until each grain is soft, stirring constantly. Serves 4 to 6.

Fried corn is an excellent breakfast or luncheon dish, with whole strips of bacon on top.

For more fancy varieties, mix 1 cup chopped crisp bacon or minced ham into corn. One-half cup chopped celery, pimientos and green peppers do a bang-up job!

For a yellow and green platter, use parsley and olives. The results will definitely surprise you.

CORN CHEESE

Combine 2 cups corn cut from cob, or creamed corn, ¼ cup milk, salt, 1 teaspoon pepper, 1 teaspoon sugar, 1 cup grated cheese. Heat well. Do not brown. Serves 4.

CORN PUDDING

2 cups grated corn cut from cob or 1 No. 2 can cream corn	dash mace or nutmeg
	4 eggs
1 quart milk	3 tablespoons melted butter
1 teaspoon salt	2 tablespoons sugar
	1 teaspoon celery salt

Beat egg yolks. Add sugar, butter and milk. Beat well again. Mix with corn and spices. Add to egg yolks. Beat egg whites until stiff and fold into egg yolk mixture. Place in a greased casserole dish. Set in oven to bake at 350° F. about 1 hour. If pudding browns too fast, place a piece of heavy brown paper on top. Serves 6.

Who can suggest a tastier combination than corn pudding and a roast fillet of beef?

SPICY HOT CORN

2 cups fresh garden corn (yellow bantam)	2 tablespoons butter
	2 cloves
1 onion	2 tablespoons sugar
½ cup white vinegar	1 teaspoon salt
1 tablespoon Tabasco sauce or red pepper	1 teaspoon grated lemon rind
	sprig celery

Melt butter in pan. Add onion and celery, then vinegar, spices,

VEGETABLES ON PARADE

Tabasco sauce, corn, and lemon rind. Season. Simmer 20 minutes, covered. Sprinkle with paprika and serve. Serves 6. Something special with roast pork or ham!

CORN CUSTARD, SOUTHERN STYLE

3 or 4 eggs
2 cups canned, creamstyle
   corn
1 teaspoon sugar
2 tablespoons melted butter
   or substitute

2 cups warm milk
dash nutmeg
salt and pepper to taste
½ cup cracker crumbs or
   buttered bread crumbs

Beat eggs well. Add corn, sugar, melted butter and milk. Stir well. Add seasonings, and place in a greased baking dish. Sprinkle with crumbs which have been warmed in 2 tablespoons butter. Bake in a slow oven, 275° F., about 45 minutes or until custard is set. Serves 4 to 6.

CAROLYNE BRYANT'S EGGPLANT

1 eggplant
2 chopped onions
1 green pepper, chopped
½ cup chopped celery
2 tablespoons bacon fat

1 medium can minced clams
1 cup tomatoes
salt and pepper to taste
1 cup bread crumbs
2 tablespoons melted butter

Wash and pare eggplant. Cut in pieces. Parboil about 20 minutes. Drain. Sauté onions, peppers and celery in bacon fat. Add clams, eggplant, tomatoes and seasonings. Grease a casserole dish, place in it a layer of eggplant mixture, a layer of bread crumbs that have been added to melted butter, and repeat until casserole is full and top layer is bread crumbs. Bake in moderate oven, 350° F., for 40 minutes. Serves 6.

EGGPLANT CASSEROLE

1 medium eggplant
3 medium onions
1 green pepper
½ teaspoon garlic salt

4 tablespoons cooking fat
1 teaspoon salt
¼ teaspoon pepper
1 cup grated cheese

Peel eggplant and onions. Slice in medium rounds. Stem and seed pepper and cut into rings. Cook in salted water until tender. Drain. Place in casserole. Season with garlic salt and pepper. Cover with cheese and bake in hot oven, 375° F. for 20 minutes. Serves 6.

FRIED EGGPLANT

Select firm, fresh eggplant. Wash, peel and cut in slices. Sprinkle with salt, cover and let stand 1 hour. Dip in beaten egg and 1 teaspoon lemon juice, then into bread or cracker crumbs. Fry in deep fat until brown. Serves 4 to 6.

MIXED GREENS

It is amazing to realize that even in far off Cuba, where you least expect it, you run into a chef cooking dishes that are typically Southern.

One had the most charming way of making people feel that they were doing him a favor when they ate his food. He followed no set rules in his cooking. From nothing more than a description of a dish, its ingredients and taste, he was able to produce it in the shortest possible time.

To those who had never heard of the dish, a pot of "mixed greens and ham" becomes a "must."

OLD-FASHIONED MIXED GREENS

1 bunch kale	1 bunch spinach
1 bunch turnip or beet tops	1 bunch collards
1 bunch green onions	pinch baking soda
1 garlic clove	1 pound bacon, ham or
several red pepper pods	salt pork
(cabbage sprouts may be	salt and pepper to taste
substituted as a green)	

Parboil meat in about 3 cups of water. Add chopped onions, garlic and seasonings. Pick and wash greens thoroughly, making sure they are free from sand. Cut in small pieces. Add to meat. Cook moderately 1½ to 2 hours. Serves 6 to 8.

COLLARD GREENS AND KALE

1½ to 2 pounds ham, bacon	salt and pepper to taste
or salt pork	1 teaspoon celery salt
2 garlic cloves	2 red pepper pods

177

VEGETABLES ON PARADE

2 onions	1 tablespoon sugar
4 pounds greens	1 teaspoon Season-all

Wash and clean greens well through several salt waters. Boil meat in just enough water to cover. Add pepper and seasonings. Add greens which have been cut in small pieces and boil 1½ hours. Serves 4.

Serve hot with corn bread, lettuce and tomato salad and baked sweets.

If salt pork or bacon are used, cut in small pieces. Fry or render fat. Place 1 quart of water in pot.

For best results use as little water as possible when cooking greens.

BOILED TURNIP GREENS

3 bunches fresh turnip greens	1 tablespoon sugar
1 pound bacon ends or salt pork	1 garlic clove
	2 teaspoons salt
2 red pepper pods	1 quart water

Wash greens thoroughly. Cut away tough stems. Chop greens in small pieces. Cut bacon or salt pork in small pieces. Add water and boil slowly. Add pepper pods, sugar, salt and garlic, then chopped greens. Cook until tender. When done, drain water. Place on platter with meat in center. Turnips may be peeled and cooked with greens. Serves 6.

Serve with corn bread and garden salad.

Turnips may be boiled and served in a cream sauce, or baked whole with your roasts.

SWISS CHARD

2 bunches Swiss chard	1 teaspoon salt
½ teaspoon celery salt	3 tablespoons butter
½ teaspoon seasoned salt	pinch sugar

Wash well and cut green leaves from white mid ribs of chard. Trim mid ribs and cut in small pieces. Cover with salted water and boil 15 minutes. Cut green leaves in small pieces and add to rest of chard. Cook 30 minutes until tender. Drain. Season with butter and seasonings. Serve as a vegetable. Serves 6.

WILTED LETTUCE

1 head leaf lettuce	*2 tablespoons vinegar*
4 slices bacon	*¼ teaspoon salt*

Wash lettuce thoroughly. Cut into shreds with scissors or sharp knife. Measure 4 cups, put leaves into colander or sieve, and pour boiling water over them until wilted. Drain thoroughly. Fry diced bacon slowly until crisp. Add vinegar and salt. Pour hot bacon dressing over lettuce. Serves 4.

HOMINY GRITS

1 cup hominy grits	*1 teaspoon salt*
4 cups boiling water	*2 tablespoons butter*

Add salt and butter to boiling water. Then add hominy grits slowly, stirring constantly. Lower heat and cook from 40 to 60 minutes, stirring frequently. Serve hot. More butter may be added, also a bit of pepper or paprika. Serves 4 to 6.

Serve hominy grits for breakfast, or with stews, hash, fried meat and gravy at dinner.

BAKED CASSEROLE OF WHOLE HOMINY WITH
CHEESE SAUCE

1 large can whole hominy	*¼ pound grated American*
1 teaspoon celery salt	*cheese*
1 teaspoon paprika	*2 cups medium white sauce*
1 teaspoon nutmeg	*1 teaspoon Tabasco sauce*

Mix strained hominy with white sauce. Add seasonings. Place in casserole. Sprinkle with grated cheese and nutmeg. Bake 20 to 30 minutes in a hot oven. Serves 4 to 6.

SAUTÉED WHOLE HOMINY

1 No. 2 can whole hominy	*salt, pepper and paprika*
1 tablespoon chopped	*to taste*
parsley	*2 tablespoons grated onion*
	⅓ cup butter

Sauté onion in butter. Add hominy. Season with salt and pepper. Simmer 20 minutes. Place in vegetable dish. Sprinkle with parsley and paprika. Serves 6.

VEGETABLES ON PARADE

MUSHROOMS

Mushrooms add a delightful touch to the dreariest of dishes. They are tasty, and when prepared correctly will appease the appetite of the most fastidious eater.

I met an interesting old cook in the South who insisted on calling them "toadstools." I can well remember the warnings received as a child against toadstools and the poisonous distinction between them and wild mushrooms. But I did love the old woman's way of expressing herself, and her use of mushrooms. She had no set recipes but whenever her "folks" wanted something special she "threw in" a few mushrooms and produced a wonderful dish.

I wouldn't go so far as to suggest that you "throw" mushrooms into your cakes or pies or in the middle of your favorite roll dough, but I do say, try them: add them to your stews, roasts and vegetables. Be an improviser. If you follow your cooking sense, you will be able to tell right from wrong, but here are a few tips to guide you.

To clean mushrooms, wash well in a small amount of water or under running water. If they are full of grit and dirt, scrub with a brush. Cut off discolored end of stems. Peel mushrooms if they are tough. Young, tender caps do not need peeling.

Mushrooms can be fried or sautéed. Melt butter, add mushrooms, cover and cook over low heat 10 to 15 minutes (add chopped onion and celery, if desired).

Mushrooms can also be creamed. Follow method of frying. When mushrooms have cooked 5 minutes, add 2 tablespoons flour, blend and add 1 cup cream or milk. Cover and cook 5 minutes. Season with salt and pepper.

To broil mushrooms, slice or leave whole. If stems are tough, chop. Season, dot with butter and broil for 10 minutes.

PICKLED MUSHROOMS

1 cup mild vinegar	*1 clove garlic*
2 tablespoons pickling sauce	*2 tablespoons sugar*
1 bay leaf	*2 pounds mushrooms*

Place all spices and sugar in vinegar and boil for 15 minutes. Strain. Wash and cut dark ends off stems of mushrooms. Boil in salted water 10 minutes. Drain off water; pour hot strained vinegar and spices over mushrooms and bring to a boil. Cool and serve on toothpicks as an appetizer. Serves 6 to 8.

BOILED OKRA

Wash oka well and trim stems carefully. Do not cut ends too close. Sprinkle with salt. Cover okra with boiling water. Boil gently until tender. When done, drain off water. Sprinkle with onion salt, pepper and butter. Cover and let stand a few minutes.

OKRA AND TOMATOES

1 onion, diced	½ pound okra, diced
3 cups tomatoes, canned or fresh	3 tablespoons butter or bacon fat
salt and pepper to taste	pinch sugar

Sauté onion in fat, add okra and fry 5 minutes. Add tomatoes, sugar, salt and pepper. Cover and cook 15 minutes. Remove cover, and simmer 5 minutes longer. Serves 6.

If you like pepper, add a chopped green pepper to onion and proceed as instructed.

OKRA GUMBO

1 pound fresh okra	1 teaspoon paprika
2 green peppers	1 can whole kernel corn
2 cups chopped celery and leaves	2 onions
	1 garlic clove
3 tablespoons butter or bacon fat	1 No. 2 can tomatoes
	¼ teaspoon celery salt
1 teaspoon sugar	½ teaspoon thyme
¼ teaspoon garlic salt	

Sauté onion, pepper, garlic and celery in fat. Add corn and seasonings, then okra which has been washed and cut. Add tomatoes and simmer 30 minutes. Serves 6.

OKRA WITH FRESH CORN

Wash and trim 1 pound of okra. Leave enough of the pod so juices won't run out. Cover with hot water, boil until tender. When half done, add 1 teaspoon salt, 1 tablespoon sugar, ¼ teaspoon black pepper. Add 1 cup chopped onion, 1 cup fresh kernel corn cut from cob. Cook 15 minutes. Drain water and add 2 tablespoons butter. Steam for 5 minutes over very low fire. Serve hot.

ONIONS

Onions are among the healthiest vegetables we can eat. They are, therefore, a necessity in your vegetable bin, as well as on your menus; fried, steamed, creamed, baked or raw. However offensive the odor of raw onions may be to some, they are high in food value. It has been said that a glass of milk will destroy the odor of raw onions on one's breath.

On the farm we were often given onion stew as a remedy for colds and there are many folk today who can convince you that the lonely onion is an infallible remedy. But no matter what their therapeutic value, onions produce magic in your dishes.

ONIONS WITH PARSLEY

10 small onions	*2 tablespoons butter*
¼ cup parsley	*1 teaspoon lemon juice*
½ teaspoon celery salt	*1 teaspoon salt*
½ teaspoon paprika	

Peel onions, pierce with fork. Boil in salted water 15 minutes. Drain well. Melt butter, add parsley, lemon juice, celery, salt. Pour over onions. Sprinkle with paprika. Cover and steam 5 minutes. Serves 4 to 6.

Fresh green onions and tops may be cooked in the same manner.

PAN SAUTÉED ONIONS

4 large Bermuda onions	*2 to 4 slices bacon*
salt, pepper, and paprika	*dash red pepper*
to taste	

Fry bacon in skillet until crisp. Remove bacon. Peel and slice onions in rounds. Lay in pan with bacon fat, simmer slowly 15 minutes, turning carefully so as not to break. Add salt, seasonings and chopped cooked bacon. Cover and steam 15 minutes longer. Serve over meats or as a vegetable.

Green pepper rings and celery may be added if desired.

PEAS

Canned peas may be used for any recipe. Just be careful not to overcook. If you do, they will mush since they are pre-cooked and only need to be heated. If you use frozen peas, follow directions given on package.

In the country I have seen peas cooked with whole kernel corn, chopped lettuce and onions. I had my doubts at the time, but they were fine eating, and I suggest you try preparing them that way, too.

Have you ever tried chopped celery in your fresh green or frozen peas? If not, you are in for a delightful surprise. Mushrooms and pimientos cooked with peas not only improve their appearance but contribute a new, piquant flavor.

PEAS WITH MINT

At a dinner I attended, I remarked to my hostess, "These peas are something to rave about! May I be so inquisitive as to ask just how they were prepared?" Her reply floored me since I didn't expect it to be an age-old recipe. She told me, "My great grandma started this recipe by putting the peas in a pot of boiling water and mint meant for mint tea. Discovering her mistake, she made the best of the error by adding a few tricks to season them in her own inimitable way."

I heartily recommend this recipe. Nothing could be finer with lamb.

2 pounds fresh peas	*¼ cup butter*
1 teaspoon salt	*½ cup finely chopped*
4 or 5 sprigs mint	*green onion tops*
1 teaspoon sugar	

Place several sprigs of mint and stems in a pot of boiling water. Add fresh peas which have been shelled. Boil 20 minutes or until peas are done. Strain all but 1 cup water from peas. Add a few chopped mint leaves. Steam butter, salt, pepper and onion tops 15 to 20 minutes. When water has absorbed and peas are tender, sprinkle with paprika. Serves 6.

PEAS AND GREEN PEPPERS

2 green peppers (sliced)	*1 teaspoon Season-all*
1 cup diced celery	*½ teaspoon sweet basil*

VEGETABLES ON PARADE

½ teaspoon paprika   3 tablespoons butter
¼ teaspoon onion salt

Sauté peppers and celery in butter. Cook 15 minutes. Do not brown! Add seasonings and 2 cups of cooked green peas. Serves 4 to 6.

PEAS AND MUSHROOMS

2 pounds fresh peas
2 small onions
1 teaspoon salt
1 teaspoon paprika
1 cup heavy cream
pinch rosemary
1 pound mushrooms

¼ cup butter
½ teaspoon celery salt
1 teaspoon sugar
1 tablespoon Worcestershire
     sauce
1 cup boiling water

Shell and wash peas. Place in sauce pan of boiling water. Sauté onions in butter until brown. Add mushrooms. Cook 15 minutes, then add seasonings and cream. Simmer 10 minutes. Drain peas and pour mixture over peas. Add Worcestershire sauce. Serves 6.

Peas may be served in a thin cream sauce, with or without cheese.

NEW ORLEANS PEPPERS

6 large sweet green peppers
boiling water to cover
2 cups bread crumbs,
     moistened
3 tablespoons butter
1 onion, minced
1 teaspoon Worcestershire
     sauce

1 clove garlic (optional)
2 sprigs parsley or chopped
     celery tops
1 egg, beaten
1 teaspoon salt
1 cup cooked or
     canned shrimp

Place peppers in a saucepan. Cover with boiling water. Let stand 5 minutes. Drain. Remove stems and seeds. Trim bottom of each pepper to allow them to stand upright. Melt 2 tablespoons butter. Cook onion, garlic, parsley or celery 1 minute, stirring constantly. Add bread crumbs, squeezed dry. Heat well. Add cut shrimp, salt, Worcestershire sauce. Remove from heat and add egg. Season to taste. Fill pepper cups. Set in pan containing ¼ inch boiling water. Dot with butter. Bake until brown, adding more water if necessary. Baking time 20 to 30 minutes. Serves 6.

GREEN PEPPERS WITH ONION AND TOMATO SLICES

6 green peppers	4 Bermuda onions
6 firm tomatoes	¼ cup butter or oil
½ teaspoon celery salt	pinch of sugar
2 tablespoons water	½ teaspoon salt
¼ teaspoon pepper.	

Cut tops from peppers and tomatoes, slice thin. Peel onions, cut in rings. Place butter in pan. Add peppers and onions. Cook 10 to 15 minutes, stirring constantly. Lay tomato slices on top of peppers. Add seasonings and water. Cover and steam 10 minutes. Serve as vegetable. Serves 4 to 6.

STUFFED GREEN PEPPERS No. 1

1 small can corn	1 medium onion
4 fresh tomatoes	8 to 10 finely chopped green
2 tablespoons butter	or stuffed olives
½ cup bread crumbs	1 teaspoon seasoned salt
1 teaspoon paprika	1 garlic clove
pinch sugar	dash red pepper
6 green peppers, uniform in size	

Cut tops off peppers. Remove centers and seeds. Drop peppers in hot water. Cook slowly 15 to 20 minutes. Remove from water and drain. Place peppers in baking dish. Sauté seasonings, onions, tomatoes, garlic and corn in fat. Cook 15 minutes. Add chopped olives. Fill peppers and sprinkle bread crumbs on top. Dot with butter and bake until crumbs are brown.

Use small firm peppers for stuffing. Large peppers may have a tendency to be tough.

STUFFED GREEN PEPPERS No. 2

6 large peppers	1 tablespoon prepared
2 tablespoons bacon fat	mustard

VEGETABLES ON PARADE

1 chopped onion
sprig parsley or a few green
    onion tops
1 teaspoon paprika
2 ripe tomatoes

1 cup boiled rice
¼ cup chopped celery
½ cup grated cheese
salt and pepper to taste

Cut tops from peppers. Remove center and seeds. Parboil peppers about 5 minutes in boiling salted water. Drain. Sauté onions, parsley and celery in fat until brown. Dice tomatoes and add to vegetables. Cook until tomatoes are done and mixture is thick. Add water, rice and seasonings. Turn off heat. Add cheese. Mix well. Fill peppers. Set top on each pepper. Place in a baking dish. Add small amount of water to baking dish to prevent sticking. Bake about 25 minutes at 350° F. Serves 6.

Leftover meat may be chopped and added to peppers with shrimp or leftover fish.

BAKED POTATOES   (Stuffed with Leftovers)

6 potatoes
½ cup hot milk
¼ cup butter
2 cups leftover meat and
    vegetables

1 teaspoon Season-all
salt and pepper to taste
paprika, grated cheese, or
    parsley

Select large uniform-sized potatoes. Wash and grease and pierce with a fork. Bake in a moderate oven 45 minutes to 1 hour. Cut slice from top of each potato, scoop out inside and mash, adding hot milk, butter, and seasonings. Beat until fluffy. Line potato shells with mashed potatoes, leaving center unfilled. Place leftover meat and vegetables, chopped and mixed well together, in center of potatoes. Cover with more mashed potato and sprinkle with paprika, grated cheese, or parsley. Bake 10 to 15 minutes longer. Serves 6.

LYONNAISE POTATOES

2 cups diced boiled
    potatoes
salt and pepper to taste

1 whole chopped onion
2 tablespoons fat
1 tablespoon chopped parsley

The potatoes should be slightly undercooked to produce the best results. Season with salt and pepper. Sauté the onion in fat until light brown. Add the potatoes and stir with a fork until all sides are brown, being careful not to break the potatoes. Add more fat if necessary. When done, transfer potatoes to a hot dish, sprinkle parsley over top and serve hot. Serves 4.

SPECIAL FRIED POTATOES

6 *medium raw potatoes*	2 *green peppers*
2 *onions*	1 *teaspoon salt*
½ *teaspoon celery salt*	½ *teaspoon pepper*
½ *teaspoon paprika*	¼ *cup bacon fat*

Wash and peel potatoes and onions. Dice. Remove seeds and tops of peppers and dice. Heat fat in pan. Add vegetables and seasonings. Cook, turning frequently until brown and crisp.

Bits of parsley or sliced stuffed olives may be added.

SOUTHERN FRIED POTATOES

Wash and pare small potatoes, cut into lengthwise strips, ¼ inch thick, soak in cold water 1 hour. Dry, dip in slightly beaten egg, then in bread crumbs and place in a frying basket. Immerse in hot deep fat 375° F. and cook 3 to 5 minutes or until brown. Drain on absorbent paper, sprinkle with salt. Serve hot.

STUFFED BAKED POTATOES

4 or 5 *medium or large potatoes*	1 *teaspoon onion juice or onion salt*
½ *cup hot milk, or diluted evaporated milk*	4 *tablespoons butter*
½ *teaspoon salt*	1 *egg yolk*
2 *tablespoons grated cheese*	*dash cayenne pepper*

Rub skins of scrubbed potatoes with oil or fat. Bake in moderate oven until you can pierce with fork. Remove from oven. Slice in halves lengthwise. Scoop out potatoes carefully. Set shells aside. Put potato pulp through ricer into a bowl. Season with salt, pepper, butter, onion juice and hot milk. Whip. Season to taste. Fill potato shells, leaving a mound in centers. Brush with egg yolk and sprinkle with grated cheese. Brown in moderate oven. Serve hot, two halves to a portion.

VEGETABLES ON PARADE

Oven temperature: 350 to 375° F. Baking time: 45 to 60 minutes.

SPECIAL MASHED WHITE POTATOES

6 to 8 medium potatoes
½ cup milk or cream
1 teaspoon salt
pinch baking powder

¼ cup butter
½ teaspoon celery salt
¼ teaspoon white pepper

Peel potatoes and boil in salted water until done. Drain. Mash until all lumps disappear. Add butter, cream and seasonings with baking powder. Beat hard until light and fluffy. Serves 6 to 8.

For variety, add parsley, chopped pimientos or green onion tops to creamy mashed potatoes.

Add ¼ cup grated cheese to mashed potatoes for variety. Pimientos or chopped olives, grated fresh celery and carrots are also good. Bits of boiled celery and celery leaves are excellent too, as is parsley.

Add an egg to leftover mashed potatoes and form into patties to be fried or baked.

Mix leftover vegetables in mashed potatoes. Form into patties. Roll in crumbs and bake.

BAKED MASHED POTATOES WITH CHEESE

6 medium potatoes
¼ cup butter
½ cup milk
1 teaspoon salt
dash nutmeg

½ teaspoon paprika
⅓ cup parsley, chopped
½ cup grated cheese
dash pepper

Peel and boil potatoes until done in salted water. Mash with potato masher or put through a ricer. Add butter, milk and seasonings. Beat until all ingredients are light and fluffy. Whip in cheese and parsley. Place in a baking dish. Sprinkle with nutmeg. Bake 15 minutes in a hot oven. Serves 6.

MASHED POTATOES AND YELLOW TURNIPS
(Rutabagas)

3 medium potatoes
⅓ cup hot milk

3 tablespoons butter
1 teaspoon salt

188

1 medium yellow turnip   ¼ teaspoon pepper
pinch sugar

Peel and dice vegetables. Cook in salted water separately. Add sugar to rutabagas. Cook until tender. Drain. Combine the vegetables and seasonings. Mash. Add milk gradually, also butter. Beat until light and fluffy. Serves 6 to 8.

Good at holiday time!

RICE

Rice has been a problem to many of us, and cooking it according to each person's preference can certainly confuse the best of cooks. We all want one thing; dry, flaky rice where the grains stand alone! If you have invented your own method, you have indeed accomplished a feat. As the old folks say, "You may take the long way 'round, but you get there." That's what really matters, the getting there with rice. Whether you use the boiler method, brown paper, steam, frying pan, butter method or hot water and vinegar method.

During my childhood in South Dakota, rice was only served as a dessert or a breakfast dish, so I have had to become acquainted with rice. I have been educating myself to the "facts of rice-life," and now I am ready to pass them on to you!

Packaged rice is best because you can eliminate washing. There are several modern brands that are so very easy to fix that there should be no rice failures.

BOILED RICE No. 1

6 cups boiling water   1 teaspoon salt
2 cups long grained brown   1 teaspoon vinegar
   rice

Add salt and vinegar to boiling water. Add rice slowly, few grains at a time. Boil rapidly 15 minutes. Pour water off rice. Drain. Place in colander over hot water. Cover and steam until tender and dry. Serves 6.

BOILED RICE No. 2

4 cups boiling water   1 tablespoon shortening
1 cup white rice   1 teaspoon salt

Add salt and shortening to boiling water. Sprinkle rice into boiling water. Boil 20 minutes until tender. When you can crush a grain between your fingers, rice is done. Drain balance of water. Blanch with cold water, then hot water to reheat, or place in oven for 5 minutes. Serves 4.

BOILED RICE No. 3

3 cups boiling water	1 teaspoon salt
1 cup rice	½ teaspoon vinegar
2 tablespoons butter	

Add salt and vinegar to boiling water. Wash rice, pour into water slowly. Cover and boil gently 15 to 20 minutes or until water is absorbed. Add butter. Stir gently with fork. Continue to steam 5 minutes until dry. Serves 4.

PAPRIKA RICE

1 tablespoon paprika	4 cups boiling water
1 teaspoon salt	pinch white pepper
2 tablespoons butter	1 tablespoon celery salt
1 cup long-grained rice	

Wash rice well. Add salt and boiling water. Boil 5 minutes. Do not stir. Drain off water. Add paprika and butter. Stir with fork until blended. Return to heat. Cover and steam for 5 minutes. Remove cover. Continue to steam 15 minutes longer over very low heat.

BOILED RICE CREOLE

Wash rice thoroughly in cold water; place water in large pot to boil—about 1 quart for 1 cup rice, and 1 tablespoon salt. Pour rice into boiling water carefully so grains will not stick together. As soon as grains start to soften, do not stir; boil 20 minutes—at longest, 25 minutes. Test grains by mashing between your fingers. If rice is solid but soft, drain off water. Place a small amount of shortening or butter in pan; return rice and steam on very low heat. Do not cover as steam will make rice too soft.

Serve with your favorite dish!

MOLDED RICE

Add ½ cup melted butter to 2 cups cooked rice. Place in a greased mold; pack tightly, and let set 15 to 20 minutes on warm stove or in warm oven. Turn out carefully on a hot platter.

Should mold break, mold into shape with fingers.

Chopped parsley, or salted almonds with paprika make a colorful mold.

SPANISH RICE

1 cup whole grain brown rice	⅓ cup tomato sauce or
3 cups boiling water	3 tablespoons paste
1 teaspoon salt	3 tablespoons butter or bacon
1 garlic clove, chopped	fat
1 small onion	1 tablespoon celery, chopped
1 small green pepper	

Sauté onion, pepper, garlic and celery in fat in a heavy skillet. (Do not allow to brown.) When tender, add unwashed rice. Stir until well mixed and all grains are semi-fried. Add tomato paste or sauce, seasonings and hot water. Stir until well mixed. Do not cover. Cook over very low heat until rice is dry, light and fluffy. Grains should be whole and firm. (If it is necessary to stir when adding water, use a fork. Refrain from stirring, if possible.) Serves 6.

Crushed salted almonds or diced stuffed olives make this a glamorous party dish. (A bit of thyme or a bay leaf cooked in the sauce, add a spicy taste.)

Plain cooked rice may be used for Spanish rice. Simple prepare your Spanish sauce and add rice, mixing well. Steam 10 to 15 minutes.

Some folk like rice dry and some with plenty of sauce. These things have to be worked out to suit your own family taste, which only you can determine. But moist or dry, a Spanish sauce simply does things to plain rice and brightens up the meal!

SPECIAL BOILED RICE

1 cup rice	2 tablespoons Parmesan
4 cups hot water	cheese

191

VEGETABLES ON PARADE

2 slices bacon   pinch saffron
2 tablespoons butter

Wash rice, chop bacon and add to water with salt and saffron.
Boil 10 minutes. Add cheese, then rice. Continue to boil for
about 15 to 20 minutes. Drain water. Steam rice uncovered
until dry. Before removing from heat, add 2 tablespoons butter. (Do not stir rice with a spoon; use a fork.) Serves 4 to 6.

CURRIED RICE

2 cups cooked rice   1 green pepper, sliced
1 onion, diced   2 teaspoons curry powder
½ cup water   2 teaspoons butter
salt and pepper to taste

Sauté onion and pepper in butter (do not brown). Add water,
curry powder, salt and pepper, then mix well. Cover and
steam over very low heat 15 minutes. Add rice. Mix gently
and serve with your favorite meat. Serves 4.

PARSLEY RICE

This dish may be prepared in the same way as Plain Boiled
Rice. Chop and crush parsley; add to rice after straining. Parsley pressed may at times be fresh enough to have a green
juice that will color the rice and make it most unusual.

RICE WITH PINEAPPLE

2 cups boiling water   ½ cup pineapple (crushed
1 cup whole grain rice   and drained)
1 teaspoon salt   2 tablespoons butter
dash paprika

Add salt to boiling water, then unwashed rice. Boil about 15
minutes, stirring with a fork. Drain, blanch in cold water. Add
butter and pineapple. Cover and return to heat and steam 10
to 15 minutes. Turn over lightly with a fork. Serves 4 to 6.

Serve with sweet and sour spareribs, ham or pork chops.

Grated orange and lemon are also used in rice most effectively.

VEGETABLES ON PARADE

RUTABAGAS

2 pounds rutabagas	1 tablespoon sugar
¼ cup chopped parsley	½ teaspoon paprika
1 small onion, chopped	2 tablespoons butter
salt and pepper to taste	

Wash, pare and dice rutabagas in tiny squares. Add salt, pepper, onion and enough water to cover. Boil 25 to 30 minutes. Drain water. Sprinkle with sugar and paprika. Add butter and parsley. Steam 10 to 15 minutes. Serves 4 to 6.

MASHED RUTABAGAS
(Yellow Turnips)

2 pounds rutabagas	2 tablespoons butter
1 tablespoon sugar	½ teaspoon Season-all
¼ teaspoon pepper	dash paprika
2 tablespoons cream	1 teaspoon salt
pinch red pepper	

Wash, peel and cut rutabagas in small pieces. Add salt, pepper, onion and water to cover. Boil 25 to 30 minutes or until tender. Drain well. Mash with potato masher. Add butter, sugar, seasonings and cream. Beat until light and fluffy. Serves 4.

SPINACH

So they won't eat spinach! Why not try a few diced onions, 2 tablespoons of butter and ⅛ cup of tomato sauce in the bottom of the pan before you place the spinach (which has been cut fine before cooking) in the pan. No water, please. Cover, and simmer 10 to 15 minutes. Add salt and pepper. Turn upside down on the dish, and sprinkle with paprika. It's delicious!

SPINACH SURPRISE

2 pounds spinach	1 teaspoon salt
2 medium onions	½ teaspoon pepper
1 green pepper	½ teaspoon garlic salt
2 pimientos	¼ teaspoon thyme
3 tablespoons butter or bacon fat	¼ cup cream

Wash and chop spinach fine. Sauté chopped onion, green pepper and pimientos in butter. Add cream and seasonings. Simmer 10 minutes. Add spinach and continue to cook 10 to 12 minutes, stirring frequently. Serve hot. Serves 4.

SPINACH, RED PEPPERS AND OLIVES

2 pounds fresh spinach or
1 package frozen
3 slices bacon
6 to 8 ripe olives with
2 tablespoons juice

4 red sweet peppers
1 teaspoon salt
½ teaspoon pepper
¼ teaspoon nutmeg

Wash and clean spinach well. Remove tops and seeds from peppers, cut in thin slices. Chop bacon and fry slowly until brown. Add peppers, chopped olives and juice. Cover and simmer 10 minutes. Add spinach and cook 10 minutes longer. Season. Serves 4.

ZUCCHINI SQUASH WITH TOMATOES

1 to 2 pounds squash
1 garlic clove, chopped
1 onion, minced
2 tablespoons bacon fat or
butter

pinch sugar
2 fresh tomatoes, sliced
½ cup water
¼ cup grated cheese
salt and pepper to taste

Wash and cut up squash. Place in pan with garlic and onion. Add tomato slice and seasonings with fat. Pour water over mixture and steam 15 minutes. Drain off excess water and turn upside down in a vegetable dish. Sprinkle with grated cheese and paprika. Serves 6 to 8.

STUFFED ACORN SQUASH

4 acorn squash
1 egg
⅓ cup melted butter
1 teaspoon mace
⅓ cup crushed pineapple or

apple sauce
2 tablespoons honey or
sugar
1 teaspoon salt

Wash squash and cut in half. Sprinkle with salt and place cut side down in baking pan with small amount of water. Bake in moderate oven about 1 hour until soft. Cool. Scrape inside of squash into mixing bowl. Mash well. Add egg, honey and melted butter. Beat until light and well mixed. Add fruit and spice. (If mixture seems dry, add 2 tablespoons cream or milk.) Fill each shell with mixture. Dot with butter. Return to oven and bake 15 minutes longer. You can garnish each shell with cherries or pineapple slices. Serves 8.

A grand dish served with roast pork or fowl.

BAKED BANANA SQUASH

½ *banana squash*	*dash nutmeg*
1 teaspoon salt	¼ *cup melted butter*
½ *cup sugar*	

Scrub outside of squash. Cut into pieces about 4 inches square. Remove seeds and fibres. Cut off outside skin. Place in boiling water with salt. Cook 10 to 15 minutes, being careful not to break. Remove from water, place in a baking dish. Sprinkle with a mixture of melted butter, nutmeg and sugar. Bake 20 to 30 minutes in moderate oven until done. Serves 6.

Squash, like humans, change their clothes for the seasons. A heavy skin for winter, a thin one for summer.

STEAMED SUMMER SQUASH SUPREME

1 pound small squash	*dash nutmeg*
2 tablespoons butter	*salt, pepper and paprika to*
1 medium onion, diced	*taste*
2 small stalks celery,	*1 tablespoon*
chopped	*Worcestershire sauce*
1 green pepper, diced	*buttered breadcrumbs or*
⅓ *cup tomato sauce*	*grated cheese*

Select small, firm squash. Wash and remove brown ends. Sauté onion, celery, and pepper in butter. Add tomato sauce and diced squash. Steam 10 minutes; add Worcestershire and seasonings; steam 12 to 15 minutes longer. Serves 4.

After steaming, squash can be put in a well-greased baking dish, sprinkled with buttered bread crumbs or grated cheese and baked for 15 minutes.

BAKED ACORN OR HUBBARD SQUASH

3 acorn squash	*2 tablespoons butter*
3 tablespoons honey	*1 teaspoon ginger*
salt to taste	*dash nutmeg*

Wash and cut squash in half. Remove seeds. Bake, cut-side down, in moderate oven 350° F. 20 minutes. Turn over. Fill each squash with mixture made of butter, honey, salt, nutmeg and ginger. Continue to bake 30 to 40 minutes.

If Hubbard squash is used, cut in large squares and follow the same method given. Serves 6.

ITALIAN GREEN SQUASH
(Zucchini)

1 pound Zucchini	1 teaspoon salt
2 medium onions	2 tablespoons butter
1 teaspoon sugar	1 teaspoon paprika
½ cup water	½ teaspoon celery salt

Scrub squash—do not peel. Cut off ends. Slice in thin rounds as cucumbers. Arrange a layer of squash and a layer of onion which has been cut in thin rounds. Sprinkle with salt and pepper. Add sugar, celery salt, paprika and water. Cook 15 minutes covered over a low flame. Do not stir the last 5 minutes. Drain any remaining water and add butter. Steam 2 or 3 minutes to melt butter. Serve hot. Serves 4.

SWEET 'TATERS

The old adage, "You can learn something new every day" was quoted by a very "young" great-grandmother of 72 whom I happened to meet in Georgia. When I complimented her on her very fine recipes for sweet potatoes and yams, she surprised me by asking if I knew their origin. I answered quickly that they came from the South. Well, that answer was a little too quick since I was promptly told that I needed to study up on this protein vegetable. For indeed there is a great difference between the original yam and the sweet potato and yam of today.

The original yam, she told me, was brought over from Africa. As for the sweet 'taters, well, they're sort of "country cousins" to the yam. "Tain't nowhere as sweet and juicy," she said. "Course, they are still good and I can get together some fine doings with them. They always told me sweet 'taters came from American soil, and I guess they do. But as long as I can 'count for the yam, I ain't gonna worry 'bout where the sweet 'taters came from."

I guess if the truth were known and we did take time to study the origin of foods, we would have many surprises in store.

YAMS WITH APPLE SLICES

6 medium yams	1 teaspoon cinnamon
3 apples	¼ cup melted butter
6 red cherries and juice	¼ cup brown sugar
1 cup milk	2 tablespoons white sugar
1 egg	2 tablespoons lemon juice
1 teaspoon nutmeg	1 teaspoon salt

Slice apples in half. Remove core. Parboil 10 minutes. Set aside to cool. Wash and boil yams until soft. Mash. Add egg, sugar, spices, butter and milk, then lemon juice. Place in a greased baking dish. Place apples on top of mashed sweets. Place a cherry in the center of each apple. Sprinkle with white sugar and pour cherry juice over entire dish. Bake 40 minutes in a moderate oven. Serves 6 to 8.

SWEET POTATO CHIPS

6 medium sweet potatoes	2 tablespoons juice or vinegar
dash salt	pinch sugar

Select well-shaped potatoes. Wash, pare and slice thin as you would when making white potato chips. Place in a bowl and cover with water. Add salt and vinegar or lemon juice and soak for 10 minutes. Drain and wipe dry, and then fry in deep fat until brown, for 5 minutes. Drain, sprinkle with sugar or salt.

SWEET POTATOES, GEORGIA STYLE

2 cups mashed sweet potatoes	2 teaspoons butter
¼ cup corn syrup and molasses mixed	¼ teaspoon nutmeg
	salt to taste

Place mashed potatoes in a greased baking dish. Sprinkle with salt and nutmeg. Add butter to syrup mixture. Pour over potatoes. Bake until brown. Serves 4.

197

VEGETABLES ON PARADE

SWEET POTATO FLUFF

4 to 6 cooked sweet
    potatoes
3 well-beaten eggs
⅓ cup sugar
½ cup milk

2 teaspoons orange juice
¼ cup melted butter
1 teaspoon salt
1 teaspoon baking powder

Peel and mash potatoes fine. Add eggs, sugar, milk, orange juice. Beat well. Add salt and melted butter. Whip in baking powder last. Place in a greased dish and bake in moderate oven 30 minutes or until brown. Serves 6.

Serve with roast pork, chicken, turkey or duck.

SWEET POTATO PONE

1 cup sugar, white or brown
⅔ cup butter
2 eggs, beaten
2 cups raw grated sweet
    potato
grated rind of 1 orange

grated rind of ½ lemon
½ teaspoon ginger
½ teaspoon mace
dash cinnamon
½ cup milk

Cream sugar and butter. Add beaten eggs and grated potato. Beat well. Add lemon and orange rind, spices and milk. Continue to beat. Pour into a well-greased baking dish. Bake 1 hour in moderate oven. May be served hot or cold. Serves 4 to 6.

FRIED SWEETS

4 boiled sweet potatoes
3 tablespoons butter

sugar, granulated or
    powdered

Slice boiled potatoes lengthwise. Fry in hot butter until brown. Sprinkle with sugar and serve hot. Serves 4 to 6.

Leftover boiled or baked sweets will welcome this quick, easy recipe!

Uncooked sweets may be fried without boiling. Cut in rounds or lengthwise. Fry in hot fat slowly. Serve same as precooked with butter and sugar.

CANDIED SWEETS

6 medium yams
½ teaspoon salt
½ teaspoon mace

½ teaspoon cinnamon
¾ cup brown sugar
2 tablespoons butter

½ cup fruit juice (orange or   ½ cup pineapple
    pineapple)

Parboil sweet potatoes; peel and cut in half. Place slices in a flat baking dish. Sprinkle with salt, mace, cinnamon and brown sugar. Dot with butter. Add another layer and repeat until dish is filled. Add juice from lemon or orange to water. Pour over potatoes. Dot with butter and bake 30 minutes in oven (350° F.). Serves 6.

CANDIED YAMS WITH BRANDY

6 medium cooked yams   ¼ cup brandy
1 cup sugar, brown or white   3 tablespoons butter
¼ cup lemon juice   salt to taste
1 teaspoon nutmeg   ¼ cup water
1 teaspoon cinnamon

Cut yams lengthwise. Mix sugar, butter, water, lemon juice and spices. Place sliced potatoes in a baking dish. Sprinkle with salt. Pour mixture over potatoes and add brandy. Cover and place in a moderate oven 30 minutes. Uncover and brown 15 minutes. Serves 6 to 8.

Serve with turkey or roast ham.

ORANGE SLICES AND YAMS

½ cup honey   2 tablespoons lemon juice
1 teaspoon mace   4 large round yams
2 tablespoons melted butter   2 small oranges

Mix honey, butter and lemon juice and mace. Set aside. Parboil and peel potatoes. Cut round slices from thick part of yam. Place on a greased baking pan. Slice orange and put 1 slice on each potato ring. Cover each with 1 tablespoon honey mixture. Bake 15 minutes in a moderate oven. Serves 4 to 6.

FRENCH FRIED SWEET POTATOES

Boil 4 medium, uniform-size potatoes about 20 minutes. Cool, peel and slice. Cut into strips approximately 2½ inches long by ¼ inch thick (as French fries).

Heat deep fat 475° F. Drop potatoes one at a time so they

will not become too soft. Turn until brown. Remove and sprinkle with sugar if desired. Serves 6.

Serve with fried ham or chicken.

FRIED TOMATOES

Select 6 or 8 medium ripe tomatoes. Cut in slices about ¼ inch thick. Sprinkle freely with salt and pepper. Then dip in corn meal to which 1 teaspoon paprika, ½ teaspoon sugar has been added. Be sure tomatoes are well covered in corn meal. Have heavy skillet pre-heated with a small amount of fat. Place tomatoes in hot skillet. Do not crowd in the pan. Fry fast but do not burn. Turn with pancake turner. When brown on both sides, remove. Drain on brown paper. Serve hot.

FRENCH FRIED TOMATOES

4 medium, firm tomatoes	*1 cup bread or cracker*
1 teaspoon savory salt	*crumbs*
1 egg	*2 tablespoons milk*
salt and pepper to taste	*pinch sugar*

Wash and dry tomatoes. After removing thin slice from both stem and blossom ends, slice each crosswise into 3 thick pieces. Dust with salt, pepper and sugar. Roll in crumbs. Beat egg with milk. Dip crumbed slice into egg and milk mixture, then sprinkle with crumbs on both sides. Fry to a golden brown in deep fat, hot enough to brown a cube of bread in 1 minute (350° F.). Drain on unglazed paper or white paper towels. Serve plain. Also delicious served on rounds of toast with a white or cheese sauce. Serves 4.

BROILED TOMATO SLICES WITH CHEESE

1 medium onion, grated	*1 teaspoon celery salt*
2 tablespoons bread crumbs	*½ teaspoon pepper*
2 tablespoons butter	*6 large firm tomatoes*
1 cup coarsely grated	*1 teaspoon salt*
cheese	*2 tablespoons sugar*

Mix grated onion and bread crumbs. Sauté in butter. Remove from heat. Add coarsely grated cheese, celery salt and pepper. Cut tomatoes in half. Sprinkle with salt and sugar. Place about 1 tablespoon of mixture on top of each tomato. Sprinkle with paprika. Place under the broiler. Broil 15 minutes or until cheese is well melted. Serve with your favorite chops for lunch or dinner. Equally good for breakfast. Serves 6.

PAN-BROILED TOMATOES

6 medium ripe tomatoes	1 tablespoon sugar
2 tablespoons butter	1 teaspoon grated onion
salt and pepper to taste	(optional)
garlic salt	paprika

Slice tomatoes in half. (If tomatoes are large, 3 slices will do.) Sprinkle both sides of tomatoes with seasonings. Heat heavy skillet. Add butter and onion, if desired. Lay slices in pan and sauté on each side for 5 minutes. Sprinkle with sugar and simmer 2 or 3 minutes longer. Serves 6.

BAKED TOMATO SLICES

6 small tomatoes	1 small finely chopped onion
1 teaspoon salt	1 teaspoon pepper
2 tablespoons butter	1 teaspoon paprika
½ cup bread crumbs	1 teaspoon garlic salt
1 small can mushrooms (optional)	

Cut ends off tomatoes. Slice in half. Place in a long flat baking pan. Sauté onion in butter. Add salt, pepper, paprika and garlic salt. Add mushrooms, if desired. Place about 1 tablespoon of mixture on each tomato slice. Bake in oven 20 minutes or under broiler for 5 to 10 minutes. Serves 6.

Serve for breakfast with corned beef hash, for lunch with lamb chops, or for dinner with meat loaf or ham. Baked tomato slices are also good served on wilted lettuce.

STEWED TOMATOES

12 fresh or 1 No. 2 can tomatoes	pinch thyme leaf
2 tablespoons bacon fat or butter	½ cup bread crumbs
	1 sprig parsley
1 small chopped onion or 6 green onion tops	1 bay leaf
	salt, pepper and paprika

VEGETABLES ON PARADE

Scald tomatoes. Remove skins. Place butter in sauce pan. Add chopped onion. Brown. Add tomatoes and simmer. Stir in bread crumbs. Add spices and continue simmering about 45 minutes. Serve hot. Serves 6.

TOMATO GLACE

Put 6 whole peeled tomatoes on a buttered pan, season with salt and pepper. Put a small piece of butter on top of each and bake in a moderate oven for 10 minutes.

TURNIPS AND PARSNIPS

Turnips and parsnips are often neglected as vegetables. Like onions, they contain many health-giving minerals and vitamins.

On the farms and in small home gardens where turnips and parsnips are grown, they are gaining recognition with a number of good ways for preparation.

Try cooking the turnips as you would potatoes. They are excellent when diced and served as a separate vegetable with drawn butter and parsley.

Roast duck or beef doesn't seem right without turnips. They lend a special something, so try them for variety.

BOILED BUTTERED PARSNIPS

6 parsnips	*2 tablespoons parsley*
1 teaspoon salt	*3 tablespoons butter*
pinch sugar	*½ teaspoon paprika*

Wash and scrape parsnips, dice, cover with water. Add salt and sugar. Boil until tender, 20 to 25 minutes. Drain. Add butter, parsley and paprika. Serve hot. Serves 4 to 6.

Parsnips are delicious cooked in the same manner as above and served with a rich egg sauce.

Parsnips may be boiled whole in salted water and placed in a baking dish with a bit of butter and grated cheese. Bake 15 to 20 minutes in a moderate oven.

FRIED TURNIPS

6 to 8 turnips	*1 teaspoon paprika*
pinch sugar	*salt and pepper to taste*
3 tablespoons butter	

Boil turnips whole with sugar and salt for about 1 hour in hot water until very tender. Drain well. Sprinkle with salt, pepper and paprika. Heat butter in skillet. Add turnips. Brown slowly, turning on all sides. Place on a platter around roast beef or duck.

EBONY'S HEART OF PALM

½ cup butter	1 teaspoon paprika
¼ cup slivered almonds	1 cup broth or water
1 cup finely chopped celery tops	1 teaspoon salt
	¼ teaspoon garlic salt
1 small bunch finely chopped green onions	1 package frozen peas
	1 can Hearts of Palm, drained and sliced
1 cup pimiento diced, with juice	

Melt butter in heavy saucepan. Add almonds, celery and onions and stir over low heat until almonds are lightly browned. Add pimiento, broth and seasonings; cover; bring to boil. Add frozen peas; cover; boil until peas are well done, (about 8 to 10 minutes). Add Hearts of Palm, stir carefully to mix well, then heat thoroughly.

VEGETABLE CROQUETTES

2 cups cooked rice or potatoes	1 onion, grated
2 cups cooked carrots	1 teaspoon salt
2 eggs	1 cup toasted bread crumbs
1 cup tomato pulp	1 teaspoon celery seed

Combine mashed vegetables. Add seasoning and mix well. Shape in medium-size balls. Fry in deep hot fat to a golden brown. Drain on brown paper. Serves 6 to 8.

15.

Macaroni, Spaghetti, Noodles

FOR ECONOMICAL TASTY MEALS, there's nothing quite like macaroni, spaghetti or noodles served in different styles to suit various tastes. If cooked properly, they are worthy of your culinary efforts from a side dish to a main course.

Any one of the three, when overcooked, becomes soggy, but by following directions given on the package you can judge the cooking time and method to perfection. Macaroni, spaghetti, or noodles are then ready to be used in any of the following tasty dishes.

MACARONI AND CHEESE

2 cups macaroni	2 tablespoons butter
2 teaspoons salt	6 to 8 cups boiling water
2 cups grated or chopped cheese	½ teaspoon garlic salt
	1 teaspoon celery salt
1 tablespoon prepared mustard	½ teaspoon pepper
	1½ cups hot milk
½ teaspoon paprika	bread crumbs (optional)

Cook macaroni in boiling water and salt 15 minutes. Drain and rinse in warm water. Place layer of macaroni in baking dish. Add layer of cheese. Sprinkle with salt, pepper and paprika. Repeat layers until dish is full. Add mustard and butter to milk and pour over casserole. Bake in moderate oven, 350° F., 30 minutes. Bread crumbs may be sprinkled on top if desired. Serves 6 to 8.

BAKED MACARONI IN CREAM SAUCE

2 cups macaroni	6 cups boiling water
2 teaspoons salt	2 medium onions, chopped
1 large green pepper, chopped	1 cup celery, chopped
2 cups milk	3 tablespoons butter
1 teaspoon garlic salt	1 tablespoon paprika
dash dry mustard	grated cheese, salt, pepper to taste

Cook macaroni in boiling salted water for 15 minutes. Blanch and drain. Sauté onion, celery and pepper in butter until tender. Add flour and seasonings, then milk. Cook until thick, stirring constantly. Pour over macaroni in casserole. Sprinkle with cheese and bake in moderate oven, 350° F., 40 minutes. Serves 6.

Chopped olives, pimientos or almonds may be added to cream sauce if desired, or macaroni may be baked in rich mustard and cheese cream sauce. Egg noodles may be baked the same way as macaroni.

FESTIVE MACARONI

2 cups elbow macaroni	1 cup grated cheese
1 small can pimientos	1 bunch green onions
½ cup parsley	1 teaspoon paprika
2 teaspoons salt	1½ cups hot milk
3 tablespoons butter	½ cup bread crumbs

Boil macaroni in hot water and salt for 15 minutes. Drain well and blanch in warm water. Chop pimientos and onions fine (include green tops). Sauté in butter until tender. Add bread crumbs. Remove from fire. Add parsley and cheese to milk. Combine macaroni and vegetables in baking dish. Pour milk and cheese over mixture and bake 30 minutes in moderate oven. Serves 4 to 6.

MACARONI SPECIAL

½ pound macaroni	1 cup tomatoes
2 tablespoons butter	1 teaspoon salt
½ teaspoon pepper	1 small onion, chopped
½ teaspoon paprika	½ cup grated cheese
pinch thyme	½ teaspoon celery salt

MACARONI, SPAGHETTI, NOODLES

Boil macaroni in salted water until done. Drain. Blanch in warm water. Season with salt, pepper and seasonings. Melt butter, sauté onions. Add tomatoes and cheese. Bring to a boil. Pour over macaroni. Steam 15 minutes. Serves 4 to 6.

RAVIOLI

Dough for Ravioli

1 cup flour   1 egg, whole or 2 yolks
½ teaspoon salt

Mix flour and salt. Place on bread board. Add egg slightly beaten. Blend into a dough with a fork. Roll out thin and cut into squares (1½ to 2 inches).

Filling

Place in center of each square 1 teaspoon of the following fillings of your choice:

ground chicken with onion   chopped chicken livers
chopped meat; hamburger   and onion
    or veal, with onion

Place another square on top of filling. Fold or press edges together with a fork or your fingers. Drop into boiling clear beef broth or chicken soup or broth. Boil 8 to 10 minutes until they rise to top. Serve with special sauce and grated cheese.

RAVIOLI SAUCE

1 small onion, chopped   1 green pepper
1 garlic clove   salt and pepper to taste
2 tablespoons butter or olive   1 can mushrooms (stems and
    oil   pieces)
1 can tomato sauce

Sauté onion, garlic and pepper in butter. Add tomato sauce and mushrooms. Cook 15 minutes. Serves 6.

Ravioli may be filled with cheese or chopped vegetables.

NOODLE SURPRISE

1 package wide noodles   2 tablespoons cream
1 teaspoon salt   ½ cup sliced mushrooms
½ teaspoon dry mustard   ½ teaspoon paprika

2 tablespoons chopped	chopped
parsley	½ cup grated cheese
½ cup pistachio nuts,	2 tablespoons butter

Boil noodles in salted water with dry mustard. When tender, drain and cut in 1-inch pieces. Sauté mushrooms in butter. Add seasonings, cream and cheese. Mix with noodles. Place over low flame to heat through. Just before serving, add parsley and chopped nuts. Serves 6 to 8.

NOODLE RING

½ package medium egg	3 eggs
noodles	8 tablespoons cream or
3 tablespoons melted butter	evaporated milk
½ teaspoon paprika	½ teaspoon salt

Cook noodles 8 to 10 minutes in at least 2 quarts salted, boiling water. Drain and rinse in hot water. Beat yolks. Add to noodles with butter, milk and seasonings. Fold in stiffly beaten egg whites. Turn into a well-greased mold. Place in a pan of hot water. Bake 35 to 40 minutes in a moderate oven until firm, 350° F. Remove from oven. Let set 5 to 10 minutes. Turn out on a heated platter. Fill center with plain or creamed vegetables, creamed fish, chicken or turkey. Serves 6.

BOILED NOODLES WITH BUTTER AND PARSLEY SAUCE

1 package medium noodles	1 teaspoon salt
¼ cup chopped parsley	½ teaspoon celery salt
1 tablespoon grated onion	½ teaspoon paprika
¼ cup butter	¼ teaspoon white pepper
½ teaspoon savory salt	

Boil noodles until tender in salted water. Sauté onion in butter. Add parsley and seasonings. Pour over cooked noodles and steam 5 minutes. Serves 4 to 6.

NOODLES IN CURRY SAUCE

1 package fine egg noodles	4 tablespoons butter
1 small onion	2 cups warm milk
4 tablespoons flour	1 teaspoon curry powder

MACARONI, SPAGHETTI, NOODLES

2 pimientos   1 teaspoon salt
½ teaspoon white pepper

Boil noodles in salted water until done. Drain well. Sauté butter. Add pimientos and flour. Blend well. Add milk and seasonings. Cook until thick. Pour over noodles and serve. Serves 6.

NOODLES FOR SOUP

1 egg   ½ teaspoon seasoned salt
1 cup flour

Beat egg, add salt and as much flour as can be worked into egg to make a very stiff dough. Knead 3 minutes, cover, and let stand 30 minutes. Roll paper-thin and spread on cloth to dry. Roll loosely like a jelly roll and cut across into ⅛-inch strips. Unroll and allow to dry thoroughly. Cook in boiling soup until tender, about 15 to 20 minutes. Yield: 1¾ cups of sliced noodles.

SPAGHETTI

Spaghetti knows neither race, color, nor creed. Everybody loves it! I, for one, can eat it three times a day when cooked correctly.

Spaghetti is one of the simplest of foods, but the correct way to serve the dish is to your guests' taste whether it is with meat, mushrooms, or plain tomato sauce. It is not a dish that should be served to a large number of people or served elaborately. It is an informal dish or pick-up affair, always good for late evening when your party begins to lag and your guests are hungry.

Cooking spaghetti is very important. All the old tricks like blanching in cold water, placing over hot water after cooking, putting grease into a sieve when straining, are wrong. These and similar notions are simply "old wives' tales."

There is only one way to cook spaghetti. Take a large pot, and half fill with water. Add a tablespoon of salt when the water boils. Add spaghetti whole. Don't break the strands. Put the ends in water and they will soften and bend so that the rest of the spaghetti strands will fit. When water begins to boil, lower heat so that it will simmer and won't tear up spaghetti. Cooking time should be from 6 to 8 minutes.

SPAGHETTI ALEXANDER

Once while passing through Chicago, I stopped off to see an old friend, a fellow whom I had known since childhood. What makes it interesting is the fact that our fathers were both excellent chefs and buddies. Today we are close friends, which leads us back to that stop over in Chicago and a visit with the Houstons. An invitation to dinner soon renewed old times. My favorite dish—spaghetti—was served. Imagine my surprise when I discovered that the recipe they used was an old one of my father's which somehow wasn't among the ones Mother had left me. I was so thrilled that I went to work at once to perfect this wonderful recipe. I hope you like it.

1½ to 2 pounds brisket of beef	1 package long thin spaghetti
2 medium onions	pinch crushed red peppers
1 green pepper	1 No. 2 can tomatoes
2 garlic cloves	1 can tomato paste
¼ cup olive oil	1 cup Italian cheese
1 bay leaf	½ teaspoon thyme
several stalks celery	½ cup mushrooms (optional)
	salt to taste

Boil brisket of beef with 1 onion and celery chopped fine. Add bay leaf and salt. Cook until tender. (Save stock.) Sauté garlic, remaining onion, and pepper in olive oil. Remove meat from stock. Add onion mixture, tomatoes and paste, and seasonings. Cover and simmer 30 minutes. Cut brisket in small pieces and add to sauce. Simmer slowly 45 minutes to 1 hour until sauce is thickened and ready to serve.

Cook spaghetti in plenty of boiling water with salt. Drain. Pour sauce over spaghetti. Mix well. Add cheese and serve with your favorite green salad and bread sticks. A glass of beer adds zest to this dish. Serves 6 to 8.

SPAGHETTI SAUCE
(With Rolled Meat)

1 large onion, chopped fine	1 small bunch fresh spinach, chopped
3 garlic cloves, chopped fine	½ teaspoon red pepper
½ cup grated Parmesan cheese	

MACARONI, SPAGHETTI, NOODLES

2 pounds round steak, cut
　very thin
1 large can tomato purée
1 teaspoon cumin seed
½ teaspoon sweet basil
1 green pepper, finely
　chopped
1 cup celery and leaves,
　chopped

several sprigs parsley
2 eggs
¼ cup bread crumbs
1 can tomato paste
1 tablespoon chili powder
1 sprig leaf sage
½ cup olive oil

Chop all vegetables fine and add eggs and spices. Mix well. Lay thin round steak on board, sprinkle with paprika. Add chopped mixture. Roll as jelly roll, as tightly as possible, tucking ends under. Tie with fresh clean string. Put skewers through meats so that it will hold together on all sides. Place olive oil in a heavy Dutch oven. Add meat roll and brown on all sides. Sprinkle with garlic salt and pepper. Add several bay leaves, cumin seed, leaf sage, sweet basil and tomato purée. Cook 1 hour. Add tomato paste, diluted in equal amount of water. Cook at least 3 hours. Serves 6.

SPAGHETTI WITH ROLLED FLANK STEAK

2 pounds flank steak
1 package long thin spaghetti
2 tablespoons chopped
　parsley
3 medium onions, chopped
3 cloves garlic
2 tablespoons Parmesan
　cheese
1 cup bread crumbs
1 tablespoon Worcestershire
　sauce

2 chili peppers
1 teaspoon each salt, paprika,
　chili powder
2 bay leaves
½ teaspoon thyme
½ cup olive oil or bacon fat
2 8-ounce cans tomato purée
1 6-ounce can tomato paste
2 cups water

Mix parsley, onions, garlic, bread crumbs, spices (except bay leaves), salt, pepper and Worcestershire sauce. Spread on steak. Roll tightly and tie well with clean white string. Pour oil into heavy pot. Place rolled steak in pot and sauté on all sides until brown. Add tomato paste, tomato purée and bay leaves. Cook slowly, adding water as needed, for 3 hours.

Cook spaghetti in boiling water. Drain and rinse in hot water. Place meat on a platter and slice. Pour sauce over spaghetti. Sprinkle with cheese. Serve with garlic bread. Serves 8.

SPAGHETTI SAUCE WITH MUSHROOMS

1 can tomato sauce	*2 small garlic cloves*
2 onions or 1 bunch green	*1 can tomato paste*
onions and tops	*1 teaspoon salt*
1 pound mushrooms	*½ teaspoon paprika*
½ cup olive oil	*pinch sweet basil*
1 bay leaf	*1 cup water*
several stalks celery, chopped	*Parmesan cheese*

Sauté onion, celery, garlic in olive oil. Add mushrooms and seasonings, then tomato sauce diluted with water. Cook ½ hour. Add tomato paste, diluted by filling can with water. Cook another 30 minutes. Serves 4 to 6.

SPAGHETTI WITH BACON

1 package thin spaghetti	*1 onion*
1 can tomato paste	*3 or 4 strips bacon*
½ cup grated cheese	*1 teaspoon salt*
½ teaspoon garlic salt	*½ teaspoon sweet basil*
¼ teaspoon pepper	

Boil spaghetti according to directions. Drain. Cut bacon in small pieces. Cook until brown and crisp. Remove from pan. Add chopped onion to fat. Sauté until done. Add tomato sauce, seasonings and cheese. Cook until cheese is melted. Blend in spaghetti. Serves 6.

SPAGHETTI SAUCE WITH HAM

1 small onion, chopped	*1 can tomato sauce*
1 green pepper, chopped	*½ teaspoon pepper*
several stalks celery, chopped	*½ teaspoon thyme*
1 garlic clove	*1 teaspoon salt*
2 tablespoons bacon fat	*1 teaspoon chili powder*
2 cups chopped ham	*½ lb spaghetti*

Sauté onion, pepper, celery, garlic in bacon fat. Add ham, tomato sauce and seasonings and simmer for 15 minutes. Cook spaghetti in salted boiling water according to directions. Drain and rinse in hot water. Pour sauce over spaghetti and serve. Serves 4.

MACARONI, SPAGHETTI, NOODLES

SPAGHETTI AND SHRIMP

1 pound fresh shrimp	1½ teaspoons salt
1 green pepper	2 tablespoons parsley,
1 garlic clove	chopped
2 medium onions	4 strips bacon
2 cups tomato purée	2 tablespoons butter
½ pound spaghetti	pinch salad herbs
1 bay leaf	

Chop bacon and brown. Add chopped pepper, garlic, and onion. Simmer 15 minutes. Add butter, bay leaf, and parsley. Clean and shell shrimp. Cut in halves and add to bacon mixture. Stir in tomato purée and rest of seasonings. Cover and cook over low flame 20 minutes.

Break spaghetti into small pieces, and cook in boiling salted water 8 to 10 minutes. Drain. Sprinkle with paprika, and add sauce. Heat and serve. Serves 4.

16.

Salads

SALADS ARE VITAL to good health, especially those containing green vegetables and fruit. They are not expensive, and are chockful of vitamins and minerals that we need so much in our daily routine. They also supply part of the roughage that our diets require.

Good salads should be simple. In making a salad, it is well to remember that "what pleases the eye, pleases the stomach."

The proper use of salad dressing is also very important. Just a tiny bit of dressing is all that is necessary; whether mayonnaise, French dressing, salad dressing, or your own mixture of oil and vinegar. Nothing in the world can be less glamorous than a soggy, wet dish of salad.

If you prefer to mix your dressing of vinegar, oil and spices directly on the salad in the salad bowl, do so. A well-trained hand knows the amounts. But when in doubt, don't trust to luck—use a good recipe!

SOME GARNISHES FOR SALADS

Olives	Radishes
Red or green peppers	Green onions
Pimientos	Egg yolk, grated or sliced

SALADS

Celery
Pickles, sliced or chopped
Capers

Nuts
Cherries
Cucumbers

SALAD GREENS

Iceberg lettuce
Chicory
Water cress
Endive
Romaine
Napa

Garden lettuce
Spinach
Parsley
Nasturtium leaves
Escarole

VEGETABLE SALAD À LA HOUSTON

½ cup grated carrots
1 cup shredded cabbage
6 to 8 sliced radishes
½ cup string beans
2 teaspoons sugar
1 teaspoon paprika
¼ cup salad oil
½ cup diced celery

½ cup shredded red cabbage
6 green onions
¼ teaspoon pepper
1 teaspoon salt
1 head Romaine lettuce
3 tablespoons Tarragon
   vinegar

Line salad bowl with Romaine lettuce. Cut string beans very fine, lengthwise, French style. Mix all vegetables. Add seasonings, oil, vinegar. Mix well. Place on lettuce and serve. (Peas may be added, if desired.) Serves 6.

CARROT AND CHEESE SALAD

1 head lettuce
1 cup cottage cheese
2 tablespoons grated onion
1 bunch water cress

1 bunch endive
4 to 6 shredded carrots
French dressing
chicory

Wash and drain greens. Rub salad bowl with grated onion. Shred lettuce. Cut up chicory and endive. Add carrots and water cress. Pour French dressing over salad, sprinkle with salt and toss lightly. Arrange cottage cheese around bowl on top of salad and serve. Serves 4 to 6.

RED AND GREEN SLAW

3 cups green shredded
   cabbage

1 large onion, grated
2 tablespoons sugar

214

1 teaspoon prepared mustard   1 teaspoon celery seed
⅛ teaspoon pepper   1 teaspoon paprika
2 tablespoons lemon juice   2 teaspoons salt
3 cups red shredded cabbage   ½ cup salad dressing
1 green pepper, grated

Combine vegetables. Add salt, pepper, celery seed, sugar.
Combine lemon juice, mustard and salad dressing. Add vege-
tables to dressing and mix thoroughly. Sprinkle with paprika.
Serves 6 to 8.

GARDEN SALAD BOWL

½ head Romaine   ½ head lettuce
½ bunch endive   ½ bunch water cress
2 tomatoes, cut in wedges   2 stalks celery
½ cup crumbled Roquefort   6 radishes, sliced
   or bleu cheese   ¼ cup French dressing
3 or 4 green onions

Break lettuce in pieces. Tear endive and water cress in small
pieces. Arrange tomatoes, celery, radishes on top of greens.
Sprinkle with salt and pepper. Pour dressing over salad and
toss very lightly. Garnish top with green onions. Sprinkle
with crumbled cheese. Serves 6 to 8.

TOSSED GREEN SALAD WITH AVOCADOS

1 whole avocado   1 bunch water cress
1 bunch Romaine lettuce   1 bunch endive
½ head iceberg lettuce   1 green pepper, sliced thin
6 green onions and tops   1 tablespoon sugar
pinch of salad herbs   ⅓ cup vinegar
¼ cup olive oil   several sprigs parsley
½ head Napa cabbage
   (optional)

Rub bowl with garlic. Break greens into small pieces. Do not
cut. Slice pepper. Sprinkle with salt, pepper, paprika, salad
herbs and sugar. Cut avocado in medium pieces. Arrange artistically on top of greens after tossing salad lightly. Add vinegar and oil.
   Serves 6 to 8.

CHOPPED BEET SALAD

6 cooked beets
1 tablespoon grated onion
1 tablespoon sugar
1 teaspoon salt
¼ cup salad dressing

1 tablespoon lemon juice
1 tablespoon vinegar
parsley to taste
dash paprika

Drain juice from beets. Place in bowl and chop fine. Add grated onion, salt, sugar, lemon juice and vinegar to salad dressing. Mix well. Add beets. Let stand in refrigerator for 1 hour. Mold into a ball. Place on a lettuce leaf. Add a piece of parsley and a dash of paprika. Serves 6.

SUMMER SALAD WITH SOUR CREAM DRESSING

1 head chicory
1 head lettuce
1 bunch radishes
dash salt
1 bunch water cress
pinch sugar

¼ pound Roquefort cheese
½ cup sour cream
1 teaspoon prepared mustard
4 to 6 green onions
1 tablespoon lemon juice

Rub bowl with garlic. Blend cheese, sour cream and mustard in salad bowl with sugar and lemon juice. Mix well. Break or cut greens and vegetables into bowl. Sprinkle with salt. Toss salad lightly so that each green is covered with salad dressing. This salad should be served at once. Serves 8.

MOSS GREEN SALAD

1 bunch spinach
2 green peppers sliced thin
½ cup green onion tops or
    chives

½ pound strings beans (cut
    French style)
1 bunch water cress
½ bunch endive

Wash and cut spinach, water cress, endive, peppers and onion tops. Add string beans. Pour garlic dressing over salad. Toss lightly. Serves 4 to 6.

VEGETABLE COMBINATIONS FOR THE SALAD PLATE

Beets sliced around a center of chopped green beans.
Beets quartered, eggs quartered, green pepper wedges.

Pickled artichokes, asparagus tips, tomato slices, pepper rings.

Shoestring carrots, asparagus spears, string beans.

Peas, chopped onion tops, celery.

Diced green beans, carrots, beets.

These combinations may be served with mayonnaise or any salad dressing of your choice.

When cooking vegetables for salad, season well with garlic salt or celery salt, and a teaspoon lemon juice or vinegar to pep up the flavor. Don't *over-cook!* Soft, soggy cooked vegetables lose their salad glamor.

EBONY'S GREEN SALAD WITH CLARET

½ head lettuce	*French dressing made with*
½ head escarole	*4 tablespoons claret*
1 unpeeled cucumber	*wine instead of vinegar*
½ head chicory	*2 hard-cooked eggs*
1 green pepper, cut in rings	*garlic salt*

Wash greens and tear into pieces. Slice pepper, eggs and cucumber thin. Sprinkle with garlic salt and dressing. Serves 6.

STUFFED AVOCADO WITH GRAPEFRUIT

2 grapefruits	*mustard*
3 green onions and tops	*2 tablespoons salad*
2 hard-cooked eggs	*dressing*
salt and pepper to taste	*3 small avocados*
dash sugar	*1 bunch water cress*
1 tablespoon prepared	*1 tablespoon lemon juice*

Peel grapefruit and cut in sections. Add onions and eggs, chopped fine, but save yolk of 1 egg. Mix salt, pepper, sugar, and mustard in salad dressing and combine with grapefruit mixture. Peel avocados, remove pits, and place half an avocado on each plate on a bed of water cress. Squeeze lemon juice over avocados and sprinkle with salt. Fill centers with grapefruit mixture and sprinkle with crumbled egg yolk. Serves 6.

Crushed pineapple may be used instead of grapefruit and the egg may be omitted.

SURPRISE SALAD BOWL

1 head lettuce	*12 strips Swiss cheese*
1 bunch Romaine	*4 slices boiled ham*

217

1 cup diced chicken
12 green onions
salt, pepper to taste
1 bunch water cress
4 tomatoes

12 strips yellow store cheese
1 cup chopped celery
garlic salt to taste
French dressing

Arrange lettuce in bowl. Mix celery and chicken and lay on lettuce. Cut tomatoes in wedges. Sprinkle mixture with garlic salt. Arrange tomatoes, ham, cheese and onions in pyramid style around bowl. Cover with French dressing and paprika and serve. Serves 6.

SPANISH SLAW

1 small head green cabbage
2 green peppers
¾ cup Roquefort dressing
1 teaspoon sugar

salt and pepper to taste
2 pimientos
1 Spanish onion, sliced thin
1 teaspoon paprika

Grate cabbage and peppers. Add onion slices with pimientos. Sprinkle with sugar, salt, pepper and paprika. Add dressing and mix well. Let stand, then serve. Serves 6.

FRESH STRING BEAN SLAW

2 pounds string beans
1 small head of cabbage
2 onions
2 green peppers
½ cup chopped parsley
2 tablespoons sugar
1 teaspoon celery salt

1 teaspoon salt
1 teaspoon paprika
1 cup salad or French
    dressing
¼ cup cream
2 tablespoons vinegar

Slice string beans very thin, French style. Add shredded cabbage and grated onion with diced green pepper and parsley. Mix sugar, vinegar, celery salt, paprika, cream and salad dressing in bowl. Add vegetables. Mix lightly and serve. Serves 8.

OLD-FASHIONED COUNTRY SALAD

4 medium tomatoes, ripe
1 large cucumber
1 Spanish onion
1 green pepper (optional)

1 tablespoon sugar
1 teaspoon salt
½ cup vinegar
paprika and pepper to taste

Wash tomatoes and slice thin in a large bowl. Peel cucumber and onion. Slice thin. Mix with tomatoes. Sprinkle with salt, pepper, sugar and paprika. Pour vinegar over vegetables. Set in refrigerator to chill 1 hour.

If green pepper is desired, slice thin and add to other vegetables. Serves 6.

A famous old salad served with greens and boiled dinners with corn bread. Good on hot days with cold meats. Cucumber may be omitted.

POTATO SALAD WITH SOUR CREAM

4 cups sliced or diced potatoes (cooked)	*2 tablespoons chopped parsley*
1 small cucumber, diced	*1½ cups sour cream*
1 onion, minced	*½ cup mayonnaise*
1 teaspoon celery seed	*⅓ cup vinegar*
2 hard-cooked eggs	*dash sugar*
1 teaspoon prepared mustard	*salt and pepper to taste*

Combine potatoes, cucumber, onion, salt and pepper. Blend. Dice egg whites and add to potato mixture. Blend yolks into sour cream and mayonnaise and add sugar and vinegar. Heat over low flame 5 minutes. Pour over potato mixture and chill. Serve on a bed of lettuce, if desired. Serves 8.

CREAM CHEESE BALLS ON WATER CRESS

3 packages cream cheese	*2 tablespoons salad dressing*
⅓ cup parsley, chopped	*1 teaspoon paprika*
⅓ cup carrots, grated	*1 hard-cooked egg, chopped*
1 bunch water cress	*½ teaspoon salt*
celery salt	

Put parsley, carrot and egg each in a separate flat dish. Sprinkle with celery salt and paprika. Roll 4 cheese balls in egg, 4 in carrots and 4 in parsley. Be sure they are well covered. Place on a bed of lettuce or water cress. Allow 3 cheese balls to each person. Add 1 teaspoon salad dressing or French dressing and serve. Serves 4.

POTATO SALAD No. 1

3 cups diced potatoes (cooked)	*½ cup grated carrots (uncooked)*

SALADS

⅓ cup chopped beets
1 can pimientos, chopped
bunch green onions,
    chopped
2 or 3 sweet or dill pickles,
    or 1 tablespoon chow-chow

1 cup French dressing
¹₂ cup celery, chopped
⅓ tablespoon salad
    dressing
¼ cup green peppers
salt and pepper to taste

Mix diced vegetables, salt, pepper and pickles. Marinate well with mixed French dressing and salad dressing. Serve on a bed of water cress with your favorite cold cuts. Serves 6.

Serve your favorite potato salad with home-made mustard dressing.

For a party: Garnish potato salads with cucumbers, olives, carrot strips, eggs, capers or radishes.

Instead of placing lettuce under your salads, garnish with bits of water cress, parsley or any variety of lettuce after salad has been placed in the bowl. Place an extra bowl of fresh, crisp lettuce beside your salad bowl. Let folks help themselves. It is not only thrifty, but it is also very appetizing.

Sprinkle carrot strips, radishes or celery with plain or garlic salt before serving.

POTATO SALAD No. 2

½ cup mayonnaise
2 tablespoons mustard
2 tablespoons sour cream
1 tablespoon lemon juice
1 tablespoon vinegar
1 teaspoon sugar
salt and pepper to taste

2 cups diced, cooked
    potatoes
1 grated onion
½ cup chopped celery
½ cup minced parsley
2 hard-cooked eggs

Combine mayonnaise, mustard, sour cream, lemon juice and vinegar in a bowl. Add sugar, salt and pepper, diced vegetables and eggs cut in wedges or chopped. Mix well and let stand about 1 hour before serving. Serves 6.

SIMPLE POTATO SALAD

6 medium potatoes, cooked
    and diced
¼ cup chopped parsley
½ cup celery

⅓ cup grated onion
1 cup salad dressing
½ teaspoon celery seed
salt and pepper to taste

1 teaspoon paprika   *dash sugar*
1/4 cup vinegar

Combine potatoes, celery, onion and parsley. Mix celery seed, salt, pepper, vinegar and salad dressing. Pour over potatoes. Mix well. Chill and serve with tomato slices. Garnish with parsley and paprika. Serves 6.

HOT POTATO SALAD

1/2 pound bacon, diced   *1 tablespoon sugar*
5 potatoes, boiled in jackets *1/4 teaspoon paprika*
1 onion, chopped fine   *1/4 cup vinegar*
1/2 teaspoon salt   *1/2 teaspoon celery seed*
1/2 cup cooked celery, diced *1 teaspoon prepared mustard*
few sprigs parsley, chopped *1/4 teaspoon pepper*

Peel and dice potatoes. Cook bacon until crisp. Remove from pan and drain. Add potatoes, celery and seasonings to bacon drippings. Sprinkle with crumbled bacon and chopped parsley. Serves 6.

MACARONI SALAD

1 pound macaroni, salad cuts *1/2 cup parsley, chopped*
1/2 cup green pepper,   *1 onion, grated*
  chopped   *1 tablespoon paprika*
1/4 cup vinegar from pickle or *1/2 cup salad dressing*
  juice of 1/2 lemon   *1 small can chopped*
1 teaspoon celery seed   *pimiento*
1/2 cup celery, chopped

Boil macaroni 10 to 15 minutes in boiling water with salt and 1 tablespoon vinegar. Drain, blanch in cold water and cool. Add chopped vegetables, salt and pepper, vinegar and salad dressing. Mix well. Serve on a bed of lettuce with tomato slices for decoration. Serves 6.

Pimiento may be omitted and 1/3 cup grated carrots substituted. They add color and variety to the salad.

COMBINATIONS FOR THE SALAD BOWL

Here are a few unusual salad combinations at a glance, which can be mixed right in your salad bowl and arranged attractively.

SALADS

(1)

6 beets
1 jar ripe olives
½ cup capers
Russian dressing

3 hard-cooked eggs
1 can fillet of anchovies
1 head shredded lettuce
1 pound green beans

(2)

4 tomatoes, cut in wedges
1 green pepper, cut in rings
1 head lettuce, shredded

1 cucumber, sliced
6 green onions
garlic dressing

(3)

1 can asparagus tips
½ cup chopped ham
¼ pound Swiss cheese,
    slivers
mustard dressing

2 eggs, hard-cooked
several slices pimiento
1 bunch water cress

(4)

½ head lettuce
½ head chicory
1 clove garlic, or rub bowl
⅓ cup oil
salt and pepper
½ head escarole

1 bunch water cress
1 pound black cherries
1 tablespoon tarragon or
    wine vinegar
2 tablespoons lemon juice

TOMATO AND CREAM CHEESE ASPIC

3 cups tomato juice
1 small onion, chopped
2 whole cloves
1 tablespoon vinegar
½ cup chopped parsley
1 cup cream cheese

2 bay leaves
1 teaspoon salt
2 tablespoons plain gelatin
¼ cup cold water
2 tablespoons grated onion

Soften gelatin in water and add vinegar. Boil tomato juice, bay
leaves, onion, salt and cloves. Strain and add gelatin mixture.
Blend together well. Pour into a mold and put in icebox to cool.
When slightly congealed, remove from refrigerator and mix in
cream cheese, onion and parsley which have been blended
together. Return to refrigerator to become firm. Turn out on a
cold plate on a bed of shredded endive. Serve with a spicy
salad dressing.

Aspic may be placed in square baking pans to be cut into squares, if desired.

STUFFED TOMATOES

Combinations for stuffings

Cottage cheese and chive.

Cream cheese and chive or green onion tops.

Grated red and green cabbage with salad dressing.

Chicken salad.

Egg salad.

Shredded shrimp, salad dressing and chow-chow pickle.

Shrimp salad.

Tuna salad.

Green pepper, chopped celery and salad dressing.

For tasty stuffed tomatoes, be sure to season with seasoned salt, onion or garlic salt inside and out before serving. Tomatoes may be quartered before filling. Do not cut all the way through.

TUNA SALAD

1 small can tuna fish	*6 pineapple slices*
½ cup chopped onions	*½ cup chopped peppers*
1 tablespoon prepared mustard	*⅓ cup salad dressing*
	1 bunch endive
½ cup minced celery	*8 to 10 minced olives*
1 tablespoon lemon juice	*1 teaspoon paprika*

Blend ingredients. Add dressing. Mold with a small tea cup or custard cup. Place molds on beds of chopped endive on slices of pineapple. Garnish with parsley. Serves 4.

CHICKEN SALAD WITH PINEAPPLE

1½ cups diced cooked chicken	*1 head lettuce*
	1 bunch chopped chives, or green onion tops
½ cup diced celery	
½ cup green peppers	*1 tablespoon lemon juice*
1 cup diced apples	*10 small pineapple slices*
salt, pepper and paprika to taste	*10 olives, green or ripe*
	celery curls
1 cup salad dressing	

Combine chicken, green peppers and celery. Pour lemon juice

over apples and add to chicken. Moisten with salad dressing. Add salt and pepper to taste. Shred lettuce on plate and lay a slice of pineapple on lettuce bed. Add a mound of salad. Place another slice of pineapple on top of mound. Sprinkle freely with chopped chives and paprika. Place 2 olives and celery curls on each plate with salad. Serve with toasted cheese straws. Serves 4.

CHICKEN AND APPLE SALAD WITH ALMONDS

3 cups chopped chicken
1 cup diced apples
1 cup salad dressing
2 cups firm green peas
½ cup salted almonds, crushed
¼ cup parsley

1 cup diced celery
½ lemon
1 small grated onion
1 tablespoon sugar
2 hard-cooked eggs, chopped
salt, pepper, paprika to taste

Sprinkle lemon juice on apples. Mix chicken and vegetables. Add seasonings, nuts, salad dressing, apples and chopped eggs. Arrange in mounds on a bed of water cress or endive. Garnish with paprika, ripe olives, and pimiento. Serve with tiny hot honey biscuits. Serves 6.

MOLDED HAM AND CHEESE SALAD

3 cups tomato juice
1 tablespoon lemon juice
½ cup grated green pepper
2 cups ham, chopped
2 tablespoons gelatin
2 tablespoons tomato catsup
dash garlic salt

1 tablespoon Worcestershire sauce
1 tablespoon Tabasco sauce
4 to 6 cloves
2 tablespoons onion, grated
1 cup grated snappy cheese
1 cup cold water
½ cup minced parsley

Cook vegetables and tomato juice with spices 20 minutes. Remove cloves. Soak gelatin in cold water. Add to tomato and vegetable mixture. Stir until dissolved. Cool. Mix ham, cheese and catsup. Stir into mixture. Place in mold and chill until firm. Serve on lettuce with mustard sauce. Serves 6.

When serving molded salads, fit a small bowl into open center of salad. Place sauce or dressing in bowl. This will help keep your salad firm and neat. Parsley or lettuce can be used to conceal the bowl.

HAM AND APPLE SALAD

2 cups boiled or baked ham, diced
4 apples, diced
1 teaspoon paprika
½ teaspoon Season-all
1 cup celery and leaves, diced
1 head lettuce
½ lemon
mustard dressing

Squeeze lemon juice over diced apple. Combine all ingredients, adding enough salad dressing to coat well. Toss together in a salad bowl and serve on bed of lettuce. Serves 6.

Bits of fresh pineapple may be added, if desired.

SHRIMP SALAD SUPREME IN PINEAPPLE BASKET

1 large pineapple
2 cups cooked shrimp
½ cup salted almonds
½ teaspoon salt
1 cup salad dressing
2 tablespoons lemon juice
½ cup chopped celery
½ teaspoon celery salt

Cut pineapple in half. Do not remove green top. Scoop out center and chop fine. Strain juice. Combine shrimp, celery, almonds and pineapple. Add lemon juice and salad dressing. Sprinkle with paprika. Arrange a bed of lettuce in pineapple center. Refill with salad, garnish with paprika and serve. Serves 6.

All fruit salads may be attractively arranged and served in pineapple or melon baskets.

CRANBERRY RING

Mrs. Hattie McWarter of St. Louis, Missouri, has been catering for years, and knows all the answers. In her well-appointed home whenever she gives a party, her fresh cranberry ring has become a truly fabulous dish. So, for your parties, The Little Brown Chef gives you:

1 quart cranberries
2 cups sugar
1 package gelatin
2 apples
grated rind 1 orange
¼ cup hot water
juice of 3 oranges
1 package lemon Jello
¼ cup cold water
mayonnaise

SALADS

Grind cranberries. Add chopped apples with sugar. Dissolve gelatin in water. Add to berry mixture. Add hot water to lemon Jello. Add grated orange peel and juice. Mix all ingredients well. Pour into ring. Allow to stand overnight until firm and turn out of mold onto a bed of lettuce. Fill center with mayonnaise. Serve. Serves 8 to 10.

Excellent with cold meat platter or turkey.

FRUIT COMBINATIONS FOR SALADS

Pineapple, apple, pear.
Pineapple spears, melon spears.
Peaches, apricots, cream cheese.
Pears, peaches, oranges.
White grapes, pineapple, red cherries.
Pears, strawberries.
Chopped red cherries, apple.
Bananas, Queen Anne cherries.
Melon balls of watermelon, cantaloupe, honeydew.
Apple, nuts, pineapple.
Honeydew melon, white grapes, pineapple.
Orange slices, grapefruit, cherries.
Diced pineapple, strawberries.
Pineapple slices, raspberries, pears.
Banana, orange, grapefruit.

Serve fruit salads with whipped cream dressings, French dressing with fruit juice, mayonnaise or cooked salad dressing.

PEANUT SALAD

1 small head cabbage	1 teaspoon flour
2 teaspoons salt	1 teaspoon dry mustard
1 teaspoon sugar	1 cup vinegar
1 teaspoon butter	½ teaspoon pepper
2 egg yolks	1 pint peanuts

Chop cabbage and peanuts fine. Add salt and pepper. Cream butter, mustard, sugar and flour together. Stir in vinegar. Cook in double boiler until stiff. Add egg yolks. Pour over the nuts and cabbage. Serves 6 to 8.

ZESTFUL SALAD

6 raw carrots, grated
1 tablespoon tartar sauce
juice of 1 lemon
1 medium head crinkly cab-
    bage, finely chopped

1 tablespoon horseradish
    (optional)
salt to taste

Mix ingredients well and see if this isn't one of the nicest econ-
omy salads you have yet tasted. Serves 6.

JELLIED PINEAPPLE SALAD

2 heaping cups crushed
    pineapple (1 No. 2 can)
juice of 1 lemon
¾ cup sugar
2 tablespoons gelatin

½ cup cold water
¾ cup grated American
    cheese
½ pint whipping cream

Add sugar to pineapple. Heat and stir until sugar is dissolved.
Add lemon juice. Soak gelatin in cold water for 10 minutes.
Add to hot mixture and stir until dissolved. When mixture
cools and begins to stiffen, fold in cheese and stiffly beaten
cream. Place in mold in refrigerator for several hours before
serving. Serve with mayonnaise. Serves 6.

EBONY'S GREEN SALAD WITH CHEESE

½ head lettuce
½ head escarole
½ head chicory
2 hard-cooked eggs

1 unpeeled cucumber
1 green pepper, cut in rings
garlic salt

French dressing made with ¼ cup claret wine in place of
vinegar.

Wash greens and tear into pieces and place into a large
salad bowl. Slice eggs and cucumber and add green pepper
rings to salad greens. Sprinkle with garlic salt and dressing.
Toss together lightly but well. Yield: 6 servings.

RED AND GREEN SLAW

3 cups shredded green
    cabbage
3 cups shredded red cabbage

1 green pepper, finely
    chopped
1 large onion, finely chopped

SALADS

1 teaspoon celery seed	*½ cup salad dressing*
1 teaspoon salt	*½ teaspoon paprika*
⅛ teaspoon pepper	*1 teaspoon prepared mustard*
2 tablespoons sugar	*2 tablespoons lemon juice*

Combine vegetables into large bowl. Toss together. Add celery seed, salt, pepper and sugar. Mix well. Combine all remaining ingredients. Mix well, pour on top of vegetables and mix thoroughly. Yield: 6 to 8 servings.

SALAD DRESSING

2 eggs	*1 teaspoon salt*
1 tablespoon flour	*½ cup vinegar*
2 tablespoons sugar	*1 cup milk*
¼ teaspoon cayenne	*1 teaspoon dry mustard*
¼ teaspoon paprika	

Mix together all dry ingredients. Add to slightly beaten eggs. Beat until smooth. Add milk and vinegar. Cook in double boiler 20 minutes. Yield: 1½ cups.

COOKED SALAD DRESSING

½ cup sugar	*1 teaspoon dry mustard*
1 teaspoon salt	*½ cup white vinegar*
3 whole eggs	*2 tablespoons butter*
½ teaspoon salt	

Combine dry ingredients. Add vinegar and heat to boiling point. Pour over well-beaten eggs, stirring constantly. Return to heat. Cook until thick, beating with rotary egg beater. Add butter.

Just before serving, add ½ cup whipped cream or ⅓ cup heavy cream (plain), or evaporated milk. Yield: 2 cups.

MAYONNAISE

2 teaspoons salt	*1 teaspoon dry mustard*
dash cayenne	*2 egg yolks*
1 pint olive or salad oil	*¼ cup cider and tarragon*
1 tablespoon lemon juice	*vinegar, in equal parts*

Combine dry ingredients with unbeaten yolks in a mixing bowl and beat together until stiff. Add part of the oil, beating it into

the mixture drop by drop at first, then proceeding more rapidly, always keeping the mixture stiff. When it begins to thick-
en, add a little of the vinegar; alternate the oil, vinegar and
lemon juice until blended. Yield: 2½ cups.

THOUSAND ISLAND DRESSING

To 1 cup mayonnaise dressing, add 2 tablespoons chili sauce,
2 tablespoons minced stuffed olive, 1 tablespoon chopped
green pepper, 1 tablespoon minced onion or chives, ¼ cup
heavy cream, whipped or plain. Makes 2 to 2½ cups.

FRENCH DRESSING

½ cup peanut oil	½ teaspoon paprika
½ cup vinegar	½ tablespoon salt
dash pepper	

Put all ingredients into a bottle or jar. Just before using, shake
vigorously until well mixed.

SIMPLE FRENCH DRESSING

1 cup olive oil	2 tablespoons chopped
¼ cup vinegar	parsley
½ teaspoon sugar	½ teaspoon salt
pinch dry mustard	½ teaspoon paprika
	¼ teaspoon pepper

Combine ingredients, shake well. Yield: 1⅓ cups.
Wine vinegar may be used, if desired.
Using 1 cup of simple French dressing as a foundation, try
the following variations:

2 tablespoons minced capers	2 tablespoons Roquefort
¼ cup chopped chives	cheese, crumbled fine and
1 tablespoon salad herbs	creamed into dressing
1 small minced garlic clove	¼ cup tomato juice, 2 table-
½ small onion, grated	spoons tomato catsup
	¼ cup claret or white wine
	substituted for vinegar

FRENCH DRESSING FOR FRUIT SALADS No. 1

½ cup olive oil	½ cup lemon juice, or
1 teaspoon salt	pineapple juice
dash paprika	2 tablespoons sugar or honey

Combine all ingredients and shake well. Yield: 1 cup. Juice of ½ lime may be combined with lemon juice. 1 tablespoon chopped mint or parsley may be added.

FRENCH DRESSING FOR FRUIT SALADS No. 2

¼ cup lemon juice
¼ cup orange or pineapple juice
½ cup salad oil

salt, pepper, paprika to taste
3 tablespoons sugar
1 tablespoon vinegar
1 teaspoon grated onion

Combine ingredients in jar and mix well. Set aside to ripen. Use on any fruit salad desired. Yield: 1 cup.

FRENCH DRESSING SUPREME

1 grated onion
2 tablespoons sugar
1 teaspoon salt
1 teaspoon paprika
½ cup tarragon or wine vinegar
1 tablespoon Worcestershire sauce

1 cup olive oil
1 tablespoon prepared mustard
1 tablespoon catsup
2 garlic cloves (on toothpicks)

Mix onion, garlic and dry ingredients. Place in a jar. Add wet ingredients. Cover jar and shake well. Set in refrigerator to ripen. Yield: 1 pint.

FRENCH DRESSING

yolks of 4 hard-cooked eggs
2 teaspoons paprika
2 teaspoons powdered sugar
1 teaspoon celery salt

1 bunch finely chopped chives
½ cup oil
¼ cup lemon juice
few sprigs parsley

Mash egg yolks, making into a paste with vinegar. Blend all ingredients. Set in jar to ripen. Yield: 1 pint.

AVOCADO DRESSING

4 tablespoons cream
2 tablespoons lemon juice
6 drops Tabasco sauce

1 teaspoon salt
½ avocado, mashed
½ teaspoon dry mustard

Beat cream, lemon juice, mustard and Tabasco sauce. Add avocado. Cover. Shake well. Set in refrigerator to ripen. Yield: 1 cup.

ROQUEFORT OR BLEU CHEESE DRESSING

½ cup Roquefort cheese	juice 3 lemons
¼ cup cream cheese	1 pint cream

Mash cheese and add juice. Add cream slowly. Stir until smooth. Place in jar. Set in refrigerator to ripen. Yield: 1 quart.

ROQUEFORT DRESSING

½ teaspoon dry mustard	6 tablespoons crumbled
½ teaspoon sugar	Roquefort cheese
½ teaspoon onion salt	6 teaspoons anchovy paste
½ teaspoon celery salt	(optional)
¼ teaspoon paprika	¼ teaspoon Worcestershire
⅛ teaspoon cayenne	sauce
3 tablespoons mild vinegar	1 small finely chopped
3 tablespoons lemon juice	garlic clove (optional)
⅔ cup salad oil	

Mix dry ingredients. Then add vinegar and oil alternately. Place in a jar or bottle which has a tight-fitting cover. Crumble cheese with a fork. Beat in anchovy paste. Add Worcestershire sauce and lemon juice. Add to ingredients in a jar or bottle. Shake well. Add salt and pepper to taste. Finely chopped garlic may be added. Always shake dressing before using. Yield: 1 pint.

QUICK WHIPPED CREAM SALAD DRESSING

1 cup salad dressing or	½ teaspoon lemon juice
mayonnaise	1 cup heavy cream
1 tablespoon confectioners'	¼ teaspoon salt
sugar	

Whip cream, beat in sugar and salt. Blend lemon juice in dressing and fold into cream. Mix well. Yield: 2½ cups.

MUSTARD DRESSING

1 tablespoon olive oil or	1 tablespoon sugar
butter	1 egg

231

1 cup milk, sweet or evaporated	*1 teaspoon salt*
2 tablespoons dry mustard	*½ cup vinegar*

Blend together oil, mustard, sugar, salt and beaten egg in double boiler. Add vinegar which has been heated. Stir in milk. Cook 10 to 15 minutes until thick, stirring frequently. Chill. Yield: 1½ cups.

PORK AND APPLE SALAD DRESSING

1 cup mayonnaise	*1 teaspoon celery seed*
½ teaspoon curry powder	*1 teaspoon sugar*
1 teaspoon paprika	*2 tablespoons lemon juice*
1 teaspoon salt	

Mix all ingredients thoroughly. Use half with pork and apple slices and set remainder in separate dish for dressing.

BASIC GARLIC AND HERB DRESSING

4 cloves garlic	*¼ cup pepper (black or white)*
1 cup salt	
juice of 1 lime or 1 lemon	*1 tablespoon paprika (optional)*
2 tablespoons basil or thyme or salad herbs	

Place unpeeled garlic in large bowl; crush slightly and remove peel. Crush garlic thoroughly, adding ¼ cup of the salt; mix well and crush together. Add all remaining ingredients; mix thoroughly. Pack in tightly covered glass jar and store on shelf for one month before using. Use to rub on steaks, lamb, veal, pork, fish and chicken before cooking. May be used as directed for seasoning in vegetables, sauces and stews.

HERB DRESSING

2 tablespoons lemon juice	*½ teaspoon salt*
½ teaspoon basil	*⅔ cup salad oil*
1 teaspoon marjoram	*⅓ cup vinegar*

Combine all ingredients in quart jar; seal tightly and shake vigorously. Chill before using. Serve on green salads, vegetable salads, some fruit salads and some meat salads.

ALMOND AND OLIVE BUTTER

1 small bottle stuffed
 pimiento olives
4 ounces toasted blanched
 almonds
½ cup butter

1 teaspoon paprika
1 teaspoon celery salt
1 teaspoon onion or garlic
 salt

Drain olives and chop very fine. Crush almonds or grind fine. Combine olives, almonds, soft (not melted) butter. Sprinkle seasonings on hot, cooked cauliflower or broccoli. Spread with prepared butter.

LEMON ALLSPICE DRESSING

½ cup mayonnaise
¼ cup powdered sugar
juice of half lemon
⅛ teaspoon salt

1 teaspoon paprika
½ teaspoon allspice
½ cup heavy cream whipped

Blend mayonnaise with sugar, lemon juice, salt, allspice and paprika. Fold in whipped cream. Makes 1½ cups dressing. Delicious with fruit salads.

17.

Breads

BREAD

For biscuits, rolls, and muffins, your favorite recipe will do. But where you have been using 4 tablespoons of other shortening, 3 tablespoons of peanut oil will be sufficient.

THREE-HOUR ROLLS

¾ cup scalded milk	¼ cup lukewarm water
1 teaspoon salt	1 well-beaten egg
¼ cup sugar	¼ cup shortening
2 cakes fresh yeast	4 cups flour

Crumble yeast into water. Melt shortening in milk. Add sugar and salt, then yeast. Beat with egg beater until well mixed. Add 1½ cups flour, then egg. Beat again. Add balance of flour until dough can be handled. Turn dough onto lightly floured board. Cover dough and let stand 10 minutes to loosen up. Knead until very smooth and elastic. Place in a greased bowl and cover with a damp cloth about 1½ hours at room temperature. Turn on lightly floured board again and shape into rolls. Cover and let rise once more until double its bulk. Bake 15 to 20 minutes in hot oven 425° F. Yield: 24 rolls.

BOSTON BROWN BREAD, STEAMED

1 cup white flour	1 teaspoon salt
1 cup corn meal	¼ cup molasses

1 cup floured raisins	2 cups sour milk
1 cup graham flour	½ cup sugar
1½ teaspoons soda	

Sift dry ingredients together and then add molasses, milk and raisins. Mix thoroughly and pour into a greased mold or coffee tin. Do not fill mold or tin more than ⅔ full. Place cover on tightly and steam for 2½ hours. Yield: 1 small loaf.

BROWN BREAD

1½ cups milk and water	¼ cup brown sugar
½ cup molasses	¼ cup shortening or butter
1 teaspoon soda	1 cup raisins
½ cup grated orange rind	1¼ cups white flour
1¼ cups wheat flour	½ teaspoon salt
2 teaspoons baking powder	2 eggs

Cream sugar and shortening. Add molasses and well-beaten eggs. Beat in sifted ingredients and fold in fruit. Mix well, place in greased loaf pans and bake 1 hour at 350° F.

APRICOT BREAD

1½ cups dried apricots	1½ cups hot water
2 tablespoons butter	1 cup sugar
1 teaspoon salt	

Chop apricots fine. Add hot water, sugar, butter and salt. Mix well and set aside to cool. Add 2 eggs, well beaten. Sift together:

1 cup wheat flour	1 cup pastry flour
1½ teaspoons soda	2 teaspoons baking powder

Add to apricot mixture. Blend in 1 cup chopped almonds. Pour in a greased loaf pan and bake in a moderate oven, 350° F., for 1 hour. Makes 2 large or 3 medium loaves.

ORANGE NUT BREAD

2¾ cups sifted flour	1 cup honey
3 teaspoons baking powder	1 egg, beaten slightly
½ teaspoon salt	2 tablespoons grated
½ teaspoon baking soda	orange rind

BREADS

¾ cup chopped pecans or   ¾ cup fresh orange juice
    walnuts   ½ cup butter

Sift together flour, baking powder, salt and soda. Combine
butter and honey until well blended. Add egg and orange rind;
beat to blend. Add dry ingredients alternately with orange
juice; stirring after each addition until blended, no longer. Stir
in nuts. Turn into greased and floured 9½ x 5½ x 2½ inch loaf
pan. Bake in 325° F. (moderately slow) oven 60 to 70 minutes.

COCONUT BREAD

1 fresh coconut, grated   ½ cup butter
    (save water)   2 cups flour
1 cup sugar   1 teaspoon vanilla
2 teaspoons baking powder   1 teaspoon salt
2 eggs   1 cup raisins (optional)

Cream butter and sugar. Add eggs and blend well. Mix coconut and raisins. Sift in dry ingredients and add coconut water
to make a soft dough for kneading. Knead lightly on floured
board; divide in half and shape into loaves. Place in greased
loaf pan. Let rise 30 minutes. Bake in slow oven one hour.

If there is not enough coconut water to mix flour to knead
soft dough, use approximately ⅔ cup milk as substitute.

CHRISTMAS BREAD

1 package instant dry yeast   1 teaspoon cloves
½ cup warm water   5½ cups sifted flour
1½ cups milk   4 eggs
¾ cup butter   ½ cup currants
1 cup brown sugar   1 cup raisins
1 cup white sugar   1 cup finely cut candied
1 teaspoon mace   citron
1 teaspoon nutmeg   1 cup finely cut mixed
1 teaspoon cinnamon   candied fruits
1 cup chopped pecans   ½ cup chopped, blanched
1 teaspoon salt   almonds

Dissolve yeast in warm water. Scald milk and pour into large
bowl. Add butter, sugar, spices and salt. Mix well. Beat eggs

slightly and add to milk mixture; blend well. Add yeast and mix thoroughly. Add flour gradually; beat in after each addition; add enough flour to make a very soft dough. Add ¼ cup flour to all fruits and nuts; add to dough and mix in thoroughly to distribute all through dough. Turn onto lightly floured board. Knead dough for at least 5 minutes. Shape dough into a round mound, flat ball-shaped, and place on a large, greased baking sheet. Brush top with melted shortening. Cover with waxed paper or foil and a dry cloth. Let rise until double in bulk. Bake in a 350° F. (moderate) oven about 1 hour. When bread is still slightly warm, frost with icing made of 2 tablespoons butter, 2 cups confectioner's sugar and 1 cup well drained crushed pineapple.

CLOVER LEAF ROLLS

Use same recipe as for three-hour rolls. Cut small pieces of dough the size of a walnut. Shape into a ball. Dip in melted butter. Place 3 rolls in each greased muffin tin to rise. Bake as directed. Yield: 24 rolls.

POPPY SEED ROLLS

Use basic 3 hour roll dough. Form into desired shapes. Brush with mixture of 2 tablespoons of Dutch Poppy Seed and egg white or melted butter. Set aside to rise. Bake as directed.

CINNAMON AND NUT BUNS

Use same recipe as for three-hour rolls. Place one tablespoon brown sugar and one teaspoon butter in bottom of each muffin tin. Set in oven to melt. Add pecans or walnuts. Roll dough into rectangular shape. Sprinkle with cinnamon and sugar and roll as a jelly roll. Cut in ½ inch slices with a sharp knife. Place each slice in muffin tin with sugar and nut mixture. Let rise about 40 minutes. Bake 20 to 25 minutes at oven temperature of 350° F. Yield: 24 rolls.

BASIC SWEET DOUGH FOR SPECIAL ROLLS

2 cakes compressed yeast,   ½ cup warm water
dissolved in ½ cup luke-   3 tablespoons shortening
warm water   2 tablespoons sugar

1 teaspoon salt	3½ cups all-purpose
1 egg, beaten	flour, sifted

Add shortening, sugar and salt to warm water. Beat in one cup of the flour until smooth. Add dissolved yeast. Mix until smooth. Stir in egg. Add flour, mixing well, until dough can be handled easily. Thoroughly knead dough in bowl. Add just enough flour to prevent dough from sticking. Keep dough soft. Knead lightly until surface is satiny. Cover with cloth. Let stand for 15 to 20 minutes.

Shape dough as desired. Place on greased pans, and brush lightly with melted fat. Cover. Let rise until double in bulk, 30 to 45 minutes.

Bake for 15 minutes in oven pre-heated to 400° F. While baked rolls are still hot, brush tops with beaten egg mixed with ¼ cup water. Yield: 1 dozen rolls and one tea ring.

ORANGE FILLING FOR ROLLS

2 tablespoons grated orange rind	½ cup butter
	½ teaspoon nutmeg
½ cup unstrained orange juice	1 cup sugar

Squeeze juice from orange. Mix orange rind, unstrained juice with sugar and butter in a sauce pan. Place over direct heat and gradually bring to a boil, stirring constantly. Boil rapidly from 8 to 10 minutes. Remove from heat. Cool in refrigerator until thick. Spread on dough. Roll as jelly roll and slice with a sharp knife. Place cut side down on greased pan or muffin tins. Bake in a hot oven, 400° F., for 25 minutes. Turn upside down so filling will make glaze on top. Serve warm.

Pineapple may be substituted for orange, if desired.

NEVER-FAIL ROLLS

1 cup milk	6 cups flour
1 small can evaporated milk	1 cake yeast
3 medium potatoes, boiled	1½ teaspoons salt
⅔ cup shortening	¾ cup sugar
2 eggs	

Mash potatoes and stir in shortening and sugar while potatoes are still hot. Beat well and add milk and salt. Then beat in yeast cake and 1 cup flour. Let stand in warm place until light and foamy, then add well-beaten eggs and remainder of the flour, beating until dough is elastic and easy to handle. Knead until well blended and smooth. Let stand in warm place until bulk is doubled and then make into rolls. Let rise until very light and bake in moderate oven, 375° F. Makes approximately 3 dozen rolls.

These rolls are just as good 3 to 4 days after baking, when reheated, as when they were first made.

HOT ROLLS

2 cups milk or water	*1 egg*
⅓ cup sugar	*2 cups flour*
⅓ cup shortening	*1 teaspoon salt*
1 cake yeast	

Scald milk. Add shortening and sugar. Set aside to cool. Break yeast in bowl, dissolve with a little warm water, and add to milk.

Add beaten egg, flour and salt gradually to make a soft dough. Knead lightly to hold together and place in a greased mixing bowl. Let rise until double its bulk. Place on floured board, roll out and cut into desired shape or make into a clover leaf roll. Place in muffin tins or on greased baking pans. Let rise again. Brush with milk or cream. Bake 15 to 20 minutes in a hot oven. Yield: three dozen rolls.

BOSTON PARKER HOUSE ROLLS

6 cups flour	*1 teaspoon salt*
2 tablespoons lard or butter	*1 yeast cake*
¼ cup sugar	

Mix all dry ingredients together in a large mixing bowl, then blend in lard well. Dissolve yeast cake in about ¼ cup luke-warm water and add to other ingredients. Use just enough warm water to hold together. Knead. Let rise until the dough is double in bulk. Turn out on a floured board, cut into roll sizes. Flatten each roll, dip in butter and fold in half. Again let rise until bulk is again doubled. Place in a 400° F. oven and bake 30 minutes. Yield: 3 dozen rolls.

REFRIGERATOR ROLLS

Bread just wasn't bread when grandmother was a girl unless it was made with potato water. Though modern methods have helped us save effort and time, some of the old folk won't listen to reason and still insist that the lowly potato be used, at least in bread.

Here is a modernized bread recipe utilizing grandma's potato water as well as mashed potatoes.

1 cake yeast	*1½ teaspoons salt*
1½ cups lukewarm potato water	*2 eggs*
	6 to 7 cups flour
⅓ cup butter	*1 cup potato (mashed*
⅓ cup vegetable shortening	*without milk)*
⅔ cup sugar	

Crumble yeast in bowl. Add small amount of lukewarm water. When dissolved, add well-beaten eggs. Add shortening to potatoes with sugar and salt. Mix well. Add to egg and yeast. Beat well. Add remaining lukewarm water and 2 cups of flour at a time, beating well after each addition. When dough is too stiff to use spoon, work in flour with hands until dough is easy to handle without sticking to hands. Don't let dough get too stiff!

Knead on a floured board for 10 to 15 minutes or until smooth and elastic. Cover with a damp cloth and let rise in a warm room 1½ to 2 hours. Knead and save amount needed for meal. Mold into rolls as desired. Brush surface with melted shortening. Set aside to rise double in bulk. Bake 15 to 20 minutes in hot oven, 425° F. Yield: 2 dozen rolls.

Place remaining ball of dough in greased bowl. Cover tightly using waxed paper and a damp towel. Place in refrigerator until ready to use. Dampen cloth from time to time if dough has tendency to dry out. Should dough rise, don't be afraid to knead it. When ready to use, remove from refrigerator and take amount needed. Leave remaining dough and let stand in warm room 1½ to 2 hours before shaping into rolls.

FILLINGS FOR COFFEE CAKE

The following combinations may be used to fill coffee rolls and cakes that are made with sweet roll dough:

(1)

1 cup chopped dates   ½ cup chopped nuts

(2)

1 cup chopped raisins   1 teaspoon nutmeg
2 tablespoons brown sugar   1 orange, ground

(3)

1 cup cooked mashed prunes   2 tablespoons butter
2 tablespoons brown sugar

(4)

1 cup crushed almonds   1 package cream cheese
1 teaspoon cinnamon

(5)

¼ pound orange peel   ¼ pound lemon peel
½ cup dates   ½ cup cherries
2 tablespoons honey   1 teaspoon mace

(6)

½ cup crushed pineapple   6 red cherries, chopped
2 tablespoons butter   ¼ cup brown sugar

(7)

1 cup cooked mashed   2 tablespoons honey
  apricots   1 teaspoon lemon juice

(8)

2 tablespoons brown sugar   1 tablespoon flour
1 tablespoon butter   ½ cup crushed salted nuts

BREAD STICKS

1 cake yeast   2 tablespoons melted
1 cup lukewarm water   shortening
1 tablespoon granulated   3½ cups sifted all-purpose
  sugar   flour
1 teaspoon salt   2 eggs

BREADS

Soften yeast in ¼ cup of the water. To remainder of water add sugar, salt, shortening and 1 cup of the flour. Mix thoroughly. Add yeast, stiffly beaten egg whites and enough flour to make a soft dough. Turn out on a lightly floured board and knead until smooth. Form into a ball, place in greased bowl, and cover. Let rise until double in bulk and let rise again. To make bread sticks, divide dough into small portions about two inches in diameter. Cover for 10 minutes. Roll each piece on board with hand to the size of a pencil. Place one inch apart on a greased baking sheet sprinkled with corn meal. Cover and let rise until double in bulk. Brush with egg yolks mixed with two tablespoons cold water. Bake in a very hot oven, 450° F., for 20 minutes, first placing a large, shallow pan of water in bottom of oven to remain throughout entire baking process. Yield: 36 bread sticks.

HOT CROSS BUNS

¼ cup shortening
1 cup boiling water
½ cup sugar
1 teaspoon salt
1 cup milk
¼ cup lukewarm water
1 cup seedless raisins, or currants
¼ cup shredded citron
¼ cup orange peel
½ teaspoon cinnamon
4 cups sifted flour
1½ cakes yeast
2 eggs

Scald milk. Add shortening, sugar, salt, hot water and cool until lukewarm. Dissolve the yeast in the lukewarm water and add to the first mixture. Stir in the eggs, one at a time. Add the fruit, cinnamon and flour. Knead lightly on a floured board, adding more flour if necessary. When smooth, place in a greased bowl and cover. Let rise in a warm place until double in bulk. Cut off small pieces and form into balls. Place in greased baking pans. Let rise until double in bulk. Bake in a very hot oven until brown. Remove from oven and brush with melted butter. When cool, mark a cross with white icing on the top.

First rising: 2 hours or more. Second rising: 1 hour or more. Oven temperature, 425° F. Baking time 20 minutes. Yield: 24 buns.

BISCUITS

Hot biscuits do a lot for any meal but they are more likely to be appreciated for Sunday breakfast when folk have more time to enjoy and prepare a meal. Of course you can't overlook the fact that it is not necessary to bake biscuits as soon as they are mixed. If you are going shopping, make your biscuit dough in the morning. Roll dough, cut, place biscuits on sheet of paper and set aside. Bake at dinner.

Garnish the top of your biscuits with cranberries, or add dates and raisins to the dough for variety.

Create some special recipes of your own! Stale biscuit, bread, and cake can be made into crumbs by drying them in the oven. Roll out fine and place in a covered jar or tin to be used as needed.

CREAM OF TARTAR BISCUITS

2½ cups flour	1 cup milk
1 teaspoon salt	¼ teaspoon sugar
2 teaspoons cream of tartar	2 tablespoons shortening

Sift dry ingredients. Work in shortening with fingertips. Add milk. Mix well. Knead lightly on a floured board until smooth. Roll out about ½ inch thick. Cut in rounds or squares. Bake in a greased pan in a hot oven, 425° F. Yield: 12 to 16 biscuits.

HONEY BUTTER BISCUITS

2 cups sifted flour	½ cup shortening
½ teaspoon salt	¾ cup milk
1 teaspoon sugar	3 tablespoons soft butter
4 teaspoons baking powder	3 tablespoons honey

Sift together flour, salt, sugar and baking powder. Work shortening into flour mixture with fingertips lightly until the consistency of coarse corn meal. Add milk. Knead dough gently on lightly floured bread board. Pat or roll out to ½ inch thickness; cut with biscuit cutter. Hold biscuits between fingers and place thumb in center to make indentation. Place biscuits on baking sheet. Combine honey and soft butter; blend well. Place ½ teaspoon of mixture in each biscuit hole. Set aside to rise about 10 minutes. Bake in a 425° F. (hot) oven for 10 to 12 minutes until biscuits are golden brown.

BREADS

LEMON BISCUITS

⅓ cup shortening
1 teaspoon salt
2 cups flour
¼ teaspoon soda

1 teaspoon grated lemon rind
4 teaspoons baking powder
⅔ cup milk
3 tablespoons lemon juice

Cut shortening into sifted dry ingredients. Mix lemon rind and juice with milk. Let stand ½ hour before adding to flour mixture. Roll out dough. Cut in rounds. Brush with melted butter or cream. Let rise 15 minutes. Bake in hot oven 10 to 12 minutes. Yield: 24 biscuits.

BEATEN BISCUITS

2 cups flour
½ teaspoon salt

½ cup shortening
⅓ cup sweet milk

Measure and sift dry ingredients into mixing bowl. Measure shortening, then milk. Cut shortening into flour as in biscuit making. Add milk gradually. Mix thoroughly, making a stiff dough. Flour board or block. Put dough on board and knead for about 5 minutes. Beat dough with smooth wooden stick for 20 minutes, about 1,000 strokes. Beat dough until flat, fold, and continue beating as hard as possible. Roll dough to ⅓ inch thickness. Fold and roll ½ inch thick. Cut the dough with biscuit cutter. Prick each biscuit with fork about three or four times. Place on oiled baking sheet ½ inch apart. Bake at 375° F., 25 minutes or until light brown. Serve hot or cold. Yield: 24 biscuits.

TEA BISCUITS

2 cups flour
½ teaspoon salt
2 tablespoons sugar
4 tablespoons baking powder
pinch cream of tartar
    (optional)

½ cup shortening
½ cup milk
1 whole egg
¼ cup chopped parsley

Sift dry ingredients. Blend shortening with fingertips. Add slightly beaten egg to milk, and then to dry mixture. Add parsley. Mix well. Place on lightly floured board and roll out ½ inch thick. Brush with melted butter. Cut with small biscuit cutter, then form into Parker House roll shapes. Place on a greased sheet and let rise 20 to 30 minutes. Bake 15 minutes in hot oven, 400° F. Yield: 24 small biscuits.

Chopped pimiento may be substituted for parsley. Water cress or grated celery may be used. To be really different, try grated cheese and a dash of nutmeg.

SOUR MILK BISCUITS

2 cups flour	½ teaspoon soda
1 teaspoon baking powder	1 cup sour milk
1 tablespoon sugar	1 teaspoon salt
3 tablespoons shortening	

Mix and sift dry ingredients. Cut in shortening. When mixed, add sour milk gradually. When mixture is partly blended, turn onto floured board. Pat lightly together and roll to ½ inch thickness. Cut in rounds and stick with fork. Place on a well greased baking sheet and bake about 20 minutes at 400° F., until brown and fluffy. Yield: 24 biscuits.

SOUR CREAM BISCUITS

2 cups flour	1 teaspoon sugar
2 tablespoons butter or shortening	1 teaspoon salt
	1 cup sour cream
1 teaspoon soda	¼ teaspoon nutmeg

Melt shortening and add to sour cream. Sift dry ingredients and add cream slowly. Mix thoroughly. Place on floured board. Roll lightly or pat into shape. Cut in squares or round. Bake in hot oven 12 to 15 minutes. Yield: 24 biscuits.

SOUTHERN YEAST BISCUITS

5 to 6 cups flour	2 teaspoons salt
¼ cup shortening	1 tablespoon sugar
1 yeast cake	2 cups milk
¼ cup warm water	1 egg
2 tablespoons melted butter	

Scald milk, add shortening and sugar. Cool. Dissolve yeast in warm water and stir into milk. Stir in 2 cups flour and egg. Blend well. Set aside to rise in a warm place. When double its bulk, place dough on bread board, and knead in balance of flour until smooth and elastic. Roll dough out to ½ inch thickness. Cut with biscuit cutter. Dip each biscuit in a bit of melted butter. Place on a cooky sheet, about 1 inch apart, to rise. When double in bulk, bake in a hot oven, 400° F., 20 to 25 minutes.

BUTTERMILK BISCUITS

2 cups sifted flour	⅓ cup shortening
1 teaspoon baking powder	¾ cup buttermilk
½ teaspoon baking soda	1 tablespoon light corn
½ teaspoon salt	syrup

Sift together twice the flour, baking powder, baking soda and salt. Put shortening into dry ingredients. Combine buttermilk and syrup; add to mixture. Stir together until well mixed; turn onto lightly floured board. Knead lightly several times with fingertips. Roll or pat to ½ inch thickness; cut in desired shapes. Place on baking sheet. Bake in a 450 degrees F. (hot) oven about 12 minutes.

QUICK CINNAMON BUNS AND DATE BRAID

4 cups flour	1 cup milk
6 teaspoons baking powder	1 egg
½ cup shortening	1 cup brown sugar
1 teaspoon salt	1 cup raisins
1 teaspoon sugar	

Cinnamon Buns: Mix and sift dry ingredients (except brown sugar) and combine with milk and egg. Knead lightly. Roll half of the dough to ¼ inch thickness (saving rest for Date Braid). Spread with soft butter and sprinkle with cinnamon, brown sugar, and raisins. Roll like jelly roll and cut in ¼ inch thick slices. Place slices in greased pan and bake 20 minutes in moderate oven.

Date Braid: Roll dates and nuts into dough. Fold over and roll again. Cut in 3 strips and braid loosely. Place in greased pan and bake 20 minutes in moderate oven. Remove from oven and frost with mixture of ½ cup powdered sugar and 2 tablespoons of milk.

Or, instead of Braid: Cover dough with nuts, dates, and

raisins or mashed prunes. Roll, join ends to form a ring. Place on greased baking sheet. Snip outer edge with scissors at 2 inch intervals. Pull sections apart, twist lightly and brush with beaten egg yolk. Bake as above.

BREAKFAST CRUMB CAKE

An amusing story was told to me concerning a cook who, when asked by her employer if she could make a crumb cake for breakfast, immediately answered, "Of course." She added that she could make anything, and crumb cake was her "specialty." Here is the result, and though her employer knew it was not exactly what she had in mind, she was wise enough to realize her cook had created a masterful crumb cake of her own.

1½ cups flour	1 cup bread or cake crumbs
3 tablespoons baking powder	¼ cup crushed walnuts
½ teaspoon salt	1 teaspoon cinnamon
¼ cup sugar	4 tablespoons sugar
2 eggs	1 teaspoon flour
1 cup milk	3 tablespoons butter

Sift dry ingredients. Blend shortening with fingers. Add crumbs, then eggs and milk. Mix well. Spread in a greased, flat cake pan. Sprinkle with walnuts, cinnamon, sugar, flour and butter. Bake in a hot oven, 400° F., 25 minutes. Cut in squares and serve for breakfast. Serves 4 to 6.

GOLDEN COFFEE CAKE

1 8-ounce can crushed pineapple	2 cups sifted flour
4 teaspoons baking powder	½ teaspoon salt
2 tablespoons sugar	4 tablespoons shortening
1 egg	⅓ cup milk
2 tablespoons strained honey	2 tablespoons softened butter

Place pineapple into strainer to drain. Sift flour, add baking powder, salt and sugar. Sift twice. Blend shortening until evenly distributed. Beat egg well, add milk and ⅓ cup of the juice drained from pineapple. Add to flour mixture and blend thoroughly. Turn into well-greased eight-inch square baking pan. Blend strained honey with softened butter. Add well-drained pineapple. Mix well, then spread over dough in pan. Bake in hot oven, 400° F., 30 minutes. Serves 6.

COFFEE CAKE

1/3 cup sugar	2½ cups flour
1/4 cup butter	3 teaspoons baking powder
1 teaspoon mace	½ cup pineapple
1 teaspoon cinnamon	½ cup nuts
2 eggs, beaten	½ teaspoon salt
3/4 cup milk	

Topping

2 tablespoons butter	1 tablespoon nutmeg
1/4 cup brown sugar	

Blend sugar, butter, and spices with fingers. Add eggs and milk. Add flour, salt, baking powder, pineapple and nuts. Mix well. Pour into greased pan. Mix brown sugar, butter, and nutmeg. Sprinkle over cake and bake 40 minutes.

QUICK COFFEE CAKE

Here is a coffee cake that you can mix and bake while you are making your coffee and preparing the rest of the breakfast.

1 cup flour	1 beaten egg
½ cup sugar	2 tablespoons melted
1 teaspoon salt	shortening
2 teaspoons baking powder	1/4 cup white or brown
1/4 cup shortening	sugar
3/4 cup milk	1 tablespoon cinnamon

Combine flour, sugar, salt, and baking powder. Cut in shortening. Add milk and egg. Mix well, but don't beat; dough will be a little stiff. Spread over a well greased square cake tin. Sprinkle top of cake with mixture made from melted shortening, brown sugar, and cinnamon. Bake 20 to 25 minutes in a moderately hot oven. Cut in squares and serve.

DATE AND NUT BREAD

2 cups flour	1/4 cup sugar
2 eggs	1/4 cup melted shortening

1 teaspoon salt
¾ cup milk
½ cup finely chopped dates
½ cup finely chopped nut
    meats

½ teaspoon nutmeg
4 teaspoons baking powder
1 teaspoon mace

Beat eggs. Add sugar, melted shortening, and spices. Mix. Sift in flour and dry ingredients. Add dates and nuts, which have been finely chopped. Mix well, and turn into greased loaf pan. Bake at 350° F. for 45 minutes. Cool and slice. Yields 1 loaf.

BANANA BREAD

½ cup butter or substitute
⅓ cup sugar
1½ cups mashed bananas
1 teaspoon nutmeg
½ teaspoon soda

2 cups flour
½ cup walnuts or pecans
1 teaspoon salt
2 eggs
2 teaspoons baking powder

Cream butter and sugar and add unbeaten eggs. Mix and beat well. Blend in bananas. Sift dry ingredients. Add nuts and blend into banana mixture. Beat about 2 minutes until well blended. Pour into greased loaf pans and bake 45 minutes to 1 hour in a moderate oven, 350° F. Yield: 1 large or 2 small loaves.

BOSTON BROWN BREAD, BAKED

1 cup white flour
1 cup whole wheat flour
¾ cup molasses
2 cups sour milk
1 cup raisins

1 cup corn meal
½ teaspoon salt
1½ teaspoons soda
¼ cup melted shortening

Mix and sift dry ingredients. Blend in raisins. Add sour milk, shortening, and molasses. Beat well. If desired, steam 2 hours in greased molds, filled ¾ full, and cover very tightly. May be baked in greased bread pan in slow oven (325° to 350° F.) for one hour. Makes one loaf.

CORN BREADS

WHOLE KERNEL CORN BREAD

¾ cup white or yellow
    corn meal

3 teaspoons baking powder
1 tablespoon sugar

BREADS

2 eggs, beaten
1½ cups milk
½ cup white flour
1 teaspoon salt

3 tablespoons melted butter
or substitute
1 can whole kernel corn

Mix dry ingredients. Add eggs and fat to milk and corn. Add to dry ingredients. Stir quickly until mixed. Place in a very hot skillet or casserole. Bake in a moderate oven, 375° F., for 40 minutes or until done. Serves 6.

KANSAS CORN BREAD

1 cup white corn meal
½ cup flour
½ teaspoon salt
1¼ cup milk
⅓ cup melted shortening

1 cup yellow corn meal
2 tablespoons sugar
4 teaspoons baking powder
3 eggs

Sift dry ingredients into a bowl. Beat eggs, add milk and shortening. Blend into dry ingredients. Beat until smooth. Pour into well-greased baking dish and bake in a moderate oven, 350° F., 20 to 25 minutes.

CORN CAKE

½ cup yellow corn meal
3 teaspoons baking powder
½ teaspoon salt
1 cup warm milk

1½ cups flour
¼ cup sugar
2 eggs
⅓ cup shortening

Sift dry ingredients into a bowl. Blend in shortening. Add warm milk. Beat well. Blend in eggs which have been beaten until light. Bake in a well-greased square cake pan 30 minutes with oven temperature of 400° F.

CRACKLIN' BREAD

Cracklin's are little pieces of pork fat, fatty meats, or ham skin which are left crisp and brown after the lard or fat has been rendered from them.

1 cup cracklin's
    (broken in pieces)
1 teaspoon soda
1 teaspoon sugar

½ teaspoon salt
2 cups white corn meal
1 cup sour milk
2 tablespoons melted fat

Mix and sift dry ingredients. Add milk. Stir in cracklin's and sour milk. Form into oblong cakes. Roll in shortening. Bake in a greased baking dish 30 minutes in a hot oven. Serves **6.**

CORN BREAD

1 cup corn meal	*2 eggs*
½ cup flour	*1 cup milk*
2 teaspoons baking powder	*½ cup finely chopped green*
½ teaspoon salt	*onion*
3 tablespoons melted butter	*1 tablespoon sugar*

Sauté onion tops in butter. Do not brown. Mix and sift dry ingredients, add milk and eggs which have been beaten together with onion tops. Pour into a greased baking pan or muffin tins. Bake 20 to 30 minutes in a moderate oven. Serves 4 to 6.

For real surprises, in place of onions try ½ cup chopped celery leaves, or ½ cup coarsely grated American cheese.

SOUR MILK CORN BREAD

2 cups sifted corn meal	*2 eggs*
1 teaspoon soda	*2 cups sour milk*
1½ teaspoons salt	*2 tablespoons melted*
2 tablespoons sugar	*shortening*

Sift dry ingredients together. Beat eggs. Add sour milk and melted shortening. Add egg mixture to dry ingredients. Stir well but do not beat. Pour into a greased baking pan or muffin tins. Bake in a hot oven 25 to 30 minutes. Serves 6.

SPOON BREAD No. 1

2 cups corn meal	*2 cups sweet milk*
1 cup boiling water	*1 teaspoon salt*
1 tablespoon sugar	*¼ cup melted butter*
3 eggs	*dash nutmeg*

Sift meal. Scald with boiling water and mix until free from lumps. Add melted butter and sugar, salt, nutmeg, and milk. Separate eggs and beat whites until light. Add yolks to dough. Mix well. Fold in whites. Pour into a greased baking dish. Bake in a moderate oven, 350° F., 35 minutes. Serve in baking dish. Serves 6.

BREADS

SPOON BREAD No. 2

1 cup yellow corn meal	2 tablespoons butter
2 eggs	2 tablespoons sugar
1 teaspoon salt	1 cup cooked bacon, or
1 teaspoon baking powder	leftover turkey or chicken
2½ cups milk	

Cook corn meal in milk until thick. Beat yolks and add melted shortening, salt, sugar, baking powder, bacon. Beat egg whites until stiff. Fold in. Bake in a greased casserole in a moderately hot oven 40 minutes.

SOUTHERN SPOON BREAD

½ cup corn meal	2 cups milk
½ teaspoon salt	2 eggs
1 teaspoon sugar	

Put corn meal and salt in a sauce pan. Stir in 1½ cups milk. Cook until a thick mush is formed, or about 2 minutes. Remove from stove. Stir in 1 egg, unbeaten. Mix thoroughly and turn into a buttered baking dish. Beat the second egg slightly. Stir in the remainder of the milk. Pour the egg and milk mixture over the mush, cutting with a knife so that the two mixtures are only partly combined. Bake in a moderate oven, 375° F., for 30 minutes or until the top is puffed and brown. Serve at once from the baking dish with a spoon. Serves 4.

Some people like to eat spoon bread with butter and syrup. Others prefer just butter, salt, and pepper.

CORN STICKS No. 1

1 egg, beaten	1½ cups buttermilk or
½ teaspoon soda	sour milk
1 teaspoon salt	1½ cups corn meal
¼ cup melted shortening	2 teaspoons baking powder

Beat eggs and add milk. Add dry ingredients to milk mixture. Add shortening and beat well. Grease hot corn stick pans well. Fill almost full. Bake in a hot oven, 425° F. Brush tops with shortening or cream. Place under broiler or in oven to brown from 2 to 3 minutes. Don't overbake! Serve hot. Yield: 12 to 14 corn sticks.

CORN STICKS No. 2

2 cups corn meal
1 cup milk
1 egg
½ teaspoon salt

2 tablespoons shortening
1 tablespoon sugar
2 teaspoons baking powder

Heat milk, add shortening and sugar. Beat in egg. Sift dry ingredients. Add to milk and egg mixture. Pour in hot greased corn stick pans and bake in a quick oven, 450° F., 12 to 15 minutes.

CORN STICKS No. 3

½ cup yellow corn meal
1 cup milk
1 egg
½ teaspoon nutmeg
½ cup white corn meal

2 tablespoons shortening
½ teaspoon sugar
½ teaspoon salt
1 cup flour
2 teaspoons baking powder

Heat milk, add shortening and sugar. Beat in egg. Sift dry ingredients. Add to milk and egg mixture. Pour in hot greased corn stick pans and bake in a quick oven, 450° F., 12 to 15 minutes.

DOCTOR'S MUFFINS

2 cups flour
1 teaspoon salt
2 teaspoons sugar
1 cup milk
2 tablespoons melted
    shortening

2 teaspoons baking powder
2 beaten eggs
2 teaspoons sugar
dash nutmeg

Beat milk, eggs and shortening. Sift dry ingredients and mix together. Do not beat, but mix well. Pour in greased muffin tins. Bake 25 minutes in a hot oven. Yield: 12 muffins.

For tea muffins add two tablespoons sugar and ½ cup finely chopped nuts.

ONE-EGG MUFFINS

2 cups flour
4 teaspoons baking powder
½ teaspoon salt
1 egg

2 tablespoons sugar
1 cup milk
2 tablespoons shortening

BREADS

Mix and sift dry ingredients. Do not over-mix. Add milk gradually, and well-beaten egg, to which melted butter has been added. Bake in buttered pans 25 minutes. If old-fashioned iron pans are used, heat first.

MUFFINS

2 cups flour	½ teaspoon salt
2 teaspoons sugar	3 teaspoons baking powder
1 cup milk	2 eggs
4 tablespoons melted butter	

Sift together flour, salt, sugar, and baking powder. Mix milk, eggs and melted shortening with dry ingredients. Stir until mixture is moist, but not smooth. Don't worry if the batter is lumpy. Fill greased muffin tins a little over half full, and bake in a very hot oven, 400° to 425° F., about 25 minutes. Makes approximately 1 dozen large or 2 dozen small muffins.

For variations try adding any of the following to your basic muffin dough.

½ cup finely chopped dates	½ cup cranberries
½ cup finely chopped raisins	1 cup cherries
	1 cup raspberries
½ cup finely chopped figs	1 cup whole kernel corn
1 cup blueberries	

When fresh berries are used, eliminate ¼ cup of milk and add fresh fruit to dry ingredients.

Another muffin trick: Add 1 teaspoon jam, jelly, or cranberry sauce on top of each raw muffin before baking.

FRESH CORN MUFFINS

2 cups flour	1 cup milk
2 teaspoons baking powder	2 tablespoons sugar
½ teaspoon salt	1 cup fresh white kernel corn
1 egg	3 tablespoons butter

Melt butter and add corn. Set aside to cool. Sift dry ingredients. Beat egg and add milk. Add butter and corn mixture. Pour over dry ingredients. Mix quickly but well. Do not beat. Bake in greased muffin tins, ¾ full, in a hot oven, 400° F., 20 to 30 minutes. Makes 1 dozen muffins.

Instead of corn, you can add bits of chopped cooked ham, bacon or grated cheese to this batter.

If you are a business wife or busy mother, and pressed for time, try using 1 cup of fresh corn or canned whole kernel in your favorite corn muffin mix.

WHOLE KERNEL CORN MUFFINS

1 cup sifted flour
3 teaspoons baking powder
½ teaspoon salt
4 tablespoons sugar
1 cup yellow corn meal
¼ cup melted butter
1½ cups milk
2 eggs, beaten slightly

2 tablespoons drained canned whole kernel corn
¼ cup finely diced pimiento
2 tablespoons finely chopped green onions and tops

Sift together flour, baking powder, salt and sugar; stir in corn meal lightly but well. Combine melted butter, milk and beaten eggs; mix well; add to dry ingredients and stir just enough to moisten all dry ingredients. Stir remaining ingredients gently. Place about ¼ cup of mixture in each greased muffin pan. Bake in a 400° F. (hot) oven 20 to 25 minutes.

18.

Sandwiches

HINTS ON SANDWICHES

Don't make dry, tasteless sandwiches. Try mustard, horse-radish, dressings, catsup, chili sauce, seasoned salts, lemon juice, and all sorts of zesty spices to pep them up.

Gravies and cream sauces are most appetizing over sandwiches on cold days!

A FEW OPEN SANDWICH SUGGESTIONS

Cooked asparagus with melted cheese
Cooked asparagus with tomato and melted cheese
Bacon, asparagus and cream sauce
Creamed crab meat, tuna or lobster with grated cheese
Ham, asparagus, melted cheese
Sliced chicken, tomato slices, bacon
Sliced chicken, water cress, sliced egg, bacon

SANDWICH FILLING WITH FRUITS

Dates, nuts, cheese
Chopped prunes, nuts, salad dressing
Pineapple, raisins, nuts, salad dressing
Apple, celery, nuts, salad dressing
Pistachio nuts, cherries, salad dressing
Pineapple, cheese, parsley, salad dressing

1 cup cottage cheese, ¼ cup grated green pepper, ¼ cup grated celery, 1 tablespoon onion juice, ½ teaspoon salt, paprika to taste

1 cup cottage cheese, dash Season-all, 1 tablespoon chopped pickle, ½ cup chopped or ground ham

1 cup cottage cheese, dash garlic salt, 1 tomato diced fine, 1 tablespoon grated onion

1 cup cottage cheese, 1 tablespoon mayonnaise, 1 medium apple, chopped fine, dash salt and pepper

1 cup cottage cheese, ¼ cup chopped parsley, 1 tablespoon grated onion, 1 teaspoon salad dressing

AMERICAN CHEESE SANDWICH SPREADS

1 cup grated American cheese, 2 slices bacon, fried and chopped; ½ teaspoon grated onion, 1 tablespoon chow-chow or chopped pickle, 3 tablespoons mayonnaise

1 cup grated American cheese, 3 tablespoons anchovy paste, 1 teaspoon catsup, 2 tablespoons salad dressing, one teaspoon minced onion

1 cup grated American cheese, 2 hard-cooked eggs, chopped; 2 tablespoons chopped pimiento, 2 tablespoons salad dressing, dash garlic salt, 1 tablespoon chopped sweet pickle

½ pound grated American cheese, ¼ cup tomato catsup, 1 teaspoon dry mustard, 1 teaspoon Worcestershire sauce

CREAM CHEESE SANDWICH SPREADS

1 package cream cheese (8 ounces), ¾ cup chicken, cooked and chopped, 1 tablespoon onion, grated, 1 tablespoon parsley, 1 tablespoon salad dressing, salt, pepper and paprika to taste

1 package cream cheese, 1 tablespoon salad dressing, ½ cup chopped water cress, salt and paprika to taste

2 packages cream cheese, 2 hard-cooked eggs, chopped, 1 teaspoon prepared mustard, 1 tablespoon chopped pickle

1 package cream cheese, ¼ cup grated carrots, ¼ cup chopped nuts, two teaspoons mayonnaise, dash salt, pinch sugar, paprika to taste

1 package cream cheese, ¼ cup crushed pineapple, ½ teaspoon lemon juice

SANDWICHES

1 package cream cheese, 6 to 8 red cherries, 2 tablespoons chopped nuts, 1 tablespoon mayonnaise

Cream cheese is also excellent with raisins, dates, pickles, jams, vegetables and chopped nuts

Canned or fresh fish such as salmon, crab meat, shrimp, lobster, or tuna may be made into fillings with the following:

SALMON

1 small chopped cucumber, 1 cup salmon, ½ cup mayonnaise, 1 tablespoon onion juice

½ cup chopped pickle, 1 cup salmon, ½ cup salad dressing, salt and pepper

¼ cup mustard pickle, 1 cup salmon, 2 chopped pimientos, ¼ cup salad dressing

¼ cup green pepper, 1 small chopped tomato, 2 tablespoons onion, ¼ cup chopped celery, 2 cups salmon

TUNA

1 cup flaked tuna, 1 tablespoon lemon juice, ½ teaspoon paprika, 2 tablespoons celery, ½ cup mayonnaise

1 cup flaked tuna, 1 tablespoon lemon juice, ½ cup chopped apple, ½ cup salad dressing

½ cup crushed pineapple, ½ cup mayonnaise, 1 cup tuna, ½ cup celery

1 cup tuna, ½ cup pickle relish, ½ cup salad dressing

1 cup tuna, 1 small pepper, chopped, 1 small bunch water cress, ½ cup chives, ½ cup mayonnaise

1 cup tuna, 1 tomato chopped, ½ cup salad dressing, ½ cup avocado

RED TOMATO SNACK

¼ cup butter
4 tablespoons flour
1 cup grated cheese
1 teaspoon paprika
1 teaspoon garlic salt
pinch of sugar

2 cups tomato sauce or soup
6 pieces buttered toast
1 tablespoon grated onion
2 stalks celery, chopped
1 cup warm milk
salt to taste

Sauté celery and onion in butter. Add flour and seasonings. Do not brown. Add milk and stir until thick. Add cheese and stir until melted. Place over hot water or in double boiler. Heat tomato sauce or soup. Add a pinch of sugar. Add to cheese mixture, stirring constantly. Pour over toast on plate and sprinkle with parsley. Serve with assorted pickles and tea as an afternoon snack. If desired, add hearts of lettuce and salad dressing. Serves 6.

HAMBURGERS WITH CHEESE

1 pound hamburger or chopped meat	1 teaspoon chopped onion
1 tablespoon prepared mustard	4 thick slices American cheese
1 chopped pickle	1 teaspoon salt
dash red pepper	paprika to taste

Combine beef, onion, salt, pepper and pickle. Form into about four patties. Cover both sides with paprika. Sauté in a small amount of fat on top of stove. Place in a flat baking dish and lay a slice of cheese on each hamburger. Place in oven 5 minutes, then under broiler from 2 to 3 minutes. Serves 4.

Serve on toast. Use red and green cole slaw to top off this dish.

POOR BOY SANDWICH

Those wonderful days when sandwiches were a nickel have passed into oblivion, but the memory of some mighty good combinations still lingers.

When Trav Crawford and Lee Gaines of the Delta Rhythm Boys went to Dillard University in New Orleans, they lived partially on a sandwich that was a meal; a real New Orleans "special" called "Poor Boy Sandwich." Although it has passed out of the five cent class, the idea is good and can certainly be utilized for stags, children's parties, or mid-night snacks. Their version would read: A loaf of French bread, split in half, dipped in gravy, several slices of meat, cheese, pickle or ham between the bread. Oh, boy! But to make it easier to eat, try:

4 hard rolls	4 thin slices beef, pork or ham
½ cup thin gravy	several slices pickle

SANDWICHES

Heat beef in gravy. Split rolls. Dip cut side of rolls into gravy. Place meat on roll. Add pickles. Creole sausages may be used as well. Serves 4.

FRIED OYSTER SANDWICH

3 dozen large oysters
24 slices toast
2 eggs
¼ cup water
1 head lettuce

1 cup bread crumbs
1 teaspoon garlic salt
1 cup salad dressing
¼ cup pepper relish
1 teaspoon celery salt

Drain oysters. Beat eggs and add water. Add garlic and celery salt to crumbs. Dip oysters into egg mixture, then into crumbs. Fry in hot deep fat. Place in a baking dish in oven to dry out. Mix salad dressing and relish. Spread on toast. Shred lettuce, sprinkle with salt. Place a bit of lettuce on each slice of toast. Place oysters on top of lettuce and toast. Make into sandwiches and hold together with toothpicks. Cut sandwiches in 4 sections. Place a stuffed olive and a ripe olive on each toothpick.

Put a small mound of fresh string bean slaw in center of a large plate. Arrange sandwich sections around slaw. Lay a few crisp French fried potatoes between each section and serve.

SANDWICH BREADS

White
Whole wheat
Rye
Banana
Chocolate
Pineapple
Brown
Prune

Bran
Raisin
Nut
Fig
Peanut Butter
Orange
Apricot

19.

Waffles, Fritters, and Pancakes

FRITTER BATTER No. 1
(For Fruits and Vegetables)

2 eggs, separated
1 cup flour
dash salt
1 tablespoon melted butter
½ cup milk

2 tablespoons wine or
    brandy
dash nutmeg
1 teaspoon lemon juice
1 tablespoon sugar

Beat egg yolks well and add flour and salt. Beat until light. Add melted butter and flavoring. Add milk to egg mixture. Fold in egg whites, which have been beaten with sugar until stiff. Batter should be thick enough to coat fruit or vegetables well. Drop with teaspoon into fat. Serves 4 to 6.

FRITTER BATTER No. 2

2 eggs, separated
1 cup flour
1 teaspoon baking powder
1 tablespoon melted butter
    or shortening

1 teaspoon lemon rind,
    grated
½ teaspoon mace
½ cup milk
1 tablespoon sugar

Beat egg yolks well and add flour, baking powder and salt. Beat until light. Add melted butter and flavoring. Add milk to egg mixture. Fold in egg whites, which have been beaten with sugar until stiff. Batter should be thick enough to coat fruit or vegetables well. Drop with teaspoon into fat. Serves 4 to 6.

FRITTER BATTER SUPREME
(For Fruits)

1 cup flour	*½ teaspoon salt*
1½ teaspoons baking	*¼ teaspoon mace*
powder	*¼ teaspoon nutmeg*
⅓ cup milk	*2 eggs*
2 tablespoons sugar	

Mix and sift dry ingredients. Beat eggs until light and fluffy. Add milk and pour into flour mixture. Mix well. Drop fruit into batter. Be sure it is well coated. Fry in deep hot fat until well brown. Drain on brown paper.

Use this batter for your bananas or fresh apricot, peach, apple or pineapple slices. You may add a few drops of lemon juice or sprinkle white wine on your fruits before placing them in the batter. This gives an extra taste treat.

SWEET POTATO FRITTERS

3 boiled sweet potatoes	*½ teaspoon mace*
1 teaspoon sugar	*1 cup white wine or brandy*
juice of ½ orange	*juice of ½ lemon*
powdered sugar	

Cut potatoes in slices. Place in a sauce pan. Cover with wine, and simmer ½ hour on a very low heat. Remove from heat. Mix into a batter with lemon juice, orange juice and sugar. Fry in deep fat until brown. Remove from fat. Drain on paper. Serve hot, sprinkled with powdered sugar. Serves 6.

APPLE FRITTERS

1½ cups flour	*1 egg*
2 teaspoons baking powder	*⅔ cup milk*
¼ teaspoon salt	*2 sour apples*

Sift together flour, baking powder and salt. Beat eggs, add milk and stir in dry ingredients. Pare and core apples, then dice.

Drop small pieces into batter. Drop into deep fat with teaspoon and fry to a delicate brown. Serves 4 to 6.

Serve with ham, pork chops or chicken.

CORN FRITTERS No. 1

1 cup canned corn	2 teaspoons baking powder
¾ cup flour	1 teaspoon sugar
½ teaspoon salt	dash nutmeg
2 tablespoons butter	1 egg

Sift dry ingredients. Add corn and egg. Then melted butter. Mix well. Drop in deep hot fat with teaspoon. Fry 8 to 10 minutes until brown. Serves 6.

CORN FRITTERS No. 2

1 can cream corn	1 tablespoon baking powder
4 egg yolks	dash salt
1 cup flour	1 teaspoon sugar

Mix corn and egg yolks. Add salt and sugar. Blend with flour and baking powder. Drop each fritter in deep fat with tablespoon at 450° F. Fry until brown, about three minutes. Turn if necessary. Drain on brown paper. Serve hot. Allow two fritters to each person. Serves 6 to 8.

WAFFLES

2 cups pastry flour	¼ teaspoon salt
2 eggs	4 teaspoons baking powder
2 tablespoons sugar	1¼ cups milk
½ cup peanut oil	

Sift dry ingredients together. Beat egg yolks and add with milk to dry ingredients. Beat until batter is smooth. Add peanut oil and fold in stiffly beaten egg whites. Pre-heat iron and bake 4 minutes. Makes 6 waffles.

SOUTHERN WAFFLES

1½ cups sifted flour	2 eggs
1 tablespoon corn meal	¾ cup sour cream
1½ teaspoons baking powder	⅓ cup melted butter
¼ teaspoon salt	⅓ teaspoon baking soda
⅓ cup boiling water	

WAFFLES, FRITTERS, AND PANCAKES

Combine flour, corn meal, baking powder and salt. Sift together twice. Beat eggs thoroughly and add sour cream. Add to flour mixture gradually, beating thoroughly. Add melted butter. Dissolve baking soda in boiling water, cool, and stir into batter. Cook in pre-heated waffle iron. Serve hot with butter and syrup. Serves 6.

Use half white flour, half whole wheat, graham flour or corn meal for a welcome and delicious change.

RICH WAFFLES

2 cups sifted flour	2 tablespoons sugar
2 teaspoons baking powder	4 eggs
1 teaspoon salt	1 cup milk
1/4 cup melted butter	1/2 teaspoon nutmeg

Mix and sift dry ingredients. Separate eggs, beat yolks until thick. Add milk. Add to dry ingredients and melted butter. Beat egg whites until stiff and fold into batter. Bake on a hot waffle iron, according to directions.

VARIATIONS

Add 2 teaspoons cinnamon to dry ingredients.
1 teaspoon grated orange or lemon peel may be added to batter.
1/4 cup grated coconut.
1/2 cup chopped fried crisp bacon.
2 tablespoons crushed pineapple.

HAM WAFFLES

2 cups flour	1 3/4 cups milk
1/2 teaspoon salt	1/3 cup melted shortening
4 teaspoons baking powder	1/2 cup finely minced
2 eggs, separated	cooked ham

Sift together the dry ingredients. Beat egg yolks and add to milk. Combine with dry ingredients. Add melted shortening and minced ham. Fold in stiffly beaten egg whites. Bake in hot wafflle iron. Serve with cheese sauce. Serves 6.

BLACK WALNUT AND BANANA WAFFLES

2 cups sifted flour	1/4 cup sugar
4 teaspoons baking powder	1/4 teaspoon baking soda

1/2 teaspoon salt
1 teaspoon mace
1/4 teaspoon nutmeg
1 tablespoon vanilla
3/4 cup melted butter

4 eggs, beaten until light
and fluffy
2 cups milk
1 cup mashed ripe bananas
1 cup chopped black walnuts

Sift together flour, baking soda, baking powder, sugar, salt and spices. Combine vanilla, well-beaten eggs, milk and mashed bananas; beat until well blended; add to dry ingredients; beat well but avoid overbeating. Let mixture stand 15 minutes. Stir in melted butter and black walnuts carefully but thoroughly. Bake in pre-heated waffle iron.

BACON WAFFLES
(Mrs. Earline Hicks)

1 1/2 cups flour
1 1/2 cups corn meal
3 teaspoons baking powder
1/2 teaspoon salt

8 strips bacon
1/3 cup shortening
2 eggs, beaten
1 cup milk

Mix and sift dry ingredients. Cut in shortening and mix well. Combine the beaten eggs and milk. Blend well. Bake on preheated waffle iron with two strips of bacon for each waffle until golden brown. Serve at once with butter and syrup. Serves 4 to 6.

FLANNEL CAKES No. 1

2 eggs
1 1/2 cups milk
2 cups flour
1/2 teaspoon salt

1 tablespoon sugar
1/4 cup melted butter
3 teaspoons baking powder

Sift dry ingredients into bowl. Beat egg yolks well. Add milk and melted butter to flour. Mix well. Fold in egg whites which have been well beaten. Drop with teaspoon on a hot griddle. Brown both sides. Serve hot with maple syrup. Serves 4 to 6. Serve with tasty pork sausage.

FLANNEL CAKES No. 2

2 cups milk
2 eggs

1/2 cake compressed yeast
1/2 teaspoon salt

2 tablespoons shortening   1 teaspoon sugar
3 cups flour

Heat milk. Cool and add crumbled yeast dissolved in a bit of warm milk or water. Add flour. Beat well, set aside to rise overnight or several hours before use. When ready to use, add eggs slightly beaten and melted shortening with remainder of salt and sugar. Cook on a hot griddle as pancakes. Serves 4 to 6.

SOUR MILK PANCAKES

2 cups flour   2 tablespoons butter,
½ teaspoon salt   or substitute
1¼ teaspoons baking   2 tablespoons sugar
   powder   2 cups sour milk
dash nutmeg   pinch of soda
2 eggs

Mix and sift dry ingredients. Add milk and eggs beaten together with melted butter. Beat well. Grease a hot griddle or skillet with butter. Pour on a very thin layer of batter. Make each cake about 5 inches in diameter. Bake until brown on each side. Spread each pancake with jam or jelly, or sprinkle with powdered sugar. Roll while hot. Serves 6.

Pancakes may be rolled plain and served with melted jelly or syrup.

Lemon butter syrup is good, too!

OLD-FASHIONED PANCAKES

2 eggs, beaten   2 teaspoons sugar
2 tablespoons melted fat   2 cups flour
   or butter   2 teaspoons baking powder
2 cups milk   1 teaspoon salt

Beat eggs well. Add milk, fat and dry ingredients which have been sifted. Bake on a greased hot griddle or skillet, as above. Serves 6. For variety, add ¼ cup corn meal instead of flour, and ¼ cup more milk.

CORN MEAL GRIDDLE CAKES

¾ cup corn meal   1 teaspoon soda
1 or 2 eggs   ½ cup hot water

¾ cup white flour	1 teaspoon sugar
½ teaspoon sugar	1½ cups sour milk

Scald meal with hot water. Add flour and salt. Beat eggs well. Add to corn meal. Put soda in milk and add to corn meal mixture. Beat well. Bake on hot griddle as directed. Serves 6.

Sweet milk may be used by omitting soda and adding 1 teaspoon baking powder.

SIMPLE SYRUPS
White Sugar Syrup

1 cup white sugar	dash salt
⅓ cup butter	1 cup water
1 teaspoon lemon juice (optional)	

Bring sugar and water to a boil. Add butter. Boil 8 to 10 minutes. Serve hot, on your favorite waffles or cakes.

Brown Sugar Syrup

1 cup brown sugar	dash salt
¾ cup water	1 teaspoon vanilla

Cook in same manner as white syrup. Butter may be added if desired.

SYRUP VARIATIONS
Add 1 cup of fruit juice such as pineapple, cherry or orange instead of water.

One teaspoon vanilla or lemon juice, a dash of nutmeg with cinnamon will give life to your syrups.

Crushed pineapple in your syrup is a novel innovation.

20.

Pies

ALL YEAR 'ROUND THERE
is a wealth of food ma-
terial for pie. Just about
every fruit or vegetable in the market stands at attention
awaiting your selection for pie making. You can close your
eyes and visualize almost any combination for your pie-
eating pleasure; pies as light and fluffy as cotton candy—
or the heavy rich varieties of your choice. No matter how
fine the bakery, it's hard to beat a good home-made pie.
The secret is in the crust . . . but what's a crust without a
good filling? So with a few simple rules for both, your date
with a pie should be a real success.

Remember, when baking fruit pies, use a deep plate so
that the juices will not escape.

When using flour, tapioca or corn starch to thicken
juices, mix with sugar, spices and fruit in a bowl before
placing in crust. In this way, the flour, sugar, etc. are well
distributed.

A small amount of butter and lemon juice add flavor and
pep.

Brushing the bottom crust with egg whites helps it to
stay crisp in fruit and custard pies.

In the summer, try icebox and chiffon pies. They are
light, and add that touch of sweetness to a cold summer
meal.

HINT ON MAKING PASTRY

In the country I've tasted delicious pie crust made with chicken fat, which can be bought in some of the poultry markets today. When the fat from the chicken is rendered and cooled, it may be substituted for shortening in pastry. It is very good and does its job well.

One country mother who could not afford shortening surprised me by making pie crust with cold, strained bacon fat. To tell the truth, I couldn't taste the difference. But it takes time to master all the little tricks that go into making unusual crust. So, when we are fortunate enough to have the best, let us make the most of it.

Making pie crust is not easy. Success cannot be attributed to luck, but to the simple directions and rules called for in the recipe.

It is always wise to try several recipes in order to find the one that is easiest for you, then stick to it until perfected. Remember these fundamental rules:

1. Measure accurately.
2. Handle crust as little as possible.
3. Use cold or ice water.
4. Shortening should also be cold.
5. Wet, sticky pie crust dough is sure to make tough crust.

PASTRIES, PIE CRUSTS

Peanut oil is superior for the making of delicious pastries; pie crusts made from peanut oil are so light and flaky that they melt in your mouth.

1 ¾ cups flour	*¼ cup peanut oil*
½ teaspoon salt	*¼ cup cold water*

Sift flour and add salt. Add peanut oil, a little at a time, mixing it in thoroughly. Add water (preferably ice water), a small amount at a time, mixing lightly with a fork. Roll out on slightly floured board. Bake in hot oven, 450° F. Makes sufficient pastry for 8-inch two-crust pie or two 8-inch pie shells.

PIE CRUST

1 cup flour	*½ teaspoon salt*
2 heaping tablespoons lard	*¼ cup cold water*

Place all ingredients in a mixing bowl and mix until you produce a flour as fine as corn meal. Add a little cold water at a time about ¼ cup until mixture will hold together. Roll out very thin on a floured board.

PLAIN PASTRY

2 cups sifted flour
1 teaspoon salt
1 teaspoon vinegar
cold water

⅔ cup shortening
½ teaspoon sugar
pinch baking powder

Sift flour, salt, sugar and baking powder. Add shortening. Cut in with fork or using pastry blender. Pour the vinegar and water into the flour mixture, a few drops at a time, mixing with a fork until it will hold together. Chill. Roll out as quickly as possible. Makes a double crust for one 9-inch pie or 2 pie shells.

BUTTER PASTRY

2 cups sifted flour
½ teaspoon sugar
1 scant cup butter

½ teaspoon salt
½ cup ice water

Sift flour, sugar and salt. Cut in butter with pastry blender or fork until coarse as corn meal. Add just enough water to hold together. Chill. Roll out to ⅛ inch thickness. Makes one 8-inch pie or 2 shells.

EXTRA FLAKY PASTRY

2 cups flour
1 teaspoon salt

¾ cup shortening
cold water

Mix and sift flour and salt. Cut in half of the shortening and add enough water to make a stiff dough. Roll out on a slightly floured board and dot with bits of shortening. Fold dough over and roll again. Fold once more. Add more shortening. Repeat until all shortening is rolled into dough. Chill and use same as plain pastry. Makes one 9-inch two-crust pie.

HOT WATER PIE CRUST

1 cup shortening
3 cups sifted flour

½ teaspoon baking powder
(optional)

½ *cup boiling water*   ½ *teaspoon salt*

Melt shortening into hot water. Beat and blend well. Add salt, baking powder and flour. Mix quickly. Wrap in waxed paper and place in refrigerator to cool. Chill overnight, if possible. Makes crust for two pies.

CHERRY AND APPLE SHORTCAKE

2 cups red cherries	1 teaspoon nutmeg
1½ cups sugar	2 tablespoons grated
2 tablespoons butter	orange peel
1 teaspoon cinnamon	1 tablespoon flour
2 cups diced apples	

Use Extra Flaky Pastry crust recipe but increase ingredients by 50 per cent.

Mix fruit and orange peel with flour, sugar and spices. Roll out bottom crust and place on it one-half of fruit mixture. Add another layer of pie crust, then fruit. Cover with top crust. Cut in several places so steam may escape. Seal edges. Bake in hot oven 10 minutes. Reduce heat to 350° F. Bake 30 minutes longer. Serves 6.

PASTRY FOR MEAT AND CHICKEN PIES

1¾ cups flour	⅔ cup butter or shortening
½ teaspoon salt	3 to 5 tablespoons milk
½ teaspoon baking powder	

Mix and sift the flour, salt and baking powder. Cut in the butter with two knives or use pastry blender. Add milk slowly, tossing the mixture together lightly and use only enough milk to hold ingredients together.

RHUBARB PIE No. 1

3 cups rhubarb	1¼ cups sugar
2 tablespoons flour	1 teaspoon butter
2 beaten eggs	¼ teaspoon nutmeg
dash salt	

Use recipe for Plain Pastry.

Peel rhubarb and cut in small pieces. Add spices. Line pie pan with plain pastry. Mix flour, salt, sugar, eggs and butter.

Add to rhubarb and pour into crust. Cover with top crust. Press edges together and trim. Bake in a quick oven 15 minutes. Reduce heat to 350° F. and bake 30 minutes. Makes one 9-inch pie.

RHUBARB PIE No. 2

2 cups stewed rhubarb, sweetened	1 tablespoon lemon juice
2 tablespoons butter	3 tablespoons corn starch or flour

Use recipe for Plain Pastry.

Combine rhubarb, butter, corn starch and lemon juice. Line pan with plain pastry crust. Add mixture. Cover with top crust. Press edges together, or make criss-cross top. Bake in moderate oven 40 minutes. Makes one 9-inch pie.

1 cup pineapple or strawberries may be substituted for 1 cup rhubarb, giving you a delicious rhubarb fruit pie.

BLACKBERRY ROLL

1 box blackberries	1 cup sugar
1 teaspoon lemon juice	1 teaspoon nutmeg
2 tablespoons butter	1 tablespoon flour
crust for 1 pie	

Wash berries, sprinkle with sugar and spices. Add lemon juice. Roll crust into rectangle, very thin. Sprinkle with flour and dot with butter. Pour berries over dough. Roll tightly, as a jelly roll. Place in baking dish. Bake in moderate oven, 350° F.

Mix together 1 tablespoon butter, ⅓ cup sugar, and juice of 1 orange; and baste roll with this mixture for approximately 30 minutes. Serve warm with orange sauce. Serves 6 to 8.

CHERRY ROLL

2 cups sifted flour	⅔ cup milk
3 teaspoons baking powder	1 can red cherries
1 teaspoon sugar	1½ cups sugar
½ teaspoon salt	1 teaspoon vanilla
6 tablespoons shortening	1 teaspoon mace

Sift together flour, baking powder, salt and sugar. Cut in shortening with pastry blender or fingers. Add milk gradually to form a soft dough. Knead lightly. Roll out to ¼ inch thickness.

Drain juice from cherries. Add sugar, mace and vanilla. Spread over dough. Roll like a jelly roll. Dot with butter. Pour 2 cups of water over roll which will produce its own sauce. Bake 35 to 40 minutes at 350° F. Serves 6 to 8.

PASTRY FOR FRIED PIES

2 cups flour	½ cup shortening
dash nutmeg or mace	1 teaspoon sugar
½ teaspoon salt	1 teaspoon vinegar
4 to 5 tablespoons cold water	fat for deep frying

Cut shortening into dry ingredients until small lumps are formed. Add vinegar and cold water until pastry is blended, not sticky. Chill about 1 hour. Roll thin. Cut in about 2½ to 3 inch squares. Put about 2 tablespoons of filling in each square. Press edges together to form a triangle. (Large circles may also be cut and folded over). Let pies stand a few minutes before frying. Heat fat to high temperature. Fry pies until golden brown. Remove from fat and drain. Sprinkle with sugar and serve. Makes 10 small pies.

A few of the fillings that may be used in fried pies:

Apple sauce (thick) with a bit of nutmeg.

Fresh apples sliced and parboiled with a bit of water. Drain— add sugar and cinnamon as needed. (Peaches and apricots may be used also).

Pitted prunes, mashed and a small amount of lemon juice added.

Cooked, sweet potatoes, mashed with a bit of cream or raw egg. Sugar, vanilla and spices.

APPLE PIE

2 cups brown sugar	1 teaspoon allspice
3 tablespoons flour	1 teaspoon cinnamon
⅛ teaspoon salt	½ teaspoon nutmeg
½ cup water	2 tablespoons granulated
1 cup Puerto Rican rum	sugar
1 box seedless raisins	juice of 1 lemon
3 tablespoons butter	pastry of double crust pie
3 pounds apples	

Combine brown sugar, flour and salt in heavy saucepan; mix well. Add water and rum; mix well. Wash and drain raisins and add to mixture. Cook over low heat, stirring continually until sugar is dissolved. Add butter, mix well; remove from heat; set aside to cool. Peel and core apples, and cut apples into very thin slices. Mix together spices and sugar. Add to apples and toss gently to coat all apple slices. Add lemon juice and toss carefully. Add raisin mixture and stir carefully to mix well. Line pie plate with pastry as usual. Pour filling in, then add top pastry as for any double crust pie. Stick in several places. Bake in a 425° F. (hot) oven for 35 minutes.

CRANBERRY PIE

5 cups cranberries
2 cups sugar
1 teaspoon lemon juice
1½ cups water
1 teaspoon grated orange rind
½ teaspoon salt

Boil sugar and water. Add berries which have been washed. Cook until they stop popping. Add orange and lemon. Remove from fire and cool. Line tin with pastry, fill with cool berries. Criss-cross pastry on top of pie. Brush with egg and sugar (optional), or sprinkle with sugar. Bake in moderate oven, 350° F., for 30 minutes. Finely chopped walnuts may be added to berries, if desired.

PUMPKIN CHIFFON PIE

1 cup brown sugar
2 eggs
1½ cups canned pumpkin
½ cup milk
½ teaspoon salt
½ teaspoon ginger
½ teaspoon allspice
2 teaspoons cinnamon
2 tablespoons gelatin
5 tablespoons cold water
2 tablespoons white sugar
baked 8-inch pie shell

Separate eggs, beat yolks. Place brown sugar, slightly beaten egg yolks, pumpkin, milk, salt and spices in saucepan. Simmer until thickened. Soak gelatin in cold water until softened, then add to hot mixture. Cool until slightly thickened. Fold in meringue made from stiffly beaten egg whites and sugar. Pour into baked 8-inch pie shell, and chill until firm. Makes 1 8-inch pie.

SPECIAL PUMPKIN PIE

2 cups strained, cooked or
   canned pumpkin
1 cup brown sugar
1 teaspoon ginger
½ teaspoon mace
½ teaspoon salt
4 eggs

¼ cup brandy or rum
1 teaspoon lemon juice
½ cup evaporated milk or
   light cream
3 tablespoons melted butter
1½ cups milk

(1 unbaked pie shell)

Combine pumpkin, sugar, spices and salt thoroughly. Beat eggs until light; add brandy or rum, lemon juice, evaporated milk, butter and milk; mix well. Add to pumpkin and beat carefully to mix thoroughly. Pour into unbaked pie shell. Bake in a 400° F. (moderate) oven about 30 minutes.

PUMPKIN PIE

⅔ cup brown sugar
½ teaspoon salt
1 teaspoon cinnamon
½ teaspoon ginger
½ teaspoon cloves
2 eggs

1½ cups milk
½ cup pancake or
   maple syrup
1½ cups canned pumpkin
1 teaspoon lemon juice

Use your favorite pie crust recipe for shell.

Mix sugar and spices, add eggs, beat slightly. Add remaining ingredients. Blend well. Pour in 9-inch pie pan lined with unbaked pastry. Bake in a hot oven 1 hour or until a silver knife comes out clean.

COCONUT PIE

1 cup shredded coconut
½ cup sugar
pinch salt

2 eggs, separated
2 cups scalded milk
1 teaspoon vanilla

Beat yolks with sugar and pinch of salt. Add stiffly beaten egg whites. Stir in scalded milk. Blend in one cup coconut. Bake in a deep pie plate with bottom crust only in a hot oven (475° F.) for first 15 minutes and in a moderate oven (350° F.) for naif hour.

PIES

BANANA SQUASH PIE

Leola Bulter is an excellent professional cook from Virginia, whose food was mighty fine when I had a chance to feast upon her cooking. But foremost in my mind was her delicious pie which had us all fooled because we thought it was sweet potato pie. Here is her recipe for banana squash pie. It's one of the best.

2 cups cooked mashed banana squash	⅓ cup butter
1 cup rich milk	1 teaspoon cinnamon
3 egg yolks	½ teaspoon nutmeg
½ cup sugar	1 teaspoon salt
3 egg whites, stiffly beaten	2 teaspoons vanilla

Line pan with pastry. Mix banana squash and milk. Beat egg yolks until light. Add sugar and melted butter with spices and vanilla. Fold in egg whites. Pour into pie shell. Bake in quick oven 10 minutes. Reduce heat. Continue to bake 20 to 25 minutes longer until firm. Cool and serve.

SWEET POTATO PIE SUPREME

When a sweet potato pie is *good*, it's just about tops in dessert, and you can always sell it to the male members at your table. I've selected three that are fit for royalty, so you can close your eyes and pick. The cooks who contributed these recipes deserve gold stars!

1½ cups mashed sweet potatoes	1 cup whipping cream
2 tablespoons honey	1 tablespoon grated orange peel
⅓ cup sugar	⅓ cup orange juice
½ cup crushed black walnuts	⅔ cup milk
1 teaspoon vanilla	½ teaspoon nutmeg
4 eggs	pinch salt

Beat eggs, potato and sugar together well. Add honey and milk. Add nuts, orange juice and vanilla. Pour into flaky pie crust shell and bake in quick oven 10 minutes. Reduce heat. Continue to bake 30 minutes or until firm. Cool. Whip cream. Add

grated orange peel and nutmeg. Spread on pie and serve.
Nuts may be omitted and crushed pineapple added.

SWEET POTATO PIE

3 eggs
½ cup white sugar
¼ cup melted butter
½ teaspoon salt
⅓ cup milk
1 teaspoon vanilla

1 teaspoon cinnamon
1 teaspoon nutmeg
1½ cups mashed sweet
    potatoes
2 tablespoons lemon juice

Beat eggs and sugar. Add melted butter, salt, milk, and spices.
Blend with potatoes and lemon juice. Pour into unbaked pie
shell and bake in hot oven 10 minutes. Reduce heat. Continue
to bake 40 minutes longer. Serve plain or with whipped cream.

SWEET POTATO PIE WITH WINE

2 eggs
½ cup brown sugar
1 teaspoon mace
1 teaspoon salt
2 tablespoons melted butter
½ cup wine, or
    ⅓ cup brandy or rum

½ cup milk
1 teaspoon lemon juice
1½ cups mashed, cooked
    sweet potatoes
1 unbaked pie shell

Beat eggs until light. Add sugar, mace, salt, butter; beat well.
Add wine, milk and lemon juice; blend well. Add to sweet potatoes, mix well, then beat carefully but thoroughly. Pour into
unbaked pie shell, and bake in a 400° F. (hot) oven about 30
minutes.

BUTTERMILK PIE

½ cup butter
⅔ cup sugar
3 egg yolks
3 tablespoons flour
½ teaspoon salt

⅔ cup sugar
1 tablespoon lemon juice
2 cups buttermilk
3 egg whites
1 10-inch baked pie shell

Cream butter or margarine with sugar, adding sugar gradually.
Add egg yolks one at a time, beating well after each addition.
Add flour, salt, lemon rind, juice. Mix well. Add buttermilk.

Beat egg whites until stiff, but not dry. Fold in carefully. Turn into baked pie shell. Bake in a moderately hot oven for 45 minutes. Cool.

LEMON PIE

Here are some special pie recipes made by Mrs. Edith Scott of Baltimore, who has been cooking as far back as she can remember. Although she refuses to be called a cateress, she certainly excels in culinary arts. Her specialty is Jewish dishes, but she possesses a fine knowledge of all foods. You'll be convinced of her talent after you try her delicious pies.

7 eggs	*2 lemons, juice and rind*
1 cup sugar	*¼ teaspoon salt*
1 baked pie shell	

Separate eggs. Beat yolks slightly. Add sugar and juice from lemons. Place in double boiler and cook until thick. Cool. Beat egg whites until stiff but not dry. Add salt and grated lemon rind. Fold in egg yolks lightly and pour into baked pie shell. Let stand until firm. Serve.

BEN'S LEMON PIE

2 cups milk	*3 eggs, separated*
1 cup sugar	*½ cup lemon juice*
½ teaspoon salt	*grated lemon rind*
3 tablespoons corn starch or	*baked pastry shell*
4 tablespoons flour	

Scald milk. Mix sugar, salt and cornstarch and pour milk in gradually. Cook in a double boiler for 15 minutes, stirring constantly until thickened. Beat egg yolks, and add to milk mixture. Cook 3 minutes, stirring constantly. Remove from heat, add lemon juice and grated lemon rind. Cool slightly and pour into baked pastry shell. Cover with meringue made from stiffly beaten egg whites. Brown in a moderate oven, 350° F. 20 minutes.

BANANA CUSTARD PIE

4 eggs	*1 teaspoon lemon juice*
¼ cup sugar	*¼ teaspoon nutmeg*
3 bananas	*1½ cups milk*

Beat eggs slightly. Add sugar, salt, nutmeg, and milk. Mash bananas, and add to custard mixture. Add lemon juice. Pour into pastry lined pie plate. Bake in hot oven, 450° F., for the first 10 minutes until firm, then reducing heat to moderate temperature 325° F., 35 minutes longer.

BUTTERSCOTCH PIE

1 cup brown sugar	3 tablespoons flour
3 tablespoons butter	2 eggs
¼ teaspoon salt	1 cup warm milk
1 teaspoon vanilla	1 baked pie shell

Place sugar and butter in a sauce pan, stirring gently until melted. Separate eggs, beat yolks until light. Add flour and milk. Beat until smooth. Mix slowly into sugar mixture. Cook until thick. Add flavoring. Pour into baked pie shell.

Beat egg whites. Add salt, 2 tablespoons white sugar, ½ teaspoon grated lemon rind. Spread over top of pie and brown in oven.

Whipped cream may be used, if desired.

For variety add ½ cup ground coconut or ½ cup crushed pecans to custard.

NEW ORLEANS COCONUT PIE

6 egg whites	½ cup confectioners' sugar
2 cups milk	½ pound grated coconut
¼ teaspoon salt	3 tablespoons butter
1 teaspoon vanilla	½ teaspoon mace
1 teaspoon fresh lemon juice	¼ cup white wine
1 unbaked pie shell	

Beat sugar and butter until light. Add wine, vanilla and lemon juice. Scald milk. Add coconut and cool. Add to sugar mixture. Beat whites of eggs until stiff. Add salt and mace. Blend into coconut mixture quickly. Place pie shell in oven and bake 10 minutes. Remove. Add filling and continue to bake until firm, 25 to 30 minutes in a moderate oven. Serve cold. Sprinkle lightly with confectioners' sugar.

MOLASSES PECAN PIE

1 cup sugar	½ cup molasses

1 tablespoon vinegar
¼ cup butter or margarine
3 eggs, well beaten
¼ teaspoon allspice

¼ teaspoon nutmeg
1 cup chopped pecans
1 unbaked pie shell

Combine sugar, molasses, vinegar and butter in heavy saucepan. Stir over heat until sugar is dissolved. Bring to boil; cook one minute. Pour slowly on top of beaten eggs, stirring constantly. Add spices and pecans and mix well. Pour into unbaked pie shell. Bake in a 300° F. (moderate) oven about 1 hour or until set. Yield: 6 servings.

EBONY'S BLACK WALNUT PIE

1 tablespoon plain gelatin
½ cup hot milk
4 eggs, separated
1 teaspoon vanilla
1 baked pie shell

¼ cup cold milk
2 squares chocolate
1 cup sugar
dash mace
½ cup crushed black walnuts

Soften gelatin in cold milk. Add melted chocolate and hot milk. Blend together well. Add slightly beaten egg yolks with mace, vanilla and half of sugar. Cool until thick. Beat egg whites until foamy with balance of sugar. Add nuts and fold into cool chocolate mixture. Pour into pie shell and let stand until firm. Spread with whipped cream and serve. Serves 6 to 8.

GRAHAM CRACKER PIE

Crust

16 graham crackers
½ cup butter

½ cup sugar

Roll out crackers. Mix well with butter and sugar. Line pie plate.

Filling

½ cup sugar
2 cups milk
vanilla

2 tablespoons flour
3 egg yolks

Mix sugar, milk, flour and egg yolks, and cook in double boiler. Add vanilla. When thick, pour into pie shell. Makes one 8-inch pie.

STRAWBERRY PIE

4 cups strawberries,
    fresh or frozen
4 tablespoons flour
1 tablespoon butter

2 teaspoons raw tapioca
½ teaspoon cinnamon
1½ tablespoons lemon juice

Combine sugar, flour, tapioca, lemon juice and cinnamon. Sprinkle over strawberries. Blend berries and mixture well and pour into baked pie shell. Dot with butter. Use remaining dough to cover pie. Place in pre-heated oven and bake at 400° F. for 10 minutes. Reduce heat to 350° and bake additional 10 minutes.

COUNTRY CHEESE PIE

Here is a recipe that takes time, but it is worth every minute of effort and waiting.

1 quart milk
½ cup confectioners' sugar
½ teaspoon salt
½ teaspoon nutmeg

1 cup cream
5 eggs
¼ cup butter

Use recipe for butter pastry pie crust.

Place milk in a pottery bowl and let stand in warm place until thick or curdled. When milk is thick, pour boiling water over it. Place in cheesecloth and let drain overnight. Mash 1 cup of milk curd through strainer. Stir in cream, sugar, beaten egg yolks, salt and butter. Flavor with nutmeg. Add beaten egg whites. Line heavy shallow pottery baking dish with butter pastry. Pour in cheese mixture. Bake 30 minutes. Makes one 9-inch pie.

VIRGINIA PEANUT PIE

⅔ cup sugar
¼ teaspoon salt
2 tablespoons butter
¾ cup ground peanuts
1 tablespoon vanilla
1 baked pie shell

2 tablespoons corn starch
1½ cups milk
2 eggs
4 tablespoons sugar
dash mace

Combine ⅔ cup sugar, salt, corn starch in double boiler. Add butter and stir in egg yolks. Cook until thick. Add ground peanuts. Pour into pie shell. Beat egg whites stiff. Add mace, vanilla and 4 tablespoons sugar. Beat until stiff but not dry. Cover with meringue and bake 15 to 20 minutes in a slow oven, 300° F. Serves 6 to 8.

CHRISTMAS PIE

½ pound suet, ground
1 cup raisins
1 cup ground or chopped apples
1 cup chopped nuts
⅔ cup sugar
½ cup dates

1 teaspoon cinnamon
1 teaspoon nutmeg
1 teaspoon mace or allspice
3 tablespoons flour
1 cup wine or brandy
½ cup red cherries, chopped

Mix fruits and nuts and sprinkle with flour. Add salt and sugar with brandy and spices. Line pie pan and place filling in pan. Cover with top crust. Bake in hot oven, 450° F., 20 minutes. Reduce heat to 350° F. Continue to bake 15 minutes longer. Serve with hard sauce. Criss-cross crust may be used, if desired. Serves 6 to 8.

EBONY'S SPECIAL MINCE MEAT

¼ pound beef, ground
1 pound suet, ground
1 pound raisins
1 pound currants
¼ pound citron, chopped
¼ pound orange and lemon peels
6 apples, peeled and diced
1 cup brown sugar

1 teaspoon cinnamon
1 teaspoon nutmeg
1 teaspoon mace
1 teaspoon cloves
1 teaspoon salt
1 cup honey
1 cup brandy, or rum
juice of 1 lemon and 1 orange

Cover beef in a small amount of water. Cook until tender. Add suet. Add apples, sugar and honey, then remainder of fruit and spices. Mix thoroughly. Cook 1 hour. Pour brandy or rum in mince meat. Pack in clean jars, and seal. May be placed in refrigerator or used at once. Makes two 9-inch pies. A flavor treat.

½ cup black walnuts may be added just before making into pies.

FRIED DRIED APPLE PIE

2 pounds dried apples,
     sliced
3 cups boiling water
1 cup sugar
grated rind of 1 lemon

2 cups flour
dash salt
2 teaspoons baking powder
¼ cup fat
½ cup cold water

Cook apples in boiling water until soft. Add sugar and lemon rind. Chill. Sift together flour, baking powder and salt. Cut in fat with two knives. Add water. Roll thin. Cut dough into rounds, using a saucer. Fill half with mixture. Cover with other rounds and press together with fork. Fry in deep fat and drain.

KEY LIME PIE

1 can condensed milk
1 teaspoon grated lime peel
1 teaspoon orange peel
½ cup lime juice
2 eggs, separated

2 tablespoons sugar
¼ teaspoon salt
1 baked pie shell of pastry
     or graham crackers

Blend milk, lime juice, lime peel and salt. Mix with egg yolks slightly beaten. Beat egg whites with sugar and orange peel until very stiff. Add to milk mixture. Pour into shell and sprinkle with orange peel. Bake in oven 15 minutes. Chill and serve. Makes one 9-inch pie.

DAMSON PLUM PIE

½ cup sugar
4 eggs, separated
1 tablespoon vanilla

¾ cup melted butter
1 cup damson preserves

Mix all ingredients, except egg whites. Beat egg whites until stiff. Fold into mixture. Pour into unbaked pastry shell. Bake 25 minutes in moderate oven.

PLYMOUTH ROCK SWEET POTATO PIE

4 medium yams
1 heaping tablespoon
     butter

sugar
½ teaspoon lemon extract
warm milk

Boil yams until tender and soft. Peel and mash with butter. Add sugar to taste (since some yams are sweeter than others).

Add warm milk until potatoes reach the consistency of heavy cream. Add lemon extract. Pour into an unbaked pie crust. Cut one inch pastry strips and place 6 across top of pie. Place in a 400° F. oven and bake 30 minutes. Makes one 8-inch pie.

BUTTERSCOTCH PIE SUPREME

3 tablespoons corn starch	3 eggs
3 tablespoons flour	2 cups milk
3 tablespoons butter	1½ cups brown sugar
½ cup nuts (optional)	

Sift dry ingredients. Beat egg yolks and sugar. Add milk and beat into dry ingredients. Place mixture in top of double boiler and stir constantly until thickened. Remove from heat. Add one tablespoon vanilla and beat until mixture is smooth. Pour into baked pie shell and bake until firm.

Beat egg whites until stiff, adding three tablespoons powdered sugar. When fluffy, sprinkle chopped nut meats on egg whites before browning on pie and brown in quick oven. Makes one 8-inch pie.

GINGER-SNAP PUMPKIN PIE
(Mrs. Earline Hicks)

1 cup canned pumpkin	¼ teaspoon clove
½ cup sugar	2 slightly beaten eggs
½ teaspoon cinnamon	1 cup milk
½ teaspoon salt	7 crushed ginger-snaps

Mix ingredients in order given. Bake in a pie tin lined with pastry 10 minutes in hot oven, 450° F., then lower temperature to 350° F., and continue baking for another 25 minutes.

CHESS PIE

6 tablespoons butter	4 eggs, separated
1 cup sugar	6 tablespoons milk
1 teaspoon vanilla or lemon juice	1 unbaked pie shell

Cream butter and sugar. Add egg yolks and beat well. Add milk and vanilla. Mix well. Pour into unbaked pie shell and bake in a moderate oven 30 to 40 minutes until firm. Beat egg whites with ½ teaspoon salt and 2 tablespoons sugar until stiff. Place on top of baked pie and brown in hot oven 20 minutes.

WHITE POTATO PIE
(Mrs. N. P. Bradford)

2 cups mashed white potatoes	1 teaspoon mace
⅓ tablespoon butter	½ teaspoon nutmeg
1 teaspoon cinnamon	1 cup sugar
3 eggs	2 cups milk
½ teaspoon salt	1 teaspoon grated orange peel
1 tablespoon orange juice	

Mash potatoes with butter and salt. Add sugar, slightly beaten eggs, spices and milk. Add orange peel and juice. Pour into unbaked pie shell. Bake until firm, about 40 minutes. Makes one 8-inch pie.

VINEGAR PIE

3 cups scalded milk	½ teaspoon salt
½ teaspoon grated nutmeg	4 eggs
½ cup sugar	2 teaspoons vinegar
1 unbaked pie shell	

Mix eggs and sugar. Add salt, vinegar and nutmeg, then hot milk. Pour into unbaked pie shell and bake 25 to 30 minutes. Cool before serving.

TOMATO PIE
(Mrs. Narcissa Smith)

2 cups canned or cooked fresh tomatoes	½ cup milk
	dash nutmeg
1 cup sugar	2 eggs
⅓ cup butter	1 tablespoon flour

Mash tomatoes. Beat eggs. Mix all ingredients. Pour between unbaked double pastry shells and bake as any pie.

COUNTRY GARDEN PIE
(Mrs. Narcissa Smith)

2 cups mashed turnips	1 teaspoon cinnamon
3 eggs	½ teaspoon mace
2 tablespoons butter	1 teaspoon salt

1 cup milk
¾ cup brown sugar
1 teaspoon lemon juice

½ teaspoon cloves
½ teaspoon allspice
recipe for 1 pie shell

Line pie pan with pastry and flute edges. Separate eggs. Mix turnips, milk and egg yolks beaten with sugar and spices. Add melted butter and lemon juice. Fold in egg whites. Pour into unbaked shell. Bake in a quick oven for 10 minutes. Reduce heat to 375° F. and bake 30 minutes longer until firm. Add one tablespoon of sherry wine if desired. Makes one 8-inch pie.

21.

Cakes, Cookies, and Candies

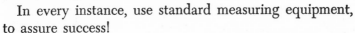

CAKE HINTS

CAKE FLOUR IS GENERALLY RECOM-mended. However, a good quality of all-purpose flour, well sifted, will give best results.

In every instance, use standard measuring equipment, to assure success!

The secret of expert cake-making is simply to follow the rules. For instance, it is basic that you pay attention to oven temperatures since some cakes require more heat than others. Always be sure your oven is pre-heated and place the cake in the center of the oven. When a cake shrinks from the sides of the pan and springs back when pressed lightly with the finger, the cake is done. Always cool a cake before frosting and then cover the sides before the top.

Other rules that should be carefully followed:

All ingredients should be room temperature. Use the best ingredients. A cake is no better than the ingredients used.

Remember a dash of salt is important. It will bring out the flavor and add a bit of zest.

Cake flour is not necessary except when making angel food or very fancy cakes. Be sure to sift flour well. Use a good bleached flour, especially in spice cakes.

CAKES, COOKIES, AND CANDIES

OLD-FASHIONED 1-2-3-4 CAKE

1 cup butter	1/2 teaspoon salt
2 cups sugar	1 teaspoon vanilla
3 cups flour	3/4 cup milk
4 eggs	3 teaspoons baking powder

Cream shortening, salt and sugar until light. Beat eggs and add to creamed mixture. Blend well. Sift flour and baking powder together. Add alternately with milk. Beat well for 5 minutes. Bake in greased layer pans or loaf pan until done. Layer cakes, 25 to 30 minutes; loaf cake, 45 to 60 minutes. Oven temperature, 350° F. Frost with Five Minute Chocolate Icing.

THRIFTY POUND CAKE

3 cups sifted cake flour	1/8 teaspoon salt
1 1/2 teaspoons baking powder	1 1/2 cups sugar
	1/2 cup milk
1 cup butter	1 teaspoon vanilla
1/4 teaspoon mace	3 eggs, beaten

Sift flour, baking powder, mace and salt together 3 times. Cream butter with sugar and vanilla until fluffy. Add eggs and beat thoroughly. Add sifted dry ingredients and milk alternately in small amounts, beating well after each addition. Pour into greased tube pan and bake in moderate oven, 350° F., about 60 minutes.

Makes one 10-inch cake.

OLD-FASHIONED POUND CAKE

1 pound butter	1 pound sugar
1 pound sifted cake flour	1 teaspoon vanilla
10 eggs, separated	1/2 teaspoon salt
2 teaspoons baking powder	

Cream butter, and blend in flour and baking powder until mixture is mealy. Beat egg yolks, sugar and vanilla until fluffy. Add to first mixture gradually, beating 15 minutes. Fold in stiffly beaten egg whites. Beat until well blended. Pour into two greased loaf pans, and bake in slow oven, 325° F. approximately one hour.

RAISIN POUND CAKE

1 pound butter	1 pound flour (4 cups)

8 to 10 eggs
1 teaspoon cinnamon
½ teaspoon mace
1 pound sugar

1 teaspoon fresh lemon juice
½ teaspoon vanilla
1 cup raisins
2 teaspoons baking powder

Cream butter with sugar until fluffy. Beat egg yolks until thick and add to creamed mixture. Fold in spices and flavoring, mixing thoroughly. Add flour, baking powder and raisins and beat vigorously 15 minutes. Fold in beaten egg whites and beat again. Pour into greased loaf pans and bake in slow oven, 325° F. for approximately 1 hour.

LOAF CAKE

½ cup butter
1 cup sugar
2 cups flour
3 eggs
½ cup milk
½ teaspoon salt

1 teaspoon lemon juice
2 teaspoons baking powder
½ teaspoon mace
½ teaspoon vanilla
pinch cream of tartar

Cream butter and sugar. Add eggs and beat with rotary egg beater 5 minutes. Add milk, mace, salt and flavoring. Sift flour into egg mixture. Beat well for 5 minutes and add baking powder and cream of tartar. Beat just enough to mix baking powder. Pour in a greased loaf pan. Bake 1 hour in a moderate oven, 350° F.

EVERYDAY CAKE

2 cups sifted flour
3 teaspoons baking powder
¼ teaspoon salt
½ cup butter

1 cup sugar
2 eggs
¾ cup milk
1 teaspoon vanilla

Sift flour, measure. Add baking powder and salt. Sift together 3 times. Cream butter thoroughly. Add sugar gradually, creaming together while adding. Beat eggs until thick and lemon colored. Add to sugar mixture and beat well. Add the sifted flour mixture alternately with the milk, stirring vigorously after each addition until smooth and blended. Add flavoring. Bake in two greased layer-cake pans in moderate oven 25 to 30 minutes.

CAKES, COOKIES, AND CANDIES

This cake may be baked in greased loaf pan in moderate oven (350° F.) 55 to 60 minutes, or baked as cup cakes, in moderate oven for 18 to 20 minutes.

For variations add fruits of your choice or nuts before final addition of flour. Using varied decorations of nuts and cherries, this cake becomes very versatile.

CAKES FOR HALLOWEEN

If you're a novice at cake-making, the month of October is a good month to try spice cakes to break the ice—and the icing.

SQUASH CAKES

2 cups flour	½ teaspoon ginger
½ cup butter	1 teaspoon nutmeg
1 cup brown sugar	2 eggs
½ teaspoon salt	¾ cup cooked Hubbard
1 teaspoon soda	squash
½ cup coconut	1 teaspoon vanilla

Cream butter and sugar. Add unbeaten eggs. Mix well. Sift together flour, nutmeg, ginger, soda, salt. Stir in squash with egg mixture. Add dry ingredients to squash and egg mixture. Stir in vanilla and coconut until well blended. Drop with teaspoon into greased muffin tins and bake about 25 to 30 minutes in a moderate oven. Frost with yellow cream icing.

Funny faces can be made with raisins. Makes 16 to 20 cakes.

SPICE CUP CAKES

1 cup sifted all-purpose flour	½ teaspoon mace
	¼ teaspoon nutmeg
¾ cup granulated sugar	¼ cup melted shortening,
2 teaspoons baking powder	or oil
½ teaspoon salt	1 egg
½ teaspoon cinnamon	½ cup milk
¼ teaspoon cloves	1 teaspoon vanilla

Mix and sift dry ingredients into mixing bowl. Pour shortening into a 1-cup measure, break in egg, then fill measure with milk. Pour into a mixing bowl, add flavoring, and gradually stir in the dry ingredients. Beat until smooth, about 1 minute. Pour into greased muffin pans and bake in a hot oven, 400° F., 10 to 15 minutes. Makes about 12 medium cup cakes.

OLD-TIME PLANTATION SPICE CUP CAKES

2 cups flour
½ teaspoon salt
½ teaspoon cloves
½ cup raisins
1 egg
½ cup shortening

3 teaspoons baking powder
½ teaspoon ginger
¼ cup ground candied
   ginger
½ cup nuts
1 cup milk

Cream butter and sugar. Add beaten egg and spices. Chop raisins, nuts and ginger, then add to egg mixture. Sift flour, salt and baking powder and add to mixture alternately with milk. Beat well. Fill greased muffin tins ⅔ full and bake in moderate oven, 350° F., 20 minutes, or until straw or cake tester comes out clean. Frost with caramel icing. Makes 16 cup cakes.

SOUR MILK CHOCOLATE CAKE

1½ cups flour
¼ teaspoon salt
1 tablespoon butter
1 teaspoon soda

3 teaspoons cocoa
1 cup sugar
1 cup sour milk
1 teaspoon vanilla

Cream butter and sugar. Add 1 cup sour milk in which soda has been dissolved. Mix and sift dry ingredients. Add to sour milk mixture. Add vanilla and bake in layers or as cup cakes in a moderate oven 20 to 25 minutes.

This may be made into a layer cake, the layers spread with an uncooked butter frosting. Or it may be baked in little cup cakes to serve with afternoon tea.

SOUR CREAM CAKE

1 cup sour cream
1 cup sugar
1½ cups flour
½ teaspoon soda

½ teaspoon cream of tartar
2 egg whites
½ teaspoon salt
1 teaspoon vanilla

Add cream to sugar. Beat well. Sift in soda and cream of tartar with flour. Mix together and beat well. Add eggs. Pour in greased square pan. Bake 30 minutes at 350° F. Frost with caramel icing.

CAKES, COOKIES, AND CANDIES

CHOCOLATE FUDGE CAKE

2 cups sugar
4 eggs, separated
4 squares chocolate
1 cup butter

2 teaspoons vanilla
1 cup flour
2 cups chopped walnuts
    or pecans

Add sugar to well-beaten egg yolks, then chocolate and butter melted together. Add vanilla, flour and nuts, and fold in well-beaten egg whites. Line pans with waxed paper and bake in a quick oven, 375° F. Frost with fudge icing.

COCOA CAKE

½ cup cocoa
½ cup hot milk
½ cup shortening
1 cup sugar
2 eggs, beaten

2 cups flour
2½ teaspoons baking powder
¼ teaspoon soda
⅔ cup cold milk
1 teaspoon vanilla

Cook cocoa with hot milk until smooth and thick. Cool. Cream shortening and sugar gradually. Add beaten eggs, cocoa mixture, sifted dry ingredients, then cold milk and vanilla. Beat 3 to 5 minutes. Bake 20 minutes in moderate oven in a square, greased pan. Cool. Spread with fudge frosting. Cut into squares.

DEVIL'S FOOD CAKE WITH COCOA

½ cup shortening
1½ cups sugar
2 eggs
4 tablespoons cocoa
1 teaspoon red vegetable
    coloring
2 tablespoons hot coffee

2 cups flour, scant
1 teaspoon salt
1 teaspoon soda
1 cup sour milk or
    buttermilk
1 teaspoon vanilla

Cream shortening, add sugar gradually, and continue creaming until fluffy. Blend in well-beaten eggs. Mix cocoa, red coloring and hot coffee together to form a smooth paste. Blend it into the creamed mixture *immediately* because cocoa mixture tends to stiffen upon standing. Sift flour once before measuring. Then sift flour, salt, and soda together, and add to creamed mixture alternately with the sour milk (or buttermilk). Blend in vanilla. Pour into well-greased and floured pan, using one 8-inch tube-center pan or one 8-inch square pan, or two layer pans. Bake cake in moderate oven, 350° F., 35 to 40 minutes if layer pans are used, 55 to 60 minutes for 8-inch pans.

When cake is cool, spread white icing or any other desired icing over top, sides and between layers.

DEVIL'S FOOD CAKE

2 cups brown sugar	½ cup sour milk
½ cup butter	1 teaspoon soda
3 eggs	2 squares chocolate
2 cups flour	½ cup boiling water
1 teaspoon vanilla	

Dissolve chocolate in boiling water. Cream sugar and butter. Add eggs, and beat well. Add soda to sour milk. Add chocolate to egg mixture. Add sour milk and flour alternately. Pour into square pan or greased layer pans. Bake 20 minutes in a moderate oven. Frost with butter icing.

MY ANGEL FOOD CAKE

1 cup cake flour	1 cup and 2 tablespoons sugar
1 teaspoon cream of tartar	
½ teaspoon salt	1 cup egg whites (10 to 12 eggs)
½ teaspoon lemon or almond flavoring	½ teaspoon vanilla

Sift flour and 2 tablespoons sugar 3 or 4 times onto a piece of waxed paper. Beat egg whites and salt 5 minutes. Add cream of tartar and beat until frothy and light. Add sugar with tablespoon, beating after each addition. Do not over-beat. Eggs should be stiff but not dry. Add flavorings. Sift a small amount of flour into egg whites, folding mixture gently until all flour is blended. *Do not beat!* After flour has been added, pour into large ungreased tube pan. Cut gently through batter with a knife to remove any air bubbles. Bake in a moderate oven 50 to 60 minutes. Turn upside down and set until cake is cool. Frost with a simple white icing or serve plain.

UPSIDE-DOWN CAKE

½ cup shortening	3 teaspoons baking powder
3 eggs	⅔ cup milk

295

1 pint fruit (strained) or	½ teaspoon salt
8 slices pineapple	1 teaspoon vanilla, or juice of
1 cup sugar	fruit to be used
2 cups flour	1 cup brown sugar

Cream shortening and sugar. Add to beaten eggs. Add sifted dry ingredients, milk, and vanilla. Mix well. Place 2 tablespoons butter in round baking dish or skillet. Add brown sugar. Place well-strained fruit in bottom of pan. Arrange artistically. Pour batter over mixture, and bake in moderate oven, 350° F., 50 to 60 minutes. When cake is done, turn pan upside down. Do not lift pan for a few minutes so that mixture will run over cake. Serves 6 to 8.

DRIED APRICOT CAKE

1 cup dried apricots	1 teaspoon baking powder
2 cups water	½ cup shortening
6 tablespoons sugar	1 cup sugar
1¾ cups sifted cake flour	2 egg yolks
½ teaspoon salt	1 teaspoon vanilla
½ teaspoon baking soda	¼ cup water

Simmer apricots, water, and 6 tablespoons sugar together for 30 minutes. Mash and measure ½ cup pulp. Sift flour, salt, soda, and baking powder three times. Cream shortening and 1 cup sugar until fluffy. And egg yolks and vanilla,˙ and beat thoroughly. Add dry ingredients alternately with water and pulp in small amounts. Bake in greased cake pan at 350° F. for 45 minutes.

MAPLE CAKE

Here is a cake from Vermont, and when you say "Vermont" that means maple syrup or sugar.

This recipe is definitely a prize-winner and has graced the table of many of the first families. It is by one of the finest Negro cooks in New England.

½ cup butter	½ teaspoon mace
½ cup sugar	⅓ cup water
1 cup pure maple syrup	2½ cups flour
2 eggs	2 teaspoons baking powder

1 teaspoon soda   ½ cup nuts (optional)
½ teaspoon salt

Cream butter and sugar. Add syrup and eggs. Beat hard for 3 minutes. Add water and sifted dry ingredients. Bake in a well-greased square or loaf pan 30 to 40 minutes at 350° F. Chopped walnuts or butternuts may be added. Frost with maple icing.

CRANBERRY CAKE

½ cup butter   1½ cups chopped seedless
1 cup sugar   raisins
2 eggs, beaten   1 teaspoon soda
1 cup strained cranberry   ½ teaspoon salt
    sauce   1 teaspoon cinnamon
2 cups sifted flour   ½ teaspoon cloves
                                   ½ cup chopped nut meats

Cream butter and sugar together thoroughly. Add beaten eggs. Add cranberry sauce which has been whipped with a fork until light. Blend together thoroughly. Sift flour, measure. Add soda, salt, and spices, and sift together. Add nut meats and raisins which have been rinsed, dried, and chopped. Add this mixture to cranberry mixture and beat together thoroughly. Turn into a greased and paper-lined eight inch square loaf pan. Sprinkle with a tablespoon of sugar and bake in a slow oven, 325° F., about 50 minutes, or until cake tester inserted in the center comes out clean. Serve in squares. If desired, serve hot, topping each serving with a spoonful of whipped cream garnished with a whole cranberry.

GRATED APPLE CAKE

½ cup butter   ½ teaspoon soda
1 cup sugar   ½ teaspoon salt
2 eggs, beaten   1 teaspoon mace
1 cup grated fresh apples   2 tablespoons cocoa
1 teaspoon baking powder   ½ cup hot water or milk
2 cups sifted flour

Cream sugar and butter. Add eggs and grated apple. Beat well. Add hot water to cocoa; then add to butter mixture. Sift flour, baking powder, soda and salt. Add to mixture and beat well.

Bake in a tube pan 45 to 50 minutes. Serve with chocolate icing.

SWEET POTATO CAKE

1½ cups sifted flour	¾ cup sugar
2 teaspoons baking powder	¼ teaspoon salt
½ cup shortening	1 teaspoon nutmeg or
2 eggs, well beaten	cinnamon
2 cups hot mashed sweet	½ cup milk
potatoes	juice ½ lemon

Sift flour and baking powder together. Add shortening and beaten eggs to potatoes while still hot. Add sugar, salt and nutmeg. Beat thoroughly. Add flour and milk alternately in small amounts, beating well after each addition. Add lemon juice. Pour into greased loaf pan and bake in slow oven, 325° F., 1 hour. Frost with lemon or maple icing.

FRUIT CAKE No. 1

½ cup finely ground suet	1½ cups flour
⅔ cup strong hot coffee	1 cup seeded raisins
½ cup sugar	1 cup currants
1 teaspoon allspice	2 cups finely chopped mixed
1 teaspoon nutmeg	candied fruits
1 teaspoon cinnamon	1 cup chopped nuts
4 eggs	½ teaspoon soda
⅓ cup molasses	

Place finely ground suet in mixing bowl. Pour hot coffee over suet and let stand a few minutes. Then stir in the sugar, spices, soda, well-beaten eggs, and molasses.

Sprinkle 2 tablespoons flour over the fruit. Add remaining flour to suet mixture, stirring until well blended. Add floured fruit. Pour mixture into a well-greased baking pan, lined with several thicknesses of wrapping paper. Bake for 2 hours and 15 minutes in slow oven (300° F.). When cool and ready to serve, cut carefully with thin, sharp knife.

FRUIT CAKE No. 2

2 cups white sugar	2 cups uncooked prunes
5 cups sifted flour	2 cups candied cherries
4 cups seedless raisins	4 cups citron

1 cup candied pineapple
½ cup candied lemon peel
1 cup candied orange peel
1 cup pecans
1 cup broken walnut meats
2 cups brandy or wine
1 cup brown sugar
1 pound butter
1 teaspoon salt

3 teaspoons baking powder
3 teaspoons cinnamon
2 teaspoons cloves
1 teaspoon allspice
2 teaspoons mace
10 eggs, well beaten
1 tablespoon vanilla
1 tablespoon grated orange
   rind

Pour boiling water over prunes, cover, and let stand 10 minutes. Drain, dry and cut from pits. Chop in very small pieces. Combine fruit, nuts and peelings. Pour wine over combined fruits. Let stand 2 to 3 hours or overnight. Sift flour, salt and baking powder together. Cream shortening, sugars and spices until fluffy. Add beaten eggs and mix thoroughly. Add flour, prepared fruit mixture and flavoring, stirring until fruits are well mixed. Pour into medium tube pans lined with two thicknesses of greased brown paper. Smooth tops of cakes and decorate if desired. Bake in very slow oven, 275° to 285° F., 3 to 4 hours. Test with toothpick or cake tester before removing from oven. Baked weight is approximately 10 pounds.

May be served as soon as cool, but improves if ripened a few days longer.

TOMATO SOUP CAKE

½ cup shortening
1 cup sugar
2 eggs
1 cup condensed tomato
   soup
2 cups sifted flour
½ teaspoon baking soda

2 teaspoons baking powder
1 teaspoon cinnamon
1 teaspoon mace
1 teaspoon nutmeg
½ cup raisins
1 cup chopped walnut
   meats

Cream shortening and sugar. Add beaten eggs, mix well. Add tomato soup, then sifted dry ingredients. Beat until smooth. Fold in raisins and nuts. Bake at 350° F. in layer pans, well greased, and sprinkled with flour, 20 to 30 minutes; loaf cake 40 to 50 minutes. Frost with cream cheese icing.

LAST-MINUTE FRUIT CAKE

⅔ cup shortening

1 cup granulated sugar

2 eggs
1 cup strained applesauce
2½ cups flour
½ teaspoon nutmeg
½ teaspoon allspice
1 teaspoon salt
1 teaspoon soda
½ cup fruit juice
½ cup finely chopped
    almonds

½ cup finely chopped
    walnuts
½ cup raisins
½ cup finely chopped dates
½ cup finely chopped
    candied cherries
½ cup finely chopped
    candied pineapple
½ cup finely chopped
    lemon rind

Cream shortening. Add sugar gradually and cream thoroughly. Add well-beaten eggs and cooled applesauce. Sift flour once before measuring. Sift together flour, spices, salt, and soda. Add flour mixture alternately with fruit juice to the creamed mixture. Add fruit and nuts which have been mixed with the last addition of flour. Pour into greased and floured pan and bake 45 minutes at 350° F. Yields 3 to 4 pounds.

DARK FRUIT CAKE No. 1

2 pounds candied cherries
2 pounds candied pineapple
2 pounds candied apricots
3 pounds currants
2 pounds citron
6 pounds seeded raisins
4½ cups sifted cake flour
1 pound butter or substitute

1 pound light brown sugar
1 dozen eggs, well beaten
1 teaspoon cloves
1 teaspoon allspice
2 teaspoon cinnamon
2 nutmegs, grated
1 teaspoon cream of tartar
1 cup strong coffee

Cut cherries in halves, and pineapple, apricots and citron in thin pieces. Put currants and raisins through meat chopper. Combine fruits with half the flour. Cream shortening. Add sugar gradually and beat until fluffy. Add eggs and beat thoroughly. Mix and sift remaining flour with spices and cream of tartar. Add alternately with coffee to creamed mixture. Add fruits, stirring until well mixed. Pour into greased and paper-lined pans and bake in slow oven, 275° to 300° F., 2½ to 4 hours, depending upon size of cake. Makes about 21 pounds.

Keep cake moist with wine, brandy or rum until ready to use. Steam in oven for 4 hours. (To steam fruit cakes in oven, place a flat pan filled with water under grill of oven. Keep filled during entire process of baking.) Makes approximately 8 cakes.

Cakes may be decorated with pieces of fruit before placing in oven.

Store cakes in crockery dishes or airtight tins.

DARK FRUIT CAKE No. 2

2 pounds seeded raisins
1¾ pounds raisins
¾ pound citron
1 pound currants
½ pound candied pineapple
¼ cup candied lemon peel
½ pound dates
½ pound candied cherries, halved
¼ cup candied orange peel
2 cups nut meats
2 cups shortening

12 eggs
1 cup molasses
4 teaspoons cinnamon
4 teaspoons allspice
1½ teaspoons mace
½ teaspoon nutmeg
½ teaspoon baking soda
½ teaspoon salt
1 cup grape juice or
    1 cup red sweet wine
1 pound flour (4 cups)
1 pound brown sugar

Grind all fruits and nuts in food chopper. Pour grape juice or wine over fruit and let stand overnight. Dredge fruit and nuts with half of the flour. Cream shortening and sugar until fluffy. Add eggs, one at a time, to the creamed mixture and continue creaming. Add molasses. Combine remaining flour with other dry ingredients and sift 3 times. Add alternately with grape juice and fruit mixture to creamed sugar and egg mixture. Blend thoroughly. Pour into greased loaf pans lined with brown paper. Bake in slow oven, 275° to 285° F., 3 to 4 hours. Test with toothpick or cake tester before removing from oven.

LIGHT FRUIT CAKE

½ pound shelled almonds
¼ pound shelled pistachio nuts
½ pound candied lemon peel
½ pound candied cherries
1 tablespoon lemon juice
10 egg whites

1 cup butter or substitute
1½ cups sugar
½ pound candied pineapple
4 cups sifted flour
1 teaspoon salt
½ teaspoon cream of tartar

Pour boiling water over nuts. Let stand a few minutes, drain,

CAKES, COOKIES, AND CANDIES

and remove skins. Cut almonds in long thin shreds. Cut fruit in thin strips. Combine fruit with nuts and 1 cup of flour. Cream shortening. Add sugar gradually and beat until fluffy. Add lemon juice. Add remaining flour sifted with salt, a little at a time. Stir in fruits and nuts. Beat egg whites with cream of tartar until stiff but not dry. Fold into batter. Pour into greased and paper-lined pans and bake in slow oven, 275° to 300° F., 2½ to 4 hours, depending upon size of pan used. A small loaf requires 2½ hours. A large 10-inch tube pan will take about 4 hours. Makes approximately 4½ pounds of cake.

CARAMEL SQUARES

1 cup light brown sugar	¼ cup butter
1 egg	1 cup flour
¼ teaspoon salt	1 teaspoon baking powder
¼ cup finely chopped nut meats	1 teaspoon vanilla

Heat butter and sugar in saucepan, stirring constantly. Cook gently until sugar is melted and mixture has cooked thick. Cool to lukewarm. Beat in egg. Sift flour with baking powder and salt. Add nut meats and stir into first mixture. Add vanilla. Turn into buttered square, 8-inch pan. Bake in slow oven, 300° F., 20 to 25 minutes. Mark in squares while still warm and then allow to cool before removing from pan. Makes 12 squares.

HOT GINGERBREAD

2½ cups flour	1 teaspoon soda
1 teaspoon baking powder	¼ teaspoon salt
1½ teaspoons ginger	1 teaspoon cinnamon
4 tablespoons sugar	1 cup molasses
1 cup water	4 tablespoons melted fat
1 egg	

Mix ingredients and beat well. Pour into a shallow well-greased cake pan. Bake 30 minutes in a moderate oven. When warm, cut in squares and serve with whipped cream or lemon sauce.

HOT WATER GINGERBREAD

2 cups sifted flour	½ teaspoon salt

2/3 cup brown sugar
1 teaspoon ginger
1/2 teaspoon cloves
1/2 teaspoon nutmeg
2/3 cup molasses

1/2 teaspoon baking powder
1/2 teaspoon baking soda
2 eggs
2/3 cup hot water
1/2 cup shortening

Melt shortening in hot water. Add brown sugar and molasses. Stir until dissolved. Blend in beaten eggs. Sift dry ingredients and beat into egg mixture. Pour into square, shallow cake pan and bake 30 minutes in moderate oven, 350° F. Serves 6 to 8.

GOLDEN GINGERBREAD

1 1/2 cups flour
1/3 cup sugar
2 teaspoons baking powder
1/2 teaspoon salt
1 teaspoon ginger
1/4 teaspoon soda

1 egg
1/2 cup honey
1/2 cup milk
1/4 cup melted butter
1/2 teaspoon cinnamon

Sift dry ingredients. Beat egg. Add honey, milk and melted butter. Blend into dry ingredients. Beat well. Pour into greased pan. Bake in moderate oven, 350° F., 30 minutes.

GINGER CAKE

2 cups flour
1/3 cup butter
1/2 cup sugar
1/2 cup molasses
2 eggs
1 teaspoon soda

1/2 cup sour milk
1 teaspoon ginger
1/2 teaspoon cinnamon
1/2 teaspoon allspice
1/2 teaspoon salt

Sift dry ingredients. Cream butter and sugar. Add beaten eggs and molasses. Mix well. Blend in spices. Add milk and flour alternately. Beat well. Pour into a greased shallow pan. Bake in a 375° F. oven for 30 minutes. Cool, cut in squares. Serve with lemon sauce, whipped cream or apple sauce.

WHITE CAKE

2 1/2 cups flour
4 egg whites
pinch salt
1 teaspoon vanilla

1/3 teaspoon almond
    extract
1/2 cup butter or shortening
2/3 cup milk

3 teaspoons baking powder   1¼ cups granulated sugar
½ teaspoon lemon juice

Mix butter, salt and sugar gradually until creamy. Add egg whites, well beaten, to this mixture. Add flour alternately with milk. Beat 150 strokes with spoon or electric mixer. Add extracts and baking powder. Place in two 9-inch cake pans or bake as a loaf cake.

Bake at 375° F. Do not open oven door for 10 minutes. Frost with pineapple icing.

BANANA CAKE

½ cup shortening   ¾ teaspoon soda
1½ cups sugar   ½ teaspoon salt
2 eggs   ¼ cup sour milk or
1 teaspoon vanilla   buttermilk
2 cups cake flour   1 cup mashed bananas
½ teaspoon baking powder   (2 or 3)

Cream shortening and sugar, and beat in eggs one at a time until very light and fluffy. Sift dry ingredients, including soda, at least three times. Combine bananas and sour milk. Add flour mixture and liquid to the first mixture. Stir in vanilla and bake in 2 layer pans at 375°F. for 30 minutes.

GRANDMOTHER'S FEATHER CAKE

4 eggs   2½ cups flour
½ cup water   dash salt
1 teaspoon vanilla   ¾ cup butter
1¼ cups sugar   2 tablespoons baking powder

Sift flour 4 times. Add baking powder and salt. Cream butter and sugar. Beat egg yolks. Add to butter with water. Mix well. Beat whites and add to creamed mixture. Fold in flour and vanilla. Pour into greased pan. Bake 45 to 50 minutes in loaf pan or as layer cakes.

SOFT MOLASSES CAKE

½ cup fat   2 cups all-purpose flour
⅓ cup sugar   ¾ cup water
1 egg   1 teaspoon baking soda

½ teaspoon salt   1 cup molasses
2¼ teaspoons ginger

Cream fat until soft. Add sugar gradually, creaming well. Beat
egg and add to fat and sugar. Sift the flour with the baking
soda, salt and ginger. Add dry ingredients alternately with the
liquid to the fat, sugar and egg. Pour into a greased, shallow
pan and bake in a moderate oven, 350° F., 30 to 35 minutes. If
a deeper pan is used, bake at 325°F. 45 to 60 minutes.

OLD-FASHIONED SPICE CAKE

½ cup butter   2 cups sifted flour
1 cup sugar   1 teaspoon soda
½ cup molasses   1 teaspoon nutmeg
2 or 3 eggs   ½ teaspoon mace
¼ cup milk   1 teaspoon cloves
½ cup raisins   dash salt

Cream butter, add sugar and unbeaten eggs. Beat well. Add
molasses and milk. Blend together. Add flour, soda, raisins and
spices which have been sifted together. Beat well for 3 minutes.
Bake in a loaf pan 375° F., 35 to 40 minutes. Frost with a
crunchy caramel nut icing.

TWO-EGG SPICE CAKE
(Mrs. Zenobia Posey)

2¼ cups bake flour   1½ teaspoons cinnamon
1½ teaspoons baking powder   ½ teaspoon cloves
1 teaspoon soda   ¼ teaspoon nutmeg
1 teaspoon salt   1½ cups sugar
½ cup shortening   1 cup milk
2 eggs

Sift together sifted cake flour, soda, salt, baking powder, spices
and sugar. Cream shortening until soft; add dry ingredients
and ¾ cup milk. Stir until flour is dampened. Beat 2 minutes.
Add eggs and rest of milk and beat. Bake in well greased loaf
pan in moderate oven (350° F.) approximately 50 minutes.

HAZEL NUT TORTE

6 eggs   ½ cup cake flour

| 2 cups ground hazel nuts | 2 teaspoons baking powder |
| 2 cups powdered sugar | 2 teaspoons vanilla |

Beat eggs thoroughly with egg beater until thick and lemon colored. Add powdered sugar, flour and baking powder mixed with nuts. Beat in vanilla. Line 2 9-inch square pans with brown paper and bake at 325° F. for 30 minutes.

Frost cake with the following mixture: Beat 1 pint heavy cream. Add 3 tablespoons sugar and 2 grated squares of chocolate. Spread between layers and on top. Place in icebox for 2 hours before serving.

MARBLE CUP CAKES

1½ cups flour	1 teaspoon vanilla
1 cup sugar	⅔ cup milk
2 teaspoons baking powder	1 egg
½ teaspoon salt	¼ cup cocoa
2 tablespoons hot water	½ cup shortening

Cream shortening. Add sugar. Beat in egg well. Sift dry ingredients. Add with milk to creamed mixture. Add vanilla and divide dough in half. Blend cocoa and hot water. Add to half of dough. Grease muffin tins. Place a bit of white, then chocolate batter in muffin tins alternately until full. Bake in hot oven, 400° F., 10 to 15 minutes. Makes 1½ dozen cakes.

ZOAH HUNT'S CAKE

½ cup plus 2 tablespoons butter	2 teaspoons vanilla
1½ cups sugar	2⅔ cups cake flour
2 egg yolks, beaten	2½ teaspoons baking powder
¼ teaspoon salt	2 whole eggs, unbeaten
	1 cup milk

Cream shortening and sugar thoroughly. Add unbeaten whole eggs, 1 at a time, then add the beaten egg yolks. Sift flour and measure. Add baking powder and salt and sift three times. Mix milk and vanilla. To the first mixture, add flour and milk alternately. Bake at 325° F. about 40 minutes.

Frosting

Use the 2 whites for icing. Put 2 unbeaten egg whites, ¼ teaspoon salt, 1 cup sugar, 1 teaspoon cream of tartar, 3 tablespoons water, and 2 teaspoons lemon juice in top of double boiler. Place over boiling water and beat with egg beater for 4 minutes or until stiff.

CHEESE CAKE

1½ cups ground bread crumbs or graham cracker crumbs
1 cup ground nuts
1 tablespoon melted butter
1 tablespoon light cream
3 tablespoons sugar
⅛ teaspoon nutmeg
4 egg yolks
2 pounds cream cheese

2 tablespoons grated lemon rind
2 tablespoons lemon juice
4 egg whites
⅛ teaspoon salt
2 cups sour cream
2 tablespoons confectioners' sugar
2 teaspoons vanilla
1 cup sugar

Combine bread crumbs, ground nuts, melted butter, cream, 1 tablespoon sugar and nutmeg. Blend ingredients well. Turn into greased spring form pan. Combine cream cheese, egg yolks, sugar, cinnamon, vanilla, lemon rind and lemon juice. Blend well and beat thoroughly. Beat ½ cup sour cream into cheese mixture and whip until smooth and well blended. Beat egg whites until firm adding sugar and salt. Beat until stiff peaks form. Fold egg whites carefully into cheese mixture. Do not beat, but blend well. Pour into spring pan. Make sure pan is securely locked. Place in heated oven 250° F. and bake 1 hour. Blend together 1½ cups sour cream, confectioners' sugar and vanilla. Mix well. Spread mixture over cake. Chill in refrigerator 4 to 6 hours before cutting.

FIVE MINUTE CHOCOLATE FROSTING

2 squares unsweetened chocolate
1 can condensed milk

1 teaspoon milk
1 teaspoon vanilla

Melt chocolate, add condensed milk and cook over boiling water until thick. Add vanilla and plain milk. Spread on cake while warm.

BUTTER FROSTING

3 tablespoons butter

¼ cup sweetened milk

> 1½ cups sifted confectioners'   ½ teaspoon vanilla
>   sugar

Cream butter and milk. Add vanilla and sugar. Beat until well blended. Spread on cake. A few drops of vegetable coloring may be added.

FUDGE FROSTING

2 squares chocolate	2 tablespoons butter
1 cup milk	2 tablespoons light corn
2 cups sugar	syrup
½ teaspoon salt	1 teaspoon vanilla

Add chocolate to milk, cook slowly until melted and blended. Add sugar and syrup. Stir until dissolved and mixture boils. Cook until mixture forms a soft ball in cold water. Add butter and vanilla. Cool until lukewarm. Beat until thick enough to spread.

CHOCOLATE ICING FOR CHOCOLATE CAKE

2 cups powdered sugar	⅔ cup hot coffee
⅔ cup cocoa	2 tablespoons melted butter
1 teaspoon vanilla	

Blend cocoa and hot coffee. Add sugar. Beat all ingredients thoroughly to consistency to spread on cake. More sugar may be added if mixture is too thin.

SEVEN MINUTE ICING

1 egg white	3 tablespoons water
¾ cup sugar	½ teaspoon vanilla
⅛ teaspoon cream of tartar	

Combine egg white, sugar, cream of tartar, and water in top of double boiler. Beat until ingredients are blended. Place over rapidly boiling water and beat with rotary beater until mixture is white and very light. Icing is ready when it holds its shape. This takes 5 to 7 minutes, depending on size of boiler and amount of beating. Remove from hot water. Fold in flavoring. This makes a generous amount of icing for square cake or baked in tube center pan, or just enough filling and icing for a layer cake.

MAPLE ICING

2 cups maple sugar 1 teaspoon vanilla
1 cup cream ½ teaspoon salt

Boil together until liquid forms a soft ball when dropped in cold water. Remove from fire and add vanilla. Cool. Beat until creamed. Spread on cake.

ICING FOR SPICE CAKE

9 heaping tablespoons 1 teaspoon vanilla
brown sugar 6 tablespoons coffee cream

Boil until mixture bubbles up and thicken with powdered sugar. Beat until a consistency to spread on cake is attained.

CARAMEL NUT ICING

1 cup brown sugar 2 tablespoons butter
½ cup sour milk or cream ½ cup crushed nuts
1 teaspoon vanilla (walnuts, butternuts or
dash salt pecans)
½ cup white sugar

Combine sugar and cream. Cook, stirring constantly, until soft ball forms in cold water. Add butter and vanilla. Cool without stirring. Beat until thick enough to spread. Add nuts. If frosting becomes too thick while beating, add a few drops of hot milk or water.

SOUR CREAM CARAMEL FROSTING

2 cups brown sugar 1 tablespoon butter
1 cup granulated sugar 1 teaspoon vanilla
1 cup sour cream few drops cream or
dash salt canned milk

Combine sugars and sour cream. Cook slowly until sugar is dissolved. Cook until a soft ball forms in cold water. Remove from heat, add butter and vanilla. Cool. Beat until stiff, adding a small amount of cream while beating to bring mixture to spreading consistency.

CARAMEL FROSTING

1 cup brown sugar pinch soda or cream of tartar

1 teaspoon vanilla
1 cup rich milk or cream
1 tablespoon butter

½ cup nuts of your choice
(optional)

Cook brown sugar, milk or cream, and soda or cream of tartar until mixture forms a soft ball in cold water. Cool. Do not stir. Add butter, vanilla and nuts. Beat until creamy and thick. If mixture begins to thicken too rapidly, add a little cream, 1 tablespoon at a time.

SNOW WHITE ICING

2 egg whites
5 tablespoons water
1½ cups sugar

1½ teaspoons white corn
syrup

Combine egg whites, sugar, water and corn syrup in the top of a double boiler. Beat with a rotary beater until thoroughly mixed. Add a pinch of cream of tartar or baking powder. Place over rapidly boiling water and cook, beating constantly 8 to 10 minutes or until mixture stands in a peak. Remove from double boiler; add 1 teaspoon vanilla and beat until thick enough to spread.

BUTTER CREAM ICING

¼ cup butter
½ teaspoon salt

2 cups confectioners' sugar
3 tablespoons cream

Cream butter gradually. Stir in sugar, adding vanilla and cream. Beat until smooth after each addition and adding just enough cream until icing is of proper consistency to spread. Vary recipe by adding 2 squares melted unsweetened chocolate to the butter.

MAMA SCOTT'S SUGAR COOKIES

¾ cup shortening
1 cup sugar
1 egg
2¼ cups sifted flour
2 teaspoons baking powder

½ teaspoon salt
2 tablespoons cream or milk
½ teaspoon vanilla
½ teaspoon lemon juice
⅛ teaspoon nutmeg

Cream shortening until soft. Add sugar and mix well. Then add egg and milk. Beat 3 minutes and add lemon and vanilla.

Sift in flour and nutmeg. Chill. Roll out very thin on a very lightly floured board. Cut in desired shapes. Bake on an ungreased cookie sheet in a hot oven, 375° F., 8 to 10 minutes.

If desired, you may sprinkle the board with sugar and cinnamon before rolling cookie dough. Then cut, place sugared side up on cookie sheet.

This versatile recipe can be changed any number of times to suit your taste for the unusual in cookies.

Coconut, nuts, jelly and spices may be used. To make chocolate cookies just add 2 squares of melted unsweetened chocolate, or ¼ cup cocoa mixed with 2 tablespoons hot water.

OLD-FASHIONED BLACK WALNUT COOKIES

2¾ cups flour	*½ teaspoon salt*
1 cup shortening	*2 cups brown sugar*
2 eggs	*1 teaspoon vanilla*
⅓ cup milk	*1 teaspoon nutmeg*
1 cup chopped black walnuts	

Cream butter and sugar. Add milk and eggs. Beat with egg beater. Sift dry ingredients and blend with vanilla into egg mixture. Drop from teaspoon onto greased sheet. Bake 10 to 15 minutes in moderate oven until brown. Makes approximately 5 to 6 dozen small cookies.

CRISP LEMON MOLASSES COOKIES

½ cup shortening	*½ cup brown sugar*
2 teaspoons grated lemon peel	*1 egg, well beaten*
½ cup molasses	*1½ cups flour*
2 teaspoons lemon juice	*½ teaspoon salt*
2 teaspoons baking powder	*¼ teaspoon soda*
1 teaspoon cinnamon	*½ teaspoon cloves*
¼ cup evaporated milk	

Cream sugar and butter. Add egg and molasses. Beat well. Add lemon juice and peel. Sift dry ingredients and blend in flour and spices with milk. Drop from teaspoon onto greased cookie sheet. Bake in a moderate oven 15 minutes. Coconut may be sprinkled on cookies, if desired. Makes 3 dozen cookies.

CAKES, COOKIES, AND CANDIES

PECAN DELIGHTS

1 cup cake flour	1/2 cup butter
1/2 teaspoon salt	1 cup broken pecan meats
1/4 cup confectioners' sugar	milk, if necessary

Sift together flour, salt and sugar. Cut in the shortening until evenly distributed. Add nut meats. Sprinkle small amount of milk into flour mixture so that it will hold together. (Use your own judgment; sometimes no milk is needed.) Chill until easy to handle. Form several pieces of dough into the size and shape of large dates. Place 2 inches apart on greased baking sheet and bake in moderate oven (375° F.) 20 minutes. Cool before removing from pan. Makes 12 cookies.

OLD-FASHIONED OATMEAL COOKIES

1/2 cup shortening	3/4 cup rolled oats
1 cup brown sugar	1/4 cup chopped nuts
1 egg	1/4 cup chopped raisins
2 cups sifted flour	1 teaspoon vanilla
2 teaspoons baking powder	1/2 teaspoon salt
6 tablespoons milk	1/2 teaspoon nutmeg
1/2 teaspoon cloves	

Cream butter and sugar. Add egg and beat well. Sift dry ingredients and add with nuts, raisins, and milk to which vanilla has been added to butter and egg mixture. Drop from spoon on a greased cookie sheet. Bake in a moderate oven 10 minutes. Makes approximately 3 dozen large or 4 dozen small cookies.

CHOCOLATE DANDIES

1/2 cup butter or shortening	3 cups flour
1 cup sugar	3 eggs
2 tablespoons lemon juice	1/2 cup chopped nuts
1 cup grated sweet	grated rind of 1/2 lemon
chocolate	1 teaspoon baking powder

Cream shortening and sugar thoroughly. Beat in eggs. Add nuts, lemon juice, and rind. Add grated chocolate to baking powder and flour which have been sifted together. Blend both mixtures thoroughly. Shape into long rolls, wrap in waxed paper and chill in refrigerator. Slice thin with sharp knife and bake on well-greased cookie sheet in moderate oven, 375° F., 10 to 15 minutes. Makes 3 dozen cookies.

CRUNCHY TEA COOKIES

½ cup shortening	2 tablespoons cream
¼ cup sugar	2 teaspoons lemon rind
1 egg, separated	1¼ cups sifted flour
½ teaspoon vanilla	½ cup chopped nuts or
½ teaspoon salt	grated coconut

Cream shortening and sugar. Add egg yolk and cream. Beat well. Add lemon rind and vanilla. Blend in flour and salt. Mix thoroughly. Cover with waxed paper and chill. Dip with teaspoon into slightly beaten egg white and one side into nuts or coconut. Place cookies nut side up on greased baking sheet. Decorate with red and green cherries. Bake 20 minutes at 325° F. Makes approximately 30 small cookies.

CHOCOLATE TEA COOKIES

½ cup butter	2 tablespoons cream or milk
1 cup sugar	2 cups cake flour
1 egg	½ teaspoon salt
1 teaspoon vanilla	2 squares chocolate, melted

Cream butter, then add sugar and egg. Beat well. Blend in milk and vanilla, then melted chocolate. Add flour. Chill. Form into small rounds and place on greased cookie sheet. Flatten with a damp spatula. Bake in a moderate oven, 350° F. Makes approximately 3 dozen small cookies.

Cookies may be decorated with nuts or coconut.

COCONUT MOUNDS

⅓ cup butter	2 cups flour
¾ cup brown sugar	¼ teaspoon salt
1 egg, beaten	2 teaspoons baking powder
⅓ cup milk	½ teaspoon cinnamon
1 teaspoon vanilla	1 cup shredded coconut

Cream butter and sugar. Add milk and vanilla to beaten egg. Sift flour, salt, cinnamon and baking powder. Add to butter and sugar mixture alternately with liquid ingredients. Add shredded coconut. Drop from a teaspoon on a greased baking sheet and bake in moderate oven 350° F. Makes 3½ dozen cookies.

DATE AND NUT COOKIES

½ cup butter	1 cup flour
¾ cup sugar	1 teaspoon mace
1 cup chopped dates	3 tablespoons grated orange
½ cup chopped nuts	rind
1 egg	1 teaspoon vanilla
3 tablespoons milk	½ teaspoon baking powder

Cream butter and sugar. Add egg and milk and beat well. Add sifted dry ingredients with dates and nuts. Chill. Place a small ball of dough on grated orange, turn plain side down on greased cookie sheet. Flatten with knife. Bake in a moderate oven 15 minutes. Makes approximately 2 dozen cookies.

BANANA TIDBITS

6 bananas	1 cup cake crumbs
1 cup ground pecans	½ cup pistachio nuts
1 tablespoon lemon juice	1 egg yolk

Peel and quarter bananas, making 24 pieces in all. Dip in slightly beaten egg to which lemon juice has been added. Then roll in cake crumbs and nuts. Coat well. Place on a greased baking dish and bake 30 minutes in a slow oven.

TEA TEASERS

The days when I ate bread, spread with butter and sprinkled with sugar, seem to have passed with childhood. But here are two recipes born out of that bread-and-butter combination as Mama Scott used to fix them for tea.

(1)

6 slices bread	½ cup brown sugar
¼ cup ground nuts	1 tablespoon cinnamon
¼ cup butter	

Remove crusts from bread. Melt butter. Add sugar, nuts and cinnamon. Blend together and spread on bread. Cut in thin strips and set under a low flame in the oven. Toast 10 minutes. Serve hot with tea or cocoa. Makes 24 strips.

(2)

6 to 8 slices white bread	¼ cup chopped peanuts
⅓ cup peanut butter	1 tablespoon cream
1 teaspoon mace	¼ cup white sugar

Remove crusts and cut bread in 4 triangular or square sections. Blend all ingredients together except sugar, and spread on bread. Dip bread in sugar. Place on greased baking dish and set in a hot oven to bake 15 to 20 minutes. Serve hot. Makes 24 to 32 sections.

CHOCOLATE CHIP COOKIES

½ cup shortening	½ teaspoon salt
¾ cup brown sugar	½ teaspoon baking soda
½ teaspoon vanilla	1 package chocolate chips
1 egg	½ cup walnuts, chopped
1½ cups flour	

Cream shortening and sugar. Add vanilla and egg. Beat well. Add sifted dry ingredients, chocolate chips and walnuts. Drop from teaspoon on a greased cookie sheet. Bake in moderate oven 350° F., 20 minutes. Makes 40 to 50 cookies.

BREAD CRUMB COOKIES

1 cup dry bread crumbs	2 tablespoons melted butter
¼ cup molasses	½ teaspoon baking soda
2 eggs, beaten	½ teaspoon salt
½ cup brown sugar	1 teaspoon vanilla

Combine bread crumbs and molasses. Beat eggs. Add sugar, melted butter, soda, salt and vanilla. Mix with bread crumbs. Beat well. Drop from spoon about 2 inches apart on a greased cookie sheet. Bake in hot oven, 400° F., 15 to 20 minutes. Makes 2 dozen cookies.

SUGAR COOKIES

1 can sweetened condensed milk	½ teaspoon salt
½ cup melted butter	½ teaspoon grated lemon rind
1 egg, well-beaten	1 teaspoon mace
2½ cups flour	1 teaspoon vanilla
3 teaspoons baking powder	

Blend together milk, butter, and beaten egg. Sift flour, adding baking powder, lemon rind, spices, and salt. Add milk and egg. Blend well to form a medium soft dough. Chill several hours. Roll out ⅛ inch thick. Cut with floured cutter. Decorate with coconut, nuts, cinnamon, or sugar. Bake on greased cookie sheet 10 minutes at 400° F. Makes 3 dozen cookies.

GRAHAM CRACKER COOKIES

12 graham crackers	4 tablespoons brown sugar
2 teaspoons butter	1 teaspoon cinnamon

Mix brown sugar, cinnamon and butter. Spread on crackers lightly. Slide under broiler from 2 to 3 minutes, or until sugar is melted. Serve with tea or cocoa. A good wholesome, inexpensive dessert for the kiddies.

NEW ORLEANS PRALINE COOKIES

4 tablespoons butter	1 cup pecans, chopped or
1 cup brown sugar (light)	broken in large pieces
1 teaspoon vanilla	3 tablespoons flour
1 egg	

Melt butter and blend in sugar. Add egg and beat well. Blend in vanilla, nuts and flour. Drop from tip of teaspoon on a well-greased cookie sheet 4 or 5 inches apart as they spread. Bake 10 minutes at 350° F. Let stand 5 minutes before removing from the pan. Use a spatula to loosen edges before lifting from pan. Cool on a cake rack. Do not store in a cookie jar or airtight container because cookies will stick together. Makes approximately 2 dozen large or 3 dozen small cookies.

SHORT'NIN' BREAD

4 scant cups flour	1 teaspoon salt
1 cup brown sugar (light)	1 pound or 1⅔ cups butter

Combine flour and sugar. Blend in butter when smooth. Place on floured board and roll out (with waxed paper on top) or pat with hands to approximately ½ inch thickness. Cut in squares or desired shapes. Bake in a moderate oven, 325° to 350° F., for 25 minutes.

BROWNIES

½ cup flour	⅓ cup butter or substitute
¼ teaspoon baking powder	2 eggs
¼ teaspoon soda	1 cup sugar
2 squares chocolate	¾ cup nuts, chopped
1 teaspoon vanilla	pinch salt

Cream butter, sugar and add eggs. Beat well. Add melted chocolate. Sift dry ingredients together and add to butter mixture with vanilla and nuts. Beat about 15 strokes. Pour in a greased square pan. Bake in moderate oven 25 to 30 minutes. Remove from oven. Cool and cut in squares. Makes 16 brownies.

GINGER SNAPS

2 cups flour	¼ teaspoon salt
¾ cup butter	1 cup brown sugar
2 teaspoons baking powder	1 egg
4 tablespoons molasses	½ teaspoon soda
½ teaspoon cloves	1 teaspoon cinnamon
1 teaspoon ginger	

Mix all ingredients and chill until very stiff. Make into balls the size of a walnut. Place on a cookie sheet about 1 inch apart. Flatten with the bottom of a small glass, which has been slightly dampened. Bake 10 to 15 minutes at 375° F. Makes 3 dozen small cookies.

TEA CAKES

18 marshmallows	1 can condensed milk
½ cup cake crumbs	½ cup ground or crushed
3 squares unsweetened	nuts
chocolate	

Melt chocolate in double boiler. Add milk and stir until thick. Remove from fire. Dip marshmallows in chocolate mixture with fork, coating well on all sides. Drop into cake crumbs and nut mixture and roll until chocolate is completely covered. Set aside to cool.

Cake crumbs may be omitted; coconut substituted.

CHOCOLATE TIDBIT COOKIES

½ cup shortening	1 cup flour

5 tablespoons brown sugar	½ teaspoon baking soda
½ cup white sugar	1 teaspoon vanilla
1 egg	dash mace
4 tablespoons cream	½ cup broken nut meats
2 tablespoons cocoa	1 package chocolate chips

Cream shortening with white and brown sugar. Add eggs and beat well. Add cream to cocoa, blend, and mix with creamed shortening. Blend in sifted flour, baking soda, flavorings, nuts, and chocolate chips. Mix well and drop from a teaspoon onto a greased cookie sheet. Bake 15 minutes in a hot oven. Makes 4 dozen.

JAM PINWHEELS

1 tablespoon sugar	½ cup jam (raspberry,
2 tablespoons melted butter	strawberry or
1 teaspoon mace	blackberry)
1 teaspoon grated lemon or orange rind	

Use favorite pie crust recipe and add ½ teaspoon baking powder.

Roll pie crust very thin. Mix mace, sugar, and butter. Spread over crust. Fold crust in half. Roll again lightly until spice and sugar blend into crust. Add lemon or orange rind to jam. Spread on crust. Roll tightly like a jelly roll and cut in very thin slices. Bake on a cookie sheet in hot oven, 400° F., 10 to 12 minutes. Makes 3 dozen.

Serve with tea, cocoa, or coffee.

PLAIN SODA COOKIES

1 cup sugar	5 tablespoons milk
½ cup butter	1 cup flour
1 egg	1 teaspoon soda

Cream sugar and butter. Beat in egg and milk. Add small amount of flour to which soda has been added until mixture is stiff enough to handle. Roll out. Cut in desired shapes. Sprinkle with sugar, cinnamon, or nuts. Bake on a greased cookie sheet 15 minutes in a hot oven. Makes 18 cookies.

EGGLESS COOKIES No. 1

1 cup sugar	1 cup sour cream

1 teaspoon baking soda   nutmeg
1½ cups flour

Mix sugar and cream. Add soda and nutmeg. Mix well. Sift in flour. Be careful not to make too stiff. Place on floured board. Roll thin. Cut in fancy shapes. Sprinkle with sugar or cinnamon. Bake on greased cookie sheet in a hot oven 15 minutes or until brown. Makes 2 dozen cookies.

ORANGE COOKIES
(Mrs. F. Alexander)

6 tablespoons shortening
¼ teaspoon salt
2 tablespoons orange juice
1 teaspoon orange rind,
    grated
½ cup sugar

½ cup nuts, chopped
½ teaspoon vanilla
1 cup flour
1 egg, beaten
1 teaspoon baking powder

Cream shortening and sugar. Add egg and orange. Beat well. Sift flour, baking powder and salt, and add nuts. Drop from teaspoon onto well-oiled cookie pans. Bake 15 minutes in a hot oven. Yield: 24 cookies.

OLD-FASHIONED SUGAR COOKIES

½ cup butter
1½ cups sugar
2 eggs

2½ cups flour
1 teaspoon baking powder
½ cup milk

Cream butter and sugar. Add beaten eggs. Sift dry ingredients and add to egg mixture with milk. Place on waxed paper. Chill 1 hour. Roll thin. Cut into squares with knife. Bake on cookie sheets 15 minutes in a hot oven. Yield: 40 cookies.

PEANUT COOKIES

3 cups flour
½ cup butter
1½ cups ground peanuts
1 teaspoon baking powder

1 cup sugar
2 eggs
1 cup sweet milk

Cream butter and sugar. Add eggs, well beaten. Add milk and flour. Flavor to taste with vanilla. Add peanuts. Drop from spoon onto greased cookie sheet. Bake quickly. Makes 45 cookies.

BUTTERSCOTCH COOKIES

7 cups sifted flour	1 teaspoon cream of tartar
1 cup butter	4 cups brown sugar
4 eggs	1 tablespoon soda
dash salt	

Cream butter and sugar. Add beaten eggs. Mix well. Sift flour, and dry ingredients. Blend into creamed mixture. Stand overnight. Form into a roll and slice very thin. Bake on a greased cookie sheet in a hot oven for 10 minutes. Makes approximately 8 dozen cookies.

GRANDMOTHER'S PICNIC FRUIT COOKIES

1½ cups sugar	1 cup butter
3¼ cups flour	1 cup chopped nuts
½ cup chopped raisins	½ cup currants
3 eggs	1 teaspoon cinnamon
½ teaspoon salt	1 teaspoon soda
3 tablespoons hot water	

Cream butter and sugar. Add beaten eggs. Add raisins, nuts and currants to creamed mixture. Blend in sifted dry ingredients with hot water. Drop from spoon onto greased cookie sheet. Bake in moderate oven, 350° F. for 15 minutes. Makes approximately 36 cookies.

MRS. A. MAE SCOTT'S PEANUT BUTTER COOKIES

½ cup butter	½ cup peanut butter
½ cup granulated sugar	1¾ cups flour
¼ teaspoon salt	1 teaspoon baking powder
½ teaspoon soda	1 egg, well beaten

Cream butter and peanut butter. Add sugar gradually and cream thoroughly. Add well-beaten egg. Sift flour, soda, baking powder and salt together. Chill dough well, form in small balls. Place on well-greased baking sheet. Flatten out with fork dipped in flour, making any design desired. Bake in hot oven 10 to 20 minutes (375° F.). Makes 36 cookies.

PECAN PRALINES

2 cups brown sugar	¾ cup pecan meats
1 tablespoon butter	4 tablespoons water

Place sugar and water in pan. Bring to a boil. Add nuts and butter. Stir until mixture begins to thicken. When it begins to bubble, remove from fire. Time—3 to 5 minutes. Drop with teaspoon on a buttered dish. Let cool.

LADY FINGERS

1 teaspoon vanilla	2 egg yolks
3 egg whites	¼ cup flour
½ cup powdered sugar	pinch salt

Beat egg whites until stiff and dry. Add sugar gradually and continue beating. Beat and add yolks of eggs which have been well beaten. Add vanilla, then flour. Put through pastry tube on unoiled paper. Sprinkle with powdered sugar and bake in moderate oven 8 minutes. Remove from paper with knife. Yield: 12 lady fingers.

CHOCOLATE KRISPIES

4 squares chocolate	2 eggs
½ cup butter	½ cup finely chopped pecans
½ cup sugar	½ cup flour
1 teaspoon vanilla	

Cream butter until light and fluffy. Add sugar gradually, creaming constantly. Beat eggs well and add to creamed butter and sugar. Melt chocolate and add to creamed mixture. Add flour. Mix well. Add vanilla. Grease baking sheet and spread batter in baking sheet. Sprinkle finely chopped pecans over batter. Bake at 350° F. 12 to 15 minutes. Remove from oven and cut in squares while warm. Yield: 24 cookies.

PEANUT WAFERS

2 cups flour	1 cup powdered sugar
1 cup water	½ cup rolled peanuts
½ cup butter	

Cream butter and sugar together until light and creamy. Add flour and water alternately. Add the peanuts. Drop on buttered tins and bake quickly. Cut in squares while hot since it soon becomes brittle after cooling. Yield: 36 wafers.

BROWN BABIES

4 squares baking chocolate	½ pound melted butter or
4 eggs	margarine
1 cup flour	½ teaspoon vanilla
½ to 1 cup nut meats, broken	1 teaspoon baking powder
2 cups sugar	

Melt chocolate and butter together. Blend in well-beaten eggs. Sift dry ingredients and add to chocolate mixture. Fold in nuts. Pour in oblong or square greased baking pan. Bake no longer than 30 minutes. Remove from oven. Cool. Cut in squares. Makes 36 cookies.

CARAMEL STICKS

2 cups brown sugar	½ cup melted butter
2 whole eggs	½ teaspoon baking powder
½ teaspoon salt	1 cup flour
1 teaspoon vanilla	2 cups finely chopped pecans

Beat sugar with eggs until very light and fluffy. Melt and add butter. Measure and sift flour with salt and baking powder. Add flour mixture and beat well. Add vanilla and beat well. Grease a baking pan and pour batter evenly on it. Sprinkle chopped pecans evenly on batter. Bake 10 to 12 minutes at 350° F. Cut in sticks while warm. Cool in pan. Yield: 50 sticks.

HOLIDAY FUDGE

3 cups sugar	2 teaspoons grated lemon
¼ teaspoon cream of tartar	rind
1 cup light cream	2 teaspoons grated orange
2 tablespoons butter	rind
½ teaspoon salt	½ cup candied cherries,
1½ teaspoon vanilla	chopped
	1 cup nuts, chopped

Combine sugar, cream of tartar, salt and cream in a large heavy saucepan. Bring to boiling point slowly. Stir until sugar has been dissolved. As mixture begins to boil, carefully wipe down sides of pan with wet cloth to remove sugar crystals.

Boil without stirring until a small amount dropped in cold water forms a soft ball. Remove from heat. Add butter. Do not stir. Cool to lukewarm. Add vanilla and beat fudge until it begins to lose its gloss. Quickly stir in lemon and orange rind, cherries and nuts. Turn into buttered pan to set and cut into pieces.

PEANUT BUTTER FONDANT

½ cup butter
2 packages confectioners'
*   sugar, sifted*
1 cup peanut butter

2 tablespoons maple syrup
2 to 3 tablespoons thick
*   cream*

Cream butter until soft. Add peanut butter and blend thoroughly. Add sugar gradually; mix well. Add maple syrup and cream. Knead until smooth and satiny. Place in a covered dish to ripen for 3 to 4 days. Keep well covered. Knead again and shape into desired sizes. Dip into chocolate if desired.

SHERRY CREAM PRALINES

1 cup brown sugar
1 cup granulated sugar
½ cup evaporated milk

2 cups pecans
3 tablespoons sherry

Mix brown sugar, granulated sugar and evaporated milk in heavy saucepan. Stir over medium heat until sugars are dissolved. Cover and bring to a boil. Boil 3 minutes. Uncover; cook until a small amount dropped in cold water forms a soft ball. Remove from heat. Add pecans and sherry. Beat until mixture begins to thicken. Drop from tablespoon onto waxed paper to form patties.

22.

Desserts

MOLASSES PUDDING

1 cup flour
pinch salt
½ teaspoon soda
½ cup molasses
½ cup buttermilk

1 tablespoon sugar
1 egg
6 tablespoons butter
½ teaspoon allspice

Beat egg. Add sugar and melted butter. Continue to beat. Fold in molasses and allspice. Mix and sift dry ingredients. Add to mixture with buttermilk. Do not beat, but mix well. Pour into a small, square cake pan. Bake 25 minutes. Serve hot with caramel or whipped cream sauce. Serves 6.

CARROT PUDDING No. 1

3 tablespoons butter
1 cup sugar
½ teaspoon salt
½ teaspoon cloves
½ teaspoon cinnamon
1 teaspoon grated lemon rind

2 eggs
2 heaping cups grated raw carrots
1 cup flour
1 teaspoon soda
1 teaspoon lemon juice

Cream butter and sugar. Add eggs. Beat well. Add carrots, spices, salt and sifted flour and soda. Beat well. Add lemon rind and juice. Pour into a greased mold or coffee can. Steam in hot water for 2 hours. Serve with ice cream sauce or hard sauce. Serves 6 to 8.

Don't be afraid to use a coffee tin if you don't have a mold. It does a nice job as a substitute.

CARROT PUDDING No. 2

5 slices whole wheat bread
    (toasted, if desired)
½ cup milk
1 cup raw grated carrots
½ cup raisins

3 tablespoons sugar
1 egg separated
1 tablespoon butter
¼ teaspoon salt

Soak bread in milk. Add carrots, raisins, sugar, egg yolk and fat. Beat whites with salt. Fold in bread mixture. Pour in greased baking dish and steam 45 minutes, or bake 35 minutes in a moderate oven. Serve with lemon sauce or hard sauce. Serves 6 to 8.

STEAMED SUET AND FRUIT PUDDING

2¾ cups flour
1 tablespoon soda
½ tablespoon salt
½ teaspoon cinnamon
1 cup milk
1 cup chopped suet or
    ⅔ cup butter

1 cup chopped raisins or
    currants
½ teaspoon nutmeg
1 cup molasses or light corn
    syrup
½ cup ground nuts

Mix and sift dry ingredients. Add molasses and milk to suet. Combine mixtures. Cut and flour raisins, then add to mixture. Turn into buttered mold. Cover and steam 3 hours. Serve with foamy sauce. Serves 6 to 8.

If water and butter are used, 3 cups of flour will be required since these thicken less than milk and suet. This pudding may be steamed in small stone cups.

INDIAN PUDDING

½ cup raisins
3½ cups milk
2 eggs
1 teaspoon nutmeg
1 teaspoon salt

⅓ cup corn meal
½ cup corn syrup
¼ cup butter
1 teaspoon cinnamon

Combine raisins, milk, and corn meal. Cook in double boiler, stirring constantly for 10 minutes. Cover and cook 10 minutes longer. Add mixture to slightly beaten eggs. Continue to stir. Add melted butter and syrup with spices. Pour into a greased baking dish and place in a pan of hot water. Bake in a moderate oven, 350° F., about 1½ hours. Serve warm with your favorite sauce or ice cream. Serves 6.

DARK PRUNE PUDDING

1 cup brown sugar	1 pound prunes
½ cup melted butter	1 cup flour
2 eggs	dash salt
½ teaspoon nutmeg	1 teaspoon soda

Cook prunes until tender and remove stones. Mash into a pulp. Melt butter. Blend in sugar, well-beaten eggs and smashed prunes. Stir in flour, soda and spices. Beat well. Pour into greased mold. Steam 1 hour. Serves 8 to 10.

Serve this pudding with ice cream sauce.

STEAMED CHERRY PUDDING

1 cup flour	½ cup sugar
¼ teaspoon salt	¼ cup milk
¼ cup butter	2 egg whites
2 cups red cherries	

Sift dry ingredients. Cream butter. Add sugar, milk, dry ingredients and fold in egg whites. Grease custard cups. Place 1 tablespoon cherries in each cup. Fill cups ⅔ full with uncooked batter. Place cups in large kettle with a small amount of water. Steam 30 minutes. Serves 6.

For Cherry Sauce

Use remainder of cherries and juice. Add:

1 tablespoon cornstarch	¼ cup sugar
juice of ½ lemon	

Boil together until thick. Serve over pudding.

STEAMED CHOCOLATE PUDDING

1 egg	¼ cup butter
2 cups flour	

2 squares melted
   unsweetened chocolate
½ teaspoon lemon juice
½ cup chocolate chips or
   grated chocolate

1 cup sugar
½ teaspoon salt
1 cup milk
4 teaspoons baking powder
1 teaspoon vanilla

Beat egg and sugar. Add melted chocolate and butter with milk and flavoring. Sift dry ingredients and fold in with chocolate tidbits or chips. Steam in pudding mold or tightly covered tin for 2 hours. May be steamed in double boiler if desired. Serve with foamy sauce or whipped cream. Serves 6 to 8.

RICE PUDDING

1 cup boiled rice
2 eggs
½ cup sugar
2 tablespoons butter
3 cups milk, scalded

1 teaspoon nutmeg
½ cup crushed fresh peaches
   or apricots
½ teaspoon salt
1 teaspoon vanilla

Beat eggs slightly. Add sugar, crushed fruit and rice. Mix well. Add salt and vanilla. Add butter to scalded milk. Pour over mixture. Pour in a baking dish, sprinkle with nutmeg and place in a pan of hot water. Set in oven. Bake 45 to 50 minutes until a knife inserted comes out clean. Serves 6.

If you desire, you may stir pudding several times after the first 15 minutes of baking. It keeps the rice from going to the bottom of the pan.

APPLE PUDDING

4 to 6 apples
½ cup brown sugar
1 teaspoon nutmeg
1 teaspoon cinnamon

2 cups toasted bread crumbs
1 cup raisins
2 tablespoons melted butter
½ cup syrup

Peel apples and slice; parboil 15 minutes. Drain. Combine sugar, spices, bread crumbs and raisins. Place alternate layers of apples and sugar in greased 1½ quart shallow casserole. Combine melted butter and syrup and pour over apples. Bake in a 350° F. oven about 30 minutes.

DESSERTS

GRATED SWEET POTATO PUDDING

2 cups grated raw sweet
    potatoes
½ cup sugar
pinch salt
dash nutmeg

1 teaspoon vanilla flavoring
    or brandy
2 eggs, separated
2 cups milk
2 tablespoons melted butter

Add sugar, salt, nutmeg and vanilla or brandy to potatoes. Beat yolks. Add milk and melted butter. Add to mixture. Beat whites until stiff. Fold into mixture. Bake in a greased baking dish in a moderate oven until firm. Pudding may be topped with whipped cream. Serves 6 to 8.

SWEET POTATO PUDDING
(Mrs. Zenobia Posey)

3 large sweet potatoes
1 cup sugar
1 teaspoon vanilla
1 unbaked pie shell

3 eggs
¾ cup milk
2 tablespoons butter

Boil potatoes until tender. Peel and put through a sieve or mash well. Add unbeaten eggs, sugar and milk. Beat well. Add melted butter. Pour in unbaked pie shell. Bake 30 minutes in a moderate oven, 350° F. Serve hot or cold with whipped cream.

BAKED PLUM PUDDING

¾ cup beef suet
1 cup bread crumbs
¾ cup flour
1 cup raisins
½ cup currants
½ teaspoon mace
½ teaspoon salt
1 cup milk

½ cup assorted candied
    fruit peels
2 eggs, beaten
1 teaspoon baking powder
½ teaspoon nutmeg
½ teaspoon cinnamon
1 jigger brandy

Mix and sift all dry ingredients except baking powder. Add milk and eggs. Beat well and let stand 1 to 2 hours. Stir in baking powder. Beat again. Bake in a greased baking dish 1½ to 2 hours. Cool. Pour 1 jigger of brandy over pudding. Serve with hard sauce or brandy sauce. Serves 6.

BREAD CRUMB PUDDING

3 cups toasted bread crumbs	2 teaspoons baking powder
1/2 teaspoon salt	1/2 cup suet, chopped fine or
1 cup sugar	melted shortening
1/2 cup chopped raisins	1 teaspoon cinnamon
1/4 cup jam (peach, apple,	1/2 cup ground walnuts or
apricot)	pecans
3 eggs, well beaten	2/3 cup milk or fruit juice

Combine ingredients in order given. Stir until well blended. Pour into buttered mold. Steam in oven or steamer 2 hours. Serve with hard sauce. Serves 6.

BREAD PUDDING THAT SLICES

4 cups bread or cake crumbs	1/2 teaspoon nutmeg
2 cups milk	1 teaspoon cinnamon
3 eggs, well beaten	1/2 teaspoon almond extract
2 tablespoons melted butter	1 cup raisins
1 cup sugar	1/2 cup chopped toasted
1/2 teaspoon salt	blanched almonds

Soak crumbs in one cup milk. Squeeze dry. To crumbs add the remaining cup of milk, beaten eggs, melted butter, sugar, salt, spices and almond extract. Mix thoroughly. Stir in raisins and almonds. Turn into greased 9 x 5 x 2 inch loaf pan or 9-inch tube angel cake pan. Bake in a 350° F. oven 1 hour. Slice and serve warm with whipped cream.

EBONY'S ROSE PETAL PUDDING

Wash the petals from 6 to 8 large fragrant roses. Remove the white pulpy matter at the base of the petals. Drain and chop finely. Place in a flat dish and run in the oven for 10 minutes at 250° F.

Then combine:

2 cups toasted bread crumbs	3 teaspoons baking powder
1 cup sugar	1/2 teaspoon salt
1/2 pound ground almonds or	1/2 teaspoon mace
pecans	rose petals

Add:

2/3 cups soft butter to bread crumb mixture; mix thoroughly.

DESSERTS

Beat:
> *3 eggs*

Then add:
> *¾ cup milk*
> *1 teaspoon fresh lemon juice*
> *1 teaspoon rose flavoring*
> *¼ cup rose water*

Add to bread crumb and butter mixture. Blend well. Pour into greased mold or 1 quart coffee can. Fill no more than ⅔ full. Cover tightly and steam about 1½ hours on top of stove. Turn pudding on dish and cover completely on all sides with sauce while pudding is warm. Decorate with rose petals that have been crystallized.

To Make Sauce:

2 cups powdered sugar	*½ teaspoon mace*
¼ cup melted butter	*1 teaspoon rose flavoring*
¼ cup currant or raspberry jelly	

Cream as hard sauce, adding three tablespoons cream while blending.

* Rose flavor may be obtained at most fine food stores.

* Rose water may be obtained at drug stores.

* To crystallize rose petals, dip fresh petals in slightly beaten egg whites; then in extra fine granulated sugar. Place in freezer overnight.

COBBLERS

Deep dish cobblers are country favorites. When everything in desserts fail, the unforgettable cobbler takes a bow. When sugar was scarce and pennies low, maple syrup and even molasses made delightful eating, added to apples which were topped with a crunchy, flaky crust. One of the nicest crusts I've had the pleasure of eating was made with black walnuts.

To your favorite pie crust recipe, add ½ teaspoon mace and ½ cup ground black walnuts. Do not roll your crust too thin.

Here is another recipe for cobbler crust which will surely have your family and guests asking for second helpings.

SPECIAL COBBLER CRUST

*1½ cups bread or cake
  crumbs, toasted and
  ground extra fine*
⅓ cup brown or white sugar
⅓ cup shortening or butter

2 tablespoons flour
*1 cup ground pecans or
  walnuts*
1 teaspoon cinnamon
¼ cup cold water

Cream shortening and sugar. Add cinnamon, flour, crumbs and nuts. Moisten with enough cold water to hold together. Spread mixture in baking pan. Add filling, then spread crust mixture over top. Bake 30 to 40 minutes.

BLUEBERRY DUMPLINGS

There is nothing comparable to hot blueberry dumplings. It is hard to believe that anything hot for dessert could be that delicious!

Where these dumplings originated is hard to say, but Aunt Lucy learned to make them as a girl in South Carolina, and although she was raised in Boston and was accustomed to all the traditional New England recipes, she never lost the knack of making these unforgettable dumplings.

1 cup flour
½ teaspoon salt
1 cup sugar
*1 tablespoon lemon juice or
  vanilla*
1 tablespoon sugar
½ cup milk or water
dash nutmeg

2 teaspoons baking powder
*2 cups blueberries (cherries
  or raspberries may be
  substituted)*
1 cup water
2 tablespoons shortening
2 tablespoons butter

Mix fruit, 1 cup sugar, butter, nutmeg, lemon juice and water. Bring to a boil in a large, open pan. Mix flour, baking powder, salt and 1 tablespoon of sugar. Cut in shortening and add milk. Drop dumplings with teaspoon into hot mixture. Cover. Steam for 15 minutes and serve hot with whipped cream. Serves 6.

BOILED APPLE DUMPLINGS

2 cups sifted flour
3 teaspoons baking powder
½ teaspoon salt

6 tablespoons shortening
cinnamon
⅔ cup milk

8 *small apples*	4 *teaspoons butter*
8 *tablespoons sugar*	1 *tablespoon sugar*

Sift together flour, baking powder, salt and 1 tablespoon sugar. Cut shortening in with pastry blender. Add milk gradually to form a soft dough. Knead lightly. Roll out to ¼ inch thickness. Cut into 8 squares. Pare and core 8 apples. Place one in the center of each square. Fill each cavity with 1 tablespoon sugar and sprinkle with cinnamon. Add ½ tablespoon butter and 1 tablespoon crabapple jelly. Fold dough over apple lightly. After dipping in hot water, tie cloth securely, but allow room for dumpling to swell. Place in pot of boiling water and boil 45 minutes. Serve with sweet sauce. Serves 8.

MAPLE PARFAITS

¾ *cup maple syrup*	1 *cup heavy cream, whipped*
2 *eggs, separated*	1 *teaspoon vanilla*
dash salt	

Heat syrup in a double boiler. Add slowly to unbeaten egg yolks. Mix and return to double boiler. Cook 3 minutes. Beat until creamy while mixture is hot. Fold in stiffly beaten egg whites. Chill. Fold whipped cream, salt and vanilla into chilled mixture. Freeze in ice tray. Garnish with cherries and nuts. Serves 6.

OLD-FASHIONED SHORTCAKE BISCUIT

2 *cups flour*	½ *cup milk*
1 *quart strawberries, black-*	1 *cup sugar*
berries, or peaches	4 *tablespoons butter or*
4 *teaspoons baking powder*	*shortening*
	½ *teaspoon salt*

Sift dry ingredients in bowl and blend in butter. Add milk. Place on a floured board, divide dough in half and pat into 2 large rounds about ¼ inch thick. Dot bottom round with butter, place other round on top. Bake in a hot oven, 450° F., 15 to 20 minutes.

Wash berries. Cut or crush berries and sweeten. Add 1 teaspoon lemon juice. Split cake in half. Cover with ½ of crushed berries. Add top half of cake and cover with rest of berries and juice. Serve with whipped cream. Shortcake may be cut in individual biscuits and served the same way.

Fresh peaches may be used. Peel and slice. Use same as berries.

SPONGE CAKE CUSTARDS

1 cup sugar	*¼ cup flour*
3 tablespoons melted butter	*1 tablespoon lemon juice*
grated rind of 1 lemon	*3 egg yolks, well beaten*
1½ cups milk, scalded	*3 egg whites, stiffly beaten*
1 teaspoon vanilla	

Combine sugar, flour, salt and butter. Add lemon juice, rind, and vanilla. Add to the combined egg yolks and milk. Mix well. Fold in egg whites to which a dash of nutmeg has been added, and pour in greased custard cups or muffin tins. Bake in a pan of hot water in a moderate oven, 325° F., 45 minutes. When baked, each little cake will have a custard on the bottom and cake on the top. Serves 6.

PUMPKIN CUSTARD

1 cup mashed pumpkin	*3 eggs*
(canned or fresh)	*1 teaspoon lemon juice*
1 cup sugar	*1 teaspoon nutmeg*
1½ cups hot milk or cream	*1 unbaked pie shell*
1 tablespoon melted	
shortening	

Beat eggs and add sugar and pumpkin. Add shortening, milk and spices. Pour into an unbaked pie shell and bake 35 to 40 minutes. Serve plain or with whipped cream.

INDIVIDUAL RICE CUSTARD WITH MERINGUE

3 eggs, separated	*½ teaspoon nutmeg*
¼ teaspoon salt	*3 cups scalded milk*
1 teaspoon vanilla	*⅓ cup sugar*
½ teaspoon grated lemon	*½ cup cooked rice*
rind	

Beat egg whites until stiff, adding a teaspoon of sugar and salt. Set aside. To slightly beaten egg yolks, add sugar, lemon rind, vanilla, nutmeg, rice and scalded milk. Mix well. Pour into individual baking cups. Top with one tablespoon meringue. Place in a pan of hot water. Bake 35 to 40 minutes in a moderate oven, 350° F.

This custard may be baked in one large mold or pan, if desired. Bake same method 50 minutes to 1 hour. Cool. Serve plain with whipped cream, or your favorite sauce. Serves 6.

FLAN

1¾ cups sugar	2 tall cans evaporated milk
3 egg whites	1 teaspoon vanilla
6 egg yolks	1 teaspoon lemon
½ teaspoon salt	dash nutmeg

Place one cup sugar in deep baking dish or loaf pan. Place over heat. Stir constantly until sugar melts and turns golden. Remove from heat. Tilt pan from side to side until all sides are coated. Mix custard. Beat eggs, add sugar and beat again; add milk and flavoring. Pour into coated pan. Cover custard and place in larger pan containing about 1 inch water. Bake 1 hour at 350° F. Remove from pan by turning upside down. Serves 8.

Pour a jigger of heavy rum over pudding just before serving.

RICE CUSTARD

½ cup rice	¾ cup sugar
1 tablespoon vanilla	½ teaspoon grated lemon rind
1 teaspoon grated orange peel	½ teaspoon nutmeg
2 cups warm milk	3 eggs

Use left over rice or boil fresh rice until very soft. Beat eggs. Add sugar and spice with lemon and orange rind. Add milk. Mix well. Pour into a baking dish or individual cups. Place in a pan of hot water and bake 40 minutes. Serves 6.

Serve hot or cold with a sauce or whipped cream. One half cup of raisins or ½ cup grated coconut may be added to the custard before baking if desired.

ORANGE CUSTARD

3 eggs	2 teaspoons grated orange rind
1 cup orange juice	

⅓ cup sugar
2 tablespoons flour
⅛ teaspoon salt

1 cup evaporated milk or
cream

Separate eggs. Beat yolks slightly. Mix flour, sugar, salt and egg yolks. Pour in orange juice and rind. Mix well. Add milk. Place in double boiler, stirring frequently until thick. Place in dish for serving. Fold in or cover with meringue, which is made with egg whites (stiffly beaten), 1 teaspoon sugar, dash of mace and a dash of salt. Serves 6.

BAKED CUSTARD

3 eggs, slightly beaten
½ teaspoon salt
⅓ cup sugar

3 cups scalded milk
1 teaspoon vanilla
½ teaspoon nutmeg

Combine eggs, salt and sugar. Add milk, then vanilla. Pour into custard cups or baking dish. Sprinkle with nutmeg and mace. Place in a pan of hot water and bake in a moderate oven, 350° F., 45 minutes or until a silver knife inserted in the center comes out clean. Serves 4 to 5.

NUT CAKE CRUNCH

½ cup flour
½ teaspoon baking powder
½ teaspoon mace
dash salt
3 eggs

1 teaspoon vanilla
⅔ cup sugar
1½ cups finely chopped
walnuts or pecans

Sift flour, baking powder, mace and salt. Beat egg whites very stiff and fold in half of the sugar. Beat egg yolks with remaining sugar until thick and well mixed. Add vanilla. Stir in flour and nuts. Fold in egg whites. Pour into a well greased square cake pan and bake in a moderate oven, 325° F., 45 minutes. When done, turn cake on a rack to cool; cut cake in half. Fill with whipped cream filling. Put halves together and spread filling on top. Cut in squares. Serves 8.

PEPPERMINT SURPRISE

½ pint whipping cream
¼ cup sugar

2 tablespoons flour or
1 tablespoon cornstarch

½ cup apricots or pineapple 1 cup milk
1 egg, beaten   ¾ cup crushed peppermint

Mix sugar and flour. Add milk. Cook until thick. Remove from heat. Add slowly to beaten egg. Return to fire and cook 35 minutes. Cool and add fruit. Place in refrigerator ice tray and cool with salt. Add peppermint and fold into custard mixture. Chill to freezing point and garnish with mint leaf and cherry. Serves 6 to 8.

Use cream style soft mints, white or butter mints. Do *not* use peppermint sticks.

BLACKBERRY SURPRISE

1 pint blackberries   1 cup whipped cream
⅔ cup sugar   ⅓ cup butter
1 cup flour   1 egg
½ teaspoon salt   2 teaspoons baking powder
1 teaspoon nutmeg   ⅓ cup milk
1 tablespoon grated orange   1 tablespoon lemon juice
    rind   1 tablespoon sugar

Wash berries and sprinkle with sugar, nutmeg, lemon juice and orange rind. Fill only half of greased muffin tins or custard cups with berries. Cream butter and sugar. Add egg yolk and beat well. Fold in egg white. Pour over berries in cups. Bake in moderate oven 25 to 30 minutes. Turn upside down and serve with whipped cream.

QUICK PRUNE WHIP

1 pint whipping cream   ½ cup confectioners' sugar
1 cup mashed prunes   1 tablespoon lemon juice
1 teaspoon grated lemon   dash salt
    rind

Whip cream. Add sugar, lemon juice, and rind to prunes. Blend together and chill. Serve in sherbet glasses. Serves 6.

JELLY ROLL AND FILLINGS

1 cup flour   2 teaspoons baking powder
½ teaspoon salt   ¾ cup sugar
3 tablespoons milk   1 teaspoon lemon juice
grated rind of 1 lemon   2 eggs

Sift flour, salt and baking powder twice. Set aside. Beat eggs until light, then add sugar. Beat well. Add flour alternately with milk, lemon juice, and rind. Pour into a shallow pan which has been lined with waxed paper. Bake in a moderate oven 15 to 20 minutes. Turn out on a clean damp cloth or waxed paper to cool slightly. Spread with jam or your favorite filling. Roll tightly. Wrap with towel or paper to set. When cool, slice and serve. Serves 8.

Jelly roll is most versatile and once you get the knack of making it, you'll repeat it often. If the edges become crisp in baking, trim off crust before rolling.

Fillings

> Lemon cream filling
> Chocolate custard and crushed nuts
> Jams and jellies
> Whipped cream and fruits
> Crushed fresh fruits

APPLE DELIGHT

Here's a dessert that has pleased a great number of *Ebony's* readers. Easy to make and a real time-saver. It is bound to be a family favorite.

6 to 8 large apples	1 teaspoon nutmeg
½ cup brown or white sugar	½ cup raisins
2 tablespoons butter	1 teaspoon cinnamon
2 cups stale cake crumbs, or toasted bread crumbs	1 cup table syrup

Peel and slice apples. Parboil about 15 minutes. Mix sugar and spices with bread crumbs. Alternate layers of apples and bread crumbs in greased baking dish until full. Mix raisins, butter and syrup. Cook 10 minutes and pour over top layer. Bake ½ hour in moderate oven. Serve with whipped cream or lemon sauce.

BAKED APPLES WITH DRIED FRUIT FILLING AND HONEY

6 baking apples	½ cup cooked and
½ cup finely chopped dates	chopped prunes
¼ cup hot water	¼ cup brown sugar

337

2 tablespoons chopped nuts ½ cup honey
2 tablespoons butter

Wash and core apples. Do not peel. Place in a shallow baking dish. Combine prunes with dates, nuts and ¼ cup brown sugar. Stuff apples with this mixture. Place in hot oven (400° F.) and bake for 45 minutes or until tender. Mix honey with water and use to baste apples frequently during the baking period. Serves 6. Serve with whipped cream.

BAKED BANANAS No. 1

6 bananas   *2 tablespoons melted butter*
⅓ cup sugar   *2 tablespoons lemon juice*

Remove skins from bananas and cut in halves lengthwise. Put in a shallow granite pan. Mix melted butter, sugar, lemon juice. Baste bananas with ½ of the mixture. Bake 20 minutes in slow oven, basting during baking with remaining mixture. Serves 6.

BAKED BANANAS No. 2

2 tablespoons butter   *1 teaspoon mace*
½ cup rolled cornflakes   *4 medium ripe bananas*
1 teaspoon powdered sugar

Melt butter, add corn flake crumbs, mace, and sugar. Roll peeled bananas in mixture. Place in baking dish. Bake 15 minutes until brown. Serves 6.

BANANA CHIPS

6 to 8 green bananas   *sugar*
dash salt   *fat for deep frying*

Slice bananas with a very thin knife or potato chip slicer at an oblique angle. Sprinkle with a dash of salt. Heat fat to 450° F. Drop in banana slices and fry three to five minutes or until brown and crisp. Remove and drain. Sprinkle with sugar and serve. Serves 4 to 6.

DESSERT SAUCES

Hard Sauce

⅓ cup butter   *1 cup sugar, granulated or*
                                confectioners'

1 teaspoon lemon juice   nutmeg
few drops of brandy or rum   dash salt

Cream sugar and butter until very fluffy. Add lemon juice, brandy or rum, nutmeg and salt. Yield: 2 cups.

Yellow Sauce

2 eggs   1 tablespoon vanilla
1 cup sugar   1 tablespoon brandy
dash salt

Beat eggs until very light. Add sugar gradually and continue beating. Add brandy, salt and vanilla.

Foamy Sauce

½ cup butter   2 tablespoons sweet wine or
1 cup powdered sugar   1 teaspoon vanilla
1 egg

Cream butter. Add sugar gradually, egg (well beaten) and wine. Beat while heating over hot water. Yield: 2 cups.

ICE CREAM SAUCE

1 egg   3 tablespoons sugar
dash salt   ½ cup heavy cream
2 teaspoons vanilla or rum

Beat egg white until stiff. Add salt. Add sugar and continue to beat. Add egg yolk, beating well. Beat cream stiff and add to egg mixture. Yield: approximately 1½ cups.

EASY CARAMEL SAUCE

1 egg   ½ cup brown sugar
1 teaspoon vanilla   1 cup cream
1 tablespoon butter   1 tablespoon flour
¼ cup evaporated milk

Melt butter and add flour. Beat egg and sugar. Add milk. Cook until well blended and sugar and vanilla are dissolved. Cool. Whip cream, add to sauce, and serve.

DEE'S PUDDING SAUCE

⅓ cup soft butter   2 egg yolks, beaten
1 cup powdered sugar   1 cup milk

Blend butter, eggs, and sugar in double boiler. Add milk. Cook until thick, stirring constantly. Add vanilla, then cool. (Serve warm, if desired.) Whipped cream or egg whites may be added when cool. Yield: 1½ cups.

FLUFFY BRANDY SAUCE

1 egg, separated
¼ teaspoon salt
4 tablespoons brandy

¾ cup confectioners' sugar
1 cup heavy cream,
  whipped

Beat egg whites until stiff. Add sugar and beat until stiff. Beat salt and egg yolks. Fold in whipped cream and brandy. Chill thoroughly. Yield: 1¼ cups.

QUICK CARAMEL SAUCE

1 cup syrup or brown sugar
⅓ cup cream

¼ teaspoon salt
½ teaspoon vanilla

Combine syrup and cream. Stir over heat until mixture begins to boil. Add vanilla and cook 3 to 5 minutes without stirring. Yield: approximately 1 cup.

WHIPPED CREAM FILLING

2 tablespoons sugar
1½ tablespoons flour
dash salt
1 whole egg

1 teaspoon vanilla, rum or
  fruit juice
1 cup warm milk
½ pint whipping cream

Place sugar, flour and salt in bowl. Blend in slightly beaten egg. Stir in milk. Cook over low heat until thick. Set aside to cool, then add flavoring. Whip cream very stiff and fold into cooled sauce. Spread on cake, decorate with cherries or fruit.

LEMON SAUCE

½ cup sugar
1 tablespoon cornstarch or
  1½ tablespoons flour
1 cup boiling water

2 tablespoons butter
1½ tablespoons lemon juice
1 teaspoon nutmeg

Mix sugar and cornstarch. Add water slowly, stirring constantly. Boil five minutes, then remove from fire. Add butter, lemon juice, and nutmeg. One tablespoon brandy may be used instead of lemon juice and nutmeg. Yield: 1 cup.

COCOA SAUCE

½ cup cocoa
½ cup milk or water
dash salt
2 tablespoons butter

1 cup sugar
2 tablespoons cream
vanilla

Mix cocoa with a small amount of milk to make paste. Add sugar and milk. Cook slowly, stirring constantly until it begins to boil. Add butter, cover, and boil 5 minutes. Yield: 1½ cups.

ORANGE SAUCE

¼ cup sugar
1 tablespoon flour or
  cornstarch
2 tablespoons grated orange
  rind

¼ teaspoon salt
1 cup orange juice
⅓ cup cream

Mix sugar, salt, and corn starch. Add orange juice and rind, stirring constantly about 10 minutes until thick. Cover and cook 15 minutes. Stir in cream and serve. Yield: 1¼ cups.

ROSE PETAL ICE CREAM

1 pint milk
3 eggs
1 quart cream
¼ cup honey
1 tablespoon cornstarch
1 cup crushed or chopped
  red or pink rose petals

several drops red coloring
  (beet or cherry juice)
1 teaspoon rose flavoring
2 cups confectioners' sugar
¼ teaspoon salt

Blend sugar, eggs, corn starch, and milk. Cook over hot water until thick. Add rose petals and cool. Whip cream, but not stiff. Add coloring and honey, salt and flavoring. Pour in freezer. Freeze until firm. Remove dasher. Pack. Serve on rose petals which have been washed and dried. Makes 2 quarts.

SNOW ICE CREAM

Being a kid is fun and the thrill of your first sled or bike is never forgotten. Popping corn, roasting wieners, these things always remain pleasant memories. Snow ice cream represented all the joy of childhood to Carl Jones. Though born in Kansas, he was raised in California and the memory of snow passed into oblivion for him. On a tour with the Delta Rhythm Boys, with whom he chirps first tenor, he encountered snow again. What a kick to recall his kid days and that snow ice cream!

Carl says, "Remove the top layer, and be sure the snow is clean."

Mix ½ cup sugar and 1 cup cream or milk with 1 tablespoon vanilla in a large bowl. Add snow gradually until you get the consistency of ice cream. For variety, says singing Chef Jones, Add:

> *1 cup crushed pineapple*
> *1 cup mashed bananas*
> *1 cup crushed sweetened apricots, peaches,*
> *   or frozen strawberries*

ICE CREAMS

If you are a busy housewife and time is your problem, sweetened condensed milk will help you make ice creams.

Here are several ice cream recipes that can be frozen in your refrigerator.

RASPBERRY SHERBET

2 cups fresh raspberries
⅔ cup sweetened condensed milk
2 tablespoons lemon juice
⅓ cup confectioners' sugar
2 egg whites

Crush berries and combine with sugar, lemon juice and milk. Chill about 30 minutes. Remove from refrigerator and fold in egg whites which have been stiffly beaten. Place in freezing unit until about half frozen. Scrape sides of pan. *Beat well* but do not allow to melt. Place in freezer until frozen. Makes 1 quart.

Apricots may be substituted for berries.

FRESH PEACH ICE CREAM

1 cup crushed peaches
1 can condensed milk
1 cup whipping cream
½ cup cream
½ cup confectioners' sugar
1 teaspoon vanilla

342

Blend milk, cream, and peaches which have been sweetened with sugar. Chill. Whip cream. Add vanilla and fold into mixture. Pour into freezing pan. Place in ice compartment to freeze. After mixture is half frozen, remove from refrigerator. Scrape mixture from sides of tray. Beat until smooth but not melted. Place in freezing unit and freeze until firm. Makes 1 quart.

VANILLA ICE CREAM

1 quart milk	2 teaspoons vanilla
2 cups sugar	1 pint cream
6 eggs	1 teaspoon salt
dash nutmeg	

Boil milk and cream. Beat yolks of eggs and sugar until light. Pour milk over yolks and sugar. Fold in vanilla, nutmeg and egg whites which have been stiffly beaten. Set aside to cool. Pour into freezer and freeze. Makes two quarts.

PISTACHIO ICE CREAM

1 quart milk	1/4 pound chopped pistachio
1 1/2 cups sugar	nuts
1 pint cream	1/4 teaspoon green vegetable
dash salt	coloring
1 tablespoon flour or	3 eggs
cornstarch	1 teaspoon vanilla or
	lemon juice

Blend sugar, cornstarch and egg yolks. Boil to make a thin custard. Cool, add nuts, coloring and cream. Fold in egg whites stiffly beaten. Cool, pour into freezer and freeze until firm. Remove dasher. Pack until ready to serve. Makes two quarts.

CHOCOLATE ICE CREAM

1 square unsweetened	1 teaspoon vanilla
chocolate	1/2 cup whipping cream
2/3 cup condensed milk	1/2 teaspoon salt
2/3 cup milk	

Melt chocolate in double boiler. Add sweetened milk and stir until thick. Add milk and vanilla and mix well. Chill thoroughly. Whip cream, fold into chilled mixture and freeze.

DESSERTS

When half frozen, remove from pan and beat until smooth. Return to refrigerator and freeze. Serves 6.

PEANUT ICE CREAM

1 pint peanuts	*1 pint cream*
2 cups sugar	*2 teaspoons vanilla*
2 quarts milk	*3 eggs*

Roast, shell, and roll the peanuts until they are quite fine. Brown one cup of sugar and add to milk, then add remainder of sugar, cream, vanilla, beaten eggs, and peanuts. Freeze. Makes ½ gallon.

WATERMELON SHERBET

Cut ripe watermelon in half. Scoop out the inside pulp and press until dry. Strain the juice. To each pint of juice, use 1 cup sugar, 1 cup water and ½ lemon. Flavor with mint. Pour mixture into freezer and freeze with equal parts of salt and ice. When sherbet is frozen and ready to serve, scoop it back into chilled watermelon rind and serve.

APRICOT ICE

juice of 4 lemons	*2 quarts rich milk or light*
juice and pulp of large can	*cream*
apricots	*juice of 6 oranges*
3 cups sugar	*1 cup water*

Make a syrup of sugar and water. Put apricots through sieve. Mix and freeze. Add cream when half frozen. Yield: 1 gallon.

MANHATTAN FREEZE

1½ cups orange juice	*¼ cup white sugar*
¼ cup lemon juice	*½ pint heavy cream*
¼ cup powdered sugar	*¼ teaspoon vanilla*
⅔ cup crushed macaroons	*pinch salt*

Mix orange and lemon juices, and sugar. Pour in freezing tray. Whip cream and powdered sugar and vanilla. Add macaroons which have been crushed into a powder. Pour this mixture over chilled fruit juice. Cover freezing pan with waxed paper and freeze. The two mixtures will not mix but will have the appearance of brick ice cream.

344

BUTTERMILK ICE CREAM

1 cup buttermilk
1 cup cream
1 cup sugar
1 teaspoon vanilla

1 cup crushed pineapple, drained
2 tablespoons sugar

Mix buttermilk, cream and sugar. Freeze until thick. Add pineapple blended with sugar, and vanilla. Continue to freeze until hard. Serves 6 to 8.

BANANA FREEZE

4 ripe bananas
1 cup evaporated milk

20 marshmallows, cut

Mash bananas and beat until creamy. Add marshmallows cut with scissors and melt over hot water. Cool. Scald milk. Cool and chill 5 minutes in refrigerator tray. Whip, fold in banana mixture and freeze in refrigerator tray. Serves 6.

BAKED STUFFED PEACHES

1/3 cup nut meats, broken
6 whole marshmallows

6 peach halves
1/3 cup brown sugar

Drain peaches well. Fill centers with nut meats. Top with brown sugar and a marshmallow. Place in shallow baking dish and bake 20 minutes at 300° F. Serve with game or poultry. Serves 6.

SWEET POTATOES ON HALF SHELL

6 sweet potatoes
1/4 cup sugar
1/4 teaspoon salt

1/4 cup chopped nuts
12 marshmallows
3 tablespoons butter

Scrub potatoes. Oil and bake in hot oven until soft. Cut in halves lengthwise and scoop out insides. Mash and add butter, salt, sugar and nuts. Whip until light. Refill the shells. Top each half with 2 marshmallows, and brown in a moderate oven. Serves 6.

This same method is used to prepare potatoes for orange cups. Scoop out pulp from orange halves, fill with potato mixture and bake until marshmallows are browned.

345

DESERTS

SWEET POTATO PONE
(Mrs. Narcissa Smith)

2 cups grated raw sweet
  potatoes
3 eggs
½ teaspoon cinnamon

½ cup milk
½ cup sugar
½ teaspoon nutmeg
pinch salt

Beat eggs together or separately. Add other ingredients, mixing thoroughly. Place in greased pan and let brown slightly. Serve hot. Serves 6.

APRICOT SOUFFLÉ

6 eggs
1 cup sugar
¼ teaspoon salt

1 cup mashed or strained
  cooked apricots
1 teaspoon grated lemon rind
½ teaspoon cream of tartar

Separate eggs, beat yolks until thick. Add sugar and salt, beating well. Stir in mashed apricots and lemon rind. Beat egg whites and cream of tartar until stiff, and fold into yolk mixture. Place in a buttered baking dish and put dish in a pan of hot water. Bake in a moderate oven, 350° F. for one hour until set. Serve at once with or without sauce as desired. Serves 6.

Peaches, apples or any fruit of your choice may be used.

LEMON SOUFFLÉ

6 eggs
1 cup sugar
¼ teaspoon salt

¼ cup lemon juice
1 teaspoon grated lemon rind
½ teaspoon cream of tartar

Separate eggs, beat yolks until thick. Add sugar and salt, beating well. Stir in lemon juice and rind. Beat egg whites and cream of tartar until stiff and fold into yolk mixture. Place in a buttered baking dish and put dish in a pan of hot water. Bake in a moderate oven, 350° F. for 1 hour until set. Serve at once with or without sauce as desired. Serves 6.

SEA-FOAM MERINGUES

⅛ teaspoon salt
½ teaspoon vinegar
¼ teaspoon vanilla

3 egg whites
1 cup sugar

346

Add salt, vinegar, and vanilla to egg whites. Beat until stiff. Add sugar slowly and continue beating until mixture is very stiff, then drop by spoon on brown paper (not greased) and bake on a flat baking tin in oven, 300° F., for 45 minutes. Leave meringues in opened oven 10 minutes or less to dry. Remove from tin and place on waxed paper to cool.

These meringues are simply lovely used as salad boats filled with any number of delectables, and as confections to accompany ice cream, pudding and so on.

SPICED APPLES

¼ cup butter	1 teaspoon cinnamon
½ cup finely chopped black walnuts	¼ cup maple syrup
	½ cup bread crumbs
1 teaspoon mace	

Blend all ingredients together except apples. Wash apples and partially core with tip of paring knife, cut skin around center outside of apples. Place in shallow baking dish. Fill center with mixture. Bake in 350° F. oven for 45 minutes. Baste occasionally.

CHOCOLATE CRINKLE CUPS

⅛ ounce package (8 squares) Bakers Dot Chocolate	8 to 10 paper baking cups (about 3-inch diameter)
2 tablespoons butter	

Place chocolate and butter in top of double boiler. Stir until chocolate is melted. Remove from heat; mix well. (Mixture should be thick, or cooled until thick). With the back of a teaspoon, "brush" or swirl the mixture around the bottom and inside the paper baking cups, covering entire surface with thin layer of chocolate. Place in muffin tins and chill in refrigerator until quite firm. When ready to use, peel off paper. Fill chocolate cups with ice cream, sherbet, whipped cream or coconut tapioca pudding. Garnish with lightly toasted shredded coconut.

WHITE GRAPES AND MELON IN COGNAC

1 pound white seedless grapes	juice from 1 lemon
	1 tablespoon sugar
1 cup cognac	1 honeydew lemon

347

1 teaspoon salt
1 tablespoon grated orange rind

juice from 1 orange
mint

Wash and pick grapes from stems. Dry on absorbent paper. Place grapes in shallow bowl. Mix cognac with lemon juice and sugar. Pour over grapes. Cover and chill overnight. Cut honeydew melon in half and remove seeds. Scoop out balls or dice in 1-inch squares. Sprinkle with salt, grated orange rind and orange juice. Combine with grapes. Cover and chill several hours or until thoroughly chilled. Serve. Garnish with mint.

FROZEN SANDWICH

2 egg whites
½ pint whipping cream
¼ cup powdered sugar
1 tablespoon lemon juice
1 teaspoon vanilla

1 round sponge cake (sliced)
6 bananas
⅛ teaspoon salt

Whip egg whites until stiff. Add salt and beat in the powdered sugar. Whip cream. Add vanilla and fold whipped cream into beaten egg whites. Line a mold with sponge cake. Peel and slice bananas thinly. Add lemon juice to bananas and fold into cream and egg white mixture. Fill mold ¾ full of cream and fruit mixture. Cover with additional sponge cake. Press cake down lightly into place. Freeze 2 or 3 hours. Slice and serve with whipped cream and bananas or nuts. Serves 10 to 12.

PINEAPPLE FANTASY

For a quick cooling dessert. It can be served as an appetizer, salad or dessert. Fresh or canned pineapple, surround with frosted strawberries, add pineapple chunks dipped in crème de menthe.

23.

Creole Dishes

EVERY COOK IN EVERY NOOK knows about New Orleans, the Creoles, and all the fabulous stories about the folk, as well as the food. To fully explore this land of intrigue and unique recipes, we would have to add hundreds of extra pages, so since we are trying to include everyone, we will just let THE LITTLE BROWN CHEF momentarily stick his nose into a few pots and kitchens. As you read these pages, remember that there are thousands more, but we can't include all of them.

Some of our recipes are from the famous family of Maxwell caterers and other families, plain cooks, good chefs, fancy chefs and young Creole girls who THE LITTLE BROWN CHEF say are just about tops in cooking. He has his eye set for a wife from either South Carolina or New Orleans.

ABOUT SAUCES

Creoles are famous for sauces of every variety, which come from the basic three—white sauce, brown sauce, and glaze. The making of the sauce depends greatly on the mixture of the roux. Be sure that the butter and flour *do not burn*. If you follow a basic recipe for these, any sauce you attempt to make should be a success!

CREOLE DISHES

MAMA SCOTT'S OMELET

Step 1:

1 tablespoon butter	1 tablespoon grated onion
1 tablespoon flour	or onion juice
1 teaspoon salt	1 tablespoon chopped
1/2 teaspoon paprika	parsley or celery tops
1 cup milk	

Sauté onions in butter for 10 minutes. Add 1/2 cup of cooked mixed vegetables, 1/2 cup of cooked diced potatoes and add pepper and salt to taste.

Step 2:

4 eggs	1 teaspoon salt
1/3 cup milk	1 tablespoon butter

Beat eggs and add milk and salt. Melt butter in a large hot skillet and add egg mixture. Cook slowly. When nearly done, shake skillet or turn in cooked ends so that eggs will cook through. Pour vegetable mixture over eggs. Fold over. Brown and serve.

CREOLE CAKES

1/2 cup grated lemon peel	1/3 cup sugar
1/2 cup peach jam	2 tablespoons sugar
1/2 cup orange marmalade	1/2 teaspoon salt
4 egg whites	

Mix lemon and jams. Beat 3 egg whites, 1/3 cup sugar and salt until stiff. Combine with lemon mixture. Drop from a spoon on clean white or brown paper on a baking sheet. Bake 10 minutes in a hot oven. Remove from oven and cover with a meringue of 1 egg white, stiffly beaten with 2 tablespoons sugar. Return to oven and bake until light brown.

RICE DUMPLINGS
(Echaudes de Riz)

1/2 cup flour	3 cups ground rice
8 apples, tart and not	2 quarts milk
overripe	2 tablespoons grated
sugar and cinnamon to	orange peel
taste	1/2 teaspoon salt
1/2 teaspoon grated nutmeg	

Pare and core apples. Mix ground cinnamon and sugar and fill apples with this mixture. Boil rice and salt in milk until it becomes thick and gummy. Add grated orange peel, nutmeg and flour. Remove from heat and cool. Cover each apple with thick coating of rice. Tie each dumpling tightly in a cloth. Put in pot of cold water. Bring water to boil; boil apples for ¾ hour. When done, untie cloth and place dumplings on large dish. Sprinkle with nutmeg, dot with butter and place in oven for 5 to 10 minutes to brown. Serve with cream sauce.

FISH CHOWDER
(Melee Creole)

2 to 3 pounds fresh fish	2 small onions
1 clove garlic	1 bay leaf
4 small potatoes, diced	¼ cup parsley
pinch or sprig thyme	¼ pound salt pork or bacon
1 cup tomatoes	end, chopped fine
1 quart hot water	1 cup milk
½ teaspoon cayenne pepper	2 teaspoons salt

Cut fish (of your choice) in small pieces. Dice onions and meat. Sauté meat in own fat. Add diced onions and spices, salt and pepper to taste. Do not fry. Simmer slowly. Place in pot and cover with boiling water. Add fish, tomatoes and potatoes. Cover and simmer 30 minutes. Scald milk. Add to hot fish mixture and serve with crackers.

GUMBOS

To include the many things said of New Orleans and Creole dishes, I would have had to confine this book to one subject and include the whole state of Louisiana. My collection of recipes from this vicinity dates from 1906 to the present time. I have so many recipes, each one with authentic quality, that I am at wit's end as to what The Little Brown Chef should sanction for your "Date with a Dish."

No two people seem to have the same recipe for the same dish, yet each is sworn to be authentic, so for New Orleans Gumbos, after days of concentration, I've selected a few that I think are excellent. If you are from Louisiana, remember that the contributors are, too. Their way is as authentic to them as your way is to you. When it comes to food and recipes, it is almost impossible to establish authenticity because of various likes and dislikes ... each person feels his way is correct.

CRAB GUMBO

6 to 8 hard-shelled crabs	1 large can tomatoes
3 medium onions	½ cup celery and leaves
2 pounds okra	salt and pepper to taste
1 garlic clove	several red pepper pods
1 sprig thyme leaf	few sprigs parsley
1 bay leaf	⅓ cup bacon fat

Sauté onions, garlic, parsley and celery in fat. Use a large pot. Add spices and okra. Stir to keep from burning. Cook 15 minutes.

Wash, clean and crack claws. Remove outside shell. Cut in quarters. Add crab to sautéed ingredients with tomatoes, parsley and about 1½ quarts of water. Simmer slowly about 1 hour. Season to taste. Serve with rice.

Shrimp, oysters and ham may be added if you are not serving this as a fast-day dish. In fact, one recipe requires the ham ends and bone to be boiled to make the stock. Then add the vegetables, spices and turkey base for gumbo, adding crab and shrimp. The same recipe applies to chicken and turkey base for gumbo, adding crab and shrimp. I personally love the mixture as it is a complete meal in itself! There are delicious gumbos made of green leafy vegetables with a meat base of beef or veal brisket, cabbage, radish, spinach, parsley, water cress, turnips, onions, peppers and spice cloves, marjoram and thyme. They are not as popular as the other varieties but they are good.

GUMBO FILÉ NO. 1

For your information, filé powder is a powdered sassafras made first by the Indians in Louisiana from the dried leaves.

1 large chicken or the carcass of a baked or roasted chicken or turkey	2 cups of ham
	4 sprigs parsley
	1 sprig thyme leaf
	several red pepper pods

2 large onions
2 tablespoons filé powder
2 to 3 dozen oysters
salt and pepper to taste
1 bay leaf

several red pepper pods
1 cup celery leaves
1 cup celery with leaves
1 cup fresh or canned
   tomatoes

Clean and cut fowl and sprinkle with salt and pepper. Sauté onion, garlic, celery and chicken until brown. Crush bay leaf and thyme and add chicken with diced ham. Sauté for 15 minutes, stirring frequently to prevent burning. When brown, add oyster juice and boiling water to cover 2 inches above ingredients. Add pepper pods, tomatoes and parsley. Cover and cook at low heat for 1 hour until done. Add oysters ½ hour before serving and cook 5 minutes. Remove from heat and add filé powder. Serve over rice.

Once filé is added, gumbo should not be re-warmed. Some people prefer adding filé powder to rice. It's only a matter of choice. (Allow 2 to 3 tablespoons of rice per serving).

GUMBO FILÉ No. 2

I prefer a recipe from the Pryce family of Lake Charles, La. They cover a turkey carcass well with water. Cook 1 hour. Remove meat and skin from bones, cut in fine pieces and add to stock. Then add:

2 cups chopped ham
1 hot sausage
sprig parsley
2 to 3 onions, chopped
sprig thyme
bits of green pepper
   (optional)

several stalks celery and
   leaves finely chopped
1 finely chopped garlic
   clove
salt, pepper, paprika, red
   pepper to taste
2 bay leaves

Simmer for 2 hours. Add 2 pounds of fresh shrimp, cleaned and cut or 1 pound of dry shrimp, 1 pound fresh or canned okra. Simmer until shrimp is done. Cook rice. Place ⅓ cup rice in each plate. Sprinkle with filé powder if desired. Serve gumbo over rice. This is delicious with a green salad.

GUMBO FILÉ No. 3

1 small young hen

½ pound hot sausage
   (Chaurice)

CREOLE DISHES

1 pound crab meat
2 onions, finely chopped
6 cloves garlic
2 green peppers, chopped
6 tablespoons chopped
    parsley
4 sprigs thyme
½ cup bacon fat

4 tablespoons flour
1½ to 2 quarts water
6 fresh tomatoes
½ teaspoon sugar
1 pound prepared shrimp
2 dozen oysters
salt, pepper, cayenne to taste
4 tablespoons filé

Fry chicken in bacon fat until partially done. Add Chaurice, crab meat, onions, garlic, green peppers, parsley, and thyme. Fry for 3 minutes, add flour and brown. Add water, tomatoes, sugar and boil for 15 minutes. Add shrimp and cook for 10 minutes, then oysters and cook for 5 minutes. Remove from heat and, for best results, keep top off pot until served.

SHRIMP GUMBO FILÉ

2 pounds shrimp
1 tablespoon flour
1 tablespoon butter or
    shortening
3 sprigs parsley, chopped
1 large onion, chopped
1 sprig thyme

1 bay leaf, chopped
2 quarts oyster juice
1 quart hot water
dash cayenne
salt and pepper to taste
filé to taste

Shell shrimp and boil. Make a roux by adding flour to melted fat. Brown and add chopped parsley, thyme, onion, and chopped bay leaf. Add hot oyster juice and hot water, or use strained juice from boiled shrimp. Cook. Before serving, add shrimp to mixture and remove from stove. Filé (about 2 tablespoonfuls) may be added to thicken according to taste. Season with salt and pepper.

Serve immediately with boiled rice.

OKRA GUMBO No. 1

1 small chicken
bacon fat
1 cup chopped ham
1 bunch green onions
¼ cup chopped parsley
sprig thyme
1 teaspoon paprika

pinch marjoram
2 small hot red peppers
8 fresh tomatoes or 1 can
    tomatoes
2 pounds okra
salt and pepper to taste

Clean and cut chicken. Sauté in heavy large pot with fat until brown. Add ham, onions, parsley, spices and tomatoes. Cook 20 minutes stirring frequently. Add okra and cook until tender. Add 2 or 3 quarts boiling water and simmer at least 1 hour. Season to taste and serve with rice.

If boiling chicken is used, add a few celery leaves. Season and boil as any other chicken for stew. When tender, use stock instead of water.

OKRA GUMBO No. 2

1 pound fresh okra	1 pound shrimp
2 onions, chopped fine	2 fresh crabs
6 garlic cloves	½ cup fat
2 green peppers, chopped fine	½ pound hot sausage (Chaurice)
2 sprigs fresh thyme	1 teaspoon sugar
2 fresh tomatoes	4 tablespoons flour
6 tablespoons fresh parsley	salt, pepper to taste
½ cup celery	cayenne to taste
1 quart water	

Sauté okra, onions, garlic, bell peppers, parsley and celery until lightly brown, stirring constantly. Add flour and cook 3 minutes. Then add Chaurice, crabs, tomatoes, thyme, water, salt, pepper, sugar, and let boil for 20 minutes. Add shrimp and cook for 15 minutes or depending upon desired thickness.

LOUISIANA OYSTER LOAF

2 to 3 dozen oysters	large loaf French-type bread
1 cup corn meal	1 teaspoon salt
1 teaspoon paprika	butter
dash garlic salt	⅛ teaspoon pepper

1. Mix corn meal, salt, pepper and paprika. Sprinkle oysters with garlic salt and dip in corn meal. Deep fry until crisp in hot fat.

2. Split loaf of bread lengthwise about 1 inch from top to make a lid. Make a basket by scooping out soft bread, leaving crust. Butter the inside and the lid generously. Place oysters in basket along with thin slices of pickle. Make a cocktail sauce

of catsup, Worcestershire sauce, horseradish or mustard and pour over oysters. Place top on bread and serve in portions, with cole slaw, olives, radishes and pickles.

Some folk fill bread basket or shell with creamed or broiled oysters, then place it in oven until brown. It's a matter of choice.

JAMBALAYA

1½ cups cold chicken, veal
  or mutton
2 large stalks finely
  chopped celery
1 large onion
1 large finely chopped
  onion
1 bay leaf

pinch thyme
1 cup boiled rice
½ finely chopped green
  pepper
1½ cups stewed tomatoes
1 garlic clove
salt and pepper to taste

Mix chicken, rice and tomatoes. Cook for 10 minutes. Add onion, green pepper and celery. Place mixture into a baking dish and cover with buttered crumbs. Bake for 1 hour in moderate oven, 350° F. Serve very hot.

CREOLE JAMBALAYA

1 pound fresh pork, diced
6 to 8 pork sausages
3 medium onions, finely
  chopped
2 garlic cloves, finely
  chopped
2 sprigs thyme leaf, finely
  chopped
1 green pepper, finely
  chopped

few sprigs parsley
salt, pepper and cayenne
  pepper to taste
1 cup ham
2 tablespoons butter
3 bay leaves, finely
  chopped
1 teaspoon cloves
1 teaspoon chili powder
3 quarts water or broth

Place butter in saucepan and add onions, garlic, parsley and pork and sauté until brown. Add ham and herbs. Add sausage and cook 10 minutes. Add water or broth. Cook 15 minutes. When mixture begins to boil, add rice, chili powder and pepper. Cook until rice is done. Serve hot.

OKRA CREOLE

2 pounds okra	1 clove garlic
3 tablespoons butter	1 medium green pepper
2 tablespoons chopped parsley	3 fresh tomatoes
1 medium onion	1 cup tomato juice
	salt and pepper to taste

Wash okra and cut off ends. Sauté butter in pan. Add onion, parsley, garlic and green pepper, diced. Cook 10 minutes. Add tomatoes, chopped fine, and juice. Add seasonings. Add okra and parsley. Cook 20 minutes. Serve.

POT ROAST WITH HAM
(Carne Mechada)

2 or 3 garlic cloves	4 or 5 small pieces boiled ham
salt and pepper	
1 teaspoon paprika	½ cup tomato sauce
1 pot roast, chuck or sirloin	1 onion, chopped

Crush garlic and add salt, pepper and paprika. Make into a paste. Cut 6 to 8 small pockets in roast and line with small amount of garlic mixture. Place ham in pockets. Place roast in heavy Dutch oven which has been pre-heated with fat. Brown well on all sides. Add tomato sauce and chopped onions. Cover tightly and cook until tender, turning about every half hour. When tender, remove roast and make gravy. Serve with rice, green peas and salad.

RELLENOS
(An unusual potato and meat cake)

4 to 5 large potatoes boiled in jackets	pepper to taste
	2 tablespoons butter
1 teaspoon salt	½ cup flour

Boil, cool and mash potatoes with salt, pepper and butter. Add flour. Make into balls about size of a small orange. Roll into flour. Make a pocket in the center of potato ball and fill with the following mixture which has been sautéed in butter:

¾ pound chopped meat	2 tablespoons miced green pepper
1 small onion	

CREOLE DISHES

6 to 8 chopped stuffed olives	pinch salt, pepper, paprika

Cover filled pocket with potatoes and roll into flour. Fry in hot fat until brown on both sides.

This unusual and tasty Spanish dish may be made with plantains instead of potatoes. Boil plantains like potatoes and mash. Follow same method.

MAKING A SIMPLE ROUX

Heat fat in frying pan or pot. Add equal amount of flour. Stir until the two mixtures are well blended. Where onions are added to roux, add chopped onions and cook to a golden brown stirring constantly. If roux is used as base for gravy or vegetables, add liquids or vegetables when flour is brown or the fat and flour are blended. Butter roux is made in the same order for quick cooking processes.

ABOUT SAUSAGE

Creoles are noted for their fine spicy sausages which excel in flavor and are used for breakfast as well as seasoning for Gumbos. Many old Creole families make their own. Chaurice or Creole sausages are delicious, served in a rich Spanish sauce.

STEWED TURTLE
(Ragout de Totue)

2 pounds turtle meat	1 finely chopped onion
1 tablespoon butter or shortening	1 tablespoon flour
1 bay leaf	1 finely chopped garlic clove
1 sprig thyme, chopped	1 cup water
1 wine glass sherry or Madeira	salt and pepper to taste

Cut turtle meat into 1-inch cubes. Sauté onion in fat until brown. Add flour, bay leaf, garlic, thyme and mix thoroughly with the turtle meat. Add wine and a cup of water and cook for half an hour.

24.

Menus

Your menus, whether for breakfast, lunch, bridge, or supper, should be in keeping with your personality and home. If you are the formal type, be sure your menu takes on the formal air. Foods have feelings, and they like to be placed in the right places on the right menus.

During my trips about the country, I have been the recipient of invitations to many tasty meals where I observed the menus carefully to determine what helps constitute successful parties and menus. About as close as I could come to finding perfection in this was Mrs. Evelyn Reynolds of Philadelphia, known to her readers as Eve Lyn, a poet, newspaper-woman, civic leader, and charming hostess. Her personality alone was a guarantee for a successful party!

When I complimented her on her beautiful, well-equipped home, her easy way of entertaining, and her clever menus, she informed me that she felt she must *live* her menus and give them as much thought as execution. Not every menu was planned according to set rules, because she knew the tastes of her guests and tried to include their preferences in the food and because she made it her business to see that her guests felt at home as soon as they arrived. Her menus were planned for beauty as well as taste appeal.

MENUS

JUNE BRIDE MENU

What is June without a bride? And what is the bride without the groom? Of course, once the ceremony is over, how to keep your husband happy is the important question.

Orange blossoms and lilies, white satin and lace, parties and honeymoon, these things can't last forever. There has to be a practical side, such as taking care of the home, planning good substantial meals, and building a future home and generation.

It isn't smart to say, "I just don't know how." There are no excuses for not trying. When it comes to a home and kitchen, one *should* know. You knew the answers in order to get married; you must know the answers to stay happily married.

So, try "Dating Our Dishes" for a date that lasts from the orange blossoms to the golden anniversary stage.

Your first party menu is very important. The first impression must be a lasting one. The menu need not be intricate. It need consist only of simple, tasty, well-prepared food, pleasantly presented. If you follow directions carefully, your new hubby will be very proud of your efforts and your guests will marvel at your ingenuity.

Stuffed Tomatoes
with
Shrimp on Crisp Endive
Baked Chicken in Quarters   *with*   *Mushrooms and Wine*
New Potatoes   *with*   *Parsley Butter*
Fresh Peas with Celery

Rolls   *Iced Tea*
Angel Cake   *Ice Cream*

ALTERNATE MENU

Baked Ham Slices
with
Spiced Pears
Macaroni Salad   *Peas and Carrots*
Tomato and Green Pepper Slices
Assorted Small Hard Rolls
Tiny Rum Cakes with Sauce   *Coffee*

CANADA LEE'S STEAK HOUSE

Many years ago, Canada Lee, one of America's number-one
Negro actors, opened a tiny basement dining room and called
it "The Chicken Coop." Strikingly designed and decorated to
resemble a barnyard, it was indeed delightful and a good place
for good food. The menus were designed after the famous
playbills seen in the New York theaters. So, for your reading
pleasure and your gastronomic tastes, here are two menus.
May they give you as much pleasure as I had in creating them
for Canada Lee.

OVERTURE

Tomato Juice Tang

ACT I

Starring

Miss Fried Chicken   *with*   *Her Supporting Cast of*

Gay Garden Vegetables

The French Fried Sweet Potato Chorus and

Mr. Cabbage Cole Slaw

with the

Chicken Biscuit Boys

INTERMISSION

Fresh Fruit Family

with the

Butter Cookie Twins

FINALE

Coffee Carnival

assisted by

Sugar and Cream

COMMAND PERFORMANCE

Starring

Mr. Filet Mignon   *Mushroom Dancers*

Shoestring Potato Singers

French Bean   *Comedian*

The Lettuce and Tomato Adagio Dancers

Hot Biscuit Specialty

FINALE
Miss Pumpkin Chiffon Ballet
with
The Coffee Cup

BREAKFAST MENUS

Did you ever go for a visit in Virginia, South Carolina, or Tennessee, and receive an invitation to breakfast? If not, then definitely you've missed the thrill of a lifetime . . . and was I confused! One look at the table and I consulted my watch! Had I overslept, was it dinner time? Just how many did they expect? All that food and only six people, impossible! But that's the way they do things.

In the South, some of their breakfast menus read like our dinner menus. You vow you can't eat a thing, but start out with a bit of this and that, then end up eating a good healthy serving of Virginia Ham, Hominy Grits, Fried Chicken, Scrambled Eggs, Sliced Tomatoes, Hot Biscuits and Honey, with cold milk or hot coffee. And you "didn't want a thing"!

It seems these "breakfasts" are "the thing." Now I can well understand what Southern Hospitality means. I won't go so far as to say "A Date with a Dish" has planned breakfast menus like this for you, but several well-balanced and different ones for all the seasons of the year and parts of the country are suggested.

You will enjoy the gay variety created for your family or party menus. There are ideas for every housewife.

BREAKFAST MENU AND RECIPES AT A GLANCE
(For serving 10 persons)

Melon Rings with Fresh Black Cherries

2 melons, 5 slices to each melon, honeydew or cantaloupe	1½ pounds cherries

Cut your melon in circles. Remove skin and seeds. Soak in lemon juice and salt. Wash cherries, leave stems on. Place at least 6 cherries in center of melon. Serve on rose or nasturtium leaves, or paper doilies.

Ham Slices with Tomato Rings

5 slices ham, cut in half   5 tomatoes
5 tablespoons brown sugar

Sauté small slices of ham in butter. Turn once. Lay ¼ inch thick tomato slice on each slice of ham. Sprinkle with ½ teaspoon brown sugar, paprika and chopped parsley. Cover and simmer 10 minutes longer.

Scrambled Eggs with Onion Tops

16 eggs   1 bunch onion tops
½ cup milk, canned   salt and pepper to taste
⅓ cup butter   paprika

Chop onion tops fine, and sauté in butter. Add eggs which have been beaten with milk and seasonings. Scramble quickly 5 to 8 minutes. Turn heat off and let stand. Serve in center of ham and tomato slices, on a bed of water cress.

Cinnamon Toast Strips

1 sandwich loaf   1 cup sugar
⅓ cup butter   2 tablespoons cinnamon

Slice bread in ½ inch slices. Cut into strips 4 inches long. Spread with soft butter on all sides. Roll in sugar and cinnamon. Toast in oven 15 to 20 minutes. Serve hot.

Coffee   Milk

BREAKFAST MENU

(Serves 8)

Fresh Orange and Grapefruit Juice
with Sherry
Sautéed Lamb Patties on Pineapple Slices
Chopped Browned Potatoes with Parsley
Scrambled Eggs with Corn and Pimientos

Hot Honey Biscuits   Jelly
       Coffee   Tea   Milk

FRUIT JUICE

8 oranges   1 cup sweet sherry
4 grapefruit   2 tablespoons sugar

MENUS

Juice oranges and grapefruit. Mix with sugar. Add wine. Chill and serve in small fruit juice glasses, or in a large pitcher so that each diner can serve himself.

LAMB PATTIES, PINEAPPLE AND POTATOES

Sauté pineapple in 2 tablespoons butter. Set aside. Mix ground lamb (2 pounds) with 1 teaspoon salt, pepper, paprika, 1 teaspoon mustard. Sauté in hot skillet to brown on both sides. Place on pineapple slices and run into oven to bake 15 to 20 minutes. Sprinkle with fresh chopped mint. Serve around potatoes which have been boiled with 1 onion, 1 cup celery leaves and finely chopped. Fry in patty form until brown on both sides.

EGGS AND CORN

Fry 8 slices of bacon crisp. Remove bacon. Sauté corn (kernel) in fat with pimientos. Beat 8 eggs, add salt and pepper. Add to corn. Scramble well until done. Arrange on round flat dish. Garnish with parsley and bacon slices. Sprinkle with paprika.

HONEY BISCUITS

Can be made from your favorite recipe for biscuits. During the last 8 minutes of baking, remove from oven and brush with a mixture of melted butter and honey in equal parts.

FOR MEN ONLY

If there is anything men dislike, it's dainty sandwiches and fussy menus at a man's party.

Here are a few menus that are sure to dazzle the gang and get that extra kiss or diamond bracelet you are working on.

Hamburgers on Buns
Onion and Pepper Sauté
Corn-on-the-Cob, buttered
Mustard Sauce   Dill Pickles
Bowl of Lettuce
A Plate of Assorted Vegetables
Tomato Slices, Cucumbers, Green Onions
Beer

After frying your hamburgers, pile them into a large roaster. Keep in oven, covered until ready to use.

WARM ROLLS—BUTTER

Sauté a large skillet of onions and green pepper slices, keep hot.

Slice ½ dozen large dill pickles in rounds.

Add ½ cup catsup and 2 tablespoons hot pepper sauce to mustard.

Boil corn. Place in large pot. Salt, pepper and butter. Serve.

BUFFET FOR MEN

In center of platter, place 1 large medium rare Roast Beef, sliced thin.

One platter of home-made Veal Loaf
Assorted Salami
Liverwurst
Ham Sausage

Large Platter of Cheese
(Alternate Slices)
Swiss   *Roquefort*
American   *Camembert*
A dish of Wine Cheese

A large bowl of Mixed Salad Greens
Lettuce
Endive
Romaine

Dish of Stuffed Eggs with Anchovy Paste
Assorted Pickles   *In Slices*
A large bowl of Green Onions
A dish of Hot Potato Salad
surrounded by
Tomato Slices

Plates of Buttered:
Rye Bread
Whole Wheat   *White Bread*

MENUS

Dishes of:

Mustard	Catsup	Horseradish
French Dressing		Hot Peppers

A large plate of Pound Cake
Plenty of Hot Coffee   Beer

BREAKFAST FOR 25

Oh, what a beautiful morning! A start for a lovely day. As grand as the morn, thus shall my breakfast be. I will produce a masterpiece in foods! And I'll start with a colorful assortment of juices and fruits to pep up the appetites of my guests.

To the left on my buffet I shall arrange juices in graduated glasses and color. Grapefruit juice, pineapple, then orange, with bits of mint, lemon and orange to decorate. To the right I shall arrange around the edge of a large plate, assorted melon slices on a bed of lemon leaves decorated with lemon wedges and sprinkled with salt. In the center of the plate, a bowl of sliced peaches or berries in season. Luscious cold, rich cream and fruit sugar waiting to be added for the final touch!

Can't you visualize the expression of pleasure on the guests' faces? What a sensational start for a wonderful breakfast! After giving my guests time to drink their cold, snappy juice or eat their favorite fruit, I turn their attention to a gay table set with shining, colorful dishes and silver, a gay low centerpiece of fresh flowers that catch the eye, but hold second place to the dish of light, fluffy sun-kissed scrambled eggs with corn piled high, surrounded by sausage cakes, bacon strips and fried apple slices; bite-size honey coated biscuits with plenty of home-made jam or jelly and loads of fresh butter.

Now, back to the buffet which by this time has been cleared of the glasses, plates and remnants of fruits and instead, loads of fresh, hot coffee with brandy for those who care and glasses of cold milk for those who don't.

A perfect meal—a beautiful starter for a perfect day!

You can graduate this lovely breakfast to the brunch class by serving:

Creamed Chicken on Toast Rounds
with Sauté Pineapple

Peas and Celery in Butter Sauce
or
Baked Tomato Slices with Mushrooms

ALTERNATE BREAKFASTS

(1)

Assorted Juices   *Tomato juice*   *Apricot juice*
Baked Apples with Cream
Corn Beef Hash Cups with Baked Eggs
Corn and Green Peppers Sauté
or
Lyonnaise Potatoes with Chopped Parsley in Cream

(2)

Chilled Honeydew Melon and White Grapes in Wine
Ham Slices with Spanish Omelet
Sausage and Potato Cakes on Wilted Lettuce with
Chopped Pimiento
Hot Muffins   *Coffee*

EBONY'S LUNCHEON MENUS

Whenever The Little Brown Chef has a chance to stop off in
Chicago, it becomes his duty to appease the palates of EBONY's
staff, so here are two menus "dated" just for staff luncheons
and you!

(1)

Assorted Cream Cheese Ball Salad
East Indian Chicken   *Pineapple Rice*
Parsley Biscuits
Flan with Hot Rum Sauce   *Coffee*

(2)

Special Turkey Salad
Hot Spiced Peas   *Assorted Salad Greens*
Banana Bread Sandwiches
Tomato Soup Cake Squares   *Coffee*

BREAKFAST OR BRUNCH MENUS

(1)

Grapefruit Sections in Wine

MENUS

Sausage—Bacon with Fried Apples
Scrambled Eggs   Whole Kernel Corn
Honey Butter Biscuits   Jam
Coffee

(2)

Orange Slices and White Grapes
Beef Hash   Hominy Grits
Poached Eggs
Biscuits   Coffee

(3)

Melon Slices
Creamed Chicken on Toast Rounds
Baked Bananas
Potato and Parsley Patties
Coffee   Assorted Coffee Rolls

(4)

Tomato Juice
Fried Chicken in Cream
Sautéed Sliced Pineapple   Pan Fried Potatoes
Corn Muffins   Coffee

(5)

Baked Apple
Sautéed Kidneys and Bacon
Browned Potato Cakes   Corn Sauté
Muffins   Coffee

(6)

Assorted Fresh or Dried Stewed Fruit
Ham and Chicken Ring with Whole Hominy
Broiled Tomatoes on Wilted Lettuce
Berry Muffins   Coffee

DINNER OR BUFFET SUPPER

Spiced Tomato Cocktail
Roast Ham
Baked Elbow Macaroni with Cheese and Tomatoes
Diced String Beans   Corn
A bowl of Apple, Nut, Celery Salad on Water Cress

Kernel Corn Bread   *Crackers*
Assorted Cheese
Coffee

BRIDGE LUNCHEON

Remove center from a large green raw artichoke. Wash, and
oil to make it shine. Fill with radishes, green onions, olives,
celery. Use as a centerpiece on each table.

On each plate, place on a bed of endive, ½ stuffed baked
lobster, 4 asparagus spears with pimiento butter, a small tomato stuffed with chopped celery, water cress and green pepper. A plate of tiny parsley biscuits, butter, iced tea or hot tea
with mint. Lime and cherry sherbet with pink tea cookies.

INEXPENSIVE BUFFET

Roast Ham   *Baked Beans*
Vegetable Cole Slaw
Fish Cakes   *Corn Muffins*
Assorted Pickles
Mustard
Gingercake Squares   *Coffee*

EBONY'S SPRING FISH MENUS

In spring, our pattern of life changes to the lighter side, as do
our menus! And what could be more appetizing than a delicious baked or planked fresh fish with fresh garden vegetables?

There is a wealth of fish and sea food at your command the
year 'round. But when someone in the family feels the urge of
spring and brings home a "catch," glorify and bake it to show
off the fish as well as the fisherman.

(1)
Grapefruit and Avocado Cocktail
Baked Fish
Brussels Sprouts with Parsley
Lemon Buttered Carrots
New Potatoes in Paprika Butter
Hearts of Lettuce with Mustard Dressing
Corn Sticks
Apple Delight

MENUS

(2)
Chilled Vegetable Juice
Planked Fish with Mashed Potatoes and Green Onion Tops
Lemon Sauce
Asparagus Spears   *Shoestring Beets*
Assorted Cream Cheese Balls on Water Cress
Hot Muffins
Sponge Cake Custards

ROAST BEEF DINNERS

There are definitely some dishes that lend themselves to any season. And this is true about the King of Roasts. Here he is in all his glory with his court of attendants waiting to serve you.

(1)
Fresh Fruit Cup
Roast Beef   *Brown Potatoes*
Frenched String Beans and Carrots with Parsley Sauce
Hearts of Lettuce with Roquefort Dressing
Hot Rolls
Yorkshire Pudding   *Tomato Soup Cake*
Coffee

(2)
Crawfish Bisque
Roast Beef   *Mashed Potatoes with Parsley*
Brown Gravy   *Corn Sauté with Mushrooms*
Asparagus
Lettuce and Tomato Salad
Assorted Rolls
Dark Prune Pudding with Ice Cream Sauce

RED, WHITE, BLUE

Are you patriotic? If so, try doing your foods in red, white and blue. You'll find it's fund, like playing a game of Tick-tack-toe, a real brain teaser for menus.

You'll feel that George Washington, Betsy Ross, and Abe Lincoln are all taking a bow for your patriotic creations. Date your red, white and blue dishes, and try these menus.

370

(1)
Cherry and Lemon Ice
Crab Meat in Cream Sauce with Pimiento
(served in shells)
Buttered Celery with Paprika Sauce
Baked Stuffed Tomatoes with Bread Crumbs and Olives
Tiny Hot Biscuits with Pimiento
Blueberry Upside Down Cake
with
Tinted Whipped Cream

(2)
Stuffed Tomato with Shrimp
Cauliflower with Cream Sauce and Pimientos
Red and White Cole Slaw
Blueberry Muffins   Cherry Tarts
Ice Cream Sauce
Centerpiece of gay red and white carnations,
with blue bachelor buttons

EASTER SUNDAY BREAKFAST

Dating dishes can be fun, and here's one you won't want to miss . . . all done up in a fashion befitting spring and Easter.

This breakfast or brunch can be partially prepared Saturday night, which gives you plenty of time for Church and the Easter Parade, then home again to serve your family and guests at leisure. Sharpen your appetite with a glass of cold vegetable juice with a dash of lemon, or fresh grapefruit sections and white cherries soaked in wine, served in fluted grapefruit shells. And now for our main event, baked eggs in corned beef hash cups, broiled fresh tomato slices topped with mushrooms and celery sauté on wilted lettuce, delicious coffee coils filled with creamy orange sauce, and, of course, coffee.

A menu fit for royalty, easily prepared and bearing that real professional touch. From start to finish, a table of food to be proud of. Serve buffet style.

A BASKET OF HAM AND EGGS

On a fresh spring morn when the trees are budding, grass is beginning to turn green, and the breezes are warm, what could be more appropriate than planning your Easter Sunday dinner? And if it is not lamb, it must be ham, for these meats are definitely an Easter Sunday tradition.

So, for good eating, plan your menu around a delicious baked ham and gaily colored hard-cooked eggs on a bed of water cress to form a basket. Then, scalloped potatoes in a creamy cheese sauce that graces the ham in a rich dignified manner. A dish of fresh string beans with lemon butter and a pineapple and cream cheese salad, garnished in gay Easter fashion with carrot streamers. A tasty lime sherbet with dainty tea cakes for dessert.

A bowl of daffodils will brighten your table. Put your best linen, dishes and silver on parade. Who could ask for a better view or a prettier scene than that from the kitchen to the table?

Roast your ham in pineapple juice, glaze with honey, and decorate with green cherries.

For Your Gay Eggs:

12 hard-cooked eggs	1 package food coloring
3 cups white vinegar	(assorted)
1 tablespoon salt	1 tablespoon sugar
2 tablespoons pickling spices	1 bay leaf

Cool and peel eggs. Boil vinegar, sugar and spices. Strain. Select colors of your choice. Place equal parts of vinegar in 3 bowls, sprinkle a few drops of each selected color in bowl. Color should be a little deeper than color desired. Place 4 eggs in each bowl. Cover and let stand in a cool place overnight. Drain.

Place ham in basket of washed, crisp water cress. Lay 8 colored eggs around ham. Decorate sides of ham with 8 halves. Serve with potatoes au gratin, string beans with lemon butter, pineapple chunks in cream cheese balls topped with mustard dressing.

THANKSGIVING

(1)

Avocado and Crab meat Cocktail
Roast Turkey in Wine

Corn Bread Dressing

Egg Plant Casserole   Buttered Onions and Peas

Yams and Apple Slices   Cranberry Relish

Mixed Green Salad

Assorted Rolls

Coffee   Suét Pudding with Rum Sauce

(2)

Assorted Hors d'oeuvres and Cocktail

Roast Turkey in Peanut Butter

Mashed Potatoes   Gravy

Oyster Casserole   String Beans

Green and Red Cole Slaw

Apple Chutney

Breads   Coffee

Squash Pie

HOLIDAY BUFFET

Red and green predominating in every conceivable combination, gaiety, the spirit of giving, store windows dressed for a parade of shoppers. Mother Nature lending her touch. If it isn't ice or snow, then it's the tropical touch of live green, real poinsettias, flowers, berries, and every imaginable form of life proving that it is time to celebrate.

So it's little wonder that at this time the Board of Gourmets have passed a law to "Eat, Drink and Be Merry," and this you shall do if you follow The Little Brown Chef's menu of colorful, fabulous holiday foods!

Macaroni salad with whole shrimp on a bed of Romaine lettuce, molded into a circle and decorated with parsley and pimiento to resemble a wreath of holly.

Tomato and Green Pepper Slices
around a center of
Green Peas
Tiny Hot Muffins (Cranberry)
Bowl of Assorted Greens:
Lettuce—Water cress—Endive
Hot String Beans and Chopped Stuffed Olives
with

373

MENUS

Green Onion Tops in Pimiento Butter
Tiny Individual Pumpkin Pies

FOR YOUR CHRISTMAS BUFFET

Turkey salad piled high on a round plate to resemble a pine tree, sprinkled heavily with fresh chopped parsley from top to bottom. A few red cranberries as decoration here and there like red balls.

A bowl of fresh crisp endive
Molded rounds of fresh cranberry relish
A large casserole of Green Peas and Pimientos
Stuffed Olives   Tiny Hot Parsley Biscuits
Individual Mince Meat Pies
Decorated with Red Cherries and Citron

CHRISTMAS MENU

Forget the turkey and get *duck* for Christmas. Crisp and brown, roasted in tangy juices or wine, vegetables as sophisticated as their quack master. Sweet and sour mixtures that do so much for the fastidious epicurean tastes. The real holiday spirit, the colorguard, perfect formation for your eating pleasure. Something different for the family. Give them something to quack about!

(1)
Lobster Bisque
Roast Duck—basted in Orange Juice and Wine
Sweet Potato in Fluted Orange Cups
Waldorf Salad
String Beans and Corn Succotash
Hot Rolls   Coffee
Steamed Cranberry Pudding

(2)
Crabmeat Cocktail
Roast Duck   Rice Dressing
Stuffed Baked Apple and Currants
Buttered Broccoli   Creamed Potatoes
Rolls   Coffee
Pumpkin Chiffon Pie with Rum

374

Index

Index

INDEX

INDEX

INDEX